Youth Voting Rights

Democracy in Times of Upheaval

Series Editor
Matt Qvortrup, Coventry University

Volume 5

Youth Voting Rights

Civil Rights, the Twenty-Sixth Amendment,
and the Fight for American Democracy
on College Campuses

Edited by
Jonathan Becker and Yael Bromberg

DE GRUYTER

ISBN (Paperback) 978-3-11-157516-2
ISBN (Hardcover) 978-3-11-157707-4
e-ISBN (PDF) 978-3-11-157549-0
e-ISBN (EPUB) 978-3-11-157631-2
ISSN 2701-147X
e-ISSN 2701-1488
DOI https://doi.org/10.1515/9783111575490

Library of Congress Control Number: 2025941313

Bibliographic information published by the Deutsche Nationalbibliothek
The Deutsche Nationalbibliothek lists this publication in the Deutsche Nationalbibliografie;
detailed bibliographic data are available on the internet at http://dnb.dnb.de.

© 2026 with the author(s), published by Walter de Gruyter GmbH, Berlin/Boston, Genthiner Straße 13,
10785 Berlin. This book is published with open access at www.degruyterbrill.com.

Cover image: © Common Cause North Carolina, reproduced with permission, depicting press
conference and rally at North Carolina A&T State University on March 26, 2019, the day the
United States Supreme Court heard arguments in the organization's gerrymandering challenge in
Rucho v. Common Cause

www.degruyterbrill.com
Questions about General Product Safety Regulation:
productsafety@degruyterbrill.com

Endorsements

"Generations of young Americans, from Freedom Summer in 1964 to the passage of the 26th Amendment in 1971 to the college campus struggles happening today during the Trump period, have been on the front lines of the fight to vote. This book is a stirring analysis of this important history and a powerful call to action."
– Rep. Jamie Raskin, Ranking Member of the House Committee on the Judiciary and author, *We the Students: Supreme Court Decisions for and about Students*

"At a moment of democratic peril, this desperately needed book arrives on the eve of the 250th anniversary of America's founding—*with* promising insight and powerful analysis of young voters and the youth vote. *If* America is to celebrate future anniversaries as a democracy, it will be because we heed the rich scholarship, practical lessons, trenchant case studies, and inspired wisdom inscribed on these pages."
– Cornell William Brooks, Professor, Harvard Kennedy School, 18th President & CEO, NAACP

"This book is an essential look at the hard-fought and hard-won voting rights victories of young Americans. College students and young people have always been at the forefront of change in America. It's no wonder anti-democratic forces are cracking down on university campuses—where organizing, protest, and youth-led movements are born."
– David Hogg, President, Leaders We Deserve; Co-founder, March For Our Lives

"The struggle to secure the right to vote for college students and young people did not end with the passage of the 26th Amendment in 1971. *Youth Voting Rights* shows with passion and detail that community organizing, savvy legal strategy, and perseverance are necessary to secure the promise of equal voting for young and old and for black, brown, and white."
– Richard L. Hasen, UCLA Professor and author, *A Real Right to Vote*

"This is an exceptionally important book on the too-often dismissed problem of voter suppression laws aimed at young voters. I highly recommend."
– Marc E. Elias, Partner, Elias Law Group LLP and Founder, Democracy Docket

"When colleges, students, and the broader community have organized, they have won victories and made great progress. This book shows you how that happened in the past, with important lessons for the present and future."

– Heather Booth, Founder, Midwest Academy, and 1964 Freedom Summer volunteer

"This must-read book explains in great clarity why this work is so important in this moment and time. I have worked closely with Jonathan Becker and Yael Bromberg upholding the promise of the 26th Amendment, which was supposed to bring equal access to the ballot box for young voters in America."

– David Goodman, Board Member of the Andrew Goodman Foundation, and brother of Andrew Goodman, Student Civil Rights worker murdered in Mississippi, 1964

"In this vitally important, original, and timely book, legal scholars and voting rights advocates Becker and Bromberg present a compelling, collaborative picture of the history, litigation, and future of youth voting rights and the 26th Amendment. The innovative emphasis on the role of students, faculty, and institutions of higher education, particularly HBCUs, provides new historical insights and new practical ideas to protect and defend the voting rights of young Americans in our democracy."

– Jennifer Frost, University of Auckland, and author, *"Let Us Vote!": Youth Voting Rights and the 26th Amendment*

"A compelling example of students and institutions working together to protect voting rights. An inspiring resource for anyone advancing civic engagement and access to the ballot."

– Bobbie Laur, President, Campus Compact

"College and university campuses are essential and powerful sites for democracy that ensure students graduate with the knowledge, skills, and experiences necessary for informed participation and leadership in our communities—from our town halls to the ballot box. This book describes how higher education institutions have served to shape voting rights jurisprudence and continue to work toward a democracy that includes the voices of college students and others who face systemic barriers to participation."

– Jennifer M. Domagal-Goldman, Executive Director, ALL IN Campus Democracy Challenge

Preface

We write this preface in May 2025, more than 100 days into a new presidential administration, just ahead of the 250th commemoration of the signing of the Declaration of Independence. Yet again, the struggle for the nation's identity is at a crossroads. Nowhere is this more evident than in the field of voting rights. Much ink will inevitably be spilled on the clash between the current administration's assault on basic constitutional rights, legal norms and civic society, and the rights of We The People. The United States has often struggled on its uneven path to become a more perfect union. We are in the midst of one of those times, as the forces of reaction threaten basic liberties which have made the country a beacon of democracy. The core achievements of the Second Reconstruction are under attack over 50 years later, especially in the area of voting rights. Also under assault are America's institutions of higher education, the main focus of this book: colleges and universities are in a fight not seen since the McCarthy era to preserve their autonomy and maintain their reputation as bastions of learning, rigorous research, and knowledge production. As this book shows, the United States has also been the home of resistance and reform, what the late Congressman John Lewis called "good trouble." Much of the book focuses on how civic actors in college communities, including students, faculty, and academic administrators, abetted by committed lawyers and advocates, have resisted threats to the right to vote, and in particular the youth vote.

This book was born from an academic project supported by The Andrew W. Mellon Foundation Higher Learning Team that was developed in response to a call for academic proposals on the theme of civic engagement and voting. The proposal to Mellon was a continuation of the collaboration of the two editors of this volume, Jonathan Becker, professor of political studies and vice president for academic affairs at Bard College, who is also the founding director of Bard's Center for Civic Engagement, and Yael Bromberg, a 26th Amendment legal scholar, adjunct law professor, and constitutional rights litigator. Becker and Bromberg previously worked together on litigation to establish a polling station on the Bard campus in upstate New York and subsequently, together with good government groups, on legislation that mandated on-campus polling sites on qualifying colleges across New York State. The proposal was informed by a symposium that Bromberg organized at Rutgers Law School on the promise of the 26th Amendment that included legal scholars, election administrators, members of the advocacy community, and university administrators, and which resulted in the first legal volume on the constitutional amendment to be published, by *The Rutgers University Law Review.*

The Mellon proposal envisioned the development of an academic course and teaching materials that focused on three overlapping questions: *What has been the role of college communities in the fight for suffrage? How has the fight for student voting rights been shaped by past voting rights struggles? What are the lessons for organizing, advocacy, and strategic litigation for student voting rights within the broader struggle for American democracy?*

The course, entitled "Student Voting: Power, Politics, and Race in the Fight for American Democracy," chronicles the histories of the fight for the vote on four college campuses—Bard College, North Carolina Agricultural and Technical State University, Prairie View A&M University (PVAMU), and Tuskegee University—and uses them as a prism through which to explore the history and evolution of voting and American democracy, with particular attention to issues of youth, race, and political power, and the role of various civic actors within college communities.

The ideas in the book emerge from this shared curriculum, co-designed and taught across the four institutions featured in this book, each of which possesses a distinct history related to voting, all of which have overcome tremendous obstacles involving multiple state and federal lawsuits which included students, faculty, and/or administrators acting as litigants, including two U.S. Supreme Court cases that have established precedents related to student voting and gerrymandering.

Three of the partner colleges are Historically Black Colleges and Universities (HBCUs) which offer distinct perspectives on the mission of higher education as they address and deal with the legacy and consequences of America's original sin of slavery.

Faculty from each of these colleges contributed to the ideas and understanding of the book's subject matter, and authored the individual case studies found in this book:

- North Carolina A&T State University (Greensboro, North Carolina), with historian Dr. Jelani M. Favors, United Negro College Fund Vice President and Senior Director of the Frederick D. Patterson Research Institute, and formerly the Henry E. Frye distinguished professor of history at NC A&T, and inaugural director of the Center of Excellence for Social Justice. Dr. Favors' previous publications include *Shelter in a Time of Storm: How Black Colleges Fostered Generations of Leadership & Activism*, a book which focuses on the prominent role of HBCUs as essential institutions for the African American community, fostering what he calls a "second curriculum" which has shaped the political destiny of the United States.
- Prairie View A&M University (Prairie View, Texas), with endowed professor of political science Dr. Melanye T. Price, the inaugural director of the Ruth J. Simmons Center for Race and Justice. Dr. Price's research focuses on Black politics

and political psychology. She authored the books *The Race Whisperer: Barack Obama and the Political Uses of Race,* and *Dreaming Blackness: Black Nationalism and African American Political Opinion.* The case study herein for Prairie View A&M was co-authored by PVAMU political scientist Dr. Michael J. Nojeim, whose research focus is on peace and non-violent resistance, and whose publications include the book *Gandhi and King: The Power of Nonviolent Resistance.* Co-author Dr. Alexander Goodwin is a Prairie View A&M alumnus and assistant professor of political science at Southwestern University whose research focuses on race and ethnic politics.

– Tuskegee University (Tuskegee, Alabama), with Dr. Lisa Bratton, a historian whose primary research focuses on resistance by the enslaved at Historic Brattonsville, the South Carolina plantation on which her ancestors, Green and Malinda Bratton, were enslaved. She also served as a historian for the National Park Service Tuskegee Airmen Oral History Project and interviewed over 250 of the Tuskegee Airmen.

– Bard College, with political scientist Dr. Simon Gilhooley, who specializes in American politics and political thought. His research addresses issues of constitutionality and authority within the American polity. His book, *The Antebellum Origins of the Modern US Constitution: Slavery and the Spirit of the American Founding*, explores the development of the idea of the Constitution as representative of a historical spirit and the emergence of this idea within the historical context of antebellum slavery. Bard administrator and vice president of civic engagement Erin Cannan authored a separate chapter in this book, focused on the practical work that institutions of higher education can do to support election administration in service of student voting rights.

By exploring these institutions' voting rights legal struggles in chronological order, the book teaches readers about the evolution of the right to vote, and examines the fight to vote from the perspective of college communities, which collectively host approximately 40 % of 18- to 24-year-olds in the nation, and in concentrated populations averaging 6,350 students, and up to 50,000 students. Undergraduate students make up approximately 6.5 % of the voter-eligible population in the United States. These young voters comprise an overlooked and underexamined protected constitutional classification with respect to ballot access pursuant to the 26th Amendment, and their decision to participate, or not to participate, in local, state, or national politics has the power to determine electoral outcomes.

This book captures a vision of what can exist when democracy functions in its fullest forms; the dynamic footwork required to fulfill that vision through a combination of persistent organizing, advocacy, education, and, when necessary, litigation; and a gasp of what may result if we fall short of achieving accountable and reflective representation.

Acknowledgements

There are many people whom we would like to acknowledge and thank for their contributions to this book.

We would like to thank our fellow teachers Lisa Bratton, Jelani Favors, Simon Gilhooley, and Melanye Price for their contributions to the jointly designed course, "Student Voting: Power, Politics and Race in the Fight for American Democracy," which served as the launching pad for this book, as well as Erin Cannan, Alexander Goodwin, and Michael Nojeim, who contributed chapters to this book.

We would like to thank Charles Euchner, for his preparation of written case studies for the course; Seamus Heady and Mariia Pankova who, with the assistance of Adam Stepan, prepared the video case studies which complement the course and this book; Clarence Bronte for his great help with references; and Saidee Brown for her invaluable organizational ability and thoughtful coordination of our many moving parts of this project.

For Jonathan Becker's chapters, thanks to Carol Pearce, Stephen Tremaine, and Erin Cannan for their editorial comments and suggestions and to Anna L and Natallia N for their valuable research assistance. Special thanks to Jessica Becker, Joseph Becker, and Sarah Becker for their edits and feedback, as well as for their general support over the decades of the fight for the student vote at Bard, and more broadly Jonathan's work to promote Bard as a private institution acting in the public interest.

For Yael Bromberg's chapters, special thanks to inspiring colleagues in the democracy field, including those who have fought for the ratification of the Twenty-Sixth Amendment, and those who keep its promise alive today. Their efforts and collaborations have shaped the ideas of this book and field of work. It is rare to have the opportunity to get to know the original founders of a constitutional amendment; for those who have been so generous with their time, thanks to Jason Berman, Patricia Keefer, Les Francis, Ian MacGowan, Charles Gonzalez, and Alan Di Sciullo. Thanks to the generations of youth organizers, all of whom have gone on to do great things to advance the cause of public interest, too many to name, including but not limited to: Cyrus Commissariat, Tamia Fowlkes, Evan Marlbrough, Maydee Martinez, Ava Mazzye, Eva Quinones, Jonian Rafti, Valencia Richardson, Sadia Saba, and Matthew Tolbert. And to David Hogg of March for Our Lives and Leaders We Deserve, who transmuted his pain as a survivor of the Parkland High School massacre to national youth-focused leadership. Gratitude to my husband, Rabbi Scott Perlo, and parents Assia and Joshua Bromberg, for their endless support so that I may focus on the time-intensive demands of constitutional litigation and writing.

Thanks to partners and colleagues who continue to invest in and expand this body of work, including David Goodman of The Andrew Goodman Foundation; Cornell Williams Brooks of the Harvard Kennedy and Divinity Schools and The William Monroe Trotter Collaborative for Social Justice; Duke University American historians Nancy Maclean and Gunther Peck, who has integrated these concepts in his pedagogy in the Research Triangle; Joshua Douglas of the University of Kentucky J. David Rosenberg College of Law; American historian Jennifer Frost of the University of Auckland; Aderson B. Francois of Georgetown University Law Center's Civil Rights Clinic; Elizabeth Matto of the Eagleton Institute of Politics; and Nancy Thomas of the American Association of Colleges and Universities.

In terms of the broader efforts to promote student voting rights in the Hudson Valley, which served as the inspiration for creating the voting rights course, thanks to colleagues at Bard's Center for Civic Engagement who have helped with registration and voting rights issues over the years, including Ruth Zisman, Lisa Whalen, Micki Strawinski, Bonnie Goad, Sarah deVeer, Cicily Wilson and many others too numerous to name here. Thanks to Bard's dean of studies, David Shein, vice president for administration, Jim Brudvig, and local lawyer John Pelosi, who acted as poll watchers during numerous elections to support and protect student voters, and to Bard associate professor of political studies, Simon Gilhooley, and particularly vice president for civic engagement, Erin Cannan, who regularly put in very long election days at the Bard, and in Erin's case the Barrytown, poll site. Special thanks to Bard's President, Leon Botstein, who supported student voting rights from the start and demonstrated leadership by serving as a litigant in two important cases: the more one studies college responses to attempts to suppress the student vote, the more special one realizes his response has been. Thanks to public interest advocates and lawyers, including people like Arthur Eisenberg, Alan Sussman, Kathleen O'Keefe, Yael Bromberg, Doug Mishkin, Michael Donofrio and Michael Volpe, for their amazing support. And finally, heartfelt thanks to generations of student leaders of Election@Bard and its predecessors, who have shown tremendous innovation and courage in the fight for the student vote.

More broadly, we would like to thank organizations including the Andrew Goodman Foundation, Democracy Matters, Common Cause including Common Cause North Carolina, ALL IN Campus Democracy Challenge the Institute for Democracy and Higher Education, Campus Vote Project, Students Learn Students Vote Coalition and GenVote who have played such central roles in promoting student voting rights.

Finally, we would like to thank the Andrew W. Mellon Foundation and the Open Society University Network for their support in the creation of the course which served as the basis for this volume.

Last but not least, we thank our families for their love and support in making this work possible. We dedicate our efforts to our children, Lavi and Rafi Perlo, and Joe and Sarah Becker, and the nation's youth and students: may they make better of our generational follies and advance the best of our collective knowledge and abilities.

Contents

Jonathan Becker, Lisa Bratton, Yael Bromberg, Jelani Favors, Simon Gilhooley, Melanye Price

Yael Bromberg and Jonathan Becker

Introduction

> No right is more precious in a free country than that of having a voice in the election of those who make the laws under which, as good citizens, we must live. Other rights, even the most basic, are illusory if the right to vote is undermined. Our Constitution leaves no room for classification of people in a way that unnecessarily abridges.
>
> *Wesberry v. Sanders*, 376 U.S. 1 (1964)[1]

The 26th Amendment to the U.S. Constitution ratified in 1971 lowered the voting age from 21 to 18 and further prohibited voter discrimination based on age. It was passed with near unanimity due to its strong bi-partisan support, and swept through the states, marking the quickest amendment process in U.S. history. While much writing on the 26th Amendment focuses on the hypocrisy of youth being forced into a mandatory military draft while being denied the right to vote, there is a more historically nuanced vein of research which situates the fight to lower the voting age within the context of broader efforts to remove barriers to the franchise and democratize society. As Yael Bromberg put it, "the ultimate expansion of youth access to the franchise is a part of the narrative and immediate aftermath of the Second Reconstruction, and it was a natural extension of the nation's arc towards democratic inclusion."[2]

These efforts were punctuated by several important events, such as Martin Luther King's "Give us the Ballot" speech in 1957 and Freedom Summer of 1964, and realized through several legislative milestones, including the Civil Rights Act of 1964 and the Voting Rights Act of 1965 (VRA), which, among other things, introduced Justice Department pre-approval of electoral changes in counties which had a history of discriminatory practices. A 1970 amendment to the VRA lowered the voting age via statute, leading to a tipping point on the issue after its introduction over 150 times since 1942 as it pressed on for constitutional rati-

---

1 *Wesberry v. Sanders*, 376 U.S. 1 (1964), https://supreme.justia.com/cases/federal/us/376/1/.
2 Yael Bromberg, "Youth Voting Rights and the Unfulfilled Promise of the Twenty-Sixth Amendment," *University of Pennsylvania Journal of Constitutional Law* 21, (2019): 1123, https://scholarship.law.upenn.edu/jcl/vol21/iss5/1/. As Keyssar explains, "What occurred in the course of a decade was not only the re-enfranchisement of African Americans but the abolition of nearly all remaining limits on the right to vote. Poll taxes, literacy tests, understanding clauses, pauper exclusions, and good character provisions had been swept away"; Alexander Keyssar, *The Right to Vote: The Contested History of Democracy in the United States* (Basic Books, a member of the Perseus Books Group, 2009), 228.

fication.[3] The director of NAACP's Youth and College Division, James Brown Jr., summed up the sentiment of voting activists of the time: "It is high time that we realize that black people, poor people, and young people, regardless of color, have been the victims of scorn by those who make our laws. This situation will not be alleviated until all are given full franchise."[4]

The apex on this issue was finally reached after years of movement-building by a youth-led advocacy effort, coalescing in the formation of the Youth Franchise Coalition (YFC).[5] The YFC organized across college campuses and the country, especially in Appalachia, with the support of a diverse, multigenerational coalition with organizations such as Common Cause, the National Education Association, the NAACP, the American Jewish Committee, and the National Association of Autoworkers.[6]

Debates in Congress over lowering the voting age foreshadowed both the promise and challenges that would later emerge once the 26th Amendment was ratified, particularly on college campuses. In a series of reports and deliberations, legislators expressed a fear that the failure to bring America's youth into the democratic process could contribute to their alienation and fuel the radicalism and protests that were sweeping college campuses across the country,[7] as well

---

3 For a summary explanation of the circuitous ratification process, see Bromberg, "Youth Voting Rights." See Jennifer Frost, *"Let Us Vote!": Youth Voting Rights and the 26th Amendment* (New York University Press, 2022) for an in-depth explanation of the process to ratification.

4 Frost, *"Let Us Vote!"* 279.

5 As described by Frost, the YFC was initially founded by "a small group representing key organizations," including the National Education Association, the Student National Education Association, the NAACP, the U.S. National Student Association, Young Democrats, Young Republicans, and others, which met in December 1968 in Washington, D.C. and launched an interim steering committee. Frost, *"Let Us Vote!"* 177. The role of acting executive director was taken on by Tom Hipple, a campaigner from Indiana with close connections to Senator Birch Bayh, chair of the key U.S. Senate subcommittee on constitutional amendments. A separate organization, Let Us Vote, took root in late 1968 by students at the University of Pacific in Stockton, California, following a visit from Senator Bayh. Frost, *"Let Us Vote!"* 179.

6 Bromberg, "Youth Voting Rights," 1120–1123. See also Frost, *"Let Us Vote!"* 188–189. YFC's formation was "welcomed by many politicians" from across the aisle, Frost, *"Let Us Vote!"* at 191, along with their close staff such as Jay Berman, a young staff director for Senator Bayh who organized the Senate hearings and whipped votes in favor of the measure, and Carey Parker, a stalwart aide for Senator Ted Kennedy.

7 Congressman Railsback voiced concern that college students "were being encouraged to try and overthrow the system by the very vocal radical element. They were frustrated that they had no voice in decision-making"; *Extending Voting Rights Act of 1965*, HR 914, June 17, 1970, 91st Cong., 1st sess., *Congressional Record* 116, pt. 15: 20166, https://www.congress.gov/bound-congressional-record/1970/06/17/house-section.

as a confidence that young voters could reinvigorate and strengthen American democracy.

In the congressional debate on the Amendment, Democratic Congressman Spark Matsunaga of Hawaii cited the President's Commission on the Causes and Prevention of Violence's warning that "The anachronistic voting-age limitation tends to alienate [youth] from systematic political processes and to drive them into a search for an alternative, sometimes violent, means to express their frustrations over the gap between the Nation's ideals and actions."[8] Congressman John Anderson of Illinois underlined the stakes: "we will either convince them that the ballot box and the elective process is an effective means of accomplishing change," or they will inevitably "succumb to the same pressures that have brought the demise of democracy when faith in man's right to choose has begun to fade."[9]

The Senate Judiciary Committee's report on *Lowering the Voting Age to 18*, authored by Indiana's Democratic Senator Birch Bayh, took a more positive approach—one which predominated the discussion on the youth vote—as he skillfully steered the process of constitutionalism via the Subcommittee on Constitutional Amendments which he chaired with the support of Senate Majority Leader Mike Mansfield of Montana. Bayh lauded the "dedication and conviction" students brought to the civil rights movement and the "skill and enthusiasm they have infused into the political process."[10]

West Virginia Senator Jennings Randolph, known as the Grandfather of the 26th Amendment, had first introduced an identical proposal more than a quarter century earlier in 1942, and diligently continued to champion it until its ratification:

> I had then, as I have now, the utmost confidence in the ability of our young citizens to think clearly, to weigh the issues, and to make judicious decisions on matters closely affecting

---

8 The report continued, "Lowering the voting age will not eliminate protest by the young. But it will provide them with a direct, constructive, and democratic channel for making their views felt and for giving them a responsible stake in the future of the Nation"; *Lowering the Voting Age to 18*, HR 223, March 23, 1971, 92nd Cong., 1st sess., *Congressional Record* 117, pt. 6: 7538, https://www.congress.gov/bound-congressional-record/1971/03/23/house-section.

9 *Extending Voting Rights Act of 1965*, HR 914, June 17, 1970, 91st Cong., 1st sess., *Congressional Record* 116, pt. 15: 20163, https://www.congress.gov/bound-congressional-record/1970/06/17/house-section. See also Professor Paul Freund of Harvard Law School, cited in: Senator Birch Bayh, *Lowering the Voting Age to 18: A Fifty-State Survey of the Costs and Other Problems of Dual-Age Voting*, report prepared for the Constitutional Amendments Subcommittee of the Committee on the Judiciary, 92nd Cong., 1st sess., 1971, Committee Print 56–103, 6.

10 Bayh, *Lowering the Voting Age to 18*, 6.

their futures. …They share the burden of fighting our wars and carrying out our national policies, but have no real voice in making those policies. They share the burden of paying our taxes. They stand responsible and adult, not juvenile, before courts of law. They stand responsible for the welfare and the lives of their fellow citizens, traveling on our streets and highways … allowed to operate motor vehicles. They bear the burden of the future of their families, for we allow them to make wills and to purchase insurance. They bear the burden of financial consequences for their own actions, for we allow them to be sued in court. They are responsible for their own ultimate social future, for we allow them to choose their profession. … Our youth are the promise, the home, the dream of Americans. This we all recognize as we emphasize education, family, health, and vocational preparation. … They will bring these new, different ideas. They will bring these new, so necessarily needed, enthusiasms which I sense are valuable.[11]

Conservative stalwart Senator Barry Goldwater, who claimed to have had "probably visited more colleges and universities in the last decade than anyone in the country," was convinced that "some more idealism will do us all good. It will help remove the crusty, shop-worn reasons why the policies and goals which are promised to voters don't ever seem to get accomplished. It will make us find the positive answers that will put us on the right track."[12] When the Amendment was finally approved, with an overwhelming 94–0 vote in the Senate and 401–19 vote in the House, President Nixon declared "America's new voters, America's young generation" would bring "moral courage" and "a spirit of high idealism" to the country. It was the quickest amendment to be ratified in United States history, rounding the requisite 38 states in less than 100 days, in large part due to the cross-partisan support it garnered.

But the enthusiasm was not universal. During a failed 1967 effort to lower New York State's voting age from 21 to 18, the *New York Times* decried the potential addition of "inexperienced and immature voters" onto the voting rolls.[13] In the congressional debate on the eve of the 26th Amendment, Republican Congressman Robert Michael of Illinois warned about the impact that a

---

11 Jennings Randolph, statement appearing in U.S. Congress, Senate, Subcommittee on Constitutional Amendments of the Committee on the Judiciary, *Hearings on S.J. Res. 8, S.J. Res 14, and S.J. Res. 78 Relating to Lowering the Voting Age to 18*, 90th Cong., 2nd sess., 1968, 61–62.
12 *Eighteen is Old Enough*, S. 3560, March 10, 1971, 92nd Cong., 1st sess., *Congressional Record* 117, pt. 5: 5820, https://www.congress.gov/bound-congressional-record/1971/03/10/senate-section. The report cited Freund, who asserted that "the student movement around the world" was the "herald of an intellectual and moral revolution," which, if not subverted, "could portend a new enlightenment"; Bayh, *Lowering the Voting Age to 18*, 6.
13 "The Right Voting Age," *New York Times*, July 7, 1967.

large concentration of youth voters could have on local elections, specifically youth from college campuses:

> My principal concern with this particular measure is one that has to do with permitting 18-year-olds to vote, for instance, in local and municipal elections in college towns. ... For goodness sakes, we could have these transients actually controlling the elections, voting city councils and mayors in or out of office in a town in which they have a dominant voice.[14]

Congressman Thomas Railsback, another Illinois Republican, articulated similar concerns and foreshadowed future challenges by suggesting that students should only be able to register if they stated an oath before a local election official testifying to their residency and their intention to remain within a community following graduation, and providing information about things like where they banked and where they paid their taxes.[15]

No sooner had the 26th Amendment been ratified than those concerns manifested into practical challenges that threatened students' right to vote in the communities in which they studied. Local officials, often echoing the sentiments expressed by Michael and Railsback, took actions to limit youth political power. Acting at times like Jim Crow-era gatekeepers, they imposed selective residency requirements that barred students from registering to vote locally. These requirements were overturned by numerous state and federal courts across the country,[16] leading to the 1979 case *Symm v. United States*, which emerged from complaints by students at Prairie View A&M University (PVAMU). To this day, *Symm* remains the only United States Supreme Court decision to have substantively considered a 26th Amendment challenge.

Symm, however, did not end discriminatory practices that targeted students. Local and county public officials have repeatedly demonstrated that they are prepared to suppress the vote of college students, continuing to impose residency requirements, instituting bureaucratic address requirements intended to disqualify student voters, and even threatening and arresting college students for voting lo-

---

14 *Lowering the Voting Age to 18*, HR 223, March 23, 1971, 92nd Cong., 1st sess., *Congressional Record* 117, pt. 6: 7538, https://www.congress.gov/bound-congressional-record/1971/03/23/house-section.

15 Railsback mentioned several criteria to determine residency, including "where the person intends to reside, and where he does his banking, pays his taxes ... whether he is in effect a transient, which would mean his residence would be his permanent home or where he intends to return." *Lowering the Voting Age to 18*, HR 223, March 23, 1971, 92nd Cong., 1st sess., *Congressional Record* 117, pt. 6: 7539, https://www.congress.gov/bound-congressional-record/1971/03/23/house-section.

16 Bromberg, "Youth Voting Rights," 1135–1136, footnote 126.

cally. They have also created barriers to the act of voting itself, situating polling places at considerable distance from college campuses, limiting voting hours, and sowing confusion by gerrymandering college campuses into multiple election districts.[17] These and other restrictions only metastasized after the notorious *Shelby v. Holder* 2013 Supreme Court decision which eviscerated the Voting Rights Act of 1965, the crown jewel of the Second Reconstruction, and led to new restrictions pertinent to student voters such as the roll-back of accessible polling locations and stripping of student identification as a permissible form of voter identification.

Framework

The goal of this book is to use the history of the 26th Amendment, the ongoing fight to promote and defend youth voter participation and voting rights in general, and the role of college communities in that fight, as a prism through which to teach the history of the struggle for the fundamental right to vote in the United States. The hope is not simply to address a heretofore underdeveloped area of research, but also to shape teaching and inform contemporary civic engagement efforts of students and institutions across the country.

The book explores college campuses which experienced significant threats to voting rights and which, often through lengthy battles, served as host sites to precedential voting rights litigation. It is centered around the experiences of four institutions, some of which have played out over decades: Tuskegee University in Alabama, PVAMU in Texas, North Carolina Agricultural and Technical State University (NC A&T), and Bard College in upstate New York. We explore obstacles to voting and the organizing, advocacy, and legal efforts that went into surmounting them. To contextualize developments, particularly since three of the four cases occurred at Historically Black Colleges and Universities (HBCUs), we explore HBCUs' unique history and interrogate the interplay between age, partisanship, and race in motivating youth voter suppression.

Chapter one provides an overview of the evolution of the right to vote in America with an emphasis on youth political participation during the First and Second Reconstruction, through ratification of the 26th Amendment and its immediate aftermath. The chronological legal overview frames the college case studies in the context of the evolving recognition of the right to vote, and describes indi-

---

17 A reader seeking to learn more details about these restrictions may be interested in the 2022 *Rutgers University Law Review* volume, which was the first legal volume dedicated to the 26th Amendment after its ratification over 50 years ago; *The Rutgers University Law Review* 74, no. 5 (2022), https://rutgerslawreview.com/volume-74-summer-2022-issue-5/.

viduals involved in those struggles to shape the law through organizing, advocacy, and litigation.

Chapter two then contextualizes the case studies within the environment of higher education by focusing on the historic link between American higher education and democracy, and the unique mission of HBCUs in shaping civic engagement. Particular attention is devoted to the role of key constituencies—students, faculty, and administrators—in the fight for student voting rights, including the role of institutions themselves as civic actors.

The book then moves into the case studies, each of which examines the sources and nature of the threat to voting rights and the methods and mechanisms used to defend those rights. Chapter three explores Tuskegee University (then Tuskegee Institute), which in 1957 was literally gerrymandered out of the municipality of Tuskegee, along with nearly all Black voters in the city. It devotes particular attention to the work of Tuskegee faculty member and administrator Charles Goode Gomillion, who eventually became the named plaintiff in the landmark 1960 Supreme Court case *Gomillion v. Lightfoot* which addressed racial gerrymandering for the first time.

Chapter four examines the protracted fight at PVAMU, beginning with *Symm v. United States* in 1979 and extending across the experience of generations of students who suffered harassment and arrest. Chapter five explores NC A&T, whose campus was divided into two congressional districts in a partisan gerrymander that was featured in recent North Carolina state and federal cases *Harper v. Hall* and *Rucho v. Common Cause.*

Chapter six examines the case of Bard College, which over the last quarter century participated in four successful lawsuits, one federal and three state, that secured student voting eligibility based on residency, established a polling site on campus, and contributed to the adoption of a state law mandating polling sites on college campuses with more than 300 registered student voters. Chapter seven then compares and contrasts the case studies, identifying similarities and differences between the case studies and lessons from the experiences of the four institutions.

The final chapter is a more practical step-by-step guide that offers best practices and frameworks for how college communities address student voting today.

The multidisciplinary approach of the book is reflected in the different perspectives and voice that emerges from each chapter's author, and the book as a whole. The case studies have been written by historians and political scientists based in the institutions examined, the framing chapter on the right to vote and the youth vote has been written by a constitutional rights litigator and legal scholar of the 26th Amendment, while the framing chapter on the civic role of college communities and the chapter on best practices for student voter engagement have been written by university administrators. By offering the case studies in chronological order, the book offers a multidisciplinary academic tool for classrooms to study evolution of the vote and the youth vote from the locales most familiar to student-readers: their colleges and universities.

This book makes an important contribution to the study of youth voting. The 26th Amendment and its impacts as a whole have been under-studied. This has in part been remedied by a recent book by Jennifer Frost, *"Let Us Vote!"*, and a companion book of primary documents, *Achieving the 26th Amendment*, edited by Frost and Rebecca de Schweinitz.[18] Implementation of the Amendment was addressed by a special volume of *The Rutgers Law Review* in 2022. The volume offers a first-time collection of legal scholarship dedicated to the Amendment since its ratification over 50 years ago. Yet there remain significant gaps in the literature. This is particularly true for college campuses. While the 26th Amendment emerged in part in response to youth activism calling for the youth vote at the end of the Second Reconstruction, colleges and universities have been the centers of most 26th Amendment and youth voting litigation, although very little has been written systematically about the role of these communities in the promotion and defense of student voting rights.[19]

In total, the book tells the story of how institutions of higher education, and the critical actors surrounding them, have worked and can continue to work in partnership to register student voters, successfully overcome voter restrictions, and engage in the process of democracy. It demonstrates how it is possible to promote and defend voting rights with the dynamic engagement of a variety of civic actors. And while future proposed restrictions on these campuses are possible, especially if and when advocacy or leadership wanes, those who participate in this journey of participatory democracy are themselves transformed in the process as they work to expand access for others, for democracy is a journey and not a destination.

---

[18] Rebecca de Schweinitz and Jennifer Frost, *Achieving the 26th Amendment: A History with Primary Sources* (Routledge, 2023).

[19] For example, a survey of the five the most important law review articles on the 26th Amendment over the past fifteen years reveals only two mentions of college leadership (presidents, vice presidents, provosts and deans), and then only in reference to Bard College. References to student and faculty leaders tend to be episodic, and it is difficult to extract lessons for the present. Jonathan Becker and Erin Cannan, "Institution as Citizen: Colleges and Universities as Actors in Defense of Student Voting Rights," *The Rutgers University Law Review* 74, no. 5 (2022): 1877.

Bibliography

Bayh, Birch. *Lowering the Voting Age to 18: A Fifty-State Survey of the Costs and Other Problems of Dual-Age Voting.* Report prepared for the Constitutional Amendments Subcommittee of the Committee on the Judiciary. 92nd Cong., 1st sess., 1971. Committee Print 56 – 103.

Becker, Jonathan and Cannan, Erin. "Institution as Citizen: Colleges and Universities as Actors in Defense of Student Voting Rights." *The Rutgers University Law Review* 74, no. 5 (2022): 1869 – 1909. https://rutgerslawreview.com/wp-content/uploads/2023/02/07_Becker_Cannan.pdf.

Bromberg, Yael. "Youth Voting Rights and the Unfulfilled Promise of the Twenty-Sixth Amendment." *University of Pennsylvania Journal of Constitutional Law* 21 (2019): 1105 – 1166. https://scholarship.law.upenn.edu/jcl/vol21/iss5/1/.

de Schweinitz, Rebecca and Frost, Jennifer. *Achieving the 26th Amendment: A History with Primary Sources.* Routledge, 2023.

Frost, Jennifer. *"Let Us Vote!": Youth Voting Rights and the 26th Amendment.* New York University Press, 2022.

Keyssar, Alexander. *The Right to Vote: The Contested History of Democracy in the United States.* Basic Books, 2009.

"The Right Voting Age." *New York Times*, July 7, 1967.

The Rutgers University Law Review 74, no. 5 (2022). https://rutgerslawreview.com/volume-74-summer-2022-issue-5/.

U.S. Congress. *Congressional Record.* 91st Cong., 1st sess., 1970. Vol. 116, pt. 15. https://www.congress.gov/bound-congressional-record/1970/06/17/house-section.

U.S. Congress. *Congressional Record.* 92nd Cong., 1st sess., 1971. Vol. 117, pt. 5 – 6. https://www.congress.gov/bound-congressional-record/1971/03/23/house-section.

U.S. Congress. Senate. Subcommittee on Constitutional Amendments of the Committee on the Judiciary. *Hearings on S.J. Res. 8, S.J. Res 14, and S.J. Res. 78 Relating to Lowering the Voting Age to 18.* 90th Cong., 2nd sess., May 14, May 15, and May 16, 1968.

Yael Bromberg
1 Evolution of the Right to Vote and the Youth Vote: The First and Second Reconstruction

Young people have always been a part of the multigenerational writing of the Story of America. In colonial times, they fought in the Revolutionary War as teenagers, although the colonies adopted from England the legal age of 21 as the minimum voting age.[1] The United States Constitution, passed in 1789, left the determination of suffrage to the states, which largely restricted access to white male property-owners over the age of 21. The slogan "old enough to fight, old enough to vote" was born in this era, in connection with those who fought in the Revolutionary War.[2] This limitation on the franchise since the nation's founding—on account of age, race, gender, and wealth—and, critically, servitude (i.e., the institution of slavery)—set the unstable and arguably volatile framework for the evolution of the right to vote in America; one steeped in ongoing tension between who is and who is not considered a legitimate member of the American family.

This foundation is inherently in tension with the ostensible purpose of the Declaration of Independence, unanimously adopted in 1776, proclaiming that "all men are created equal," and the opening salvo of the United States Constitution—"We The People"—which established the first constitutional republic in the world recognizing that sovereignty arises from *the people*, who consent to be governed pursuant to the rule of law. On the one hand, the evolution of the right to vote is a narrative of resistance for personal autonomy and self-government, such as in the struggle of the colonists to overthrow British control to form a new nation whose core principle is the establishment of democracy by and of the people. On the other hand, it is a narrative of continued subjugation and repression of those deemed less worthy of participating on an equal basis in the enterprise

---

1 Wendell W. Cultice, *Youth's Battle for the Ballot: A History of Voting Age in America* (Greenwood Press, 1992). See also Todd Andrlik, "How Old Were the Leaders of the American Revolution on July 4, 1776? Younger Than You Think," *Slate*, August 20, 2013, https://slate.com/news-and-politics/2013/08/how-old-were-the-founding-fathers-the-leaders-of-the-american-revolution-were-younger-than-we-imagine.html. I began to develop this concept of youth leaders writing the Story of America in a piece for *Teen Vogue*. See Yael Bromberg, "The Youth Voting Rights Act Would Transform Access for Youth Voters," *Teen Vogue*, July 27, 2022, https://www.teenvogue.com/story/youth-voting-rights-act-what-is.
2 Cultice, *Youth's Battle for the Ballot*, 5.

of democracy. The tension lays in which members of the body politic are fully recognized as comprising "the people," and how they can effectuate their voice via the vote, and their rights.

This chapter offers an overview of this contested history, specifically as it relates to youth voting rights, and the dynamics of power, politics, race, and age in the fight for American democracy. When young people finally turned to their own enfranchisement via ratification of the 26th Amendment in 1971, it was after they had been actively engaged in the struggle for equality for well over a decade. As I have written elsewhere, "[a]lthough the Twenty-Sixth Amendment is not traditionally considered as being part of the Second Reconstruction (1954–1968), youth were an integral part of the era, and youth enfranchisement in 1971 was its natural outcome."[3]

We begin with the First Reconstruction (1865–1877) to appreciate 1) the continued role that young people have played in writing the Story of America through the Second Reconstruction, and 2) how the basic precepts of the fundamental right to vote and equal protection evolved over time despite the best efforts of voter suppressors. Then, we will examine youth leadership in their own enfranchisement through the ratification of the 26th Amendment, which lowered the voting age to 18 and barred the denial or abridgement of the right to vote on account of age. In so doing, we explore the legislative history of the Amendment within the arc of evolution of the right to vote, and consider the 'special burdens' on the youth vote that the 26th Amendment was intended to address. Finally, we explore the initial challenges in the decade following this expansion of the franchise to 11 million new voters, with an emphasis on the right to establish residency from a campus domicile.

As we explore the history of constitutionalism and evolution of the right to vote with a focus on youth participation in the process—with emphasis on three Historically Black Colleges and Universities (HBCUs): Tuskegee Institute (now Tuskegee University) (Tuskegee, Alabama), North Carolina A&T University (Greensboro, North Carolina), and Prairie View A&M University (Prairie View, Texas)—we examine how these principles and dynamics apply to those host institutions, which were sites of significant voting rights precedent. By offering this analysis with a focus on college communities, undergraduate students can appreciate how their access to the ballot is shaped by the institutions where they live, eat, and study. Thus, this chapter may be read independently and/or alongside the

---

3 Yael Bromberg, "Youth Voting Rights and the Unfulfilled Promise of the Twenty-Sixth Amendment," *University of Pennsylvania Journal of Constitutional Law* 21 (2019): 1120, https://schol arship.law.upenn.edu/jcl/vol21/iss5/1/.

individual chapters in this book that focus on those institutions' backgrounds and settings, and is intended to offer a larger legal framework to those case studies in the fight for the right to vote.

1 The First Reconstruction: A Brief Moment in the Sun

The bloody Civil War (1861–1865) fundamentally transformed suffrage in America with the ratification of the 13th (1865), 14th (1868), and 15th Amendments (1870). Collectively referred to as the 'Reconstruction Amendments,' they outlaw slavery, establish equal protection under law, and forbid denial or abridgement of the right to vote on account of race, color, or previous condition of servitude.[4]

The Civil War soldiers were young—nearly two-thirds were under 22 and "more than 500,000 were less than 17."[5] Despite the contributions of youth during the war, and those of women who took up increased public roles to treat and support the wounded, the franchise was extended to neither during reconstruction.

As for freed and enfranchised Black men, "[t]he slave went free; stood a brief moment in the sun; then moved back again toward slavery," said historian and sociologist W.E.B. DuBois of the First Reconstruction.[6] The Reconstruction Amendments made immediate gains evident by the election of over 1,500 African American men by their peers to public office on the local, state, and federal level.[7]

The process of democracy during this early period in American history was raucous. Newly eligible voters cast their 'virgin vote,' as the first-time voting experience was commonly called at the time. Young white men inherited the franchise

---

4 Expansion of the suffrage also occurred prior to the Civil War, and there was some variation among the states. For example, New Jersey granted a limited property suffrage to women and African Americans from 1790 to 1807. In 1790, ten of the nation's then-13 states required property ownership to vote, while only three of the nation's then-31 states did by 1855. See Alexander Keyssar, *The Right to Vote: The Contested History of Democracy in the United States* (Basic Books, a member of the Perseus Books Group, 2009), Table A.3. By 1838, African American men were denied the vote in the Connecticut, New Jersey, New York, and Pennsylvania constitutions, but maintained it in Virginia and North Carolina; William Yates, *Rights of Colored Men to Suffrage Citizenship and Trial by Jury* (Merrihew and Gunn, 1838), iii, II.
5 Cultice, *Youth's Battle for the Ballot*, 12.
6 W.E.B. Du Bois, *Black Reconstruction in America: An Essay Toward a History of the Part Which Black Folk Played in the Attempt to Reconstruct Democracy in America, 1860–1880* (Oxford University Press, 1935), 27.
7 Eric Foner, *Freedom's Lawmakers: A Directory of Black Officeholders During Reconstruction* (LSU Press, 1996).

simply by aging into it upon turning 21, and a new generation of African American men aged 21 and older had access to the franchise for the first time pursuant to ratification of the 15th Amendment.[8] During the period between 1840 and 1900, voter participation skyrocketed to 70 and 80% of eligible voters nationally, reaching up to 90% in some states[9]—rates which are hard to conceive today.

Even though they did not have the right of suffrage, young people "fueled American politics" as "[c]ampaigns became the centerpiece of the new American culture."[10] As detailed by historian Jon Grinspan in *The Virgin Vote*, "The age of popular politics coincided with the wild years of American youth." A new culture of campaigning emerged as a form of entertainment and socialization. Political party headquarters were set up in saloons where alcohol added to the din, and in barber shops, offering networking and potential job opportunities for the working class.[11] Due to the heightened attention to politics, enfranchisement upon turning 21 took on new significance—it marked a "sharp boundary between youth and adulthood," a rite of passage for manhood.[12] Young African Americans similarly "found identity and adulthood in popular politics," albeit in more discreet settings in "freedmen's schools and churches, at covert Union League meetings and bloody Reconstruction-era polling places."[13] (Figure 1)

Despite the hope of rebirth for the nation, the gains made by the First Reconstruction proved short-lived. Federal troops that had been sent south to implement the Reconstruction Amendments were withdrawn following the electoral crisis of the 1876 presidential election. Vigilante violence by racial terrorist groups such as the Ku Klux Klan and the political violence of Jim Crow laws took root.[14] Blacks were now left on their own without federal protection. Nonetheless, they "continued to vote in large numbers in most parts of the South for more than two decades after Reconstruction."[15]

---

8 Jon Grinspan, *The Virgin Vote: How Young Americans Made Democracy Social, Politics Personal, and Voting Popular in the Nineteenth Century* (University of North Carolina Press, 2016).
9 Grinspan, *The Virgin Vote*, 5, 6, 7, and 131, citing John P. McIver, *Historical Statistics of the United States, Millennial Edition*, ed. Susan B. Carter and Scott Sigmund Gartner (Cambridge University Press, 2006); Paul Kleppner, *Who Voted? The Dynamics of Electoral Turnout, 1870–1980* (Praeger, 1982), 68–69.
10 Grinspan, *The Virgin Vote*, 5, 6.
11 Grinspan, *The Virgin Vote*, 6, 7.
12 Grinspan, *The Virgin Vote*, 8.
13 Grinspan, *The Virgin Vote*, 9.
14 See, for example, Michael J. Klarman, *From Jim Crow to Civil Rights: The Supreme Court and the Struggle for Racial Equality* (Oxford University Press, 2006), 30.
15 C. Vann Woodward, *The Strange Career of Jim Crow*, commemorative ed. (Oxford University Press, 2002), 53–54.

ELECTIONEERING AT THE SOUTH.—SKETCHED BY W. L. SHEPPARD.—[SEE PAGE 467.]

Figure 1: Newly enfranchised citizens engage in the discussion of political questions upon which they are to vote, aptly listening to a young African American orator.
Source: William Ludwell Sheppard, "Electioneering at the South." Print, *Harper's Weekly,* July 25, 1868, from The New York Public Library Digital Collections, Miriam and Ira D. Wallach Division of Art, Prints, and Photographs: Picture Collection, https://digitalcollections.nypl.org/items/510d47e1-3fa3-a3d9-e040-e00a18064a99.

During this period, the moral and political courage of youth was evident, even among those who had not yet gained the suffrage. In 1883, a recently turned 21-year-old, Ida B. Wells, who had been born into slavery, boarded a train in Memphis, Tennessee. She was dragged from her seat when she refused to relocate from the quiet 'ladies car' which was designated for white women and their Black servants, to the 'colored car' where smoking and drinking were allowed, and where white men joined at their pleasure. Wells retained an attorney to sue the railroad company for racial segregation. The trial court found in her favor, a major success at the time which gave her some local celebrity, but the verdict was later reversed by the Tennessee State Supreme Court.[16] The experience informed Ms. Wells'

---

16 Seventy years after Wells, segregation in public transportation was finally overturned by the

groundbreaking journalism exposing Jim Crow segregation and documenting lynching throughout the South.

Access to the vote was first restricted through fear and physical violence, and especially lynching. The resulting limited electorate, then, selected representatives who espoused views and advanced laws to revamp government in their likeness. Legal historian Michael J. Klarman summarized in *From Jim Crow to Civil Rights:*

> Though its timing and method varied, the general pattern of black disenfranchisement was consistent across states. First, whites reduced black political participation by force and fraud. ... Then, Democratic legislatures enacted laws, such as complex voter registration requirements, which further reduced black voting and Republican representation. This facilitated state constitutional changes, such as poll taxes and literacy tests, which consummated black disenfranchisement.[17]

For example, between 1890 and 1918, all 11 former Confederate states enacted a poll tax, such as Mississippi, which adopted a $1 poll tax, among other limitations, into the state constitution in 1890. Five of the 11 enacted grandfather clauses, which allowed those on the voter registration laws prior to Black enfranchisement to remain on those lists and therefore avoid new impediments, such as Louisiana, where such a clause was adopted into the constitution in 1898. And seven enacted literacy tests, which disproportionately impacted Black voters due to the significant rates of illiteracy, such as South Carolina, where illiteracy among Black men was 55%.[18]

The struggle for women's enfranchisement was also underway during this period. Eight states fully enfranchised women prior to the turn of the 20th century.[19] Several states gradually permitted women to vote prior to ratification of the 19th Amendment in 1920, sometimes only in school board races, particularly in the period between 1876 and 1898 when a burst of 25 states expanded such access. Women would no longer be confined to influencing the vote by appealing to their male enfranchised peers. Here, too, young people were engaged in the process of constitutionalism. For example, Alice Paul was 22 years old when she went to England and joined women's suffrage efforts there, returning home to lead suc-

---

Supreme Court when five African American women in Montgomery, Alabama similarly refused to give up their bus seats. *Browder v. Gayle*, 352 U.S. 903 (1956).

17 Klarman, *From Jim Crow to Civil Rights*, 30.

18 U.S. Library of Congress, Congressional Research Service, *The Voting Rights Act of 1965: Background and Overview*, by Kevin J. Coleman, RL43626 (2015), 8–9.

19 Keyssar, *The Right to Vote*, Table A.17, A.20.

cessful congressional efforts for the 19th Amendment and to author the first Equal Rights Amendment of 1923.[20]

Just as Jim Crow disenfranchised Black men, Jane Crow suppressed Black women. Despite ratification of the 19th Amendment, it would take another century for the constitutional protections passed in the second part of the 1800s to finally take root during the Second Reconstruction through a combination of mass organizing and public pressure, coupled with a sympathetic judiciary and eventual leadership by the executive and legislative branches of federal government.

The Reconstruction Amendments ultimately transformed evolution of the right to vote for the rest of the nation. They motivated the ratification of future constitutional amendments such as the 19th Amendment for women's suffrage, the 24th Amendment to ban poll taxes, and the 26th Amendment for youth suffrage. They authorized Congress to enact new legislation to enforce these rights, such as the Voting Rights Act of 1965, discussed further below. The fundamental right to vote is recognized in the 14th Amendment's guarantee of equal protection under law, which also became the basis of future anti-discrimination rights beyond the racial context. The fundamental right to vote is also protected by the First Amendment's recognition of the freedom of association and speech, including election-related expression. Separately, the fundamental right to vote is expressly found within the state constitutions, which offer an independent, and sometimes broader, source of protection than federal rights.

2 The Second Reconstruction: A Second Emancipation

Although United States Supreme Court precedent overturned restrictions on the right to vote such as Jim Crow grandfather clauses in 1915,[21] the reality of implementation was more complicated. The culture of racial and economic power and control had to be extracted from the mores.

Some limited social gains were made in the South despite Jim Crow's stranglehold on the vote. As explained by preeminent southern historian C. Vann Woodward:

---

20 Bromberg, "The Youth Voting Rights Act."
21 See *Guinn v. United States*, 238 U.S. 347 (1915).

Six states adopted laws, aimed at regulating the Ku Klux Klan, prohibiting the wearing of masks and burning of crosses. Forty-odd private universities and colleges admitted Negro students without legal compulsion. ... Some professional associations, learned societies, lawyers, nurses, librarians and social workers [also abandoned the color line voluntarily]. Not all the reform was the consequence of outside pressure, and it would be unfair to the South and unfaithful to the facts to leave that impression. But the margin of activity for Southern liberals and moderates was never broad, and it was to narrow sharply with the rise of militant Southern resistance.[22]

Jim Crow political and physical violence dominated the law of the land until the nation's Second Reconstruction (1954–1968), a second period of constitutional renewal. The appointment of five new justices to the Supreme Court by President Eisenhower in just four years allowed for a fresh approach with the leadership of incoming Chief Justice Earl Warren.[23] The Warren Court (1953–1969) coincided with, and helped give way to, the Second Reconstruction, "enforcing norms of fair treatment and racial equality that, in their core meanings, are no longer substantially contested in American society."[24]

The unanimous, groundbreaking *Brown v. Board of Education* decision in 1954, published the first term of the new court, overturned a 60-year precedent from the turn of the century, holding segregation in public education to be violative of equal protection.[25] The ruling, and its reasoning, eventually gave way to the integration of public spaces, from elementary schools to professional schools, restaurants to beaches.[26]

---

22 Woodward, *The Strange Career of Jim Crow*, 143.
23 William F. Swindler, "The Warren Court: Completion of a Constitutional Revolution," *Vanderbilt Law Review* 23 (1970): 213; Mark Tushnet, ed., *The Warren Court in Historical and Political Perspective* University Press of Virginia, 1993), 213. See also Mark Tushnet and Katya Lezin, "What Really Happened in Brown v. Board of Education," *Columbia Law Review* 91 (1991): 1867–1930.
24 Mark Tushnet, "The Warren Court as History: An Interpretation," *The Warren Court in Historical and Political Perspective*, ed. Mark Tushnet (University Press of Virginia, 1993), 2.
25 *Brown v. Board of Education*, 347 U.S. 483 (1954), overruling *Plessy v. Ferguson*, 163 U.S. 537 (1896).
26 The landmark case was intensely developed and litigated by the NAACP, but little known at the time, and little appreciated even today, was that the central theory of the case was masterminded by a third-year Howard Law student in her early 30s. Pauli Murray, the only woman in her class, who went on to graduate valedictorian, proposed in her seminar paper that the NAACP overly focused on challenging the comparatively unequal conditions of segregation (e. g., a comparison of different quality of books used between classrooms), and that the separation itself should be challenged as unequal. See Kathryn Schulz, "The Many Lives of Pauli Murray," *The New Yorker*, April 10, 2017, https://www.newyorker.com/magazine/2017/04/17/the-many-lives-of-pauli-murray.

In the face of southern resistance, the Warren Court struggled between the idealism it set out in *Brown* and practical implementation. The Court had simply instructed, with no clear direction, that public school desegregation be implemented with "all deliberate speed." Fred Gray, a celebrated Alabama-based civil rights attorney who worked alongside the social justice movement, reflected: "Having made its ruling, the Court failed to carefully and completely spell out how this tremendous change in the social order was to be implemented and enforced by the legislature and executive branches of government. ... [I]t gave the South years of room to evade the intent of the Court's decision."[27]

Nonetheless, Americans were finally greeted with moral clarity. Despite its shortcomings, according to Gray, the *Brown* decision "was welcomed by African Americans as if it were a second emancipation."[28] An awakening was taking place in these early days of what would later be recognized as the Second Reconstruction. The *Brown* decision unearthed an indelible well of hope from which sprang rich, multigenerational community organizing and a new era of constitutionalism. This post-*Brown* emergence of dynamic community organizing and civic engagement juxtaposed the post-*Brown* backlash of racial entrenchment, illustrated by the resurgence of the Klan and the introduction of new legal obstacles to voter engagement, such as stringent literacy tests, voter purges for technical registration flaws, and the continued imposition of poll taxes in five states (Alabama, Arkansas, Mississippi, Texas, and Virginia).[29]

2.1 The Gerrymandering of Tuskegee Institute

It was a time of rapid change in the fabric of public life and social systems. As the Montgomery, Alabama bus boycotts were winding down, Alabama State Senator Sam Engelhardt, Jr.—who was also the executive secretary of the state's White Citizens Council—proposed a 1957 state law ('Act 140') to redraw the municipal boundaries of the City of Tuskegee, the county seat of his legislative district.

What made the City of Tuskegee unique—and a target—was the presence of a concentrated, highly educated Black population associated with Tuskegee Institute, a nationally renowned HBCU founded by Dr. Booker T. Washington, and the Tuskegee Veterans Hospital, the first federal hospital staffed and operated by Black physicians, initially built to offer medical care to the more than

---

27 Fred D. Gray, *Bus Ride to Justice: Changing the System by the System* (New South Books, 1995), 186.
28 Gray, *Bus Ride to Justice*, 186.
29 See Klarman, *From Jim Crow to Civil Rights*, 392.

300,000 Black veterans returning from World War I to the racially segregated South. A journalist with *The New Yorker*, Bernard Taper, observed:

> Perhaps more than in any other comparable area, here are the extremes of [African American] life in the South and nation today. In this county, black hands daily perform the most intricate and delicate surgical operations known to medicine in the large veterans' hospital while other black hands till the earth under conditions characterized by the most primitive superstition and backwardness.[30]

The presence of this wealthier, educated class of Blacks also contributed to a polite, albeit tense, southern mannerism between the races, and specifically the "absence of menace" which was so common in other parts of the South.[31]

Before the passage of Act 140, about 40% of the voters in the City of Tuskegee were Black, and Blacks comprised nearly one-third of the county's electorate.[32] Were Black residents able to register freely, their unified voting block could have overcome the political power of white domination.[33] Act 140 was a regressive response to an emerging trend of increased Black voter registration, and allowed only a handful of voter-eligible Black residents to remain within the city's limits. *Time Magazine* reported: "In the opinion of Alabama's Racist State Senator Sam Engelhardt Jr., if you can't lick 'em, the best thing to do is scatter 'em."[34] The proposal passed the state Senate and House unanimously and without any debate.

It was apparently not enough that the Macon County Board of Registrars had already imposed literacy and other exclusionary devices on Black voter registrants, including vaguely worded questionnaires and requirements to recite or write down long tracts of the Constitution. The chair of the elections board, Wheeler Dyson, twistingly justified voter suppression: "Well, they missed some

---

30 Bernard Taper, *Gomillion Versus Lightfoot: The Right to Vote in Apartheid Alabama* (University of Alabama Press, 2003), 41.
31 Taper, *Gomillion Versus Lightfoot*, 42.
32 Robert J. Norrell, *Reaping the Whirlwind: The Civil Rights Movement in Tuskegee* Alfred A. Knopf, Inc., 1985), 89.
33 Norell, *Reaping the Whirlwind*, 89. According to the U.S. Commission on Civil Rights, the 1950 Census reported a total county population of 30,561, of which Blacks were 25,784, and whites were 4,777. By 1958, the county voter registration list comprised 3,102 white voters and only 1,218 Black voters. United States Commission on Civil Rights, *Report of the United States Commission on Civil Rights*, 86th Cong., 1st sess., September 9, 1959, 75, https://www.crmvet.org/docs/ccr_rights_us_6100.pdf (pursuant to testimony by William P. Mitchell, see *infra* at note 52 and supporting text).
34 "Alabama: How to Deny a Vote," *Time Magazine*, December 30, 1957, https://time.com/archive/6612516/alabama-how-to-deny-a-vote/.

part of the questionnaire. If a fella makes a mistake on his questionnaire, I'm not gonna discriminate in his favor just because he's got a Ph.D."[35]

Journalist Bernard Taper joined accomplished Tuskegee Institute faculty outside of the registrar's office on a registration day, observing that they were forced to return multiple times to wait for their number to be called in order to take a lengthy test to affirm the right to register to vote. Tuskegee Institute's chaplain and professor of philosophy, Daniel W. Wynn, reflected to Taper as he sat outside the office on his fifth attempt to register: "[I]t shouldn't have to take me an hour and a half or two hours of reading and writing to prove that I can cope with the English language. It didn't take me that long to demonstrate my competence in French—and German as well, for that matter—when I took my Ph.D. exams in Boston University."[36]

Such was the environment from which the Tuskegee gerrymander emerged. Act 140 altered the municipality from a square shape containing nearly 5,500 Black residents (of whom 400 were registered to vote) and 1,310 white residents (of whom 600 were registered to vote) into a 28-sided 'sea dragon' which removed all but a small handful of qualified Black voters, and no white voters.[37]

Under the leadership of Dr. Charles G. Gomillion, sociology professor and dean of students at Tuskegee Institute and founder and president of the prodigious Tuskegee Civic Association (TCA), the African American community retaliated against the new law by boycotting white merchants in downtown Tuskegee. The boycott alarmed the local whites as much as the gerrymander alarmed the local African American community, as the local politics had seemed to be one of 'good manners' and no violence or harshness due in large part to the intertwinement of the local economy.[38]

The TCA retained Fred Gray for legal representation, who had just secured precedential relief from the United States Supreme Court on behalf of the nearby Montgomery Bus Boycotters, banning segregation in public transportation.[39]

---

35 Taper, *Gomillion Versus Lightfoot*, 68.

36 Taper, *Gomillion Versus Lightfoot*, 62.

37 *Gomillion v. Lightfoot*, 167 F. Supp. 405 (M.D. Ala. 1958), reversed, 364 U.S. 339 (1960).

38 Taper, *Gomillion Versus Lightfoot*, 42–43.

39 A young attorney fresh out of law school, Gray's weekly lunches with Rosa Parks proved foundational, and launched his budding public interest law career. When she was arrested for refusing to give up her bus seat immediately after one of their lunches, Gray later reflected: "That day was, for me, the beginning point of all the monumental events that soon began to unfold in my life. My immediate little world began to change. And so did the larger world. I had pledged to myself that I would wage war on segregation"; Gray, *Bus Ride to Justice*, 33. See also The Martin Luther King, Jr. Research and Education Institute, Stanford University, "Montgomery Bus Boycott," https://kinginstitute.stanford.edu/montgomery-bus-boycott.

Despite his initial success overturning segregation in public transit, Gray had trouble recruiting local counsel to challenge Act 140, because the theory of the case seemed doomed from the start.[40] Although technically a right-to-vote case, the central issue was not blatant *denial* of the right to vote on account of race, like the grandfather clause and the white primaries that the Supreme Court had previously declared unconstitutional in 1915 and 1944 respectively. Here, Black registrants could still vote in county, state, and federal races. Yet, the central issue was that the law had redrawn the municipal boundaries to effectively move Black voters out of the city's limits. After all, how could they have a right to vote in a place they were technically no longer a part of?

Worse, just a decade earlier, the Supreme Court had refused to review a gerrymandering challenge in a case called *Colegrove v. Green*.[41] That case involved a challenge to redistricting in Illinois, where the state had simply not redistricted in 45 years, resulting in unequal populations among congressional districts. The Supreme Court famously shut the door on reviewing redistricting claims, explaining that "courts ought not enter the political thicket."[42] In other words, the judiciary should not get involved in the inherent politics of the redistricting process.

The federal district court dismissed the *Gomillion* Complaint, and the Fifth Circuit Court of Appeals affirmed the lower court's decision by a two-to-one vote. Gray was encouraged by the dissenting opinion of the appeals court, and read it as a roadmap for an argument to the Supreme Court.[43] Moreover, Gray *listened* to his clients, rather than dismissing or talking over them, reflecting: "While my colleagues were saying there was no denial of the right to vote, my clients back home in Tuskegee, who formerly lived in the city, were being denied the right to vote for municipal officers. There was definitely a Fifteenth Amendment question."[44] So, Gray was encouraged when the Fifth Circuit dissenting opinion acknowledged that "the Fifteenth Amendment contemplated a judicial enforcement of its guarantees against either crude or sophisticated action of states seeking to subvert this new right" and "there comes the time" when "legislation oversteps its

40 Gray, *Bus Ride to Justice*, 114.
41 *Colegrove v. Green*, 328 U.S. 549 (1946).
42 *Colegrove v. Green*, 328 U.S. 549, 556 (1946).
43 Gray, *Bus Ride to Justice*, 116.
44 Gray, *Bus Ride to Justice*, 117. It is a testament to Fred Gray's conviction that even with the recent bad precedent of *Colegrove*, he brought the legal challenge. Gray reflected in his autobiography, "In many respects, *Gomillion v. Lightfoot* is perhaps the most important civil rights case that I have had the privilege of handling. In fact, this case was my 'brainchild,' and the one that I thought from the beginning we would win in spite of overwhelming odds." *Bus Ride to Justice*, 119.

bounds. ... In such times the Courts are the only haven for those citizens in the minority."[45]

On appeal, Fred Gray appeared with his co-counsel Robert Carter, NAACP General Counsel, to the oral argument before the United States Supreme Court with an enlarged printed map of the gerrymander. Justice Frankfurter interrupted the very beginning of Gray's oral argument to focus on Tuskegee Institute and its centrality to the community. This seemed to set the stage for the eventual outcome of the case:

J. Frankfurter:	Where is the Tuskegee Institute on that map?
Fred D. Gray:	Tuskegee Institute is here, in the northwest corner. It is no longer in the city.
J. Frankfurter:	That's—that's now outside.
Fred D. Gray:	It is now outside. Yes, sir.
J. Frankfurter:	Well, where the—this is just geographic, historical interest, when was the Institute founded by?
Fred D. Gray:	The Institute was founded in ... I believe it was 1860, in 1860 something, I'm not sure.
J. Frankfurter:	As early as that?
Fred D. Gray:	Sir? Yes, sir.
J. Frankfurter:	Well, when did Dr. Washington get there? Do you have any idea? It's about the turn of the century, wasn't it?
Fred D. Gray:	Yes, sir.

The Supreme Court unanimously ruled with Dr. Gomillion and his co-plaintiffs, finding that, notwithstanding the critical role of state legislatures, "when a legislature thus singles out a readily isolated segment of a racial minority for special discriminatory treatment, it violates the Fifteenth Amendment."[46] The Court distinguished *Gomillion* from prior cases like *Colegrove* involving "unequal weight in voting distribution" as falling more in the "political arena" and therefore improper for judicial review, because *Gomillion* presented a "differentiation on racial lines whereby approval was given to unequivocal withdrawal of the vote sole-

45 *Gomillion v. Lightfoot*, 270 F.2d 594 (5th Cir. 1959) (J. Brown, dissenting).
46 *Gomillion v. Lightfoot*, 364 U.S. 339 (1960).

ly from colored citizens." In other words, what made *Gomillion* different from other redistricting challenges was that it involved race.[47]

However, *Gomillion* was far more impactful than even this—it opened the door to future redistricting challenges, regardless of race. Only two years later, in *Baker v. Carr*,[48] the Supreme Court found that a redistricting challenge could not escape judicial review simply because of the inherent political nature of the redistricting process. The Warren Court held that where state legislative districts contained unequal populations, they violated the equal protection guarantee of the 14th Amendment. The principle 'one man, one vote' arose from this progeny, and went on to set a redistricting revolution of maps across the country.[49] The principle underscores that votes must have equal weight and political power. Where one district concentrates voters compared with another district, the elected representatives from each district represent a different number of voters—and therefore voters are afforded a different weight. The voting power of individual voters within a less populated district is aggrandized, and the voting power of voters within a more populated district is diluted.

The major precedent established by *Baker v. Carr* would not have been achieved but for the stepping stone set by *Gomillion*, and the historic, renowned Tuskegee Institute and its founder Dr. Booker T. Washington, as advanced to the courts by its longtime faculty member and administrator, the Tuskegee Civic Association, and other faculty members engaged in community affairs. The Supreme Court simply could not fathom that an institution of higher education so famous and so central to the municipality could be gerrymandered out of it, and it could not fathom that the judicial branch would not be able to review such blatantly unconstitutional race-based conduct.

Notice that the resulting principle of one man, one vote was premised on the 14th Amendment, and that *Baker v. Carr* and related emerging cases concerned population equality among districts, and not race. This is yet another example of how the Reconstruction Amendments laid the foundation for evolution of the right to vote and the democratic process at large, well beyond race. Put another

---

47 It should also be noted that concurrent to *Gomillion*'s litigation, the U.S. Department of Justice filed a separate case, *United States v. Alabama*, on discriminatory suppression of Black voter registration in Macon County, home to Tuskegee Institute. Following a remand by the United States Supreme Court, the district court found the evidence "overwhelming" and "so abundantly clear" that "the State of Alabama, acting through its agents, including former members of the Board of Registrars of Macon County, has deliberately engaged in acts and practice designed to discriminate" in voter registration; *United States v. Alabama*, 192 F. Supp. 677 (M.D. Ala. 1961).
48 *Baker v. Carr*, 369 U.S. 186 (1962).
49 See *Reynolds v. Sims*, 377 U.S. 533 (1964).

way, these originally race-based constitutional protections ratified to eradicate the vestiges of slavery created a canon that would benefit a stronger democracy for all.

In addition to the often-overlooked role that *Gomillion* served in shaping voting rights jurisprudence, also underrecognized is the role that the Tuskegee Institute's college community played in the process. Although the institution itself was not formally involved in challenging the status quo, its academic faculty shaped the nation. These faculty members self-organized in the face of the county registrar's intransigence, and they self-organized in the face of a discriminatory state gerrymandering law that purposefully targeted them. They not only bore arm's-length witness to the discrimination of others within their community, but also endeavored to affirmatively exercise their own civil rights by repeatedly returning to the county registrar to get registered, by documenting the overall process, and then by telling the story on national television.

Indeed, Dr. Wynn, the aforementioned Tuskegee chaplain, and his faculty colleagues were among the first witnesses to testify before the newly formed U.S. Commission of Civil Rights, a creation of the Civil Rights Act of 1957.[50] The very first project of the Commission was to review election administration in Alabama following voting complaints from several Alabama counties. The Commission's 1959 report noted: "Significantly, the largest number of complaints from any single county, 44, came from Macon County, Ala., where many Negroes have achieved greater independence because of a considerably higher level of education and income"—that is, because of the presence of Tuskegee Institute and the Tuskegee Veterans Hospital.[51] The Commission report described that "the first official resistance to its attempt to carry out the task assigned to it by the Congress of the United States" was by the county Board of Registrars who, by order of State Attorney General John M. Patterson, reported to the Commission that the registrar's "records would not be made available to the Commission on Civil Rights."[52]

The Commission ultimately found the witnesses testifying as to the voter discrimination they suffered to be compelling, particularly in light of the dramatic intransigence of the local public officials. The Commission noted the qualifications of the witnesses:

> Among the 33 Negro witnesses who testified that they had not been allowed to register were 10 college graduates, 6 of whom held doctorate degrees. Only 7 of the 33 had not completed

---

50 United States Commission on Civil Rights, *Hearings Before the US Commission on Voting Rights*, 85th Cong., 1958–1959, https://www.usccr.gov/files/historical/1958/58-001.pdf.
51 *Report of the United States Commission on Civil Rights*, 56.
52 *Report of the United States Commission on Civil Rights*, 70.

high school; all were literate. Most of them were property-owners and taxpayers. Some had voted in other States. Among them also were war veterans, including two who had been decorated, respectively, with four and five Bronze battle stars.[53]

The forthright recounting by these witnesses of their discrimination stood in stark contrast to the testimony offered by members of the county Board of Registrars. When Mr. Rogers, a four-year member of the board, was asked about whether white registrants were escorted into a different, larger room, he refused to answer upon the advice of State Attorney General Patterson, explaining "[b]ecause it might tend to incriminate me." Upon further lengthier consultation with the Attorney General, Mr. Rogers defiantly testified: "I am a judicial officer under the State laws of Alabama and my actions cannot be inquired into by this body."[54]

The Commission incorporated into its report data collection offered by its first witness, Mr. William Mitchell, a Tuskegee Veterans Hospital employee and Chairman of the TCA voter franchise committee who had studied with Dr. Gomillion and served as his chief deputy within the TCA.[55] Mitchell documented the rejection of Black voter registration forms in Macon County over eight years, and offered the Commission a seven-page written analysis with his testimony.[56] The Commission noted that Mitchell's statistical information "closely paralleled" that obtained by Commission staff.[57] The Mitchell analysis tracked the voter applications submitted by Black registrants each year from 1951 to 1958, with a total of 1,585 applications collected, of which only 510 were issued certificates of registration—that is, only 32% of Black applications were accepted in Macon County in an eight-year period. The percentages of accepted Black registrants changed year to year, ranging from 14% in 1951 to 46% in 1955, depending on the functioning and leadership of the county Board of Registrars.

The Commission's findings and recommendations went on to inform new protections within the Civil Rights Act of 1960, and ultimately the Voting Rights Act of 1965 which is described further below. Among these recommendations were enhanced enforcement, including the appointment of federal registrars. This was a major provision, originally developed and drafted by a young Tuskegee Institute political scientist, Charles V. Hamilton, a newer member of the TCA, in response to

53 *Report of the United States Commission on Civil Rights*, 80.

54 *Report of the United States Commission on Civil Rights*, 80.

55 *Report of the United States Commission on Civil Rights*, 76. See also Norrell, *Reaping the Whirlwind*, 61.

56 *Hearings Before the US Commission on Voting Rights*, 25–29.

57 *Report of the United States Commission on Civil Rights*, 75.

the county registrar's refusal to abide by the law, or even to function at all for an 18-month period, so as to avoid its duties.[58]

By 1960, as the federal registrar provision was incorporated into a new civil rights proposal before the U.S. Senate, former Alabama Attorney General Patterson, who campaigned on white fear to become governor, balked before the Senate committee: "We have not had anything in the South similar to 'federal registrars' as outlined in these bills since federal groups occupied the South during reconstruction days."[59]

This story of Tuskegee Institute in shaping voting rights legal jurisprudence and legislation offers some dose of inspiration of the long arc of justice. When Dr. Booker T. Washington established Tuskegee Institute in 1881—only 11 years after ratification of the 15th Amendment—he faced substantial criticism that his educational philosophy over-emphasized self-reliance and skills development rather than direct confrontation of the racial code. Nonetheless, generations later, the very academic community which he established would go on to foster economic self-improvement which white residents not only could not deny, but also relied on, and which set a foundation from which the academic community members could help themselves politically and, in the process, shape the nation.

2.2 The Student Civil Rights Movement

Throughout the South, separate though interconnected actions seemed to spark to signal the numbered days of Jim Crow. Frustrated by the continued delay in full implementation of *Brown* and its progeny, four North Carolina A&T University students engaged in direct action on February 1, 1960 to integrate a local Woolworths restaurant counter in Greensboro, North Carolina. The action was intentional; they had been meeting in their dorm rooms to discuss what could be done to manifest the promise of the 1954 *Brown* decision. They could not have predicted that this courageous action would set off an unprecedented student-led sit-in movement that rapidly spread across the country, in particular by HBCU students who were joined by northern allies.

In April 1960, a national student convergence brought together youth who participated in these decentralized, spontaneous sit-in actions. Organized with Ella Baker's guidance and support, the convergence launched the creation of the Student Nonviolent Coordinating Committee (SNCC). Here, Baker applied and shared

---

58 Norrell, *Reaping the Whirlwind*, 119.
59 Norrell, *Reaping the Whirlwind*, 120.

lessons learned from her prior experience as a field secretary with the NAACP in the Deep South, and in particular employed a model of inclusion and participatory democracy in decision-making. "It was the practice of a new type of inclusive, consensus-oriented democracy, which opened organizational doors to women, young people, and those outside of the cadre of educated elites."[60]

Youth leadership and sacrifice were prolific throughout the Second Reconstruction. For example, Freedom Summer of 1964 became a project that bridged civil rights leaders of the 1950s with the 1960s student movement, organized by the Council of Federated Organizations, which included representatives from the SNCC (the primary leader), Southern Christian leadership Conference, NAACP, and Congress of Racial Equality (CORE).[61] The goal was to move beyond the protest mobilizations of the bus boycotts, sit-ins, and freedom rides, to voter registration and freedom school projects across the South, and especially in the belly of the beast, Mississippi. The Mississippi Delta was an area of focus because of its abysmal voter registration rates among African Americans due to a combination of poverty, economic vulnerability, and intimidation by the white power structure.[62] It was a completely different terrain from wealthier, educated Tuskegee, Alabama.

Here, too, Ella Baker encouraged the young leaders to be effective organizers in their communities—they had to "form relationships, build trust, and engage in a democratic process of decision making together with community members. The goal was to politicize the community and empower ordinary people."[63] And, those youth organizers were fundamentally transformed in the process—"[i[t was a coming of age like no other ... they forged new identities at the same time that they forced new political ideas and strategies."[64]

The SNCC specifically recruited northern white allies to Freedom Summer, in part to raise national awareness of the plight of Mississippi.[65] Six hundred and fifty student volunteers joined from 37 states and abroad, most from northern col-

---

60 Barbara Ransby, *Ella Baker and the Black Freedom Movement: A Radical Democratic Vision* (University of North Carolina Press, 2003), 310.
61 James P. Marshall, *Student Activism and Civil Rights in Mississippi: Protest Politics and the Struggle for Racial Justice, 1960–1956* (Louisiana State University Press, 2013), 36.
62 Marshall, *Student Activism and Civil Rights in Mississippi*, 41–42.
63 Ransby, *Ella Baker*, 270.
64 Ransby, *Ella Baker*, 295.
65 Ransby, *Ella Baker*, 320–322; Marshall, *Student Activism and Civil Rights in Mississippi*, 85–86, 93–94.

lege communities. Half were Jewish American,[66] including Andrew Goodman (age 20) and Michael Schwerner (age 24). Goodman had just arrived in Neshoba County from a national student training, and joined Schwerner, who had been organizing the local CORE office, when they were murdered alongside local Black activist James Chaney (age 21) by the Klan with the support of the local police department and the county sheriff's office. Their disappearance captivated national attention for weeks as the FBI undertook an extensive 44-day search to discover their bodies.

The next summer, political violence would again be broadcast on living room televisions across the country as hundreds of non-violent protesters were brutally beaten by police in a march from Selma to Montgomery. The Selma march protested the killing of African American voting rights activist Jimmy Lee Jackson (age 26), and highlighted the systemic barriers preventing voter registration in the South. The actions across the Edmund Pettus Bridge, the site of the brutal Bloody Sunday beatings of civil rights marchers, marked a turning point in the call for voting rights, and significantly contributed to finally passing the long-lingering Voting Rights Act of 1965.

2.3 The Voting Rights Act of 1965

As reported by the United States Commission on Civil Rights in 1964, Black voter registration drastically dropped following the First Reconstruction, and even then was halved by 1955 due to the proliferation of Jim Crow laws.[67] (Table 1). Then, while Black voter registration among southern states mostly increased between 1956 and 1964 (with the exception of Louisiana) in the midst of the Second Reconstruction, it remained quite low overall—lowest in Mississippi (6.7%), Alabama (23%), Louisiana (32%), South Carolina (39%), and Georgia (44%).[68] (Figure 2)

---

66 Marshall, *Student Activism and Civil Rights in Mississippi*, 93. See also Assistant Attorney General Kristen Clarke, "Justice Department Recognized Jewish American Heritage Month," *U.S. Office of Public Affairs*, May 24, 2023, blog on file with author.
67 United States Commission on Civil Rights, *Report on Voting in Mississippi*, 89th Cong., 1st sess., May 18, 1965, 8.
68 *Report on Voting in Mississippi*, 11.

Table 1: Voter Registration and Race in Mississippi, 1867–1955.
Source: United States Commission on Civil Rights, *Report on Voting in Mississippi*, 89th Cong., 1st sess., May 18, 1965, 8.

Year	Negro voting age population	Negro registration	Percent of Negro voting age population registered	White voting age population	White registration	Percent of white voting age population registered
1867	98,926	60,167	66.9	84,784	46,636	55.0
1892	150,409	8,615	5.7	120,611	68,127	56.5
1896	198,647	16,234	8.2	150,530	108,998	72.4
1899	198,647	18,170	9.1	150,530	122,724	81.5
1955	495,138	21,502	4.3	710,639	423,456	59.6

Voter impediments such as literacy tests and poll taxes persisted during this period as methods of exclusion. The latter would eventually become illegal, first via ratification of the 24th Amendment in 1962 with regard to federal elections, and then via a Supreme Court case in 1964 premised on the 14th Amendment, which applied to all elections.[69]

By 1968, three years after the passage of the Voting Rights Act, Black voter registration had climbed to more than 50% of the non-white voting-age population in every state in the South, with the biggest gain in Mississippi, where non-white registration had risen from 6.7 to 59.8%.[70] Important gains had also been made in Alabama (from 19.3 to 51.6%), Georgia (from 27.4 to 52.6%), Louisiana (31.6 to 58.9%), and South Carolina (37.3 to 51.2%).

The main features of the Voting Rights Act of 1965, which has since been amended five times, were key to facilitating increased voter registration and preventing rollbacks:

1. Prohibiting voter qualifications, standards, practices, or procedures to deny or abridge the right to vote on account of race or color.[71]

2. Establishing a coverage formula for states and political subdivisions which used a test or device (like literacy tests, for example) as a condition of voter registration on November 1, 1964, and either less than 50% of people of voting age were registered on that date, or less than 50% of people of voting age voted in that November 1964 election.[72] (This section was subsequent-

---

69 *Harper v. Virginia State Board of Elections*, 383 U.S. 663 (1966).
70 United States Commission on Civil Rights, *Report on Political Participation*, 90th Cong., 2nd sess., May 1968, 12–13.
71 *Voting Rights Act of 1965*, Public Law 89–110, amended through Public Law 110–258, Sec. 2.
72 *Voting Rights Act of 1965*, Sec. 4(b).

Estimated African American Voter Registration in 11 Southern States, 1956 and 1964

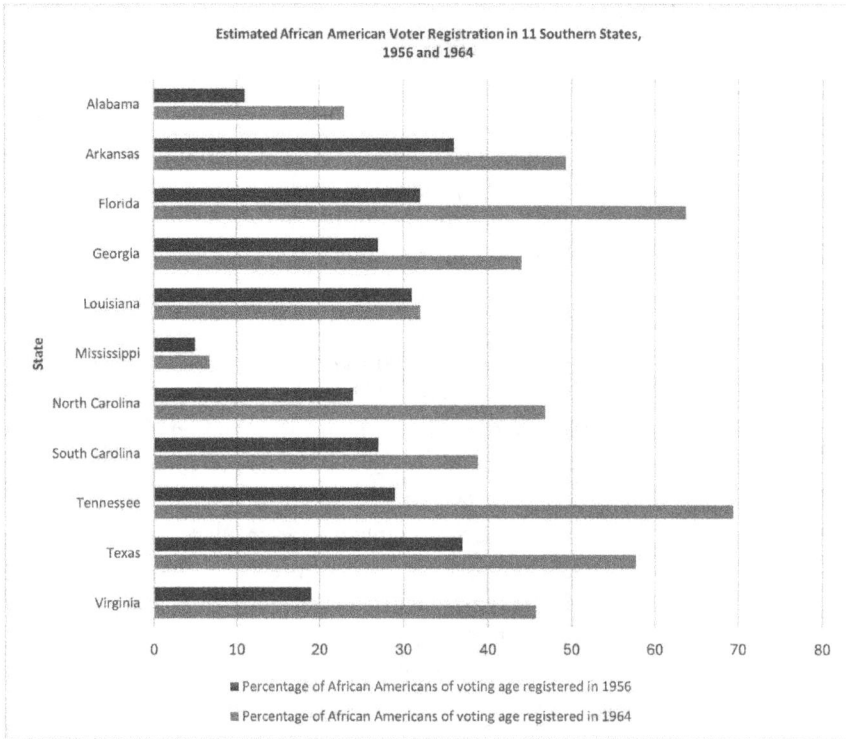

Figure 2: African American Voter Registration in 11 Southern States Prior to Passage of the Voting Rights Act
Source: United States Commission on Civil Rights, Report on Voting in Mississippi, 89th Cong., 1st sess., May 18, 1965, 11.

ly amended over time, and eventually invalidated in 2013 by the United States Supreme Court in *Shelby v. Holder.*)

3. Requiring approval of new voting laws in covered jurisdictions by the Department of Justice or a federal court (also referred to as 'pre-cleared') before going into effect.[73]

4. Authorizing the appointment of federal voting examiners to determine voter qualification and requiring enrollment by state and local officials.[74] (This proved to be a key enforcement mechanism, especially in the immediate years after passage of the Voting Rights Act.)

---

73 *Voting Rights Act of 1965*, Sec. 5.
74 *Voting Rights Act of 1965*, Sec. 7.

5. Suspending the use of literacy tests in covered jurisdictions.[75]
6. Prohibiting any person, acting under color of law or otherwise, from intimidating, threatening, or coercing any person for attempting to vote or voting.[76]

All told, youth, students, and college communities were a central force in the Second Reconstruction's call for equal protection and the right to vote. The multigenerational, diverse partnerships that emerged during the movement finally secured constitutional rights that had been ratified a century earlier during the First Reconstruction. It required mass mobilization and longer-term strategic organizing, persistence, mass media, and strategic litigation, to bend the arc of justice.

Various factors could have steered the effort off course. Had the composition of the United States Supreme Court been different, organizers and their lawyers may not have had a sympathetic ear, and landmark litigation which tapped into the public's hope likely would not have been established—or at least would have taken more time to establish. We will never know whether reason would have ultimately prevailed in the absence of violence and regular people sacrificing themselves in the process, including subjecting themselves to the risk of arrest, and even death. Had young people not committed themselves to non-violence, it is unlikely that the larger goals of the movement would have succeeded.

What is clear, however, is that a second period of constitutional renewal was finally achieved, although the work was by no means complete. For example, several initiatives introduced during this period of renewal remain outstanding today, such as eradication of the electoral college and the securement of statehood for the District of Columbia, two constitutional proposals that were advanced by U.S. Senator Birch Bayh via his critical post spearheading the U.S. Senate Judiciary Subcommittee on Constitutional Amendments.[77] By 1968, it was young people's turn for the suffrage, and they would find a home, and success, in Bayh's subcommittee.

---

75 *Voting Rights Act of 1965*, Sec. 4.
76 *Voting Rights Act of 1965*, Sec. 11.
77 See Robert Blaemire, *Birch Bayh: Making a Difference* (Indiana University Press, 2019).

Figure 3: U.S. Senator Jennings Randolph (D-WV) and his assistant Phil McGance meet with Paul Myer and Tom Hipple of the Youth Franchise Coalition during the group's early days. *"Having Randolph as a sponsor of the Twenty-Sixth Amendment lent an important historical link to our renewed effort to gain adoption. In the early days he was extremely helpful in opening other Senate doors to us."* – Paul Myer, chairman and co-founder of the Youth Franchise Coalition.[78] Photograph from approximately 1967–1968. Produced with permission by the Youth Franchise Coalition. Image courtesy of University of Indiana Archives: Modern Political Papers: 26th Amendment Collection.

3 The 26th Amendment: Youth Political Enfranchisement, an Integral Part and Natural Extension of the Second Reconstruction

A proposal to lower the voting age to 18 and outlaw age discrimination in ballot access had been introduced to Congress over 150 times during a 30-year period since 1942 in light of young people's involvement in World War II. However, bolstered by the national energy for social change in the Second Reconstruction, the late 1960s marked a tipping point for youth suffrage as the war in Vietnam festered.

---

78 Author interview with Paul Myer (July 2025).

Figure 4: Paul Myer and Tom Hipple of the Youth Franchise Coalition (YFC) attend a meeting hosted at the National Education Association headquarters and meet with representatives of the NAACP Youth & College Division. *"I and others worked very hard to gain the support of Black and Latino organizations as well as both Democratic and Republican youth organizations. While there was some initial concern about the YFC's efforts to include the 18-year-old vote as an amendment to the pending Voting Rights Act extension, ultimately the Leadership Conference on Civil Rights endorsed and worked for Congressional adoption and Presidential approval. I deeply appreciated the personal friendship and mentoring by Clarence Mitchell, NAACP lobbyist. His support was critical to achieving the YFC's goals."* – Paul Myer, chairman and co-founder of the Youth Franchise Coalition.[79] National Education Association, Joe Di Dio. Image courtesy of University of Indiana Archives: Modern Political Papers: 26th Amendment Collection, 1946–2021, Box 8.

At the end of 1968, a youth movement called "Let Us Vote" (LUV) started at the University of the Pacific in California, and spread across the country—reaching 3,000 high schools and over 300 college campuses in all 50 states in just six weeks.[80] By February 1969, a wider youth-led coalition had formed which would lead the charge: the Youth Franchise Coalition, engaging prominent civil

79 Author interview with Paul Myer (July 2025).
80 Cultice, *Youth's Battle for the Ballot*, 97–98.

rights, education, labor, and youth organizations in the first coordinated national campaign for the youth franchise.[81]

Figure 5: U.S. Senator Birch Bayh (D-Indiana) addresses the National Education Association on the status of the Twenty-Sixth Amendment. Bayh drove its ratification, along with that of several other proposed constitutional amendments, from his critical role as Chair of the U.S. Senate Judiciary Subcommittee on the Constitutional Amendments. *"It was the golden years of a remarkable U.S. Senate career that spanned three terms. He was a practical, liberal Democrat in a conservative Republican state, yet the force of his personality and his love of retail campaigning led to statewide victories in 1962, 1968, and 1974."* – Jason (Jay) Berman, long-time chief of staff to Senator Bayh. Berman was vital in organizing the congressional hearings to lower the voting age, supporting behind-the-scenes strategic coordination in Congress, and wrangling votes, first for the critical statutory approach to lowering the voting age pursuant to the Voting Rights Amendment Act of 1970, and then via constitutional ratification.[82] National Education Association, Joe Di Dio. Image courtesy of University of Indiana Archives: Modern Political Papers: 26th Amendment Collection, 1946–2021, Box 8.

---

81 The then-youth organizers leading the ratification inside and outside the Halls of Congress recently produced a one-hour documentary: Al Vanderklipp, "The 26th Amendment: The Long Road to the Fastest Ratification," Close Up Washington, 2024, 58:19, https://www.closeup.org/the-26th-amendment-and-the-history-of-the-youth-vote/. The documentary offers first-hand accounts by the Amendment's founders.
82 Author interview with Jason Berman (July 2025).

Ian MacGowan, executive director of the Youth Franchise Coalition, testified before Congress a year later in February 1970 on the vast activity of the coalition and its membership organizations such as the National Education Association; the Episcopal Church; the NAACP; the National Association of Social Workers; the Ripon Society, a Republican-oriented youth organization actively mobilizing its members in the states; the Southern Christian Leadership Conference; the U.S. National Student Association; the Young Democrat Clubs of America; and the YMCA and YWCA. MacGowan then recalled the vox publica sentiment of the nation's founding:

> The American democracy has survived for nearly two centuries. A major reason for its durability has been that, increasingly, the American form of government has been able to broaden the franchise so as to continue to be truly representative. It has become increasingly evident that to remain viable, the franchise must again be expanded so that the Government will be reflective and representative of the views of its younger citizens—those citizens aged 18 to 21. ...
>
> While America's young people have no voice in their Government, they must, nevertheless, bear the burdens of citizenship in the form of paying taxes, fighting wars, assuming family responsibilities, contributing as adults to the work force, and bearing the civil and criminal consequences of their own actions. Our Government cannot be democratically representative while there remains a group of citizens who must bear the consequences of democratic decisionmaking but have no voice in that process. ...
>
> Presently, there is widespread frustration among our Nation's youth—students and workers alike—because they do not have the opportunity for realistic and responsible expression through the use of the ballot. Granting them the right to vote would open to them the most effective, most desirable, and most legitimate channel of political participation and expression. ...
>
> No one can deny the fact that some young people have lost patience with the unresponsiveness of society. This small but significant minority has chosen more violent and radical solutions to the problems that beset us. If the disenchantment of youth increases because of a continuing unresponsiveness on our part, our society can reasonably expect more outbursts of violence. ... In Kentucky, where 18-year-olds have the vote, 80 percent of college youths of that age group voted in the last presidential election, illustrating a concern far above any other voting group. ... The political consciousness of youth needs to be channeled into meaningful involvement within the political process. The most obvious means to involve these young people is through the ballot.[83]

83 United States Senate Subcommittee on Constitutional Amendments of the Committee on the Judiciary, *Hearings on S.J. Res. 7, S.J. Res 19, and Others Relating to Proposed Constitutional Amendments Lowering the Voting Age to 18.* 91st Cong., 2nd sess., February 16–17, 1970 and March 9–10, 1970, 43–48.

Philomena Queen, a youth organizer with the NAACP, also offered the subcommittee testimony in March 1970, following the remarks of NAACP Youth Director James Brown, Jr. The previous year, the NAACP's Youth and College Division had hosted a national youth mobilization in Washington, D.C., singularly focused on lowering the voting age. It was the first coordinated outreach and lobby campaign on the issue organized on the Hill.[84] Queen testified:

> I recognize and respect the honest opinions of those who feel that age 21 should remain as the magic number to give young citizens the opportunity to effectively participate in the politics of American life and, in effect, help determine our own destiny. ...
>
> We see in our society wrongs which we want to make right; we see imperfections that we want to make perfect; we dream of things that should be done but are not; we dream of things that have never been done, and we wonder why not. And most of all, we view all of these as conditions that we want to change, but cannot. You have disarmed us of the most constructive and potent weapon of a democratic system—the vote.[85]

The path to ratification would prove to be winding. The Senate Subcommittee on Constitutional Amendments, led by Senator Birch Bayh of Indiana, held extensive hearings on youth enfranchisement in 1968[86] and 1970.[87] In 1968, approximately 50 witnesses spoke from various levels of government, including Senators, Congressmen, Governors, and the Vice President of the United States, nearly all in favor of the proposal.[88] Most of the discussion in 1968 was focused on youth enfranchisement by constitutional amendment. However, an alternative proposal was introduced in the 1970 hearings: lowering the voting age could be accomplished via legislation. Although a memorandum was originally circulated by Senator Ted Kennedy advancing this statutory approach, ultimately a different messenger was necessary to secure bipartisan support for the new strategy. Thus, the well-

---

84 Cultice, *Youth's Battle for the Ballot*, 103.

85 Philomena Queen, Youth Regional Chairman, Middle Atlantic Region, National Association for the Advancement of Colored People, United States Senate Subcommittee on Constitutional Amendments of the Committee on the Judiciary, *Hearings on S.J. Res. 7, S.J. Res 19, and Others Relating to Proposed Constitutional Amendments Lowering the Voting Age to 18*. 91st Cong., 2nd sess., February 16–17, 1970 and March 9–10, 1970, 150–155.

86 United States Senate Subcommittee on Constitutional Amendments of the Committee on the Judiciary, *Hearings on S.J. Res. 8, S.J. Res 14, and S.J. Res. 78 Relating to Lowering the Voting Age to 18*, 90th Cong., 2nd sess., May 14–16, 1968, 79.

87 United States Senate Subcommittee on Constitutional Amendments of the Committee on the Judiciary, *Hearings on S.J. Res. 7, S.J. Res 19, and Others Relating to Proposed Constitutional Amendments Lowering the Voting Age to 18*, 91st Cong., 2nd sess., February 16–17, 1970 and March 9–10, 1970, 129–130.

88 Lewis J. Paper, "Legislative History of Title III of the Voting Rights Act of 1970," *Harvard Journal on Legislation* 8 (1970): 123–157.

respected, seasoned Senate Majority Leader Mike Mansfield of Montana first introduced the proposal as a legislative amendment to the Voting Rights Act of 1965. The resulting Voting Rights Act Amendments of 1970 marked the first bipartisan federal statute to enfranchise youth.[89] The new law did not simply lower the voting age, but declared the 21-year age requirement a denial and abridgement of "the inherent constitutional rights of citizens" 18 years and older, and violative of "the due process and equal protection of the laws that are guaranteed to them under the Fourteenth Amendment."[90]

This statutory approach to lower the voting age became the subject of a challenge to the United States Supreme Court in *Oregon v. Mitchell*, which held, in an extremely divided plurality decision involving four separate dissenting opinions, that Congress could extend the youth vote via statute for federal races, but could not impede on states to determine the manner of state and local races.[91] The justices ultimately wrestled with the bounds of the 14th Amendment; the power of states to determine the time, place, and manner of elections; and Congress's supervisory powers. The justices were evenly divided as to Congress's power to alter the age-based voting requirements: four justices believed Congress did not have the power at all, neither for federal nor for state/local elections; four others believed Congress did have the power for all elections. Justice Black penned the decision and found a compromise: Congress could act for federal races, but not state and local races.

With the 1972 presidential election looming, pressure began to build due to the practical potential bureaucratic nightmare of having to administer different elections to different voting cohorts: federal ballots for those 18 and older, and state/local ballots for those 21 and older. In addition to the complications of how to practically administer such a dual electoral system, concerns also began to mount about the expense, with estimates of national cost ranging from 10 to 20 million dollars, and possibly more.[92] Congress would have to resolve the crisis, and the only path forward was a constitutional amendment—a significantly higher bar to reach. Rather than require a majority of votes in both houses, as needed for a statute to pass, a constitutional amendment needed at least two-thirds of

---

89 Bromberg, "Youth Voting Rights and the Unfulfilled Promise," 1126.

90 Bromberg, "Youth Voting Rights and the Unfulfilled Promise," setting out the legislative language of Title III of the Voting Rights Act, Public Law 91–285, §§ 301–305.

91 *Oregon v. Mitchell*, 400 U.S. 112 (1970). See Bromberg, "Youth Voting Rights and the Unfulfilled Promise," 1128–1131, describing the various findings and opinions in the case.

92 Senate Report accompanying proposal sent to the states for ratification of the Twenty-Sixth Amendment, S. Rep. No. 92–26, at 15 (1971) accompanying S.J. Res. 7, 92d Cong. (1971).

Congress, who would then send the proposal to the states, of which at least three-fourths would have to approve.

The Amendment had been introduced to Congress over 150 times since its initial proposal during World War II, but it was not until the late 1960s and early 1970s, when young people were at the helm, that it gained any real traction. While its path was circuitous, the political acumen necessary to navigate its ultimate success is undeniable, as the proposal took the shape of constitutional amendment, then statutory amendment, then intensive Supreme Court litigation generating a fairly peculiar split outcome, then potential electoral crisis, and finally ratification.

The language of the 26th Amendment ultimately ratified is identical to its original proposal in 1942:

> The right of citizens in the United States, who are eighteen years of age or older, to vote shall not be denied or abridged by the United States or by any State on account of age.
>
> The Congress shall have power to enforce this article by appropriate legislation.

While political expedience is an important part of the story, the reasons animating its ratification throughout its 30 years of introduction to Congress, and especially in the various hearings held and testimonies collected between 1968 and 1971, focused on the basic sense of fairness given young adults' increased responsibilities and capabilities:

1. The value of the idealism and moral courage that youth provide in reenergizing the practice of democracy. For example, in a ceremonial certification of the Amendment, President Nixon reflected that young people offer democracy "some idealism, some courage, some stamina, some high moral purpose that this Nation always needs, because a country, throughout history, we find, goes through ebbs and flows of idealism."[93]

2. The increased political competence of youth compared with prior generations, due to greater access to information such as, at the time, television, and due to the standardization of education during the 20th century.

3. The increased responsibilities that youth take on compared with prior generations of youth, as they fought in war, assume debt, and live independently.

4. Stemming protest and unrest by offering an on-ramp to constructively and systemically participate in the process to advance change.

---

93 Richard Nixon, "Remarks at the Ceremony Marking the Certification of the 26th Amendment to the Constitution," The American Presidency Project, U.C. Santa Barbara, July 5, 1971, https://www.presidency.ucsb.edu/node/240368.

A fifth critical theme emerged as well, connecting this increased role of youth in society with a recognition of the historical expansion of suffrage over time. Senator Birch Bayh offered the opening remarks on the Amendment's proposal on the first day of congressional hearings, May 14, 1968:

> I thought that at the beginning of the hearings it might be interesting to state that there probably have been few previous times in our history when Congress has turned more frequently and more comprehensively toward efforts to amend the Constitution of the United States. Since assuming the chairmanship of this subcommittee in 1964, I personally have presided over six major efforts to amend our basic law. ... Today, we begin the sixth effort to extend the franchise to American citizens 18 years of age or over. ...
>
> The generation of young Americans in the 1960's, this generation, is no longer docile, passive, and uninvolved. They are deeply involved in the issues of our time, the issues of war and peace, freedom and equality for all Americans, and uncompromising fulfillment of the promise of our Nation. Like any involved and active group in the United States, young people of today have among their number a few extremists, whether they be the flower children dropouts or the ultramilitant anarchists. It is unfortunate that these few attract the bulk of headlines and national attention when, in fact, the vast majority of young people today are working incessantly, if less obtrusively, toward making our Nation an even better place in which to live. They are working actively for political candidates of both parties. They are working for civil rights and equal opportunity movements; they are working for peace, whether as members of the Armed Forces of the United States or as civilian commentators in debating the merits of American foreign policy. They are students, husbands, wives, workers —anyone who has observed the young people in the Peace Corps and VISTA must be convinced of this. ...
>
> The religious and property requirements for voting were removed in colonial America. Racial barriers to voting have been coming down for a century. Women were given the right to vote in 1920. It seems to me to be in keeping with the tradition of expansion of the franchise, as well as the recognition of the greater role played by American youth in our lives today, that we should now allow the Constitution to reflect what has already become a fact of life in our land : that our young people today are well bred, well educated, and extremely well aware of the positions and needs of our Nation, and that they should now be permitted to participate in the building of our Nation through the most valued American right, the right to vote.[94]

The legislative history of the 26th Amendment includes clear guidance that it was inspired by, and was meant to further, the protections afforded by the 14th Amendment and the Voting Rights Act of 1965, at least with regard to youth voters.

---

94 Senator Birch Bayh, Chairman of the Senate Judiciary Subcommittee on Constitutional Amendments, United States Senate Subcommittee on Constitutional Amendments of the Committee on the Judiciary. *Hearings on S.J. Res. 8, S.J. Res 14, and S.J. Res. 78 Relating to Lowering the Voting Age to 18*, 90th Cong., 2nd sess., May 14–16, 1968, 2–4.

The Senate report that accompanied the proposal to the states for ratification includes a key provision of the goal of the Amendment:

> [F]orcing young voters to undertake *special burdens*—obtaining absentee ballots, or traveling to one centralized location in each city, for example—in order to exercise their right to vote might well serve to dissuade them from participating in the election. This result, and the election procedures that create it, are at least inconsistent with the purpose of the Voting Rights Act, which sought to encourage greater political participation on the part of the young; such segregation might even amount to a denial of their 14th Amendment right to equal protection of the laws in the exercise of the franchise.[95]

This language–"*special burdens*"–is key to understanding what the 26th Amendment is meant to protect, and the Senate report offers us specific, non-exhaustive examples to understand its purpose and scope: "obtaining absentee ballots"—that is, elections that are run when students are not on campus, such as during the spring or summer breaks—and "traveling to one centralized location in each city" to vote—that is, traveling far from campus to access a polling site.

What makes this constitutional history particularly interesting is both 1) the speed of the process—the quickest in U.S. history, taking less than 100 days to be approved by the requisite 38 states—in large part due to the wide, cross-partisan appeal for the youth franchise; and 2) that it was primarily led by young people who worked inside and outside of the Halls of Congress.[96] Their persistence led to the expansion of the franchise to 11 million new voters in 1971—the largest single expansion of the franchise since ratification of the 19th Amendment.

---

95 S. Rep. No. 92–26, at 14 (1971) (emphasis added).
96 Curious readers can learn more by reviewing the relatively few books and articles published on the topic. For a full history on the ratification process for the 26th Amendment, see Jennifer Frost, *"Let Us Vote!": Youth Voting Rights and the 26th Amendment* (New York University Press, 2022). See Cultice, *Youth's Battle for the Ballot*, the seminal book on the topic. See Bromberg, "Youth Voting Rights and the Unfulfilled Promise," for a legal-oriented analysis. See also the first legal volume dedicated to the 26th Amendment since its ratification, published by *The Rutgers University Law Review* 75, no. 5 (Summer 2022), featuring a variety of perspectives on the Amendment, including by U.S. Election Assistance Commissioner Ben Hovland; college faculty and students engaged in a quantitative and qualitative analysis of the treatment of provisional ballots cast by their peers; developmental scientists; a youth criminal justice legal clinician; and more.

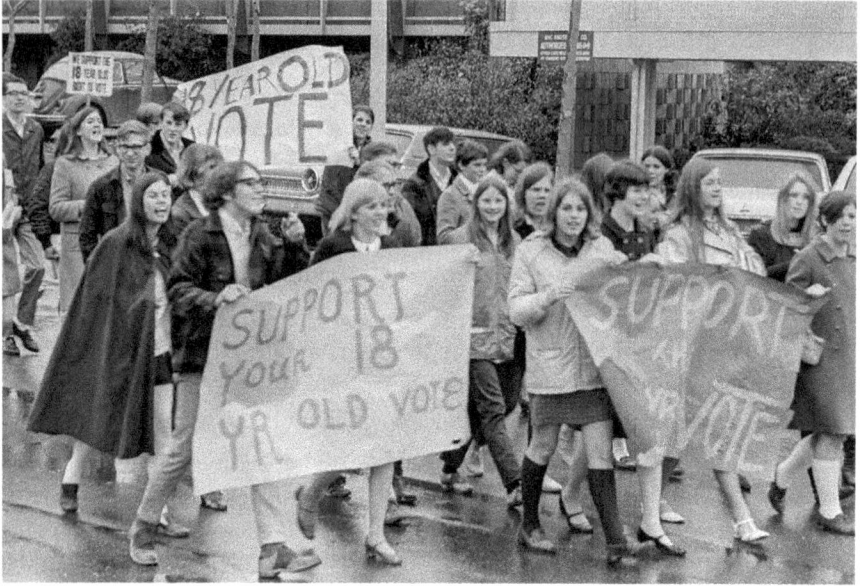

Figure 6: Demonstration for reduction in voting age, Seattle, 1969. Seattle Post-Intelligencer Collection, Museum of History & Industry, Seattle; All Rights Reserved.

4 Jim Crow Goes to College: First-Generation Challenges to the Youth Vote

As soon as the 26th Amendment was ratified in 1971, local county registrars across the nation sought to restrict the youth vote by introducing new tests for this newly enfranchised class to prove eligibility. These tests focused on the ability to establish sufficient ties to their new communities, and were primarily applied to students living on college campuses. A central problem with these residency tests was their selective distribution to young voters, which was found to be an unconstitutional abuse of discretion by election administrators under the equal protection clause of the 14th Amendment and the 26th Amendment. Another theme was that the residency tests violated other recognized constitutional rights protected by the 14th Amendment, such as the fundamental right to vote and the right to travel. Certain judicial opinions also acknowledged the impingement on the right of political expression protected by the First Amendment.

While the precise contents of the residency tests were different from the Jim Crow voter suppression devices employed until a few years earlier when they were finally invalidated by the Voting Rights Act of 1965, the pattern was the same: a grant of systemic enfranchisement was followed by the introduction of new exclusionary methods.

It only took about two years after ratification of the 26th Amendment for a flush of federal courts and state supreme courts across the nation to begin to strike down applications of these residency tests, including in, chronologically, Michigan, California, Texas, Kentucky, Vermont, New Hampshire, New Jersey, and Pennsylvania, followed by Mississippi in 1974 and 1976, and New York in 1984.[97] These tests generally inquired about the students' ties to the local campus community, whether they owned a home there, whether they were married including to local residents, and whether they had a local job arranged for after graduation. In other words, the presumption of these questionnaires was that students are temporary and not bona fide residents, and so should not vote from their new addresses.

The California Supreme Court offered context for the "new birth of freedom" of youth suffrage:

> America's youth entreated, pleaded for, demanded a voice in the governance of this nation. On campuses by the hundreds, at Lincoln's Monument by the hundreds of thousands, they voiced their frustration at their electoral incompetence and their love of a country which they believed to be abandoning its ideals. Many more worked quietly and effectively within a system that gave them scant recognition. And in the land of Vietnam they lie as proof that death accords youth no protected status. Their struggle for recognition divided a nation against itself. Congress and more than three-fourths of the states have now determined in their wisdom that youth "shall have a new birth of freedom"—the franchise. Rights won at the cost of so much individual and societal suffering may not and shall not be curtailed on the basis of hoary fictions that these men and women are children tied to residential apron strings. Respondents' refusal to treat petitioners as adults for voting purposes violated the letter and spirit of the 26th Amendment.[98]

The New Jersey Supreme Court in *Worden* also offered a fulsome analysis when undergraduate and graduate students of Trenton State College (now The College of New Jersey) and Princeton University filed a lawsuit in state court.[99] The lead

---

97 *Wilkins v. Bentley*, 180 N.W. 3 d423 (Mich. 1971); *Jolicoeur v. Mihaley*, 488 P.2d 1 (Cal. 1971); *Ownby v. Dies*, 337 F. Supp. 38 (E.D. Tex. 1971); *Bright v. Baesler*, 366 F. Supp. 527 (E.D. Ky. 1971); *Shivelhood v. Davis*, 336 F. Supp. 1111 (D. Vt. 1971); *Newburger v. Peterson*, 344 F. Supp. 559 (D.N.H. 1972); *Worden v. Mercer County Bd. of Elections*, 294 A.3d 233 (N.J. 1972); *Sloane v. Smith*, 351 F. Supp. 1299 (M.D. Pa. 1972); *Frazier v. Callicutt*, 383 F. Supp. 15 (N.D. Miss. 1974); *Latham v. Chandler*, 406 F. Supp. 754 (N.D. Miss. 1976); *Symm v. United States*, 439 U.S. 1105 (1979), *aff'g United States v. Texas*, 445 F. Supp. 1245 (S.D. Tex. 1978); *Auerbach v. Kinley*, 594 F. Supp. 1503 (N.D.N.Y. 1984).
98 *Jolicoeur v. Mihaley*, 488 P.2d 1 (Cal. 1971), 7.
99 *Worden v. Mercer County Bd. of Elections*, 294 A.3d 233 (N.J. 1972).

plaintiff, Thomas Worden, was a first-year student who testified that he hoped to obtain a "job teaching someplace" which "could be anywhere," and that he was told he could not register to vote because he was a student living on campus. *Worden* examined prior legal precedent where the right to vote could not be trampled based on a presumption of lack of sufficient connection to the community to cast a knowledgeable vote.[100]

Worden next engaged in a full legislative history of the 26th Amendment, as well as its recent judicial interpretation by various courts, and then considered the right to vote pursuant to the state Constitution. Applying these federal and state-based rights, the New Jersey Supreme Court found "little room for doubt" of denial of the right to vote. "They were subject as a class to questioning beyond all other applicants, including applicants who were freely registered though their situations indicated that they were comparably shortterm residents of their communities[.]"

The *Worden* court ordered broad relief, and specified that the right to register to vote locally includes: 1) students who plan to return to their previous residences; 2) those who plan to remain permanently in their college communities; 3) those who plan to obtain employment away from their previous residences; and 4) those who are uncertain of their future plans.

This practical application has been widely recognized and upheld in light of the purpose of the 26th Amendment and, importantly, further bolstered by the United States Supreme Court in *Symm v. United States*. By 1979, a residency challenge had finally made its way before the United States Supreme Court, on appeal from a three-judge district court panel in Texas.[101]

The case, which will be discussed in more detail in chapter four, arose from Prairie View A&M University (PVAMU), an HBCU whose history stretches back to the First Reconstruction, situated in a rural Texan county largely comprising white voters.[102] As soon as the 26th Amendment was ratified, Mr. Symm, the Waller

---

100 For example, in *Carrington v. Rash*, the United States Supreme Court in 1965 found unconstitutional a Texas law prohibiting military voters from registering to vote from their military base for fear of carpetbagging due to their transient nature. Similarly, in *Dunn v. Blumstein*, the United States Supreme Court in 1972 found that a law professor who moved to Tennessee for a new job could not be denied the right to vote because he did not satisfy the state's one-year residency requirement, which the state tried to justify as a means to ensure the engagement of "knowledgeable voters" who could exercise their rights "more intelligently."
101 *Symm v. United States*, 439 U.S. 1105 (1979), affirming *United States v. Texas*, 445 F. Supp. 1245 (S.D. Tex. 1978).
102 The name for this subsection's title is inspired by an opinion editorial by former Texas State Senator Rodney Ellis on the persistent Black student voter suppression in Waller County. See

County election official, imposed a residency questionnaire on PVAMU students, resulting in various court litigations. Even the Texas Secretary of State got involved on behalf of the students, visiting the campus ten times in just seven months ahead of the 1976 November election, to inform them of their right to register from their campus address. The Secretary of State also visited Mr. Symm to explain the proper application of the law, to no avail.

On October 14, 1976, the United States finally stepped in by filing a suit, arguing that the residency questionnaire was part of a "pervasive pattern of conduct which has the effect and intent of depriving dormitory students at Prairie View of their rights under the 14th, 15th, and 26th Amendments."[103] It was the first and only time that the United States Department of Justice brought an affirmative challenge to enforce the 26th Amendment.

Testimony was collected by PVAMU students and administrators, the Texas Secretary of State, students from the University of Texas, who confirmed that they routinely were able to register to vote, and 70 voter registrars from nearly every Texas county containing an institution of higher education—none applied Mr. Symm's presumption of non-residency when registering students to vote.[104]

After a full consideration of the record, the three-judge district court panel reached its conclusion swiftly: enjoin Mr. Symm from violating the constitutional rights of PVAMU dormitory students, as had been advocated by the State of Texas, Secretary of State, and the Attorney General of Texas. The United States Supreme Court summarily affirmed the decision on direct appeal, giving the decision below precedential value for the rest of the nation.[105] It was the only time to date that the Supreme Court has substantively ruled on a 26th Amendment challenge.

Several themes emerge from the body of case law related to evolution of the right to vote and youth voting rights, as to why students should at least have the opportunity to register to vote from their campus residential addresses:

1. Young people, as a protected class with respect to ballot access, should not be singled out from other voters to prove permanence or allegiance to a geography. In many cases, older adults may own multiple homes, for example. Older adults are also highly mobile, as are renters. Election administration must be uniformly applied in a manner which upholds the *fundamental* right to vote.

Rodney Ellis, "Jim Crow Goes to College," *New York Times*, August 27, 1992, https://www.nytimes.com/1992/04/27/opinion/jim-crow-goes-to-college.html.

103 *United States v. Texas*, 445 F. Supp. 1245, 1248 (S.D. Tex. 1978).

104 *United States v. Texas*, 445 F. Supp. 1245, 1248 (S.D. Tex. 1978).

105 For brief explanation of the precedential value of summary affirmance by the Supreme Court, see Bromberg, "Youth Voting Rights and the Unfulfilled Promise," 1134, n. 121.

2. While it may be true that students make a commitment to live in college communities for at least four years, the *class* of students remains fixed. Thus, even if we were to assume that students always come and go for a four-year interval, the class's interests must nonetheless be represented.
3. Students are included in the Census count in their college communities, and thus federal and state funds are budgeted and distributed accordingly, benefitting the entire jurisdiction. The local tax base is also often heavily derived from the student population.
4. Students have unique interests and needs, and have a right to elect local, state, and federal representatives which advance those interests. For example, young voters are interested in college affordability, environmental protection, and housing affordability on the local level when they live in off-campus communities. They have a constitutional right to be able to elect representatives that are attuned to their specific needs.
5. Young people don't always have an alternative address from which to vote. Directing election materials to a different address, or having to travel to that address to vote, may be costly or impossible.

One would think, given the unanimity of the court decisions reached by state and federal courts, and upheld by the United States Supreme Court, that the right to vote from campus would no longer be tampered with today. Yet, as history has proven in the long fight for democracy, officials empowered with the responsibilities of non-partisan election administration will nonetheless at times impose their own worldview until some combination of organizing, advocacy, and litigation halt their erroneous conduct.[106]

5 Conclusion

Given the history of constitutionalism in the United States, it should be no surprise that the promise of the 26th Amendment was not guaranteed upon ratification, and that it remains unfulfilled over 50 years later. After all, it took a century following the ratification of the Reconstruction Amendments between 1865 and 1870 for Congress to enact laws to enforce those constitutional rights, including by passage of the Voting Rights Act of 1965. Similarly, it took 60 years after ratification of

---

[106] For more on current obstacles to youth voting rights, see Yael Bromberg, "The Future Is Unwritten: Reclaiming the Twenty-Sixth Amendment," *The Rutgers University Law Review* 74, no. 5 (Summer 2022): 1685–1689, https://rutgerslawreview.com/wp-content/uploads/2023/02/01_Bromberg.pdf.

the 14th Amendment and its guarantee of equal protection under law for the 19th Amendment to be ratified in 1920 extending the suffrage to women. The nation's Second Reconstruction forced a reckoning with the perverse reversion that followed the nation's first constitutional renewal, as physical and political racial violence calcified.

When young Americans turned to expanding their own suffrage at the end of the Second Reconstruction, it was not in a vacuum. They inherited a tradition of visionary youth leadership in then-recent history, such as the freedom rides which mobilized from college communities to join south-bound buses in a public transportation desegregation campaign; the North Carolina A&T Four of Greensboro (ages 17 and 18) who sparked a restaurant desegregation sit-in campaign which inspired fellow HBCU and other students across the country, and which later went on to inspire the SNCC; and Freedom Summer volunteers like Andy Goodman (age 20) who was among the 650 student volunteers recruited from northern college communities to register Black voters in the belly of the beast, Mississippi.

This tradition of youth as constitutional architects goes back to the nation's founding, and continues through the nation's first project of constitutional renewal, such as Frederick Douglass who escaped slavery just three years before taking the stage at the Massachusetts Anti-Slavery Society in 1841 (age 23), and Ida B. Wells (age 21) who in 1883 achieved some limited success when she sued to enforce her rights against segregation on a Tennessee train, and was awakened in this process to later emerge as the nation's foremost chronologist on the viciousness of the era of lynching. The trend of youth-led constitutionalism continued through women's suffrage, such as Alice Paul (age 22) who went on to lead the push for the 19th Amendment and wrote the first Equal Rights Amendment of 1923.

Empowered by the understanding of the evolution of the right to vote, young leaders in the late 1960s and early 1970s came to Congress to advocate for their own enfranchisement, backed by a national youth-led initiative they built with a multifaceted, diverse, and multigenerational coalition. Ian MacGowan, co-founder of the Youth Franchise Coalition, testified before the Senate Subcommittee on Constitutional Amendments how "American democracy has survived for nearly two centuries ... to broaden the franchise so as to continue to be truly representative ... [and] remain viable." Philomena Queen, NAACP youth organizer, testified,

> I know that it seems revolutionary to some that the voting age should be lowered, but I submit to you that these same feelings existed during the years when women, age 21 and over, were denied the right to vote. ... [W]e the voteless minority of this country are intelligent,

interested, sensitive to the issues of our society, and have earned the right to be included. There is no justifiable reason for keeping us shut out.

There was no denying the moral and political truth of their call for youth suffrage. Patricia Keefer first joined the youth suffrage movement in an early Ohio state-based campaign to lower the voting age to 19. She was 24 years old when she quit her job to join the campaign, startled by the horrors of the war in Vietnam she learned from wartime letters from her young brother who would never return home.[107] Keefer went on to co-lead the Youth Franchise Coalition which ushered in the introduction of the 26th Amendment, and then joined Common Cause to lead the state-based efforts once the measure was sent from Congress to the states for ratification. When she reflects on the campaign for youth suffrage, Keefer often reminds listeners of its wide appeal in Appalachia and other areas of middle America. The human cost of the mandatory military draft was borne by the farming and working-class communities across the nation, which reflects the diversity of the states to formally ratify the Amendment into the United States Constitution. The Amendment became so popular that states raced to be among the requisite 38 to formally approve ratification, with some dispute as to whether North Carolina, Ohio, or Alabama actually marked the 38th state.

The collective college communities from whence these efforts often arose have been central to the process of American constitutionalism and the shaping of democracy. In Tuskegee in the 1950s, these efforts were primarily faculty-led, with some student support, challenging the state legislature and the county government. They culminated in the creation of a new voting rights legal jurisprudence and informed responsive federal legislation such as the Civil Rights Act of 1960. Throughout the Second Reconstruction, college communities were a central nexus for youth political engagement and recruitment. These efforts also culminated in multiple successful lawsuits before the Warren Court and responsive federal legislation such as the Voting Rights Act of 1965. In the decade following ratification of the 26th Amendment, youth voter suppression unfolded on campuses across the nation, be it primarily white, wealthier campuses like Princeton Univer-

---

107 Patricia Keefer, interviewed by Yael Bromberg, March 19, 2025. See also "The Lady is a Lobbyist: Pat Keefer works for Common Cause," *Cincinnati*, November 1973, in 26th Amendment Collection, Modern Political Papers Collection, Indiana University Libraries, Bloomington, Indiana. See also Center for Youth Political Participation, "Constitution Day 21: Fulfilling the Promise of the Twenty-Sixth Amendment," Eagleton Institute of Politics, 2021, Webinar Video: 1:00, https://cypp.rutgers.edu/constitution-day-2021. A rich archive of materials, including documents, interviews, and webinars of the movement for the Twenty-Sixth Amendment is archived in the Indiana University Libraries, Modern Political Papers.

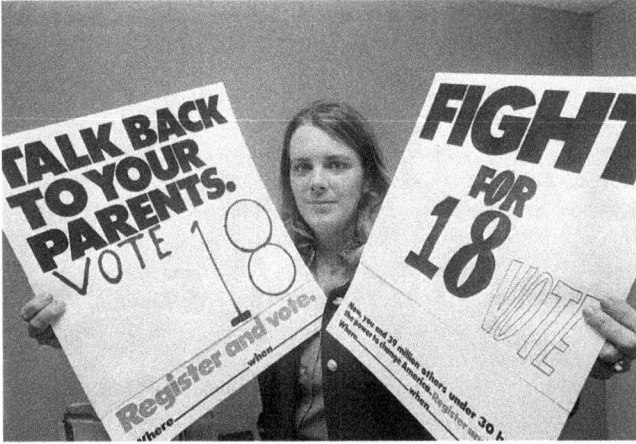

Figure 7: Patricia Keefer worked on the 19-year-old vote state-based campaign in Ohio, and then was recruited to move to Washington, D.C. to work on the Youth Franchise Coalition's national campaign to lower the voting age to 18. She then joined the newly-organized Common Cause to set up its national network of local organizations and get the Twenty-Sixth Amendment ratified by the states. Keefer is pictured here in her Washington, D.C. office on March 8, 1971. Bettman via Getty Images.

sity in New Jersey, or HBCUs like in Prairie View, Texas located in majority-white county communities. At Prairie View A&M University, response efforts were primarily student-led, and, at least in the 1970s, eventually gained support from the federal and state government to challenge the incalcitrant county election administrator.

In the case of youth voting rights, different types of 'special burdens' of the youth vote persist today, be it unnecessary restrictions on student voter residency or restrictions on other qualification proofs such as voter identification, the gerrymandering of college campuses, and situating polling places far off-campus. Several of these contemporary special burdens will be described in further detail in the case studies in this book, particularly in the chapters dedicated to Prairie View A&M University, North Carolina A&T University, and Bard College. These restrictions ignore the premise of the 26th Amendment, "to encourage greater political participation on the part of the young" in furtherance of a stronger republic, and they overlook this nation's rich social fabric of persistent and strategic resistance to voter suppression.

Bibliography

"Alabama: How to Deny a Vote." *Time Magazine*, December 30, 1957. https://time.com/archive/6612516/alabama-how-to-deny-a-vote/.

Andrlik, Todd. "How Old Were the Leaders of the American Revolution on July 4, 1776? Younger Than You Think." *Slate*, August 20, 2013. https://slate.com/news-and-politics/2013/08/how-old-were-the-founding-fathers-the-leaders-of-the-american-revolution-were-younger-than-we-imagine.html.

Blaemire, Robert. *Birch Bayh: Making a Difference.* Indiana University Press, 2019.

Bromberg, Yael. "Youth Voting Rights and the Unfulfilled Promise of the Twenty-Sixth Amendment." *University of Pennsylvania Journal of Constitutional Law* 21 (2019): 1105–1166. https://scholarship.law.upenn.edu/jcl/vol21/iss5/1/.

Bromberg, Yael. "The Future Is Unwritten: Reclaiming the Twenty-Sixth Amendment." *The Rutgers University Law Review* 74, no. 5 (Summer 2022): 1671–1696. https://rutgerslawreview.com/wp-content/uploads/2023/02/01_Bromberg.pdf.

Bromberg, Yael. "The Youth Voting Rights Act Would Transform Access for Youth Voters." *Teen Vogue*, July 27, 2022. https://www.teenvogue.com/story/youth-voting-rights-act-what-is.

Center for Youth Political Participation. "Constitution Day 21: Fulfilling the Promise of the Twenty-Sixth Amendment." Eagleton Institute of Politics, 2021. Webinar Video, 1:00. https://cypp.rutgers.edu/constitution-day-2021.

Clarke, Kristen. "Justice Department Recognized Jewish American Heritage Month." *U.S. Office of Public Affairs*, May 24, 2023. Blog on file with author.

Cultice, Wendell W. *Youth's Battle for the Ballot: A History of Voting Age in America.* Greenwood Press, 1992.

Du Bois, W.E.B. *Black Reconstruction in America: An Essay Toward a History of the Part Which Black Folk Played in the Attempt to Reconstruct Democracy in America, 1860–1880.* Oxford University Press, 1935.

Ellis, Rodney. "Jim Crow Goes to College." *New York Times*, August 27, 1992. https://www.nytimes.com/1992/04/27/opinion/jim-crow-goes-to-college.html.

Foner, Eric. *Freedom's Lawmakers: A Directory of Black Officeholders During Reconstruction.* LSU Press, 1996.

Frost, Jennifer. *"Let Us Vote!": Youth Voting Rights and the 26th Amendment.* New York University Press, 2022.

Gray, Fred D. *Bus Ride to Justice: Changing the System by the System.* New South Books, 1995.

Grinspan, Jon. *The Virgin Vote: How Young Americans Made Democracy Social, Politics Personal, and Voting Popular in the Nineteenth Century.* University of North Carolina Press, 2016.

Keyssar, Alexander. *The Right to Vote: The Contested History of Democracy in the United States.* Basic Books, a member of the Perseus Books Group, 2009.

Klarman, Michael J. *From Jim Crow to Civil Rights: The Supreme Court and the Struggle for Racial Equality.* Oxford University Press, 2006.

Kleppner, Paul. *Who Voted? The Dynamics of Electoral Turnout, 1870–1980.* Praeger, 1982.

"The Lady is a Lobbyist: Pat Keefer Works for Common Cause." *Cincinnati*, November 1973. In 26th Amendment Collection, Modern Political Papers Collection, Indiana University Libraries, Bloomington, Indiana.

Marshall, James P. *Student Activism and Civil Rights in Mississippi: Protest Politics and the Struggle for Racial Justice, 1960–1956.* Louisiana State University Press, 2013.

McIver, John P. *Historical Statistics of the United States, Millennial Edition*. Edited by Susan B. Carter and Scott Sigmund Gartner. Cambridge University Press, 2006.

Nixon, Richard. "Remarks at the Ceremony Marking the Certification of the 26th Amendment to the Constitution." The American Presidency Project, U.C. Santa Barbara, July 5, 1971. https://www.presidency.ucsb.edu/node/240368.

Norrell, Robert J. *Reaping the Whirlwind: The Civil Rights Movement in Tuskegee*. Alfred A. Knopf, Inc., 1985.

Paper, Lewis J. "Legislative History of Title III of the Voting Rights Act of 1970." *Harvard Journal on Legislation* 8 (1970): 123–157.

Ransby, Barbara. *Ella Baker and the Black Freedom Movement: A Radical Democratic Vision*. University of North Carolina Press, 2003.

Schulz, Kathryn. "The Many Lives of Pauli Murray." *The New Yorker*, April 10, 2017. https://www.newyorker.com/magazine/2017/04/17/the-many-lives-of-pauli-murray.

Sheppard, William Ludwell. "Electioneering at the South." Print, *Harper's Weekly*, July 25, 1868. From The New York Public Library Digital Collections, Miriam and Ira D. Wallach Division of Art, Prints, and Photographs: Picture Collection. https://digitalcollections.nypl.org/items/510d47e1-3fa3-a3d9-e040-e00a18064a99.

Swindler, William F. "The Warren Court: Completion of a Constitutional Revolution." *Vanderbilt Law Review* 23 (1970): 205–250.

Taper, Bernard. *Gomillion Versus Lightfoot: The Right to Vote in Apartheid Alabama*. University of Alabama Press, 2003.

The Martin Luther King, Jr. Research and Education Institute, Stanford University. "Montgomery Bus Boycott." https://kinginstitute.stanford.edu/montgomery-bus-boycott.

The Rutgers University Law Review 75, no. 5 (Summer 2022).

Tushnet, Mark, and Lezin, Katya. "What Really Happened in Brown v. Board of Education." *Columbia Law Review* 91, no. 8 (December 1991): 1867–1930.

Tushnet, Mark, ed. *The Warren Court in Historical and Political Perspective*. University Press of Virginia, 1993.

United States Commission on Civil Rights. *Hearings Before the US Commission on Voting Rights*. 85th Cong., December 8, 1958, December 9, 1958, and January 9, 1959. https://www.usccr.gov/files/historical/1958/58-001.pdf.

United States Commission on Civil Rights. *Report of the United States Commission on Civil Rights*. 86th Cong., 1st sess., September 9, 1959. https://www.crmvet.org/docs/ccr_rights_us_6100.pdf.

United States Commission on Civil Rights. *Report on Voting in Mississippi*. 89th Cong., 1st sess., May 18, 1965. https://www2.law.umaryland.edu/marshall/usccr/documents/cr12v94.pdf.

United States Commission on Civil Rights. *Report on Political Participation*. 90th Cong., 2nd sess., May 1968.

United States House of Representatives Committee on the Judiciary Subcommittee on the Constitution, Civil Rights, and Civil Liberties. *Hearing on the Enforcement of the Voting Rights Act*. 116 Cong., May 3, 2019. https://docs.house.gov/meetings/JU/JU10/20190503/109387/HHRG-116-JU10-Wstate-AllenJ-20190503.pdf.

United States Library of Congress. Congressional Research Service. *The Voting Rights Act of 1965: Background and Overview*, by Kevin J. Coleman. RL43626. 2015.

United States Senate Subcommittee on Constitutional Amendments of the Committee on the Judiciary. *Hearings on S.J. Res. 8, S.J. Res 14, and S.J. Res. 78 Relating to Lowering the Voting Age to 18*. 90th Cong., 2nd sess., May 14–16, 1968.

United States Senate Subcommittee on Constitutional Amendments of the Committee on the Judiciary. *Hearings on S.J. Res. 7, S.J. Res 19, and Others Relating to Proposed Constitutional Amendments Lowering the Voting Age to 18.* 91st Cong., 2nd sess., February 16 – 17, 1970 and March 9 – 10, 1970.

Vanderklipp, Al. "The 26th Amendment: The Long Road to the Fastest Ratification." Close Up Washington, 2024. Documentary Video, 58:19. https://www.closeup.org/the-26th-amendment-and-the-history-of-the-youth-vote/.

Woodward, C. Vann. *The Strange Career of Jim Crow.* Commemorative ed. Oxford University Press, 2002.

Yates, William. *Rights of Colored Men to Suffrage Citizenship and Trial by Jury.* Merrihew and Gunn, 1838.

Jonathan Becker

2 Civic Actors and Student Voting

This chapter examines the role of key actors—students, faculty, and colleges and universities as institutions—in promoting student voting and defending student voting rights. Underlying the analysis is a belief in the inextricable link between education and democracy. The following questions are asked: *What is the link between higher education, particularly liberal education, citizenship, and democracy? How do Historically Black Colleges and Universities (HBCUs) distinctly understand their civic role? What roles can key actors play in promoting voting and defending voting rights in colleges and universities, and what are the constraints on their actions?*

   The chapter begins with an exploration of the civic role of higher education and the relationship between higher education and democracy, and especially traditions of liberal education in the United States. In so doing, I focus on the transcendent role that civic engagement has played in HBCUs, which are the subject of three of the four case studies examined in this book. Next, key actors and the different roles they can play in the fight for student voting rights are examined, which we call 'student as citizen,' 'faculty as citizen,' and 'institution as citizen.' Finally, these actors are explored through the lens of engaged citizenship, ultimately adapting Joel Westheimer and Joseph Kahne's tripartite typology of citizenship—"personally responsible," "participatory," and "justice-oriented"[1]—to develop an understanding of the actions of the different actors as they engage with student voting and student voting rights.

1 Higher Education and Democracy

Colleges and universities in the United States have long had a civic mission. As Yale University's former president Bart Giamatti said, "I believe that the formation of a basis for how we choose to believe and speak and treat others—how, in short, we choose a civic role for ourselves—is the basic purpose of an education in a democracy."[2] The American tradition of liberal education aspires to be the embodiment of the link between higher education, democracy, and engaged citizenship. As pro-

---

1 Joel Westheimer and Joseph Kahne, "What Kind of Citizen? The Politics of Educating for Democracy," *American Educational Research Journal* 41, no. 2 (2004): 237–269.
2 A. Bartlett Giamatti, *The University and the Public Interest* (Atheneum Books, 1981), 7–8.

fessor and philosopher Martha Nussbaum declared, liberal education is "higher education that cultivates the whole human being for the functions of citizenship and life in general."[3]

This civic mission dates way back in American higher education. Even in 1749, before the founding of the Republic, Benjamin Franklin wrote a pamphlet entitled *Proposals Relating to the Education of Youth in Pensilvania* (sic.), in which he proposed the creation of a college (that first became the Academy of Philadelphia and then the University of Pennsylvania) that would cultivate in students an *"Inclination* join'd with an *Ability* to serve Mankind, one's Country, Friends and Family."[4] That same civic impulse resonated in the founding documents of numerous private colleges formed after the revolution.[5] At the turn of the 20th century, Charles Eliot, Harvard University's longest-serving president, echoed this view: "At bottom, most of the American institutions of higher education are filled with the democratic spirit. Teachers and students alike are profoundly moved by the desire to serve the democratic community."[6] The horrors of the Second World War and the rise of fascism reinforced the perception of the importance of the civic role of higher education. The Truman Commission's 1947 report, *Higher Education for American Democracy*, stated succinctly, "The first and most essential charge upon higher education is that at all its levels and in all its fields of specialization, it shall be the carrier of democratic values, ideals, and process."[7]

The civic role of higher education gained new vigor after the fall of the Berlin Wall and the end of the Cold War, with the emergence of a number of initiatives and organizations devoted to the topic, such as Project Pericles and Campus Compact. On the one hand, it was a response to the fears of the growing corporatization of higher education and neoliberal approaches that placed too much of an

---

3 Martha Craven Nussbaum, "Cultivating Humanity and World Citizenship," *Forum Futures* 37 (2007): 37–40.

4 Benjamin Franklin, *Proposals Relating to the Education of Youth in Pensilvania* (1749), https://archives.upenn.edu/digitized-resources/docs-pubs/franklin-proposals/#:~:text=Note%20from%20the%20University%20Archives,as%20the%20University%20of%20Pennsylvania. Cited by Matthew Hartley, "Reclaiming the Democratic Purposes of Higher Education," *Learning and Teaching* 2, no. 3 (Winter 2009), 12.

5 Hartley, "Reclaiming the Democratic Purposes," 12.

6 Charles W. Eliot, *University Administration* (Houghton Mifflin Company, 1908), 227–228.

7 The President's Commission on Higher Education, *Higher Education for American Democracy* (Harper & Brothers, 1947), 102, https://ia801506.us.archive.org/25/items/in.ernet.dli.2015.89917/2015. 89917.Higher-Education-For-American-Democracy-A-Report-Of-The-Presidents-Commission-On-Higher-Education-Vol-I---Vi_text.pdf.

emphasis on the careers of students and university education's economic impact.[8] On the other hand, this push was inspired by the work and writings of Central European dissidents, who emphasized the critical role of civil society and autonomous institutions in promoting and shaping democracy.[9] William Sullivan tied these threads together when he said that the university should serve "some larger public purpose as a citizen within civil society rather than simply a self-aggrandizing creature of the market."[10]

This recent renewed emphasis of the link between education and democracy is more expansive than that discussed earlier in American history and puts more of an emphasis on the role of the institution. As John Saltmarsh, Matthew Hartley, and Patti Clayton's *Democratic Engagement White Paper* underlined, many of the leading thinkers on the democratic purpose of higher education emphasize that "higher education in America has a fundamental democratic purpose—both educating for democracy and creating educational institutions that foster the revitalization of democratic society."[11] The latter, in particular, was realized through Ernest Boyer's "scholarship of engagement," which sought to connect "the rich resources of the university to our most pressing social, civic and ethical problems."[12] It was manifested through institutional support for things like engaged research, community-based learning, access programs, legal and health clinics, and an array of student-led co-curricular activities, often done in cooperation with community-based organizations. Such efforts have been supported by organizations like the American Association of Colleges and Universities (AAC&U) and

---

8 Jonathan Becker, "The Global Liberal Arts Challenge," *Ethics & International Affairs* 36, no. 3 (Fall 2022), 283–301, https://www.ethicsandinternationalaffairs.org/journal/the-global-liberal-arts-challenge.

9 Becker "Global Liberal Arts Challenge."

10 William M. Sullivan, "University as Citizen: Institutional Identity and Social Responsibility," *Civic Arts Review* 16, no. 1 (2003), 5, https://digitalcommons.unomaha.edu/cgi/viewcontent.cgi?article=1040&context=slcehighered.

11 John Saltmarsh, Matthew Hartley, and Patti Clayton, *Democratic Engagement White Paper* (New England Resource Center for Higher Education, 2009), https://scholarworks.umb.edu/nerche_pubs/45/. The movement also extended far beyond the United States: in 2005, 29 university presidents, rectors, and vice chancellors from 23 countries issued the Talloires Declaration that called for "strengthening the civic role and social responsibility of our institutions" and which committed the signatories to "expand civic engagement and social responsibility programs in an ethical manner, through teaching, research and public service"; Association of University Leaders for a Sustainable Future, "The Talloires Declaration," created October 1990, http://ulsf.org/talloires-declaration/.

12 Margaret Brabant and Donald Braid, "The Devil is in the Details: Defining Civic Engagement" *Journal of Higher Education Outreach and Engagement* 13, no. 2 (2010): 59–87, https://openjournals.libs.uga.edu/jheoe/article/view/469.

the American Council of Education, which see the heart of their work as programming and advocacy that cultivate the link between liberal education, democracy,
and citizenship.[13]

With polls showing growing distrust of institutions, and the increased doubts,
particularly among youth, about the value of democracy itself,[14] there is among
many a greater sense of importance about the potential role of colleges and universities. These were well articulated in the book *What Universities Owe Democracy* by Johns Hopkins University president Ron Daniels, who put it succinctly:

> I believe that universities should be recognized as standing firmly among the institutions
> critical to securing the full promise of liberal democracy and sharing in the responsibility
> to protect it when its legitimacy and its durability are at risk. In fact, I maintain that few
> other social institutions rival the university at its best, in the sheer breadth of its vaunted
> contributions to liberal democracy's twin promises of equality and liberty.[15]

The growing focus on the civic mission of the university has also been manifested
in efforts to encourage the civic participation of students through the franchise.
Efforts have been supported by groups like the ALL IN Campus Democracy Challenge, The Andrew Goodman Foundation, Campus Vote Project, Democracy Matters, and the Students Learn Students Vote Coalition which provide guidance
and support to students and institutions about how to promote, and in some
cases defend, student voting. The National Study of Learning, Voting and Engagement, based at the Tisch College of Tufts University, provides data on voter participation for more than 1,000 campuses on voting, registration, and yield rates,
which help institutions to measure the impact of their efforts on student voting.

---

13 For example, AAC&U's work under the rubric of "Educating for Democracy," which includes
advocacy, programming, and assessment, is framed by the claim that, "A liberal education
provides the foundational knowledge and skills that empower students to advance the common
good through responsible and engaged citizenship in local, national and global contexts."
American Association of Colleges and Universities, "What is Liberal Education?", https://www.
aacu.org/trending-topics/what-is-liberal-education.
14 Lea Wang, "Declining Youth Trust in American Institutions Shows No Signs of Stopping,"
Harvard Political Review, April 18, 2024, https://theharvardpoliticalreview.com/declining-youth-
trust-in-american-institutions-shows-no-signs-of-stopping/#google_vignette.
15 Ronald J. Daniels, Grant Shreve, and Phillip Spector, *What Universities Owe Democracy* (Johns
Hopkins University Press, 2021), 20.

1.1 The Case of HBCUs

The tradition of liberal education and the link between liberal education and democracy were not only celebrated by predominantly white institutions (PWIs). Willa Player, the president of Bennett College from 1955 to 1966, an all-women's HBCU in Greensboro, North Carolina, who with her students played an underrecognized role in the civil rights movement, reflected on the meaning of liberal education as follows:

> It was living up to your ideals, building a quality of life in the community that was accept-able to all. It was respect for human dignity and personality. And it was a recognition of val-ues that applied to all persons as equals and all persons who deserved a chance in a demo-cratic society to express their beliefs.[16]

At the same time, the position of HBCUs within American academia, and particu-larly the link between education at HBCUs and democracy, are a distinct product of the history of African Americans in the United States. There is often a misun-derstanding of the roles of HBCUs, born out of an overly narrow interpretation of the education that takes place on campuses, which at times have had terms like "Agricultural and Technical" or "Agricultural and Mechanical" in their names. It is true that leaders like Booker T. Washington, the founder of Tuskegee, saw HBCUs as a pathway to economic advancement and a way to create circum-stances in which Blacks could fulfill their basic needs, such as health care. But that was always a means to an end, because, in Washington's mind, with economic im-provement in the Black community, "civil rights would follow."[17] Moreover, many HBCUs had diverse formal curriculums, including an emphasis on humanities and social sciences, that are more traditionally associated with a liberal education. For W.E.B. Du Bois, whose views are often juxtaposed with those of Washington, these institutions would prepare the "thinkers and leaders" who would create "an intel-lectual elite that could advance the civil rights of all black people."[18]

More importantly, it should be underlined that HBCUs played a radically dif-ferent and more central role in Black culture and the shaping of Black citizens than PWIs did for white citizens. Although this is often overlooked, it was precise-

16 Willa Player, "Oral History Interview with Willa Player by Eugene Pfaff," interviewed by Eugene Pfaff, *Greensboro Public Library Oral History Program*, Greensboro Public Library, De-cember 3, 1979, transcript, 18, https://gateway.uncg.edu/islandora/object/gpl:7381.
17 Marybeth Gasman, Dorsey Spencer, and Cecelia Orphan, "'Building Bridges and Not Fences': A History of Civic Engagement at Private Black Colleges and Universities, 1944–1964," *History of Education Quarterly* 55, no. 3 (August 2015): 358.
18 Gasman, Spencer, and Orphan, "Building Bridges and Not Fences," 357.

ly the exclusion of African Americans from US democracy and democratic institutions, including from institutions of higher education, that made the civic role of HBCUs so important.[19] Indeed, for many, particularly some of the leading Black educators, the purpose of HBCUs was "inextricably linked" with "rooting out white supremacy and other antidemocratic practices found deeply embedded within the soul of America," and which PWIs benefitted from and perpetuated.[20] Indeed, Black leaders and generations of HBCU faculty and students no doubt looked on with some irony as the leaders of America's elite white institutions, including revered people like Eliot and Woodrow Wilson, who served as president of Princeton, celebrated the link between higher education and democracy while at the same time implementing policies that reinforced America's anti-democratic and violent racial hierarchy. A more genuine civic role was woven into HBCUs' very fabric, whether or not outsiders recognized this as being the case. As Gloria Dean Randall Scott put it:

> The construct of civic development was the right auricle of the heart of HBCUs, joined by the left auricle of teaching and learning, and the left ventricle of creating new knowledge, all of which combined to make up the core of American higher education: teaching, research, and public service. Historically black institutions, however, always had, as the right ventricle, a fourth purpose—the pursuit of social justice, which is the core of civic engagement, and the strengthening of democracy.[21]

Jelani Favors (author of chapter 5) unpacks this in his magisterial book *Shelter in a Time of Storm*, in which he explores how HBCUs, even those that focused more on agricultural and technical subjects, had a "second curriculum," offering a "pedagogy of hope" that emphasized idealism, cultural nationalism, and race consciousness.[22] This was not a 'hidden curriculum,' as others have argued, but an infusion of purposeful and inescapable race consciousness "into the curriculum and extracurricular activities of the day-to-day campus life."[23]

---

19 Gasman, Spencer, and Orphan wrote, "While historically white institutions have experienced a fairly recent resurgence of interest in developing the civic learning outcomes of students and creating strong, mutually beneficial bonds with their communities, historically black colleges and universities (HBCUs) were founded with and, in many cases, have maintained these purposes throughout their histories." "Building Bridges and Not Fences,'" 348.
20 Jelani M. Favors, "The Second Curriculum," *The Point* 25 (August 2021), https://thepointmag.com/politics/the-second-curriculum/.
21 Gasman, Spencer, and Orphan, "'Building Bridges and Not Fences,'" 359.
22 Jelani M. Favors, *Shelter in a Time of Storm: How Black Colleges Fostered Generations of Leadership and Activism* (University of North Carolina Press, 2020), 5.
23 Favors, *Shelter in a Time of Storm*, 7.

Favors deploys the term 'communitas' to describe "the vital space that Black colleges provided," offering both an open venue for engagement between and among students and faculty and "shelter from the worst elements of white supremacist society that sought to undermine, overlook and render impotent the intellectual capacity of Black youths."[24] Within the "fortified interstitial space" of the HBCU what was important was not so much the bricks and mortar, but the relationships and the sense of purpose among numerous students and faculty who saw it as "their duty to inculcate the second curriculum in their peers, students, or colleagues who resided within the same space."[25] It was in this second curriculum that the "hopes and dreams of the entire race"[26] rested because it prepared graduates to "serve as social and political change agents in the communities they were destined to serve."[27]

Despite the fact that they often operated in overwhelmingly constrained environments, the formal and second curriculums, and communitas, shaped a who's who of the leaders in the fight for civil rights in the United States, including such luminaries as Dubois (Fisk University), Ida B. Wells (Shaw University), James Weldon Johnson (Atlanta University), Martin Luther King Jr. (Morehouse College), Ella Baker (Shaw University), John Lewis (American Baptist College and Fisk University), and Thurgood Marshall (Lincoln University). And it was not only alumni; enrolled HBCU students played a central role in many of the key activities of the civil rights movement, whether it was the A&T (Greensboro) Four, who stood up to segregation at the Woolworth lunch counter, or the members of the Congress on Racial Equality and the Student Nonviolent Coordinating Committee, who played a central role in the battles that led to the Voting Rights Act of 1965.

With this understanding of the broad links between higher education and democracy, we can now turn to the civic actors who play an important role in the fight for student voting rights.

---

24 Favors, *Shelter in a Time of Storm*, 5.
25 Favors wrote, "Black students and faculty did not simply replicate the routine carried out at white institutions. The relationships that were built and the lessons learned through a second curriculum buoyed the hopes and dreams of the entire race. Much more would be expected of the products of this space." Favors, *Shelter in a Time of Storm*, 6.
26 Favors, *Shelter in a Time of Storm*, 6.
27 Favors, "The Second Curriculum."

2 Civic Actors

The role of colleges and universities in the fight for student voting rights has been, and remains, variegated. To understand better the role of different constituencies, this analysis is divided into three main types of agents: 'student as citizen,' 'faculty as citizen,' and 'institution as citizen.' The role of each in the fight to realize the 26th Amendment is complex and varies according to several factors. But exploring how a student, a professor, and an institution can all work to create the conditions in which voting rights are advanced can help us to understand how lofty ideals about the relationship between higher education and democracy espoused by Giamatti and others are realized, and whether institutions are living up to those ideals.

2.1 The Student as Citizen

When educators in the United States speak of the link between higher education and democracy, they often refer to what can be called the 'student as citizen' approach. This emphasizes the role of the educational process in cultivating democratic values and students' capacity to be active and informed citizens. Giamatti, for example, expresses the view that "Every classroom is an act of making citizens in the realm of that room, and every room is a figure for the larger community."[28] For Willa Player, who faced head-on the challenges of integration in Greensboro as the president of an HBCU, the link between education and active citizenship was closer to the surface. As Gasman puts it, "critical thinking was essential to learning and protest was, in many ways, a manifestation of thought."[29]

History shows that students have exercised their role as civic actors in the fight for student voting rights not simply after they have absorbed the lessons of the classroom and gone out into the world, but while they have still been enrolled in college. Students played a central role in the fight for Black voting rights, whether registering voters, protesting inequities, or advocating and lobbying for change. Some even lost their lives in these efforts, as the deaths of James Chaney, Andrew Goodman, and Michael Schwerner in Mississippi during Freedom Summer illustrate. During the Second Reconstruction, they took many of these lessons

---

28 Giamatti, *The University and the Public Interest*, 137.
29 Marybeth Gasman, "Perceptions of Black College Presidents: Sorting Through Stereotypes and Reality to Gain a Complex Picture," *American Educational Research Journal* 48, no. 4 (August 2011): 863.

and applied them to reduce the voting age. As Frost points out, in her excellent book *Let Us Vote!*, college students were central to oft-overlooked 'bottom-up' efforts to pass the 26th Amendment. They advocated, publicized, and protested on campus and through state-based and national organizations and coalitions that were devoted to promoting youth voting rights by changing state and federal laws, and ultimately the Constitution.[30]

As our case studies show, students had, and continue to exercise, an important civic role in promoting youth franchise and in the fight for voting rights in the decades following the passage of the 26th Amendment in 1971. While popular writing often focuses on youth apathy and dis-engagement, a study of the history of the struggle for youth voting rights reveals something different: idealism, determination, and a fearlessness among young Americans, particularly students, that have challenged hostility, prejudice, and discriminatory practices. Students have agency and exercise it, and are very much involved in the day-to-day election process.

Much of the student engagement is non-partisan. Students, often demonstrating the idealism that advocates of the 26th Amendment lauded, work with their college/university or with non-profits to register students and others to vote. They also create and disseminate information about candidates and host candidate forums that sometimes focus on issues of particular interest to students and youth voters. They host get-out-the-vote events on campus. They disseminate information to their peers, who are often first-time voters, about regular and early voting hours, the locations of poll sites, locations where they can find transportation to the polls, and rules governing critical issues like necessary forms of identification. Many also participate in partisan activities, volunteering for candidates and political parties, canvassing, and door knocking.

As far as the primary interest of this book is concerned, which is promoting and defending students' right to vote, students' work can be divided into three primary and overlapping areas: publicizing, advocating, and litigating. They publicize voting impediments and the infringement of voting rights by producing posters and videos, and publishing articles in student newspapers and local and national media. They disseminate information through tabling on-campus and social media platforms, speaking out at on-campus and off-campus forums, holding press conferences, appearing before government bodies, and participating in marches and other forms of protest. They advocate for change by researching and disseminating information on pertinent issues, by pressing local and state officials to remove

---

30 Jennifer Frost, *"Let Us Vote!": Youth Voting Rights and the 26th Amendment* (New York University Press, 2022), 186.

voting restrictions, and by developing practices that encourage youth voter participation. They also encourage and pressure institutional leaders to denounce violations of voting rights, provide support for efforts to redress infringements, and, more broadly, help facilitate the student voting process. Finally, they litigate, serving as plaintiffs and witnesses in cases that challenge discriminatory practices and procedures that limit student voting.

Students act through student organizations and student governments, but also partner with other student groups, be they at neighboring institutions or through national networks. They also work with NGOs and legal defense funds, such as Common Cause, the National Association for the Advancement of Colored People, and the League of Women Voters. Finally, they learn from, and partner with, faculty and administrators, as we will discuss in more detail below.

In spite of the important role they play, there are limits to the capacity of students to serve as effective civic actors in the fight for youth voting rights. Students are still students: they are learning and developing civic knowledge and their civic identities. They often are new to the communities in which they are situated and unfamiliar with complex local political structures where voting conflicts often take place. They tend not to have resources, certainly not of the magnitude that can support protracted legal battles or lengthier advocacy campaigns that require contributions from successive generations of students. Many have part-time jobs and most have full-time jobs as students, with regular reading and assignments and intense work periods during their finals. As they near graduation, they think of what is next and often attempt to position themselves for careers. Most importantly, their presence on campus is ephemeral. Students by definition cycle in and cycle out; they leave campus for holidays and study abroad, they drop out, transfer, and graduate. And yet our case studies vividly illustrate that such impediments have not imposed insuperable barriers to students mobilizing and fighting to protect their voting rights.

2.2 The Faculty as Citizen

The civic role of faculty, or 'faculty as citizen,' can be found in their teaching, research, and service. Faculty are educators who day in and day out, as the principles of liberal education suggest, not only transmit knowledge, but also develop in students critical thinking and analytic skills, ways of thinking and understanding, and means of communicating that fundamentally shape them as student-citizens.

Some faculty are more purposeful than others in connecting their teaching with citizenship, whether in the design of course subject matter or fostering community-based learning that puts special emphasis on civic engagement. This can include voting: faculty members, regardless of their field, may choose to devote class time to announcing opportunities to register to vote, or inform students about where they can learn about absentee ballots and when and where early voting is available. Some walk with eligible students to the poll site. Sometimes entire courses are constructed around issues of voting, including community-based learning courses that encourage students to work with public officials, volunteer for campaigns, participate in registration efforts based at their colleges or nonprofits, and even volunteer to serve as poll workers. Some assign or employ students to conduct engaged research that can shape our collective understanding of important voting issues and even create opportunities for students to participate in problem-solving and in improving election administration locally and statewide. A good example of this is Gunther Peck from Duke University, who together with students from his class produced important research that highlighted the perils of provisional ballots in North Carolina.[31]

But faculty engagement with students does not end at the boundaries of the classroom as traditionally understood. Indeed, a core part of the 'second curriculum,' about which Favors wrote, is co-curricular and involves engagement outside of the classroom. Faculty advise students informally and formally. They are sources of information and strategy, sounding boards and bridges to advocacy organizations and legal defense funds that are well positioned to support student voting rights and with which the faculty are sometimes affiliated. Student leaders from Prairie View A&M University (PVAMU), North Carolina Agricultural and Technical State University (NC A&T), and Bard, three of our case studies, reported that they were guided and advised at critical points by faculty members who helped them navigate challenges they would otherwise be incapable of surmounting.

Faculty also play a civic role through their own engaged research that can explore the complex mosaic of laws and practices that govern voting in the U.S. Research can expose disparities in voter participation based on characteristics such as age, race, and gender, and analyze the sources of those disparities. It can reveal the impact of 'voter integrity' laws and laws designed to encourage the franchise. It can assess the compliance of boards of election with state and federal laws. It can explore the attitudes of student voters. This research can be disseminated through journals, opinion pieces, commentaries, and public talks.

---

31 Gunther Peck, Ameya Rao, Kathryn Thomas, Delaney Eisen, Miles King, Hannah McKnight, and Luhan Yao, "Provisional Rights and Provisional Ballots in a Swing State: Understanding How and Why North Carolina College Students Lose their Right to Vote, 2008-Present," *Rutgers University Law Review* 74, no. 5 (Summer 2022): 1799–1838, https://rutgerslawreview.com/wp-content/uploads/2023/02/05_Peck_et-al..pdf.

Finally, faculty themselves can facilitate litigation, advising students, linking them with advocacy and legal defense organizations, or serving themselves as litigants, as did Charles Gomillion, a professor of sociology and head of the Division of Social Studies at Tuskegee Institute, who was the named litigant in *Gomillion v. Lightfoot*, that plays a central role in our first case study.[32]

As for students, there are constraints to the activism of faculty members. Faculty members have tremendous burdens in teaching, research, and service, and may view themselves as unlikely to gain recognition for work that colleagues may perceive as being unrelated to their core activities. Worse, they may fear alienating fellow faculty colleagues and members of the administration who determine critical career issues like renewal of employment, promotions, and tenure, as well as access to internal grants. Finally, many faculty have tenuous relationships to their home institutions, serving as adjuncts and in visiting roles, which limit the duration of their presence on campus as well as their accumulated knowledge of relevant issues, and even exposes them to potential retaliation should their interventions with students be viewed as problematic.

2.3 The Institution as Citizen

Less often discussed in the literature is what can be called the 'institution as citizen,' which views universities as civic actors in their own right. As Erin Cannan and I argued in our article, "Institution as Citizen: Colleges and Universities as Actors in Defense of Student Voting Rights," this view emerged increasingly in the 1980s and 1990s, both from a fear of a neoliberal marketization of higher education and from a desire to ensure the legacy of the link between higher education

---

32 Ironically, the decision in *Gomillion v. Lightfoot* expressly rejected the applicability of a previous court decision, *Colegrove v. Green*, that was brought by Kenneth W. Colegrove, a professor of political science at Northwestern University, although the *Colegrove* case was not related to student voting rights. In a more recent case, Vassar College professor Rebecca Edwards spearheaded a 2022 effort to implement in a timely manner New York State law mandating polling places on college campuses with 300 or more registered voters, working with the League of Women Voters and mobilizing a student and fellow faculty member, Taneisha Means, as litigants. Their efforts led to a decision on election eve requiring the polling place and unifying the Vassar campus into one election district, instead of the three that had hitherto existed; *League of Women Voters of the Mid-Hudson Valley v. Dutchess County Board of Elections*, 2022–53491 (N.Y Sup. Ct. 2022), https://www.democracydocket.com/cases/new-york-vassar-college-polling-location-challenge/; Clara Alger, "Fighting for the Youth Vote in the Hudson Valley," *The River*, November 2, 2023, https://www.chronogram.com/river-newsroom/fighting-for-the-youth-vote-in-the-hudson-valley-19347760.

and democracy discussed above.[33] In this context, an academic institution as a corporate entity commits itself to finding ways to use resources, be they organizational, human, financial, or reputational, to promote civic engagement and protect core democratic principles.[34] Benson, Harkavy, and Puckett summed it up well in their book *Dewey's Dream*, asserting: "To become part of the solution, higher education institutions must give full-hearted, full-minded devotion to the painfully difficult task of transforming themselves into socially responsible civic universities and colleges."[35]

Student radicals of the 1960s recognized the potential of a civic role for colleges and universities. The 1962 *Port Huron Statement* by the Students for a Democratic Society declared: "Social relevance, the accessibility to knowledge, and internal openness—these together make the university a potential base and agency in a movement of social change."[36] More recently, the 2011 report by The Civic Learning and Democratic Engagement National Task Force to the U.S. Department of Education, *A Crucible Moment: College Learning and Democracy's Future*, suggested that this civic role extends to economic development and a large range of social problems: "The more civic-oriented colleges and universities become, the greater their overall capacity to spur local and global economic vitality, social and political well-being, and collective action to address public problems."[37] But the common thread running through the discourse on the civic mis-

---

33 Jonathan Becker and Erin Cannan, "Institution as Citizen: Colleges and Universities as Actors in Defense of Student Voting Rights," *Rutgers University Law Review* 74, no. 4 (Summer 2022): 1877.
34 Ira Harkavy and Matthew Hartley, "Integrating a Commitment to the Public Good into the Institutional Fabric: Further Lessons from the Field," *Journal of Higher Education Outreach and Engagement* 16, no. 4 (2012): 17–36, https://openjournals.libs.uga.edu/jheoe/article/view/980/979.
35 Lee Benson, Ira Harkavy, and John Puckett, *Dewey's Dream: Universities and Democracies in an Age of Education Reform, Civil Society, Public Schools, and Democratic Citizenship* (Temple University Press, 2007), 84.
36 Tom Hayden, *The Port Huron Statement* (Students for a Democratic Society, 1962), 62, http://www.progressivefox.com/misc_documents/PortHuronStatement.pdf; "We believe that the universities are an overlooked seat of influence. First, the university is located in a permanent position of social influence. Its educational function makes it indispensable and automatically makes it a crucial institution in the formation of social attitudes. Second, in an unbelievably complicated world, it is the central institution for organizing, evaluating, and transmitting knowledge" (Hayden, *The Port Huron Statement*, 61). It should be noted that there was also a clear wariness of the university administration, which was often viewed as a source of reaction (see Hayden, *The Port Huron Statement*, 62–63).
37 The Civic Learning and Democratic Engagement National Task Force, submitted to U.S. Department of Education, *A Crucible Moment: College Learning and Democracy's Future* (October 2011), 6, https://www.ed.gov/sites/ed/files/rschstat/research/pubs/college-learning-democracys-future/crucible-moment.pdf.

sion of universities is the connection between education and democracy. This is well exemplified in Campus Compact's 1999 "Declaration on the Civic Responsibility of Higher Education," which challenged higher education "to re-examine its public purposes and its commitments to the democratic ideal." The statement concluded succinctly: "We believe that now and through the next century, our institutions must be vital agents and architects of a flourishing democracy."[38]

Institutions and institutional leaders played little role in the passage of the 26th Amendment. For example, the dense *Congressional Record* of the Senate and House debates on the days before the amendment was passed contain references to only two college presidents, both of whom were cited in reference to violence on college campuses, not on the substance of the Amendment.[39] A survey of the most important books and journal articles on the 26th Amendment found almost no mention of institutional leaders, defined as presidents, provosts, vice presidents, and deans.[40] And yet they can be critical actors.

How does this notion of 'institution as citizen' translate into issues related to student voting? First and foremost, institutions can support many of the actions of students and faculty described above, providing resources for student activities and clubs, supporting engaged research and community-based learning, and protecting and defending students, administrators, and faculty who are criticized for their work, as Tuskegee did with Charles Gomillion, whose work with the Tuskegee Civic Association drew the ire of local and state politicians.[41]

As we move to the present, one of the important areas where institutions are engaged is in voter registration. Here, we note that since the 26th Amendment, the federal government has explicitly involved colleges in the electoral process. The

---

38 Thomas Ehrlich and Elizabeth Hollander, "Presidents' Declaration on the Civic Responsibility of Higher Education," Campus Compact, drafted in 1999, https://compact.org/resources-for-presidents/presidents-declaration-on-the-civic-responsibility-of-higher-education/.

39 U.S. Congress, *Congressional Record*, 92nd Cong., 1st sess., 1971, vol. 117, pt. 5: 5707–6017, https://www.congress.gov/bound-congressional-record/1971/03/10/; U.S. Congress, *Congressional Record*, 92nd Cong., 1st sess., 1971, vol. 117, pt. 6: 7338–7650, https://www.congress.gov/bound-congressional-record/1971/03/23/.

40 Becker and Cannan, "Institution as Citizen," 1885, footnote 94. The same is true of Frost's recent book *"Let Us Vote!"*, in which college and university leadership is mentioned in passing, and only in reference to campus protests.

41 Frederick D. Patterson, Martia Graham Goodson, and Harry V. Richardson, *Chronicles of Faith: The Autobiography of Frederick Douglass Patterson* (University of Alabama Press, 1991), 109–110. See also Gabriel Antoine Smith, "A Hollow Inheritance: The Legacies of the Tuskegee Civic Association and the Crusade for Civic Democracy in Alabama" (PhD diss., Auburn University, 2016), https://etd.auburn.edu/bitstream/handle/10415/5334/smith_gabriel_ma_thesis_auetd_resubmit_20160729.pdf?sequence=2&isAllowed=y.

1998 Reauthorization of the Higher Education Act of 1965 brought colleges into the voter registration process by including a mandate that requires higher education institutions to make a "good faith effort to distribute a mail voter registration form ... to each student enrolled in a degree or certificate program and physically in attendance at the institution, and to make such forms widely available to students at the institution" during years in which there are federal or gubernatorial elections.[42] This followed the National Voter Registration Act of 1993, which, in section 7, allowed states to designate state colleges, universities, and community colleges as voter registration agencies.[43] This begs an immediate question, why have states not availed themselves of this opportunity? Second, the question, for the purposes of this book is, what roles do the institutions of higher education choose for themselves?

Often the institutions take a tepid approach. It is easy to simply email a link to voter registration websites, and this is the path that many choose to follow, leaving more engaged efforts to student groups or third parties. For example, a 2022 open letter from a group called Ivy League Votes, published in *Inside Higher Ed*, stated:

> Many of us have met with administrators only to be told that it is not their job to make voting easier and that, rather, the onus should be on students to make it to the ballot box. Indeed, administrators have told us it is actually beneficial for students to face barriers to voting while we are in college so that we get used to the barriers we will face after graduation. There seems to be an all-too-pervasive idea that voting should be mired in difficulty and inconvenience.[44]

For those institutions that choose to engage, there are many actions that they can undertake. In terms of registering students, they can make a comprehensive effort, developing complete action plans with groups like ALL IN Campus Democracy Challenge, designed to actively register students and prepare them to vote.

---

42 U.S. Congress, *Higher Education Amendments of 1998*, H.R. 6, 105th Cong., 2nd sess., 1998, https://www.govinfo.gov/content/pkg/BILLS-105hr6enr/pdf/BILLS-105hr6enr.pdf; The Help America Vote Act, which was passed following the disastrous 2000 election, created a special program to encourage student participation as poll workers or assistants, to foster student interest in the election process, and to encourage state and local governments to use students as poll workers. See U.S. Election Assistance Commission, "Past HAVCP Programming," last updated November 15, 2023, https://www.eac.gov/payments_and_grants/help_america_vote_college_program.

43 U.S. Congress, *National Voter Registration Act of 1993*, H.R. 2, 103rd Cong., 1993, https://www.congress.gov/bill/103rd-congress/house-bill/2.

44 Members of Ivy League Votes, "Student Voting is Not Where it Should Be," *Inside Higher Ed*, January 2, 2022, https://www.insidehighered.com/views/2022/01/03/college-students-face-many-unnecessary-obstacles-voting-opinion.

Rather than taking the path of least resistance to voter registration, they link opportunities to register to a range of mandatory activities like first-year orientation, class registration, and housing placements. They can empower offices, such as centers for civic engagement, to promote registration and voting, either on their own or through the supervision of students and student groups. They can respond to growing impediments to voting by providing resources that help students register and vote, be it by issuing student identity cards that comply with state regulations needed for first-time voters or voting in general, or providing notaries to help students fulfill absentee ballot requirements.[45] They can make their campuses open and available as poll sites and offer centrally located buildings with access to parking.[46] When off-campus poll sites are not easily or readily accessible via public transport, they can offer institutional transportation to the polls. They can encourage people affiliated with the institution to serve as poll workers, especially at locations where students vote, to ensure that there are friendly faces that can help students navigate voting challenges. They can ensure that they have administrators who understand the challenges students face and are knowledgeable about the local political environment. These opportunities are described in more detail in chapter 8.

When students' voting rights are violated, as in our case studies, institutions can actively support them. They can make clear the institutional position through statements by the leadership and resolutions by boards of trustees. They can, where appropriate, support litigation by facilitating links with legal defense funds and financing litigation. They can even, as was the case with Bard College's long-serving president Leon Botstein, serve as plaintiffs in voting rights cases, standing side by side with students in court. Most of all, when they are engaged they can provide the continuity that students (and often faculty) cannot; voting rights battles, our cases have demonstrated, play out over decades, not years.

There are limits to what institutions can do, in part based on the enabling environment in which they are situated. Some leaders and institutions have incentives to take a passive approach. Leaders of public institutions are particularly vulnerable, even if they enter the political fray in a non-partisan way in defense of democracy. They may face threats over budget cuts from governors and legislatures, and their leaders may face threats of dismissal because they report to a

45 See for example, Amaia Clayton, Olivia Schramkowski, and Gunther Peck, "Duke Must Do More to Protect Student Voting Rights," *The Chronicle*, September 5, 2024, https://www.dukechronicle.com/article/2024/09/090524-schramkowski-clayton-peck-duke-must-protect-voting-rights.
46 Johanna Alonso, "A N.Y. Law Mandates Campus Polling Sites. Why Are There Still So Few?" *Inside Higher Ed*, March 4, 2024, https://www.insidehighered.com/news/students/free-speech/2024/03/04/ny-law-polling-sites-campuses-not-fully-implemented.

Board of Trustees situated within a state system and who are often appointed by elected officials. This is particularly the case for public HBCUs like PVAMU and NC A&T, which witnessed the dismissal of many leaders during the battle for civil rights.[47] However, even private institutions can face threats. Almost every institution is dependent to some extent on public funds and all institutions may be exposed to threats from local and municipal officials in terms of building permits, zoning, and access to public transportation. Leaders of private institutions may also fear losing the support of their board of trustees, particularly if their actions are viewed as partisan or too provocative. Indeed, a number of presidents of private Black colleges lost their positions because of the role they played in supporting the civil rights movement.[48] Recent calls for 'institutional neutrality' may well reinforce passive and laissez-faire attitudes, as leaders withdraw from democratic engagement in an unfortunate effort to remove themselves from the political fray and accusations of partisanship.[49]

Despite the risks that have accompanied their actions, many institutional leaders have found ways to use their authority and resources to support democracy. This was well illustrated during the civil rights movement, where the Second Reconstuction began. As Eddie Cole points out in his excellent book *The Campus Color Line*, some leaders of public and private colleges and universities, HBCUs, and PWIs showed uncommon courage and creativity as they mapped out responses to issues like desegregation during the civil rights era.[50] While the issue of student voting does not have the same resonance as the civil rights movement, key actors, including institutional actors, whether at public or private institutions, can choose to engage or remain on the sidelines.

2.4 Other Actors

It should also be noted that advocacy for student voting rights often occurs in coordination with external actors, including political actors, non-profits, voting advocacy groups like the League of Women Voters, Common Cause, and The Andrew Goodman Foundation, and legal defense funds affiliated with organizations like the NAACP and branches of the American Civil Liberties Union. Indeed, in

---

47 Eddie Cole, *The Campus Color Line: College Presidents and the Struggle for Black Freedom* (Princeton University Press, 2020), 7.
48 Cole, *The Campus Color Line*, 7.
49 Jonathan Becker, "Deeds Not Words," *Liberal Education*, May 21, 2024, https://www.aacu.org/liberaleducation/articles/deeds-not-words.
50 Cole, *The Campus Color Line*.

many cases these groups have played a central role in shaping advocacy and strategy, inspiring students and faculty to take action and giving tools to administrators to address challenges. As our case studies will show, the purpose here is not to overlook these groups, but to discuss how they interact with the three actors which form the heart of colleges and universities.

3 Types of Citizenship and Voting Rights

As we examine the role of different actors, our conception of citizenship is shaped by Westheimer and Kahne, who, in their article "What Kind of Citizen?" focus on three types of citizenship: "personally responsible," "participatory", and "justice-oriented." The personally responsible citizen is characterized by duty, honesty, integrity, self-discipline, and hard work.[51] Her focus is on the individual and on how a citizen may act responsibly in their community by working, paying taxes, and obeying laws.[52] The participatory citizen "actively participates in civic affairs and the social life of the community at local, state and national levels."[53] She is an engaged member of community organizations and develops strategies to work with partners in civil society and government to accomplish collective tasks.[54] She endeavors to develop relationships, common understandings, and trust that reinforce a collective commitment to solve social problems and improve society.[55] The justice-oriented citizen takes things a step further and critically assesses social, political, and economic structures, calling "explicit attention to matters of injustice and to the importance of pursuing social justice."[56]

In elucidating the differences among the three, Westheimer and Kahne speak of how each category of citizen might respond to the issue of hunger. A personally responsible citizen "contributes food to a food drive." A participatory citizen "helps to organize a food drive." Finally, a justice-oriented citizen "explores why people are hungry and acts to solve root causes."[57]

These are archetypes, and there is clearly overlap between the three. An individual might act differently at different times depending on their personal cir-

---

51 Joel Westheimer and Joseph Kahne, "What Kind of Citizen? The Politics of Educating for Democracy," *American Educational Research Journal* 41, no. 2 (2004): 242.
52 Westheimer and Kahne, "What Kind of Citizen?" 242.
53 Westheimer and Kahne, "What Kind of Citizen?" 243.
54 Westheimer and Kahne, "What Kind of Citizen?" 242.
55 Westheimer and Kahne, "What Kind of Citizen?" 243.
56 Westheimer and Kahne, "What Kind of Citizen?" 240.
57 Westheimer and Kahne, "What Kind of Citizen?" 241.

cumstances and on external factors that might facilitate or discourage engagement. This is particularly the case for students. Someone might act as one type of citizen on a certain issue and another on a different issue. But if we superimpose this typology of each of the three key constituencies involved in student voting—what we call 'student as citizen,' 'faculty as citizen,' and 'institution as citizen'—we can help clarify different approaches and levels of engagement and inspire reflection about who we as individuals or institutional representatives engage with. Detailed descriptions of these three types of actors are given below:

Student:
– The personally responsible student attends class and registers to vote.
– The participatory student helps other students register to vote and participates in get-out-the-vote efforts, and/or volunteers for political campaigns. She works with on-campus and off-campus organizations that promote voting, and engages with administrators and other stakeholders on voting efforts. She signs petitions, participates in boycotts, and attends protests to fight voter suppression.
– The justice-oriented student organizes petitions, boycotts, and protests against discriminatory practices which disenfranchise students; supports and participates in lawsuits against public officials who deprive students of voting rights; and/or advocates for changes to state and federal laws that protect student voters and facilitate student voting, including poll sites on campus, by effecting longer-lasting institutional and legal reforms, often in partnership with advocacy organizations and legal defense funds.

Faculty:
– The personally responsible faculty member teaches students critical thinking skills and principles of government and democracy.
– The participatory faculty member advises students on strategies to address and overcome obstacles to voting and violations of students' rights; links students to advocacy organizations; offers community-based learning courses or tutorials that allow students to engage with voting issues; gives or arranges public talks on civics; helps register students to vote; and/or serves as a poll watcher or worker.
– The justice-oriented faculty member conducts research and/or teaches courses that expose the difficulties, inequities, and rights violations in the voting process; disseminates research outcomes publicly; advocates for changes to remedy the problems identified; works for advocacy and legal defense organizations; and/or supports litigation through their research or as plaintiffs in

an effort to effect systemic change to alleviate barriers to student voter participation.

Institution:
- The personally responsible institution fulfills the statutorily required 'good-faith effort' to register students to vote by sending out an email with a link to a voter registration website and hosts a polling place on campus when state officials ask for one. It remains strictly neutral on issues of student voting rights, leaving such matters to students and third parties.
- The participatory institution creates and implements a comprehensive plan for voter registration, education, and getting out the vote; provides transportation to the polls where needed; and makes efforts to identify and advocate for suitable and central on-campus poll sites. It defends the right of student and faculty activists to pursue voting rights issues and may offer tacit support.
- The justice-oriented institution creates and implements a comprehensive student voting plan; publicly supports the right of students to vote and the importance of voting as a part of its educational mission; mobilizes institutional resources to help students overcome barriers to voting and to defend student voting rights; supports directly or indirectly voting rights litigation; and/or advocates for systemic changes to overcome barriers to student voting.

When John's Hopkins president Ron Daniels referred to the university as playing an essential role in "securing the full promise of liberal democracy," one hopes he had in mind a justice-oriented role: encouraging institutions, and their constituent parts, not simply to be personally responsible and participatory, but also to be justice-oriented, active, vocal, and committed in defending and promoting voting rights for members of the college community, and for broader change in our society.

With this in mind, we can now turn to our case studies.

Bibliography

Alger, Clara. "Fighting for the Youth Vote in the Hudson Valley." *The River*, November 2, 2023. https://www.chronogram.com/river-newsroom/fighting-for-the-youth-vote-in-the-hudson-valley-19347760.

Alonso, Johanna. "A N.Y. Law Mandates Campus Polling Sites. Why Are There Still So Few?" *Inside Higher Ed*, March 4, 2024. https://www.insidehighered.com/news/students/free-speech/2024/03/04/ny-law-polling-sites-campuses-not-fully-implemented.

American Association of Colleges and Universities. "What is Liberal Education?" https://www.aacu.org/trending-topics/what-is-liberal-education.

Association of University Leaders for a Sustainable Future. "The Talloires Declaration." Created October 1990. http://ulsf.org/talloires-declaration/.

Bard Center for Civic Engagement. "Bard Center for Civic Engagement Prepares Report on Poll Sites on College Campuses." Posted February 16, 2024. https://cce.bard.edu/news/bard-center-for-civic-engagement-prepares-report-on-poll-sites-on-college-campuses-2024-01-06.

Becker, Jonathan. "The Global Liberal Arts Challenge." *Ethics & International Affairs* 36, no. 3 (Fall 2022): 283–301. https://www.ethicsandinternationalaffairs.org/journal/the-global-liberal-arts-challenge.

Becker, Jonathan. "Deeds Not Words." *Liberal Education*, May 21, 2024. https://www.aacu.org/liberaleducation/articles/deeds-not-words.

Becker, Jonathan, and Cannan, Erin. "Institution as Citizen: Colleges and Universities as Actors in Defense of Student Voting Rights." *Rutgers University Law Review* 74, no. 4 (Summer 2022): 1869–1909.

Benson, Lee, Harkavy, Ira, and Puckett, John. *Dewey's Dream: Universities and Democracies in an Age of Education Reform, Civil Society, Public Schools, and Democratic Citizenship.* Temple University Press, 2007.

Brabant, Margaret, and Braid, Donald. "The Devil is in the Details: Defining Civic Engagement." *Journal of Higher Education Outreach and Engagement* 13, no. 2 (2010): 59–87. https://openjournals.libs.uga.edu/jheoe/article/view/469.

Bromberg, Yael. "Youth Voting Rights and the Unfulfilled Promise of the Twenty-Sixth Amendment." *University of Pennsylvania Journal of Constitutional Law* 21, no. 5 (2019): 1105–1166. https://scholarship.law.upenn.edu/jcl/vol21/iss5/1/.

Cheng, Jenny Diamond. "Voting Rights for Millennials: Breathing New Life into the Twenty-Sixth Amendment." *Syracuse Law Review* 67 (2017): 653–678.

The Civic Learning and Democratic Engagement National Task Force, submitted to U.S. Department of Education. *A Crucible Moment: College Learning and Democracy's Future*, October 2011. https://www.ed.gov/sites/ed/files/rschstat/research/pubs/college-learning-democracys-future/crucible-moment.pdf.

Clayton, Amaia, Schramkowski, Olivia, and Peck, Gunther. "Duke Must Do More to Protect Student Voting Rights." *The Chronicle*, September 5, 2024. https://www.dukechronicle.com/article/2024/09/090524-schramkowski-clayton-peck-duke-must-protect-voting-rights.

Cole, Eddie. *The Campus Color Line: College Presidents and the Struggle for Black Freedom.* Princeton University Press, 2020.

Daniels, Ronald J., Shreve, Grant, and Spector, Phillip. *What Universities Owe Democracy.* Johns Hopkins University Press, 2021.

D'Ercole, Ryan. "Fighting a New Wave of Voter Suppression: Securing College Students' Right to Vote Through the Twenty-Sixth Amendment's Enforcement Clause." *Washington and Lee Law Review* 78, no. 4 (2021): 1659–1716.

Ehrlich, Thomas, and Hollander, Elizabeth. "Presidents' Declaration on the Civic Responsibility of Higher Education." Campus Compact. Drafted in 1999. https://compact.org/resources-for-presidents/presidents-declaration-on-the-civic-responsibility-of-higher-education/.

Eliot, Charles W. *University Administration.* Houghton Mifflin Company, 1908.

Eriksen, Helen. "Thousands March in Prairie View for Voting Rights." The Ruckus Society. Originally published February 25, 2008. https://ruckus.org/thousands-march-in-prairie-view-for-voting-rights-2/.

Favors, Jelani M. *Shelter in a Time of Storm: How Black Colleges Fostered Generations of Leadership and Activism.* University of North Carolina Press, 2020.

Favors, Jelani M. "The Second Curriculum." *The Point* 25 (August 2021). https://thepointmag.com/politics/the-second-curriculum/.

Fish, Eric. "The Twenty-Sixth Amendment Enforcement Power." *Yale Law Journal* 121, (2019): 1168–1265.

Franklin, Benjamin. *Proposals Relating to the Education of Youth in Pensilvania.* 1749.

Frost, Jennifer. *"Let Us Vote!": Youth Voting Rights and the 26th Amendment.* New York University Press, 2022.

Gasman, Marybeth. "Perceptions of Black College Presidents: Sorting Through Stereotypes and Reality to Gain a Complex Picture." *American Educational Research Journal* 48, no. 4 (August 2011): 836–870.

Gasman, Marybeth, Spencer, Dorsey, and Orphan, Cecelia. "'Building Bridges and not Fences': A History of Civic Engagement at Private Black Colleges and Universities, 1944–1964." *History of Education Quarterly* 55, no. 3 (August 2015): 346–379.

Giamatti, A. Bartlett. *The University and the Public Interest.* Atheneum Books, 1981.

Gomillion, Charles. "Civic Democracy in the South." PhD diss., Ohio State University, 1959. https://etd.ohiolink.edu/acprod/odb_etd/ws/send_file/send?accession=osu1486476430056701&disposition=inline.

Harkavy, Ira, and Hartley, Matthew. "Integrating a Commitment to the Public Good into the Institutional Fabric: Further Lessons from the Field." *Journal of Higher Education Outreach and Engagement* 16, no. 4 (2012): 17–36. https://openjournals.libs.uga.edu/jheoe/article/view/980/979.

Hartley, Matthew. "Reclaiming the Democratic Purposes of American Higher Education." *Learning and Teaching* 2, no. 3 (Winter 2009): 11–30. https://doi.org/10.3167/latiss.2009.020302.

Hayden, Tom. *The Port Huron Statement.* Students for a Democratic Society, 1962. http://www.progressivefox.com/misc_documents/PortHuronStatement.pdf.

Members of Ivy League Votes. "Student Voting is Not Where it Should Be." *Inside Higher Ed*, January 2, 2022. https://www.insidehighered.com/views/2022/01/03/college-students-face-many-unnecessary-obstacles-voting-opinion.

Niemi, Richard G., Hanmer, Michael J., and Jackson, Thomas H. "Where Can College Students Vote? A Legal and Empirical Perspective." *Election Law Journal* 8, no. 4 (2009): 327–348.

Nussbaum, Martha Craven. "Cultivating Humanity and World Citizenship." *Forum Futures* 37 (2007): 37–40.

Patterson, Frederick D., Graham Goodson, Martia, and Richardson, Harry V. *Chronicles of Faith: The Autobiography of Frederick Douglass Patterson.* University of Alabama Press, 1991.

Peck, Gunther, Rao, Ameya, Thomas, Kathryn, Eisen, Delaney, King, Miles, McKnight, Hannah, and Yao, Luhan. "Provisional Rights and Provisional Ballots in a Swing State: Understanding How and Why North Carolina College Students Lose their Right to Vote, 2008-Present." *Rutgers University Law Review* 74, no. 5 (Summer 2022): 1799–1838. https://rutgerslawreview.com/wp-content/uploads/2023/02/05_Peck_et-al..pdf.

Player, Willa. "Oral History Interview with Willa Player by Eugene Pfaff." Interviewed by Eugene Pfaff. *Greensboro Public Library Oral History Program*, Greensboro Public Library, December 3, 1979. Transcript, 1–35. https://gateway.uncg.edu/islandora/object/gpl:7381.

Saltmarsh, John, Hartley, Matthew, and Clayton, Patti. *Democratic Engagement White Paper.* New England Resource Center for Higher Education, 2009. https://scholarworks.umb.edu/nerche_pubs/45/.

Smith, Gabriel Antoine. "A Hollow Inheritance: The Legacies of the Tuskegee Civic Association and the Crusade for Civic Democracy in Alabama." PhD diss., Auburn University, 2016. https://etd.auburn.edu/bitstream/handle/10415/5334/smith_gabriel_ma_thesis_auetd_resubmit_20160729.pdf?sequence=2&isAllowed=y.

Sullivan, William M. "University as Citizen: Institutional Identity and Social Responsibility." *Civic Arts Review* 16, no. 1 (2003): 4–16. https://digitalcommons.unomaha.edu/cgi/viewcontent.cgi?article=1040&context=slcehighered.

The President's Commission on Higher Education. *Higher Education for American Democracy.* Harper & Brothers, 1947. https://ia801506.us.archive.org/25/items/in.ernet.dli.2015.89917/2015.89917.Higher-Education-For-American-Democracy-A-Report-Of-The-Presidents-Commission-On-Higher-Education-Vol-I---Vi_text.pdf.

U.S. Congress. *Congressional Record.* 92nd Cong., 1st sess., 1971. Vol 117, pt. 5–6. https://www.congress.gov/bound-congressional-record/1971/03/23/house-section.

U.S. Congress. *National Voter Registration Act of 1993.* H.R. 2. 103rd Cong. 1993. https://www.congress.gov/bill/103rd-congress/house-bill/2.

U.S. Congress. *Higher Education Amendments of 1998.* H.R. 6. 105th Cong., 2nd sess. 1998. https://www.govinfo.gov/content/pkg/BILLS-105hr6enr/pdf/BILLS-105hr6enr.pdf;

U.S. Election Assistance Commission. "Past HAVCP Programming." Last updated November 15, 2023. https://www.eac.gov/payments_and_grants/help_america_vote_college_program.

Wang, Lea. "Declining Youth Trust in American Institutions Shows No Signs of Stopping." *Harvard Political Review*, April 18, 2024. https://theharvardpoliticalreview.com/declining-youth-trust-in-american-institutions-shows-no-signs-of-stopping/#google_vignette.

Westheimer, Joel, and Kahne, Joseph. "What Kind of Citizen? The Politics of Educating for Democracy." *American Educational Research Journal* 41, no. 2 (2004): 237–269.

Lisa Bratton

3 Tuskegee Institute and the Struggle for African American Voting Rights

The 13th Amendment freeing African Americans from bondage was ratified on December 6, 1865. No longer bound by the physical chains of enslavement, emancipated men and women began the long and arduous process of building their lives among their former oppressors.

In addition to the acquiring of land and reconnecting with loved ones who had been tragically sold away, newly emancipated African Americans desired education. The first Black institute of higher learning, the African Institute (now Cheyney University) was established in 1837 – nearly 30 years prior to Emancipation – just north of the Mason–Dixon line in Cheney, Pennsylvania. The majority of Freedmen schools would be established after Emancipation across the South, as far southeast as Florida Memorial University in Miami Gardens, Florida (founded in 1879) and as far west as St. Philips Normal and Industrial School College (now St. Philip's College, founded in 1898) in San Antonio, Texas.

Participating in the 'American Dream' also included the Freedmen becoming involved in the political system through voting. Along with the 13th Amendment eradicating slavery, Black citizenship informed ratification of the 14th Amendment, establishing equal protection under law and birthright citizenship, and the 15th Amendment, extending the right to vote free of denial or abridgment on account of race, color, or previous condition of servitude. Newly enfranchised African American men used their power to elect 16 Black congressmen, many of whom were born into slavery. Today's fight for voting rights did not occur in a vacuum—it was part of a seemingly omnipresent challenge to Black citizenship rights that began immediately after Emancipation. It is perhaps because of freed Blacks' commitment to first-time voting and to upward mobility based on new access to education and opportunities for economic advancement, that they were met by hardline obstructionism in exercising their new political and social rights. In Alabama, and across the South, hindrances such as poll taxes, literacy tests, closed registration offices, and the voucher system (a form of voter identification that required registrants to have the support of two voters registered in the county) greatly infringed upon the ability of African Americans to register and vote.

During the Second Reconstruction, which occurred after the Second World War, the right to vote was challenged in a larger environment of rights suppression. Civil rights were tested in the Supreme Court through cases like *Brown v. Board of Education* in 1954, which outlawed racial segregation in the nation's public schools, and *Loving v. Virginia* in 1967, which upheld interracial marriage. There was also a series of civil rights acts that addressed discrimination in hiring, access to public accommodation, access to housing, and voting.

It is on the issue of voting that Tuskegee Institute (now known as Tuskegee University) has played a major role, not only in protecting the rights of the campus community and its Black citizens to vote in the face of democratic obstructionism, but also in creating new law that shaped the evolution of the right to vote, as discussed in chapter one of this book.

This chapter focuses on the extraordinary founding origins of Tuskegee Institute, the courageous civic actors connected with the institution of higher education, and how it shaped the community environs in which it is situated. The Tuskegee voting rights story is in some manner common in that it is a story of how an institution of higher education can serve as a space for active citizenship and democracy. However, as this chapter will reveal, the Tuskegee voting rights story is unique because of the way in which an informed and courageous African American academic community directly confronted disenfranchisement in an intense racial climate.

1 The Founding of Tuskegee University

Tuskegee University, originally Tuskegee Normal School for Colored Teachers,[1] was the eighth historically Black institution of higher education founded in the United States, and the first in the state of Alabama. It was founded in 1881 by an unlikely agreement between Lewis Adams, who was enslaved before becoming an entrepreneur; a banker and former slaveholder, George Washington Campbell; and a white Democratic state senator seeking re-election, W.F. Foster, who had previously been a Confederate officer. The Democratic party then was not what it is today. Just five years prior to the agreement, the Alabama Democratic Party was generally the white power party, contraposed to the bi-racial Republican Party which led Alabama politics during the initial years of the First Reconstruction.

How did this alliance between an enterprising former slave, an enterprising former slaveholder, and a Confederate soldier-turned-politician come to be? Adams was born into slavery in 1842 in Tuskegee, and although he received no for-

---

1 'Normal school' or 'normal college' was a teacher-training college which primarily prepared elementary-level teachers for public schools, hence, a place where 'norms' were imparted for the practice of teaching.

mal education, he could read, write, and speak different languages. After Emancipation, he opened a shop and school downtown where he taught trades like shoemaking and tin-smithing to young apprentices; at the family residence, his wife taught cooking and sewing to freed young women. A known community leader in Tuskegee, and deacon of the Butler Chapel A.M.E. Zion Church, Adams attempted to open a school at the A.M.E. Church for newly emancipated citizens to receive basic vocational education. However, he had difficulty attracting qualified teachers. And so, in 1879 when Foster ran for re-election and sought support from Adams to secure the African American vote, Adams asked that a 'colored college' be built in return for his assistance.

Foster won his bid for re-election and upheld his promise. He and fellow state senator Arthur L. Brooks co-sponsored House Bill 165 which appropriated $2,000 ($63,121 in 2025 dollars) to fund teachers' salaries. Students could attend the college tuition-free if they agreed to teach in Alabama's public schools for at least two years upon graduation. The bill required that the school hold classes, maintain at least 25 students, and that classes be held for at least nine months of the year—a key practical stipulation since youth were needed to support summer work in the fields. The bill was approved by the Alabama state legislature, and signed into law only two days later, with an effective date of July 4, 1881—the 105th anniversary of the ratification of the Declaration of Independence establishing the United States free from British rule.

The construction of the 'colored teachers' college' was not merely an act of magnanimity on the part of Alabama's white establishment, but a concession. Many whites were opposed to providing education to African Americans, but they realized that without African American labor the local farms and plantations might not survive. Fulfilling the African American desire for education, through the training of teachers, might influence them not to leave the county for opportunities elsewhere.[2] Normal schools were a part of the solution to stabilize free Blacks and assist them in becoming independent and economically self-reliant, although this process for racial uplift was also criticized as a form of racial accommodation.

The school was initially managed by a three-person Board of Commissioners consisting of Adams, Thomas B. Dryer, and M.B. Swanson, who was replaced early on by George Washington Campbell who had helped originally broker the plan. Campbell reached out to the then-president of Virginia's Hampton Normal and Industrial Institute (now Hampton University) in search of the school's first faculty

---

2 Robert J. Norrell, *Reaping the Whirlwind: The Civil Rights Movement and Tuskegee* (Alfred A. Knopf, 1985), 13–14.

member and principal. General Samuel Chapman Armstrong was a natural contact in Campbell's search for Tuskegee's first leader. General Armstrong was grounded in an educational philosophy of moral training and practical, industrial education, having been raised as a missionary in Hawaii where his father was the minister of public instruction. Armstrong went on to command Black troops in the Civil War, and then establish Hampton Institute in 1868, the same year that the 14th Amendment was ratified. When he opened Hampton, it was with a simple declared purpose:

> The thing to be done was clear: to train colected Negro youth who ohould go out and teach and lead their people first by example, by getting land and homes; to give them not a dollar that they could earn for themselves; to teach respect for labor, to replace stupid drudgery with skilled hands, and in this way to build up an industrial system for the sake not only of self-support and intelligent labor, but also for the sake of character.[3]

Armstrong recommended for the new Tuskegee role one of the best (if not *the* best) graduates of Hampton at the time: Booker T. Washington, who was only 25 years old. Washington had graduated from Hampton with honors in 1875, taught school in Virginia, and then returned to Hampton to teach in a program for Native American students. He was teaching at Hampton when Armstrong recommended him to serve as principal of Tuskegee—even though George Campbell, the banker/former slaveholder and co-founder of Tuskegee, specifically requested a white man.[4]

Washington arrived in Tuskegee in June of 1881. The school was a one-room shanty on a former plantation near Butler A.M.E. Zion Church. In approximately a month, Washington had made a "favorable impression" on the community and had purchased acreage on which to relocate the school, which students went on to construct and build, brick by brick.[5] (Figure 1)

By the time of his death on November 15, 1915, Washington had transformed Tuskegee into a first-class institution that focused on hard work and self-reliance. A student could come to Tuskegee with little money or resources and work his or her way through college. Washington also held wide influence beyond Tuskegee. On October 16, 1901, he became the first African American to dine at the White

---

3 Hampton University, "History," last modified June 27, 2022, https://home.hamptonu.edu/about/history/.

4 Norrell, *Reaping the Whirlwind*, 15.

5 Manning Marable, interviewed by Shawn Wilson, October 5, 2005, *The HistoryMakers Digital Archive*, Session 2, tape 5, story 3, "Manning Marable describes the founding of Tuskegee Institute in 1881," The HistoryMakers A2005.228, https://da.thehistorymakers.org/story/579882.

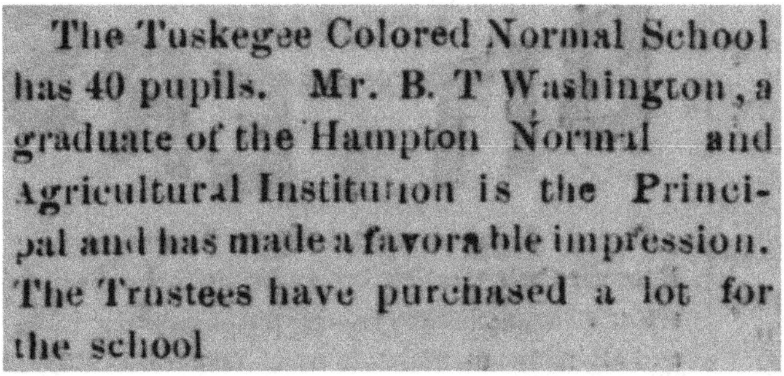

The Tuskegee Colored Normal School
has 40 pupils. Mr. B. T Washington, a
graduate of the Hampton Normal and
Agricultural Institution is the Principal and has made a favorable impression.
The Trustees have purchased a lot for
the school

Figure 1: A weekly African American newspaper serving parts of Alabama announces the arrival of
Booker T. Washington to the nascent Tuskegee Colored Normal School.
Source: "State News," Huntsville Gazette, July 30, 1881, 3. Chronicling America: Historic American Newspapers. Library of Congress. https://chroniclingamerica.loc.gov/lccn/sn84020151/1881-07-30/ed-1/
seq-3/.

House. In addition, his home, The Oaks, which still stands on Tuskegee University's
campus, was the first home in the entire state of Alabama to have electricity.

Washington believed that the best way to earn acceptance in America—particularly the South—was through economics and industriousness. His iconic "Atlanta Compromise" speech at the 1895 Atlanta Cotton Exposition encouraged a mutually beneficial economic relationship between African Americans and whites for
the progress of the south:

> [O]ne-third of the population of the South is of the Negro race. No enterprise seeking the
> material, civil, or moral welfare of this section can disregard this element of our population
> and reach the highest success. ...
>
> Ignorant and inexperienced, it is not strange that in the first years of our new life we
> began at the top instead of at the bottom; that a seat in Congress or the state legislature was
> more sought than real estate or industrial skill; that the political convention or stump speak-
> ing had more attractions than starting a dairy farm or a truck garden.
>
> A ship lost at sea for many days suddenly sighted a friendly vessel. From the mast of the
> unfortunate vessel was seen a signal, "Water, water. We die of thirst."
>
> The answer from the friendly vessel at once came back, "Cast down your bucket where
> you are." [...]
>
> The captain of the distressed vessel, at last heeding the injunction cast down his bucket
> and it came up full of fresh, sparkling water from the mouth of the Amazon River.
>
> To those of my race who depend on bettering their condition in a foreign land or who
> underestimate the importance of cultivating friendly relations with the southern white man
> who is their next-door neighbor, I would say, "Cast down your bucket where you are. Cast it
> down in making friends in every manly way out of the people of all races by whom you are
> surrounded."

> To those of the white race who look to the incoming of those of foreign birth and strange tongue and habits for the prosperity of the South, were I permitted I would repeat what I have said to my own race, "Cast down your bucket where you are. Cast it down among the eight million of Negroes whose habits you know, whose fidelity and love you have tested in days when to have proved treacherous meant the ruin of your firesides. Cast down your buckets among those people who have without strikes and labor wars tilled your fields, cleared your forests, builded your railroads and cities, and brought forth treasures from the bowels of the earth, and helped to make possible this magnificent representation of the progress of the South."[6]

Washington encouraged whites to "cast down their buckets" among the African American entrepreneurs whose work they knew well from the era of enslavement. Further, Washington believed that "brains, property, and character for the Negro will settle the question of civil rights."[7] It is important to note that Washington held this sentiment in 1888 when African Americans were just one generation removed from enslavement. Having no blueprint for how to effectively liberate a once-enslaved population, he focused on the belief that once whites saw how industrious African Americans would live as free men and women to further southern progress, that their social concerns would be eliminated, as both races would be elevated.

Washington was criticized for accommodating whites, but he established the foundation that catapulted Tuskegee into one of the premier institutions of higher learning in the country—one which would go on to make immense contributions locally and nationally in a variety of ways, illustrating Black excellence.

Renowned graduates of Tuskegee include author Ralph Ellison, best known for his novel *Invisible Man*, which won the National Book Award in 1953; civil rights leader Amelia Boynton Robinson, who played a crucial leadership role in the march on Selma which would help to secure passage of the Voting Rights Act; and Herbert Carter, one of the original 33 members of the Tuskegee Airmen who flew 77 missions during World War II and retired from the United States Air Force as a lieutenant colonel, before serving as an associate dean for student services and associate dean for admission and recruitment at Tuskegee Institute. The Tuskegee Airmen, famed African American pilots of World War II, completed ground school at Tuskegee Institute, and the City of Tuskegee was home to

---

6 Booker T. Washington, *Atlanta Compromise Speech*, September 18, 1895. Text and audio available at U.S. Library of Congress, *Exhibitions: The Civil Rights Act of 1964*, https://www.loc.gov/exhibits/civil-rights-act/multimedia/booker-t-washington.html.
7 Booker T. Washington, "The Educational Outlook in the South," July 16, 1884, *Teaching American History*, https://teachingamericanhistory.org/document/the-educational-outlook-in-the-south/.

their two training sites: Tuskegee Army Airfield (the military base that has since been demolished) and Moton Field (now the Tuskegee Airmen National Historic Site), a unit of the National Park Service. The Tuskegee Airmen fought two wars, known as the 'Double V Campaign' for a double victory: "the first V for victory over our enemies from without, the second V for victory over our enemies from within."[8]

Tuskegee residents were proud that the city was home to such an extraordinary group of men and women. Was this source of pride the very catalyst that influenced the residents of this small town in Alabama to have the 'audacity' to challenge local and state officials all the way up to the United States Supreme Court? Perhaps, but what is abundantly clear is that Tuskegee's racial divide was always stark, and would have to be directly confronted.

2 Tuskegee Institute in the Civil Rights Era

By 1950, Macon County, where the City of Tuskegee is situated, had the highest concentration of African American residents of any county in the nation.[9] Because of the presence of both the Tuskegee Institute and its associated Veterans Affairs (V.A.) Hospital, which was constructed to care for returning Black veterans in the apartheid south, the City of Tuskegee was home to an extraordinarily high concentration of African Americans with advanced degrees.

Tuskegee professor Charles Gomillion described in his 1959 doctoral dissertation the strength of an educated African American population in the South:

> In some places in the South, the handicap of a high percentage of Negroes in the population has been weakened somewhat by the presence or operation of one or more other socio-cultural factors. For example, if the Negro population in a given community is better educated than usual, and utilizes more effectively its superior educational talents and resources, as well as its economic and political knowledge, resources and opportunities, it might cope successfully with the strong resistance of white citizens.[10]

Gomillion did not simply conduct research, he was an important civic actor. He taught and served as an administrator at Tuskegee for three decades before be-

---

8 Neil A. Wynn, *The African American Experience During World War II* (Rowman & Littlefield, 2010), 40.

9 Charles G. Gomillion, "The Tuskegee Voting Story," *Clinical Sociology Review* 6, no. 1 (1988): 22, https://digitalcommons.wayne.edu/cgi/viewcontent.cgi?article=1117&context=csr.

10 Charles G. Gomillion, *Civic Democracy in the South* (Ohio State University, 1959), 91.

coming the lead plaintiff in a precedential voting rights lawsuit that centered around Tuskegee Institute.

2.1 Dr. Charles Goode Gomillion and the Tuskegee Civic Association

Dr. Charles Goode Gomillion was born in Johnston, South Carolina on April 1, 1900. When he was a child, his father killed a white man. The court ruled this incident as self-defense and from then on, his father limited his own and his children's interactions with whites.[11] Gomillion graduated from Paine College in Augusta, Georgia in 1928, studied sociology at Fisk University in 1933, and completed his Ph.D. in sociology from Ohio State University in 1959.

His doctoral dissertation, entitled "Civic Democracy in the South," offered a comprehensive sociological analysis of the state of civic democracy, involving the compilation of data from wide sources, coupled with survey responses from Black citizens in the South working closely with interracial professional and/or social action organizations.[12] He defined 'civic democracy' as:

> That type of condition of society in which all citizens are entitled to a legal status and civic opportunities and services without limitation or restriction based on race, color, creed, or national origin. It embodies the idea of equality of opportunity and treatment in the courts of law, in government and politics, in public education and employment, and in the use of public facilities and services.[13]

Gomillion sought to analyze this exercise of civic democracy across 16 southern states, and identified socio-cultural factors for consideration alongside indicia of civic status and opportunities, such as the percentage of Black adults registered to vote; the extent that they hold office; the median school years completed by Black adults; the annual per capita income of the Black population; and the percentage of Black workers in industry, in the professions, and in clerical service. Using a ten-indicia scale of civic status and opportunities for Blacks, he found that Alabama ranked in the bottom-rung of the 16 southern states, followed by Georgia and Mississippi.[14]

---

11 Jan M. Fritz, "Charles Gomillion, Educator-Community Activist," *Clinical Sociology Review* 6 (1988): 19.
12 Gomillion, *Civic Democracy in the South*, 91.
13 Gomillion, *Civic Democracy in the South*, 3.
14 Gomillion, *Civic Democracy in the South*, 4–5, 206.

Gomillion was a member of the Tuskegee Institute's faculty from 1928 to 1971, first teaching in the high school department and then, upon his return from Fisk, at the college level. He served various roles at the Institute—professor, dean of students, dean of the School of Education, and dean of the College of Arts and Science. He later served as the chair of the Division of Social Sciences. The year after he began teaching at Tuskegee, in or around 1929, he also became a single father to his young daughters, Vernita and Mary Gwendolyn.

He was best known, however, for his work in the community through the Tuskegee Civic Association (TCA), particularly for his efforts concerning the right of African Americans to vote. Gomillion's activism in Tuskegee began in 1933, upon his return from Fisk, when he started to attend meetings with a small group of socially and civically minded Black citizens including Institute faculty. They believed that "political democracy is government of the people, for the people, and by the people," and that "the ballot is the citizen's best self-help tool."[15] The group reformulated as the Tuskegee Men's Club in 1938, to which Gomillion was elected its first president.[16] It comprised 30 educators and businessmen who sought to improve the physical environment and social welfare of Macon County's African American citizens. In the first ten years of community organizing, between 1930 and 1940, the number of registered Black voters in the county increased from 30 to 75.[17]

In 1941, the group again reconstituted as the TCA for the purpose of admitting women to membership. The name was derived from Gomillion's growing focus on civic democracy, and this local field focus went on to inform the development of his dissertation on the topic. The TCA's objective was "to promote through group action the civic well-being of the community" through a three-pronged approach: "intelligent study and interpretation of local and national trends and problems; the collection and dissemination of useful civic and political data; and intelligent and courageous civic action."[18] Its primary supporters were entrepreneurs, V.A. employees, and Tuskegee Institute faculty and staff. These individuals were the most financially secure in the community, and, importantly, had the least likelihood of losing their employment in retaliation of their civic engagement. For example, V.A. workers were federal employees and thus insulated from local and

---

15 Gomillion, "Tuskegee Voting Story," 23.

16 Jessie Parkhurst Guzman, *Crusade for Civic Democracy: The Story of the Tuskegee Civic Association, 1941–1970* (Vantage Press, 1984), 9.

17 Gomillion, "Tuskegee Voting Story," 23.

18 "Crusade for Civic Democracy: First Anniversary Celebration," *Tuskegee Civic Association Magazine* (Tuskegee Institute, AL), June 24, 1958, https://digital.tcl.sc.edu/digital/collection/p17173coll38/id/15181/rec/2.

state pressure. Faculty and staff affiliated with the Institute were similarly insulated, since it was mostly funded through private, northern organizations.

In the TCA's first year, members intentionally prioritized unifying and educating the Black community, such as by sponsoring a Works Progress Administration school, a Boy Scout Troop, and the county National Negro Health Week.[19] When those efforts proved limited due to the community's lack of political power, the TCA moved increasingly towards political engagement. At the end of the TCA's first year, Gomillion wrote, "Realizing the importance of participation in politics, the Association has encouraged its members and others to register, pay their poll taxes, and vote intelligently."[20] "They did not know then," wrote Robert Norrell in his book on the civil rights movement in Tuskegee, "that voting would become their overriding concern for the next twenty-five years."[21]

2.2 Voting in Tuskegee and the State of Alabama

The issue of voting had been contentious between Tuskegee's Black and white citizens since the Alabama state constitutional convention of 1901, which was assembled with the primary goal of disenfranchising African American citizens. Advocates of the new constitution claimed that "manipulation of the black vote corrupted the election process," so "political morality demanded Black disenfranchisement."[22] Although African Americans exercised their vote in the last years of the nineteenth century, new state constitutional provisions sought their disenfranchisement in the form of literacy tests, grandfather clauses, and poll taxes. These tests and devices were intentionally discriminatory when passed, and discriminatorily applied. For example, literacy tests were administered by white registrars in Macon County who allowed illiterate whites to register with little hindrance but prevented the voter registration of the county's Black citizens, including those with Ph.Ds.[23]

Among other requirements, Alabama's state law required that African Americans seeking to vote secure two registered voters to confirm their residency in the

---

19 Norrell, *Reaping the Whirlwind*, 42.
20 Norrell, *Reaping the Whirlwind*, 42.
21 Norrell, *Reaping the Whirlwind*, 42.
22 Alabama Judicial System, Alabama Constitutions: Alabama Constitution 1901, April 11, 2023, https://judicial-alabama.libguides.com/alabamaconstitutions/alabamaconstitutionof1901.
23 Bernard Taper, *Gomillion Versus Lightfoot: The Right to Vote in Apartheid Alabama* (University of Alabama Press, 2003), 115.

county and vouch for their character. This was extremely difficult. In a 1985 interview with Professor William A. Elwood, Gomillion said,

> There were a few of us who [were] persistent enough to urge more Negroes to begin to apply for registration to vote. But at that time in order for a Negro applicant to register, he had to secure two white persons to vouch for him or her, one of whom would have to go to the courthouse and sign the register saying that this applicant is in his or her opinion worthy of registration. Many Negroes were able to get the first person who only had to sign his name to become a voucher. That person did not have to go to the courthouse. But it was very difficult for them to get the second person who would have to go to the courthouse.[24]

Gomillion himself experienced these difficulties. When he returned to Tuskegee from Fisk in 1934, he wanted to register to vote, but it would take another five years just to secure one white person to vouch for him. It was not until 1939, when a white contractor approached Gomillion about building a house, that he was able to register. Gomillion insisted that he would sign the contract for the house construction only if the contractor vouched for him before the Macon County Board of Registrars, the board responsible for registering voters. He then told the contractor that he would only sign the contract after the board approved his application, which they did at the contractor's bidding. Even then, Gomillion had to pay retroactive poll taxes of $1.50 per year from 1928, the year he arrived in Tuskegee, to the year of registration, 1939.[25]

In his various public education and advocacy endeavors, Gomillion repeatedly outlined several other techniques used to infringe upon the political participation of African Americans in Tuskegee, which he outlined in his 1988 *Clinical Sociology Review* article, entitled "The Tuskegee Voting Story."[26] These included:

1. Requiring Negroes and whites to register in separate rooms and in separate parts of the Macon County Courthouse.
2. Registrars frequently reporting for work late and leaving early, thus reducing the number of hours available to Negro applicants.
3. Permitting only two Negro applicants in the registration room at the same time.

---

24 William A. Elwood, "An Interview with Charles Gomillion," *Callaloo* 40 (1989): 584, https://www.jstor.org/stable/2931304.

25 Gomillion had to pay the equivalent of 12 years of poll taxes, amounting to approximately $400 in 2025 dollars. His second wife had to pay the equivalent of five years in poll taxes, amounting to approximately $170 in 2025 dollars.

26 Gomillion, "Tuskegee Voting Story," 24.

4. Requiring Negro applicants to read and transcribe articles from the Constitution of the United States, in addition to filling out the voter registration questionnaire.
5. Conversing with applicants as they write, which disturbs them, and stimulates making errors.
6. Permitting a Negro voter to vouch for only two applicants per year.
7. Preventing some Negroes from vouching for any applicant.
8. Failing to issue certificates of registration to Negroes immediately upon the successful completion of the requirements for registration.
9. Failing to inform unsuccessful applicants of their failures to fulfill the requirements for registration.
10. Failing to work on many registration days.
11. Resigning from the board in order not to register Negroes.
12. Refusing to appoint any Negro to serve on city or county government committees or agencies.
13. Enacting legislation which permits Board of Registrars to use 12 of their working days for clerical work only, and in even years to use up to 20 additional days in the precincts away from the courthouse.

These impediments made registration extremely difficult. According to the 1950 Census, of the 30,651 residents in Macon County, 27,384 (89.3%) were African American and 3,177 (10.4%) were white, yet data showed that in 1958 only 1,110 Blacks (4% of the Black population) were registered to vote while 3,016 whites (95% of the white population) were registered.[27]

The voter registration challenges experienced by Tuskegee Blacks were on full display in the 1945 federal case *Mitchell v. Wright*, a case brought by William P. Mitchell, a former student of Gomillion's in the high school department of the Institute, against the Macon County Board of Registrars. Mitchell, a physical therapy technician at the V.A. Hospital in Tuskegee, went on to become Gomillion's trusted deputy as the executive secretary of the TCA. He was effectively the 'chief operating officer' to Gomillion's 'chairman of the board,' and kept "meticulous records of black voting applicants."[28] Although he deferred to Gomillion on strategy, Mitchell was, in the words of Norrell, "quick witted and well spoken" and "better at per-

27 *Hearings Before the United States Commission on Civil Rights: Voting*, First Session, "Eight-Year Summary of Registration Efforts of Negroes in Macon County: Reactions of the Macon County Boards of Registrars," held in Montgomery, Alabama, December 8 and 9, 1958, January 9, 1959 (U.S. Government Printing Office, 1959), 26.
28 Norrell, *Reaping the Whirlwind*, 61.

sonal confrontation with whites than Gomillion."[29] In 1945, his application to register to vote was rejected after neither of his two 'vouchers' appeared in person before the Board of Registrars. One of the vouchers, William Campbell, had gone to the site where the board convened, but was unable to get inside the board office because of long lines, and left without signing Mitchell's application as required to effectuate the registration.[30]

Mitchell first filed a suit which was eventually heard at the U.S. District Court for the Middle District of Alabama in 1947.[31] Mitchell was represented by Thurgood Marshall, the nation's leading civil rights attorney who would go on to become a Supreme Court justice, and Arthur D. Shores, who would, in the following decade, serve as co-counsel in the *Gomillion v. Lightfoot* case which will be explored later in this chapter.

Mitchell alleged that the Macon County Board of Registrars failed to register him as a qualified voter because of his race. Judge Charles B. Kennamer ruled that while Mitchell "possesse[d] all the qualifications and none of the disqualifications necessary to be a qualified voter under the Constitution and laws of the State of Alabama," the board was within its rights to reject his registration because he had not completed the prescribed process. The judge noted that despite the fact that there "was irregularity and indefiniteness in setting a time when a person given as a reference or voucher could appear before the Board and vouch for an applicant," the decision was not discriminatory because the same voucher process was involved for "Negroes and whites alike." Kennamer concluded that "In a county where the population is predominantly Negro, the fact that there are more white than Negro electors in the county is not of itself proof of racial discrimination by members of the Board of Registrars."[32]

Mitchell appealed to the Fifth Circuit Court of Appeals, but during the appeals process it was 'discovered' that Mitchell had been registered in 1943 and that "had

---

29 Norrell, *Reaping the Whirlwind*, 61.
30 The other person whom Mitchell said vouched for him was George Washington Albert Johnston, who had also vouched for him in his earlier registration attempts. Johnston was an African American purchasing agent at the Tuskegee Institute, and a favored nephew and confidant of Booker T. Washington. During the trial, under some pressure, Johnston testified that he had not actually vouched for Mitchell. The TCA remained suspicious of his motives due to his relationship with the defendant Caro Wright representing the Board of Registrars. See Norrell, *Reaping the Whirlwind*, 66–67.
31 *Mitchell v. Wright*, 69 F. Supp. 698 (M.D. Ala. 1947), https://law.justia.com/cases/federal/district-courts/FSupp/69/698/2265832/.
32 *Mitchell v. Wright*, 69 F. Supp. 698. See the testimony of William P. Mitchell, in *Hearings*, 11–29.

Mitchell paid his poll tax he could have been voting all along."[33] With that, the case was dismissed, but this was just the start of the TCA's litigation efforts.

Following the lawsuit, the Board of Registrars became inactive, and the TCA began appealing to Alabama governor James E. Folsom, who was eventually persuaded by an open letter by the TCA to state leaders, published by a Montgomery-based paper. Governor Folsom appointed a new board member, W.H. Bentley, who was of modest but comfortable means and a New Deal Democrat. In the 13 months following Bentley's appointment in January 1949, 449 African Americans were registered—quadrupling their total in Macon County.[34] Progress was thereafter slowed after the other board members stopped attending meetings, preventing a quorum, and eventually Bentley was removed from his position in 1951 after Governor Folsom left office.[35] Nonetheless, the impact of having more Black registrants on the rolls was felt by the community. The number of Black voters in the county now comprised approximately 30% of the electorate—enough to influence outcomes.[36] The TCA was surprised, and pleased, when an incumbent sheriff politician unsuccessfully endeavored to court the organization and the Black vote in a competitive 1950 race for re-election.

The impact was also apparent in 1954 when a Black candidate for the Tuskegee Board of Education, Jessie P. Guzman (Tuskegee Institute's director of the Department of Records and Research), secured more than 500 votes in her race. Although she lost by a wide margin, according to Gomillion, it "seemed to have intensified the fear and the belief on the part of whites that Negroes were trying 'to take over' the governments of Tuskegee and Macon County."[37]

2.3 The 1957 Gerrymander of Tuskegee: Act 140

With more African Americans registering to vote locally, and the national winds shifting to favor Black voter registration, the white establishment in Macon County looked to devise creative new schemes to preserve the status quo. In 1957, Al-

---

33 Norrell, *Reaping the Whirlwind*, 68.

34 Craig Holloway, "Collared Men: Ethnographic Essays on Navigating Race and Status in Everyday Life" (PhD diss., Yale University, 2022), 88, Yale Graduate School of Arts and Sciences Dissertations, https://elischolar.library.yale.edu/gsas_dissertations/607. See also Norrell, *Reaping the Whirlwind*, 74.

35 Norrell, *Reaping the Whirlwind*, 75.

36 Norrell, *Reaping the Whirlwind*, 75.

37 Gomillion, "Tuskegee Voting Story," 25. See also, *Report of the United States Commission on Civil Rights, 1959* (U.S. Government Printing Office, 1959), 76, http://bit.ly/usccr-1959.

abama state senator Sam Engelhardt of nearby Shorter, Alabama, who was also the executive secretary for the white supremacist organization the White Citizens' Council for Alabama, introduced Senate Bill 291. This effectively redrew the boundaries of the City of Tuskegee from a rectangle to a 28-sided shape that resembled a sea dragon. (Figure 2) The municipal gerrymander excluded 99 % of Black voters from the City of Tuskegee, and the entirety of Tuskegee Institute itself, although not a single of its 600 white voters was removed.[38] The handful of African American residents who remained inside of the city boundary were exempted because they could not be removed without doing the same to a white resident; Engelhardt seemed to make sure that no whites would be disenfranchised. The gerrymandered Black voters would still be able to vote in county, state, and national elections (where their voting power was weaker) but not in local elections, where, it was feared, they would soon have the ability to outnumber whites. The bill passed unanimously and without debate, and was enacted as Act 140.[39]

Outraged by the passage of Act 140, the TCA resisted, eventually launching the Crusade for Citizenship, involving a three-year boycott of Tuskegee's white-owned businesses. Gomillion summed up his views as follows: "We are going to buy goods and services from those who help us, from those who make no effort to hinder us, from those who recognize us as first-class citizens."[40] (Figure 3) The campaign, "Buy Wisely—Trade with your Friends," lasted from June 25, 1957 to February 1961. Messaging for the boycott was important, and it was formally called a 'selective buying campaign' to avoid a state law prohibiting boycotts. It received national attention.

An observer at the first meeting, Louise Washington, described the scene as follows:

---

38 Gomillion, "Tuskegee Voting Story," 24–25. See also Tondra L. Loder-Jackson, "Hidden in Plain Sight: Black Educators in the 'Militant Middle' of Alabama's Municipal Civil Rights Battlegrounds," in *Schooling the Movement: The*
Activism of Southern Black Educators from Reconstruction through the Civil Rights Era, ed. Derrick P. Alridge, Jon N. Hale, and Roland L. Freeman (University of South Carolina Press, 2023), citing Charles Johnson and Jared McWilliams, audio recording of *Mass Meeting of the Tuskegee Civic Association #2,* July 2, 1957, featuring K.J. Burford, Fred Shuttlesworth, Ralph David Abernathy, and Martin Luther King, Jr., Tuskegee University Archives; and Guzman, *Crusade for Civic Democracy,* 23.
39 Taper, *Gomillion Versus Lightfoot,* 15.
40 "Black Citizens Boycott White Merchants for U.S. Voting Rights, Tuskegee, Alabama, 1957–1961," *Global Nonviolent Action Database,* https://nvdatabase.swarthmore.edu/content/black-citizens-boycott-white-merchants-us-voting-rights-tuskegee-alabama-1957-1961.

It was the most emotional experience I've ever had in my life. It just seemed to finally have awakened the people in the community. Dean Gomillion had tried in the past to organize 'little trade with your friends,' meaning trade with Negroes. We'd trade with our friends for about a month, and then it would sort of disintegrate. The new boycott to fight the gerrymander was the first time he really had massive and prolonged support. (We couldn't call it a boycott, of course, that was illegal. It had to be 'selective buying.') ... I dare say that our boycott wouldn't have been successful if it were not for the bus boycott in Montgomery. This was one of the rallying cries—"Aren't we going to do what the people in Montgomery did? Are we going to be less proud than the people in Montgomery?"[41]

APPENDIX TO OPINION OF THE COURT.

CHART SHOWING TUSKEGEE, ALABAMA, BEFORE AND AFTER ACT 140

(The entire area of the square comprised the City prior to Act 140. The irregular black-bordered figure within the square represents the post-enactment city.)

Figure 2: The July 1957 gerrymandering of Tuskegee's city limits that disenfranchised the Black vote.
Source: *Gomillion v. Lightfoot*, 364 U.S. 339 (1960).

To maintain the momentum and success of the campaign, African American citizens met weekly at various churches in the Tuskegee community. These meetings were fashioned after the Monday evening meetings of the Montgomery Bus Boycott. Meetings normally consisted of a devotional period, announcements, a finan-

---

41 James Forman, *Sammy Younge, Jr.: The First Black College Student to Die in the Black Liberation Movement* (Open Hand Publishing, 1986), 40, https://archive.org/details/sammyyoungejr fir0000form/page/n7/mode/2up?q=louise+washington.

Mr. C. G. Gomillion at first mass meeting, stating that "We shall buy goods and services from those who are helping us, who will help us, and who are not likely to hinder our progress." Sitting in front of Mr. Gomillion (left to right), are Mrs. D. W. Wynn and Mrs. Lois Reeves; sitting behind him in the pulpit (left to right), are Dr. D. W. Wynn, Chaplain of Tuskegee Institute; Rev. S. T. Martin, and Rev. K. L. Buford.

Figure 3: First mass meeting, Tuskegee Civic Association, June 25, 1957. Butler Chapel A.M.E. Zion Church, Tuskegee, Alabama.
Source: "Crusade for Civic Democracy," *Tuskegee Civic Association Magazine*, June 24, 1958.

cial appeal, congregational singing, the main speaker's presentation, remarks from the TCA president or a presiding officer, and a closing prayer.[42] Martin Luther King, Jr. spoke at the TCA meeting following the launch of the boycott, declaring to a large gathering of 3,500 Black attendees and scores of out-of-town visitors at the historic A.M.E. Church: "You are not seeking to put the stores out of business but to put justice into business."[43] (Figure 4)

Two months after the boycott began, Alabama attorney general John Patterson (who would later be elected to the governorship) and assistant attorney general Gordon Madison sought an injunction against it, but they were ultimately unsuccessful. Circuit Court judge Will O. Walton ruled that citizens could not be forced to shop where they chose not to.

The boycott had a tremendous impact on the local economy. Less than a year after it began, by the spring of 1958, half of the city's white retail businesses shut down, and of those remaining, sales were down at least 40–65%, and most businesses were forced to terminate some of their workers to stay afloat.[44] Tuskegee

42 Guzman, *Crusade for Civic Democracy*, 25–26.
43 Ronald Jones, "Negroes Refuse to Do Business, Theatres and Stores Closed," *Arizona Sun*, July 25, 1957, 1.
44 Norrell, *Reaping the Whirlwind*, 101; Jones, "Negroes Refuse to Do Business," 1.

Figure 4: Dr. Martin Luther King, Jr. speaks at Tuskegee Civic Association mass meeting, July 2, 1957. Photograph by P.H. Polk. (Courtesy of Tuskegee University Archives, P. H. Polk Family Collection).
Source: "Tuskegee Civic Association Materials," *Driving Through History: The Civil Rights Movement in Alabama*, https://drivingthroughhistory.org/tca.

Institute professors conducted a survey for a booklet entitled *Voting Rights and Economic Pressure, Field Reports on Desegregation in the South* that was published in 1958.[45] The 'Crisis Study' examined racial attitudes of 95 white Tuskegee residents. Forty percent of respondents said they had only recently became aware of a local racial conflict, and it was as a result of the boycott.[46]

As summarized by Robert Norwell in his masterful historical analysis on the civil rights movement in Tuskegee, *Reaping the Whirlwind:*

> The Crisis Study exposed the contours of white thinking more fully than had ever been done before. Racism pervaded the views of almost all whites; they could not conceive of dealing with the blacks on the same basis as whites. Most whites did not include blacks in their conception of democratic government. They imposed a double standard for political behavior: when whites pursued and used power to their own ends, they were merely protecting their interests, but when blacks did the same thing, they were obnoxiously aggressive and selfish. It must be noted, however, that a significant minority of whites recognized this hypocrisy and believed that blacks deserved political rights.[47]

---

45 Lewis Jones and Stanley Smith, Tuskegee, Alabama: Voting Rights and Economic Pressure, Field Reports on Desegregation in the South (Anti-Defamation League of B'nai B'rith, 1958).
46 Norrell, *Reaping the Whirlwind*, 108.
47 Norrell, *Reaping the Whirlwind*, 107–8.

The Crisis Study also revealed a general fear of what increased Black political power would look like in actuality, and a presumption that the goal of Black civic participation was to take over and control local affairs, rather than to share in democratic decision-making.

In December 1957, 61% of voters statewide approved a statewide constitutional amendment that targeted Macon County—authorizing the establishment of a legislative committee tasked with developing a study and determining the feasibility of outright abolishing Macon County or reducing its area. The committee was to develop related legislation to effectuate its proposal. That the statewide vote for such a radical proposal secured such a strong majority illustrates that the white fear that the Crisis Study captured among Tuskegee residents had wider resonance.

In February 1958, Gomillion appeared before the Macon County Abolition Committee of the House of Representatives, where he advanced the cause of 'democratic living.' The committee was deliberating a proposal, which, like Act 140, was authored by state senator Sam Engelhardt, to divide Macon County into five or six parts for redistribution to the surrounding counties in such a manner as to avoid the possibility of a Black political majority. The *Jackson Advocate*, a Black-owned and -operated Mississippi publication, described Gomillion's presentation before the committee as "one of the first direct efforts by a Negro to speak to a group of whites about so sensitive a problem in the Deep South."[48] A "verbal sparring" resulted, beginning with a question posed to Gomillion by one of the legislators, who asked whether he was afraid that the boycott of white merchants, which whites believed was sponsored by the TCA, might lead to the cutting off of funds to Tuskegee Institute. Although private, the institution received $350,000 annually from the state to guarantee the teaching of certain courses. Thus, the motivation of the proposal to abolish Macon County was revealed— the Black residents were getting too active and civically engaged, and their boycott would not be tolerated. The legislators continued to ask questions of Gomillion with great concern about whether the TCA's goal was actually "race-mixing" in schools, which Gomillion answered in the affirmative. The *Jackson Advocate* summarized the meeting as one which "accomplished little" and "simply underscores ... that the lines are very sharply drawn on integration. Even when a Negro and a group of whites meet publicly, the whole affair is cut and dried, each saying what

---

48 "Tuskegee Negro Leader Confers with Legislators," *Jackson Advocate*, March 15, 1958, 5, https://chroniclingamerica.loc.gov/lccn/sn79000083/1958-03-15/ed-1/seq-1/.

it believes and without any real discussion. This is one of the more discouraging aspects of the entire situation in the Deep South."[49]

Gomillion and the TCA's response to Act 140 was felt well beyond the state of Alabama, as it became clear that relief would have to be sought outside of the state. As Congress was readying to take up the first federal civil rights legislation, which would become the Civil Rights Act (CRA) of 1957, Gomillion appeared before the Senate Judiciary Committee in February of 1957 to discuss the numerous challenges to voting in Macon County. William Mitchell appeared in a press conference in Washington, D.C. a month after the boycott, with Senate advocates of the civil rights legislation, including Hubert Humphrey of Minnesota and Paul Douglass of Illinois, to discuss both of Englehardt's schemes: Act 140 to gerrymander Tuskegee Institute out of the city, and his latest proposal to dismantle Macon County altogether.[50] The boycott was also featured in leading publications like *Life*, *Time*, and *Newsweek*.[51] *Life* and *Newsweek* put the gerrymander into the context of the civil rights bill, with *Newsweek* calling the Tuskegee situation "a timely—though perhaps extreme—example of what the civil rights argument in the Senate is about."[52] It would be an overstatement to claim that Tuskegee's experience was responsible for the passage of the CRA, but there is no doubt that telling the story of the egregious acts of Engelhardt and others helped shape the narrative of the need for federal intervention.

The experiences of Tuskegee would only continue to inform that narrative as the United States Commission on Civil Rights, which was established by the CRA, began to report on the state of civil rights and civil society. The Commission's first public hearing took place in Montgomery, Alabama in December 1958, and its first three witnesses were from Tuskegee: William Mitchell; William Andrew Hunter, the dean of the Tuskegee Institute School of Education; and Reverend Dr. Daniel Webster Wynn, chaplain of Tuskegee Institute. Hunter had served in the U.S. Army and received his doctorate from Iowa State University. Wynn had voted in Massachusetts while studying at Harvard and then in Texas, but like many other African Americans remained unregistered in Alabama.[53]

Mitchell offered the most detailed testimony, recounting his experience of attempting to register to vote. He provided documentation including copies of questionnaires which were used to disqualify African Americans seeking to register,

49 "Tuskegee Negro Leader Confers," 5.
50 Norrell, *Reaping the Whirlwind*, 111.
51 "RACES: Boycott in Tuskegee," *TIME*, July 8, 1957, https://time.com/archive/6887897/races-boycott-in-tuskegee/.
52 Norrell, *Reaping the Whirlwind*, 110.
53 U.S. Commission on Civil Rights, *Hearings*, 1959; Norrell, *Reaping the Whirlwind*, 112.

and meticulous data which he had collected on voter registration among Blacks and whites in Macon County. Mitchell's data would be incorporated into the U.S. Commission's future reports describing the plight of Black voter registration and the need for continued federal oversight. But each of the three told incriminatory stories about the Board of Registrars being closed or meeting secretively, forcing potential registrants to fill out questionnaires with ambiguous questions, and having to write out long tracts of the U. S. Constitution, all the while knowing that the smallest of errors would lead to disqualification for Black applicants for plainly arbitrary reasons. The U.S. Commissioners also heard how potential registrants were not notified if they had failed to register, thus making an appeal impossible.[54]

From those first hearings held by the Commission in Montgomery, Alabama emerged a palpable sentiment favoring the compelling testimony offered by the approximately 30 Alabama Blacks personally impacted by voter discrimination. Their experiences unveiled repeated and systemic violations of the right to vote across the state, and stood in stark contraposition to the intransigence of the testifying Alabama southern officials, including those from Boards of Registrars. Commissioner John S. Battle forewarned at the end of the first day of the hearings: "The majority of members of the next Congress will not be sympathetic to the South, and preventative legislation may be passed, and this hearing may be used in advocacy of that legislation."[55] A former governor of Virginia, Battle was selected to serve on the Commission based on his strong southern sentiments, including his strong family roots in Alabama, where his father led the state's confederate army. He diplomatically pleaded with the southern officials that "enemies in Congress" would not take kindly to the South absent better cooperation from public officials appearing before the Commission who clearly endeavored, in the words of Battle, "to cover up their actions" and appeared "not willing to explain their conduct when requested to do so."[56] And, indeed, as history would reveal, the testimony and public records collected during these hearings went on to inform future amendments to the Civil Rights Act and eventually the Voting Rights Act of 1965 (VRA).

---

54 U.S. Commission on Civil Rights, *Hearings*, 1959; Norrell, *Reaping the Whirlwind*, 112.
55 U.S. Commission on Civil Rights, *Hearings*, 1959, 207.
56 U.S. Commission on Civil Rights, *Hearings*, 1959, 207.

2.4 *Gomillion v. Lightfoot*

The TCA was eager to challenge the state legislation which enabled the sea dragon-shaped municipal gerrymander of the City of Tuskegee which removed the Institute from the municipality along with nearly all Black voters. The TCA retained Fred Gray to bring the legal challenge—he had difficulty securing co-counsel due to the risk involved. The Supreme Court had previously ruled in *Colegrove v. Green* that the courts should not engage in gerrymandering challenges due to their inherently political nature.[57] In other words, any challenge to gerrymandering would likely be unsuccessful.

Nonetheless, Gray believed in the merits of the case, as did the unflagging TCA. He recruited NAACP general counsel Robert L. Carter to join him as co-counsel, along with an esteemed Birmingham attorney, Arthur D. Shores. Act 140 was approved by the legislature and became law without the governor's approval on July 15, 1957. That year, Gray and his colleagues filed in federal court to challenge its constitutionality naming Tuskegee mayor Philip M. Lightfoot and other city officials as defendants. The federal district court and a divided federal appeals court panel outright rejected the merits of the claim, and Gray and Carter would go on to argue the case before the U.S. Supreme Court on October 18 and 19, 1960. Also presenting before the court was Philip Elman,[58] a white attorney who briefed the legal issue as well as the moral one, and likened the travesties in Tuskegee to apartheid.[59]

The Supreme Court was in a precarious position, as precedent dictated that the judiciary was not to interfere with legislative acts of redistricting, but the court, particularly in the civil rights era, was committed to striking down discriminatory laws that deprived citizens of their full rights of citizenry, in particular constitutional rights to be free of discrimination based on race, color, or creed.[60] On November 14, 1960 the court ruled unanimously (after an unusually short period of 27 days) in favor of Gomillion, ruling that Act 140 violated Section I of the 15th Amendment which states that "the right of citizens of the United States to vote shall not be denied or abridged by the United States or by any State on account of race, color, or previous condition of servitude."[61]

---

57 Fred Gray, *Bus Ride to Justice: The Life and Works of Fred Gray* (Black Belt Press, 1995), 114.
58 Philip Elman worked with Thurgood Marshall on the *Brown v. Board of Education* case (1954) and other civil rights cases held before the Supreme Court. In the *Gomillion v. Lightfoot* case, Elman represented the United States.
59 Taper, *Gomillion Versus Lightfoot*, 97.
60 Taper, *Gomillion Versus Lightfoot*, 81.
61 *Gomillion v. Lightfoot*, 364 U.S. 339 (1960).

The court further ruled that "Act 140 was not an ordinary geographic redistricting measure even with familiar abuses of gerrymandering" and that "the city's legislation was solely concerned with segregating white and colored voters by fending Negro citizens out of town so as to deprive them of their preexisting municipal vote."[62] In a concurring opinion, Justice Frankfurter further stated that the decision should not rest on the 15th Amendment, but on the equal protection clause of the 14th Amendment which states: "No State shall make or enforce any law which shall abridge the privileges or immunities of citizens of the United States; nor shall any State deprive any person of life, liberty, or property, without due process of law; nor deny to any person within its jurisdiction the equal protection of the laws."

As explained further in chapter one, the Supreme Court therefore reversed the decision by the lower federal court and sent the matter back with instruction that the "mathematical demonstration" of the geographic redistricting is "tantamount" to proof of racial voter discrimination. Gray filed a motion for summary judgment, which the federal district court judge granted on February 17, 1961, permanently enjoining the implementation of Act 140. The original voting boundaries of the City of Tuskegee were thereafter restored and the three and a half years of litigation in *Gomillion v. Lightfoot* came to an end. African American residents who had been deemed to live outside of the city were included within its territory. The City of Tuskegee's election was held in September of 1960, before the court's ruling, and consequently only whites were successfully sworn into office. It would not be until the next election, four years later in 1964, that any African Americans would be elected in Tuskegee.

The *Gomillion v. Lightfoot* case speaks to the strength and courage of a rural community just a few generations from enslavement and their 'audacity' to challenge racist laws and appeal directly to the highest court in the country. Their actions are almost unprecedented and when considering the time in which they lived, their actions are outright heroic. In the state of Alabama, the South, and in many parts of the north and west, African Americans' upward mobility was hindered in the form of redlining, discrimination in housing, voter suppression, and almost every facet of social, political, and economic life. Without a blueprint to follow, Gomillion and his fellow activists effected change not only for themselves, but also prepared the paths for the generations of activists that would follow.

---

62 Taper, *Gomillion Versus Lightfoot*, 111, 112.

3 Other Civic Actors

While Gomillion received the greatest amount of attention for the TCA's activities and the boycott, there were other important activists associated with Tuskegee Institute.

3.1 Faculty and Administrators

3.1.1 Jessie Parkhurst Guzman

Jessie Parkhurst Guzman was born in 1898 in Savannah, Georgia. (Figures 5 and 6) She earned her B.A. degree from Howard University in 1919 and her M.A. from Columbia University in 1924. In 1923, she came to Tuskegee Institute as a research assistant to Monroe Work, Tuskegee Institute's director of records and research. Guzman served as Tuskegee Institute's dean of women from 1938 to 1944 and as the director of the Department of Records and Research until she retired in 1964. She compiled and edited two editions of the *Negro Year Book* in 1947 and 1952. She is also the author of *Crusade for Civic Democracy: The Story of the Tuskegee Civic Association, 1941-1970.*

As an active member of the TCA, Guzman held leadership and committee positions and delivered speeches at mass meetings. In February of 1954, she ran for the Macon County school board. In so doing, she was both the first African American to run for office in Macon County since Reconstruction and the first African American woman to seek office in Alabama.[63] She lost the election, but her candidacy seemed to have intensified the fear and the belief on the part of whites that African Americans were trying to take over the governments of Tuskegee and Macon County.

On August 6, 1957, she was a co-signatory of a letter published in *The Washington Post* to the U.S. Senate. The letter was entitled "An Open Letter from the South on Civil Rights"[64] and was also signed by dozens of activists including

---

[63] *Portrait of Jessie Parkhurst Guzman,* c. 1970, Tuskegee University Archives, featured in "Jessie Parkhurst Guzman," *Driving Through History,* https://drivingthroughhistory.org/jessie-parkhurst-guzman.Driving Through History.

[64] This letter was signed by 85 men and women from the South, southern border states, and the District of Columbia. The signatories contended that it would be better to pass no civil rights bill at all than to pass one that limited the enforcement power of the courts. Published in *The Washington Post* on August 6, 1957, the letter stated that African Americans would fare better under the existing legislation than if the proposed bill were passed.

Charles and Jennie Gomillion, E.D. Nixon (co-organizer of the Montgomery Bus Boycott), and Daisy Bates (strategist for the integration of Little Rock Central High School).

Figure 5: Portrait of Jessie Parkhurst Guzman, c. 1970.
Source: Portrait of Jessie Parkhurst Guzman, Tuskegee University Archives, in *Driving Through History*, https://drivingthroughhistory.org/jessie-parkhurst-guzman.Driving Through History.

3.1.2 Lewis Wade Jones

Dr. Lewis Wade Jones was born in Cuero, Texas on March 13, 1910. (Figure 7) He received his A.B. degree from Fisk University in 1931 and continued his education as a Social Science Research Council Fellow at the University of Chicago in 1931 and 1932. He was a Julius Rosenwald Foundation Fund Fellow at Columbia Univer-

Figure 6: Jessie Parkhurst Guzman and Charles Gomillion, c. 1950.
Source: Tuskegee University Archives, featured in "Tuskegee Civic Association (TCA)," *Driving Through History*, https://drivingthroughhistory.org/tca.

sity, where he earned an M.A. degree in 1939. He earned his Ph.D. from Columbia University in 1955. He pioneered studies of Black people in the rural south and hired white students from the University of Alabama to interview 95 white Tuskegee residents in the Crisis Study described above. Not surprisingly, the respondents shared their hatred of African Americans and their progress.[65] Together with Tuskegee professor Stanley Hugh Smith, he wrote an important report for the Anti-Defamation League of B'nai B'rith, *Tuskegee, Alabama: Voting Rights*

---

[65] Derrick P. Alridge, Jon N. Hale, and Roland L. Freeman, eds., *Schooling the Movement: The Activism of Southern Black Educators from Reconstruction through the Civil Rights Era* (University of South Carolina Press, 2023), 175.

and Economic Pressure, part of a series of "Field Reports on Desegregation in the South" in 1958, helping to contextualize the challenges in Tuskegee and publicize them to a national audience. The report paid particular attention to white attitudes in Tuskegee and Macon County.[66] At the time of his death in September 1979, Jones was a full professor of sociology at Tuskegee Institute and the director of the Tuskegee Institute Rural Development Center.

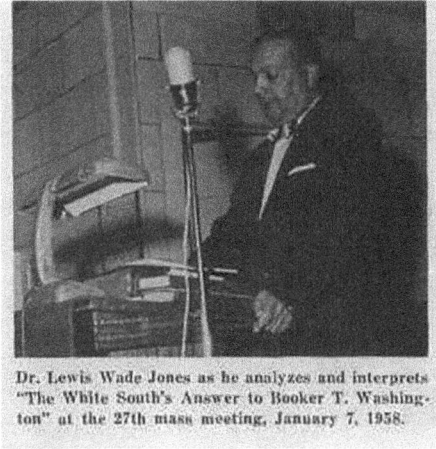

Dr. Lewis Wade Jones as he analyzes and interprets "The White South's Answer to Booker T. Washington" at the 27th mass meeting, January 7, 1958.

Figure 7: Crusade for Civic Democracy First Anniversary Celebration, June 24, 1958.
Source: "Crusade for Civic Democracy," *Tuskegee Civic Association Magazine,* June 24, 1958.

3.1.3 Frank Toland, Sr.

Frank Toland, Sr. was born in Helena, South Carolina on June 1, 1920. (Figure 8) He graduated from South Carolina State University with an undergraduate degree in History, Political Science, and English. He received his Master's degree in History from the University of Pennsylvania and was the only African American student in the department. While in Philadelphia, he worked with the NAACP. He began teaching at Tuskegee Institute in 1949, and served as chair of the History Department from 1968 to 1984. In the 1960s, he also served as president of the TCA. He retired in 2009 after 60 years of service to Tuskegee University.

---

66 Lewis W. Jones and Stanley Hugh Smith, *Tuskegee, Alabama: Voting Rights and Economic Pressure,* Field Reports on Desegregation in the South (Anti-Defamation League of B'nai B'rith, with the cooperation of the National Council of the Churches of Christ in the United States of America, 1958).

Figure 8: Jackie Robinson (second from the left), Professor Frank Toland (far right), and other supporters of the Tuskegee Civic Association at the organization's second anniversary (June 23, 1959). Robinson gave a speech in support of the TCA's crusade and praised the example that the Tuskegee movement was setting for the country. Photo Credit: P.H. Polk.
Source: Tuskegee University Archives, https://archive.tuskegee.edu/repository/digital-collection/tuskegee-civic-association-meetings-speeches-and-records/photographs/ss7731659_7731659_11926906/.

At the second anniversary of Crusade for Citizenship, Toland outlined some of the reasons for the campaign for civic democracy, namely that there had been no democracy in Macon County nor Alabama, nor in the South in the century. He further stated that citizens' petitions for redress of grievances remained ignored by white city, county, and state politicians, as African American citizens were mischaracterized as "troublemakers who endangered the good relations existing between the races, because we dare to exercise our constitutional rights to petition to redress grievances." Tolson charged that there had been "super-ordination of the white" and "sub-ordination of the Negro."[67]

---

[67] "Frank Toland Speaks at TCA Meeting, 1959," *Tuskegee Civic Association Meetings, Speeches, and Records*, Tuskegee University Archives, https://archive.tuskegee.edu/repository/digital-collec-

3.2 Tuskegee Institute Presidents

It is perhaps because of Booker T. Washington's influence that, as an institution, the Tuskegee Institute was less involved in political issues. Historically, Washington publicly represented the Tuskegee community, as did his successor, Robert R. Moton, during the first years of his presidency. Frederick Patterson assumed the presidency of Tuskegee in 1935 and did not attempt to be the 'community voice.' Though not president of the institution, Charles Gomillion filled that void.[68] The era of the *Gomillion v. Lightfoot* case marked the first time in its history that the institution was involved, even if not formally, in securing political rights for African American citizens.

While Gomillion worked at Tuskegee Institute, he was the public face of the TCA and served as the association's president three times for a total of seventeen years. The two Tuskegee presidents during this time period, Dr. Frederick Douglass Patterson (1935-1953) and Dr. Luther Foster (1953 to 1981), tacitly supported Gomillion's activities, though they insisted that he and other university employees separate their activism from their responsibilities at Tuskegee Institute.[69] Patterson defended Gomillion when his work came under attack by Alabama Governor Gordon Persons. Foster supported him even when the Highlander Folk Center, of which he was a board member, was accused of having Communist ties.[70] He was initially silent on the boycott, but due to the egregious nature of the gerrymander ultimately joined in. (Figure 9)

3.3 Tuskegee Institute Students

The Institute's leadership generally dissuaded students from engagement, fearing repercussions for the Institute's core mission. Indeed, this was not without cause: Engelhardt had threatened the institution's funding for Gomillion's work.[71] Nonetheless, Tuskegee students spoke at meetings of the TCA, contributed to programming, and were involved as groups in the boycott.

---

tion/tuskegee-civic-association-meetings-speeches-and-records/meetings/frank-toland-speaks-at-tca-meeting-1959/. A two-minute audio excerpt of Gomillion's interview is available by the link.
68 Norrell, *Reaping the Whirlwind*, 38.
69 "Tuskegee Frets Over Boycott Backed by Montgomery Leaders," *Jackson Advocate*, July 25, 1957, 1, https://chroniclingamerica.loc.gov/lccn/sn79000083/1957-07-27/ed-1/seq-6/.
70 Fritz, "Charles Gomillion, Educator-Community Activist," 17; Jones and Smith, *Tuskegee, Alabama: Voting Rights and Economic Pressure*, 76.
71 Norrell, *Reaping the Whirlwind*, 96. In Engelhardt's view, Gomillion dominated Foster.

Figure 9: Highlander participants and workshop leaders at the school during its 25th anniversary on August 31, 1957. Pictured from left to right: Ralph Helstein, Myles Horton, Rosa Parks, an unidentified man, Septima Clark, an unidentified man, an unidentified man, Charles Gomillion and Bernice Robinson.
Source: NEH Fellowship Supports Slate's Research on Civil Rights," *Carnegie Mellon University News*, February 28, 2023, https://www.cmu.edu/news/stories/archives/2023/february/neh-fellowship-sup ports-slates-research-on-civil-rights.

A 1960 march by hundreds of students in response to the nationwide sit-ins created internal controversy. The students were led by young faculty member Charles B. Hamilton, who worked closely with Gomillion but whose approach had grown more confrontational. Foster had tried to dissuade students from participating, but later, at least publicly, described it as an effort of students "to express their earnest support of efforts by many other youth groups throughout the nation to help advance the cause of full democracy in America."[72] However, months later Hamilton's position was not renewed, and he saw it as punishment.

It would not be until the mid-1960s that student activism in Tuskegee would come to the fore[73] with the tragic murder of Sammy Younge.

Sammy Younge grew up in Tuskegee and was a 21-year-old Navy veteran and Tuskegee Institute political science student and activist. He was a member of the Student Nonviolent Coordinating Committee (SNCC), the Tuskegee Institute Advancement League, a student group formed in February 1965 to support the Selma movement, and had worked to register African American voters in Alabama and Mississippi.

---

72 Norrell, *Reaping the Whirlwind*, 170.
73 Norrell, *Reaping the Whirlwind*, 170.

On the evening of January 3, 1966, Younge went into the 'Whites Only' bathroom at the Standard Oil gas station near Tuskegee Institute and was shot to death by a night watchman, Marvin Segrest. He was the first African American college student to be killed as a result of his participation in the civil rights movement.

Two days after he was murdered, 200 Tuskegee Institute students marched in the rain to the white downtown area of Tuskegee in protest. Speaking to those gathered, student body president Gwen Patton promised that the student body would "do all in its power to bring justice to Macon County."[74]

The murder of Sammy Younge had implications beyond Tuskegee and even beyond Alabama. SNCC and local Black leaders used Younge's death, in combination with the VRA, to inspire a rise in Black political participation in the region. The same was the case for Tuskegee students, whose efforts related to voting, which were particularly focused on the registration of rural Black voters in Macon County, began after the passage of the VRA in 1965 and accelerated after Younge's death, with 1,600 Black voters added to the county roles in January 1966 when the efforts reached their peak. As Norrell wrote, "The students, with the help of the new federal guarantee of the right to vote, were completing work that Gomillion and the TCA had begun twenty-five years earlier."[75]

4 Conclusion

Tuskegee Institute has historically been considered a conservative institution, dating back to the time of its first president, Booker T. Washington, who, in the years following the bloody Civil War, prioritized securing self-reliance for Blacks, and racial accommodation for surety. The formidable institution he established and shepherded would soon eclipse his greatest expectations—having secured their self-reliance, skills, and financial independence, the geographically centered academic community sought their full political rights. Moreover, faculty leveraged their academic training to secure their right to vote free of racial discrimination, and in so doing shaped the nation. Their work documenting voter suppression and contributing to public education on the poor state of civic democracy in Alabama and the South, informed the work and perspective of the United States Commission on Civil Rights and ultimately Congress, ensuring added protections in the

---

74 "Tuskegee: 'Model City' Erupts," *The Movement*, February, 1966, https://www.crmvet.org/docs/mvmt/6602mvmt.pdf.
75 Norrell, *Reaping the Whirlwind*, 179.

Civil Rights Act and the Voting Rights Act based on the experiences borne in Macon County. The persistence of faculty members such as Gomillion and colleagues secured, for the first time, the right to fair redistricting by the United States Supreme Court. The story of Tuskegee, then, and all of its accomplishments, illustrates the great measure that institutions of higher education can offer the nation when faculty engage in applied research, and work in the community to persist and advocate for political and social rights.

Bibliography

Acts of the General Assembly of Alabama Passed at the Session of 1880–1881.
Allred and Beers, State Printers, 1881. https://archive.org/stream/alabama-acts-1880-1881/Acts_1880_1881_transcript_djvu.txt.
Alabama Judicial System. *Alabama Constitution 1901.* Alabama Constitutions. https://judicial-alabama.libguides.com/alabamaconstitutions/alabamaconstitutionof1901.
Alridge, Derrick P., Jon N. Hale, and Roland L. Freeman, eds. *Schooling the Movement: The Activism of Southern Black Educators from Reconstruction through the Civil Rights Era.* University of South Carolina Press, 2023.
"Award Winners." *Ohio Sentinel*, March 21, 1959. https://digital-collections.columbuslibrary.org/digital/collection/african/id/18849/.
"Crusade for Civic Democracy: First Anniversary Celebration." *Tuskegee Civic Association Magazine.* University of South Carolina Digital Collection, McCray papers, 1958. https://digital.tcl.sc.edu/digital/collection/p17173coll38/id/15181/rec/2.
Elwood, William A. "An Interview with Charles Gomillion." *Callaloo* 40 (1989): 576–599. https://www.jstor.org/stable/2931304.
Fritz, Jan Marie. "Charles Gomillion, Educator-Community Activist." *Clinical Sociology Review* 6 (1988): 13–21.
Gomillion, Charles G. *Civic Democracy in the South.* Ohio State University Press, 1959.
Gomillion, Charles. "The Tuskegee Voting Story." *Freedomways* 2, no. 3 (1962): 22–26.
Gomillion, Charles G. "The Tuskegee Voting Story." *Clinical Sociology Review* 6, no. 1 (1988): 22–26. https://digitalcommons.wayne.edu/cgi/viewcontent.cgi?article=1117&context=csr.
Gray, Fred. *Bus Ride to Justice: The Life and Works of Fred Gray.* Black Belt Press, 1995.
Guzman, Jessie Parkhurst. *Crusade for Civic Democracy: The Story of the Tuskegee Civic Association, 1941–1970.* Vantage Press, 1984.
Hearings Before the United States Commission on Civil Rights: Voting, First Session, "Eight-Year Summary of Registration Efforts of Negroes in Macon County: Reactions of the Macon County Boards of Registrars," held in Montgomery, Alabama, December 8, 1958. U.S. Government Printing Office, 1959. https://www.usccr.gov/files/historical/1958/58-001.pdf.
Holloway Craig. "Collared Men: Ethnographic Essays on Navigating Race and Status in Everyday Life." PhD diss., Yale University, 2022. Yale Graduate School of Arts and Sciences Dissertations. https://elischolar.library.yale.edu/gsas_dissertations/607.
Jones, Lewis W. and Stanley Hugh Smith. *Tuskegee, Alabama: Voting Rights and Economic Pressure.* Field Reports on Desegregation in the South. Anti-Defamation League of B'nai B'rith, with the

cooperation of the National Council of the Churches of Christ in the United States of America, 1958.

Jones, Ronald. "Negroes Refuse to Do Business, Theaters and Stores Closed." *Arizona Sun*, July 25, 1957.

Marable, Manning. Interview by Shawn Wilson. *The HistoryMakers*, October 5, 2005. https://da-thehistorymakers-org.tuskegee.idm.oclc.org/story/579882.

"The Memphis Appeal." *Memphis Appeal* (Memphis, TN), July 9, 1867.

Mitchell v. Wright, 69 F. Supp. 698 (M.D. Ala. 1947). https://law.justia.com/cases/federal/district-courts/FSupp/69/698/2265832/.

National Park Service. *Tuskegee Institute National Historic Site Historic Resource Study*. National Park Service, June 2019. https://npshistory.com/publications/tuin/hrs-2019.pdf.

"NEH Fellowship Supports Slate's Research on Civil Rights." *Carnegie Mellon University News*, February 28, 2023. https://www.cmu.edu/news/stories/archives/2023/february/neh-fellowship-supports-slates-research-on-civil-rights.

Norrell, Robert J. *Reaping the Whirlwind: The Civil Rights Movement in Tuskegee*. Alfred A. Knopf, 1985.

"RACES: Boycott in Tuskegee." *TIME*, July 8, 1957. https://time.com/archive/6887897/races-boycott-in-tuskegee/.

Reeves, Kelly. "Lois Lambert Reeves: A York Woman Who Was Instrumental in Helping Selma Freedom Marchers." *York Daily Record*, February 24, 2004. https://www.yahoo.com/news/lois-lambert-reeves-york-woman-090057648.html.

Report of the United States Commission on Civil Rights, 1959. U.S. Government Printing Office, 1959.

Taper, Bernard. *Gomillion versus Lightfoot: The Right to Vote in Apartheid Alabama*. University of Alabama Press, 2003.

"Tuskegee Frets Over Boycott Backed by Montgomery Leaders." *Jackson Advocate*, July 25, 1957. https://chroniclingamerica.loc.gov/lccn/sn79000083/1957-07-27/ed-1/seq-6/.

"Tuskegee: 'Model City' Erupts." *The Movement*, February, 1966. https://www.crmvet.org/docs/mvmt/6602mvmt.pdf.

"Tuskegee Negro Leader Confers with Legislators." *Jackson Advocate*, March 15, 1958. https://chroniclingamerica.loc.gov/lccn/sn79000083/1958-03-15/ed-1/seq-1/.

Washington, Booker T. "The Educational Outlook in the South." *Teaching American History*, July 16, 1884. https://teachingamericanhistory.org/document/the-educational-outlook-in-the-south/.

Wynn, Neil A. *The African American Experience During World War II*. Rowman & Littlefield, 2010.

Alexander Goodwin and Michael J. Nojeim

4 The Prairie View Paradox: Age, Race, and the Evolving/Changing Landscape of Student Voting Rights at an HBCU in Texas

The right to participate in the electoral process is the most important hallmark of a representative democracy. The ability of citizens to partake in free and fair local, state, and federal elections empowers them and gives them a voice in choosing the leaders who will create policies that impact their everyday lives. If citizens are prevented from voting for arbitrary reasons, such as race, gender, or special class (such as 'student' or 'veteran'), it undermines the bedrock principle of democracy, that the authority *to* govern comes from the consent *of* the governed.

The United States' founding principles are contained and celebrated not only in the U.S. Constitution, but also in the Declaration of Independence, in which are found Thomas Jefferson's well-known notions that all men are created equal and possess inalienable rights to life, liberty, and the pursuit of happiness. However, America's fidelity to the values espoused by those famous words has proven fickle, especially as it relates to minoritized and marginalized groups, including African Americans.

For centuries, African Americans' inalienable rights were denied and then treated as though they were up for negotiation and then *re*negotiation, when, for so many other groups, there was no such need, no such question. Throughout the past 400-plus years, African Americans had their life, liberty, and pursuit of happiness severely constrained or outright denied—at the ballot box and elsewhere in the public sphere—through myriad systems of oppression, such as chattel slavery, Jim Crow segregation, convict leasing, redlining, and the prison industrial complex. In response, African Americans have consistently issued a clarion call for the United States to live up to and honor its stated values.

Throughout his leadership of the civil rights movement in the 1950s and 1960s, Martin Luther King, Jr. repeatedly echoed this sentiment. At the 1957 Prayer Pilgrimage in Washington, DC, shortly after the Montgomery Bus Boycott made him a household name, King took both Republican and Democratic officials in the federal government to task for their lack of leadership on voting rights:

> This dearth of positive leadership from the federal government is not confined to one particular political party, both ... have betrayed the cause of justice. The Democrats have betrayed it by capitulating to the prejudices and undemocratic practices of the southern Dix-

iecrats. The Republicans have betrayed it by capitulating to the blatant hypocrisy of right wing, reactionary northerners. These men so often have a high blood pressure of words and an anemia of deeds.[1]

Perhaps King's most famous and eloquent admonishments came in his "I Have a Dream" speech during the 1963 March on Washington, when he expressed his hope that the United States would "rise up and live out the true meaning of its creed."[2] King continued his exhortations until the day before his 1968 assassination in Memphis, Tennessee when, in his final public speech, he challenged America to "be true to what you said on paper."[3]

In this chapter we explore challenges and responses pertaining to the voting rights of college students at Prairie View A&M University (PVAMU), a Historically Black College/University (HBCU) located in Waller County, Texas. As we will discuss below, the paradox that is PVAMU is that, while nearly everyone involved in this case is utterly convinced that it revolves around the ugly specter of racism—the exceptions being some Waller County officials and one federal judge who was openly hostile to PVAMU students—the case was ultimately decided on the age discrimination grounds of the 26th Amendment of the U.S. Constitution rather than the equal protections provided by the 14th Amendment.

Since passage of the 26th Amendment more than 50 years ago, there have been two constants at PVAMU. First, PVAMU's students have repeatedly honored Dr. King's memory as they non-violently fought with Waller County officials for their basic voting rights. By 2006, it had become so onerous for PVAMU students to vote that *Mother Jones* ranked Waller County as ninth among its list of hardest places to (try to) vote in the United States.[4] In 2013, Rachel Maddow, citing failed efforts by states nationwide to block newly enfranchised college students from voting after the 26th Amendment was passed, called Waller County "the holdout of all holdouts."[5]

Second, the students have shown incredible courage and determination while standing up to powerful Waller County officials, especially given the County's deeply troubled racial past. While the City of Prairie View, with a population of

---

1 Martin Luther King Jr., *A Testament of Hope: The Essential Writings and Speeches of Martin Luther King, Jr.*, ed. James M. Washington (HarperCollins, 1985), 198.

2 King, *A Testament of Hope*, 219.

3 King, *A Testament of Hope*, 282.

4 Sasha Abramsky, "Just Try Voting Here: 11 of America's Worst Places to Cast a Ballot (or Try)," *Mother Jones*, September/October 2006, https://www.motherjones.com/politics/2006/09/just-try-voting-here-11-americas-worst-places-cast-ballot-or-try/.

5 Rachel Maddow, "Assault on Student Voting Rights," *MSNBC*, May 6, 2013, www.youtube.com/watch?v=d4itV4B3E48.

approximately 8,500 people, is majority Black, it has long suffered in rural Waller County, which was majority white for much of its history and which has a long history of racism and violence. Between 1877 and 1950, Waller County tied for sixth among Texas's 254 counties for the most lynchings.[6]

But Waller County's violence and racism are not just in its past. In 2015, Sandra Bland, a 2009 graduate of PVAMU, was found hanged to death in her Waller County jail cell. Bland had been stopped by State Trooper Brian Encina for failing to use her turn signal while driving. When Encina asked Bland to put out her cigarette and Bland refused, the situation escalated to the point when Encina exclaimed, "I will light you up!" and then reached inside the vehicle and forcibly removed Bland from her car and arrested and jailed her on charges of assault. Three days later, Bland was found dead in her Waller County jail cell. While her death was officially ruled a suicide, many locally suspected foul play and expressed suspicions regarding how the police handled her case.[7]

Karen Good Marable, a writer who grew up in Prairie View during the 1970s and 1980s and attended college at Howard University in Washington, D.C., reflected on her childhood in the wake of Sandra Bland's death while Bland was in police custody:

> I was not unaware of the racist attitudes that existed in Waller County. As kids, we were cautioned against driving down Field Store Road, because it was "Klan territory." My first white best friend—a thin girl with freckles, who had a ponytail that reached her butt—called me a "nigger" in our first big fight, in the second grade.[8]

The struggle for student voting rights has gone through two major phases. The first phase went from the 1970s through the 1990s and centered on the students' efforts to simply be recognized as residents of Waller County who are legally *eligible* to vote there. The second phase, which began in the early 2000s after PVAMU students seemingly won the first phase, saw the struggle shift to obtaining reasonable

---

6 Equal Justice Initiative, "Lynching in America: Confronting the Legacy of Racial Terror," 3rd ed., 2017, https://lynchinginamerica.eji.org/report/.

7 Tom Rawley, "Sandra Bland's Death Divides Texas County with Ugly History of Racism," *The Washington Post*, July 27, 2015, https://www.washingtonpost.com/national/ugly-history-of-racism-dogs-texas-county-where-sandra-bland-died/2015/07/27/e69ac168-3317-11e5-8353-1215475949f4_story.html; and Tom Dart and John Swaine, "Sandra Bland: Suspicion and Mistrust Flourish Amid Official Inconsistencies," *The Guardian*, July 25, 2015, https://www.theguardian.com/us-news/2015/jul/25/sandra-bland-suspicion-mistrust-official-inconsistencies.

8 Karen Good Marable, "Remembering Sandra Bland's Death in the Place I Call Home," *The New Yorker*, July 13, 2016, https://www.newyorker.com/news/news-desk/remembering-sandra-blands-death-in-the-place-i-call-home.

access to polling stations located on the college's campus, much like at many predominantly white institutions of higher learning.

This analysis focuses first on the legal action taken by PVAMU (and other) students that culminated with the Supreme Court ruling in *Symm v. United States* (1979), which is the only case dealing with the 26th Amendment on which the Supreme Court has ever ruled.[9] Next, the chapter examines the period after *Symm*, in which residency challenges were replaced with other forms of disenfranchisement. As will be shown, despite the students' victories in lower courts *as well as* in the 1979 Supreme Court case, officials in Waller County, including then-Waller County tax assessor-collector LeRoy Symm, continued not only to place bureaucratic obstacles in front of the students, but also made legal threats against them, going so far as to arrest 19 of them on tenuous charges of voter fraud. Finally, we will explore access to the polls, and the fight for an accessible polling place on the PVAMU campus. But first, prior to analyzing PVAMU's voting history, we will briefly examine its origins and background.

1 Background to Prairie View A&M University

PVAMU was established in 1876 during the Reconstruction Era, which was the heyday of Black political power in Texas and other southern states. The school exists thanks in large measure to the tireless efforts of African Americans elected to the Texas legislature during the Reconstruction Era, including State Representative William H. Holland from Hempstead in Waller County (about 5 miles from the City of Prairie View), whose efforts on behalf of the college led him to be known as the Father of Prairie View.[10] Holland's efforts helped lead to a provision in the Texas Constitution requiring the establishment of separate colleges for whites and Blacks. Blacks would attend what was then called the Alta Vista Agricultural and Mechanical College of Texas for Colored Youth (Alta Vista for short), which was the first public co-educational institution of higher education in Texas. Alta Vista was named after the former slave plantation on which it was founded.

While Black students would attend Alta Vista, white (male) students would attend the Agricultural and Mechanical College of Texas (later renamed Texas AM University), which would be responsible for the management of Alta Vista. To be sure, Alta Vista was poorly funded and maintained. The federal government's

---

9 Elsewhere, the authors have chronicled the students' extensive civic action, primarily protests and demonstrations, in the City of Prairie View and in Waller County. See note 104 below.

10 Michael J. Nojeim and Frank D. Jackson, *Down that Road: A Pictorial History of Prairie View A&M University* (Donning Company Publishers, 2011), 20–21.

Second Morrill Act of 1890 designated the school, and 18 other HBCUs, a land grant institution to compel former Confederate states to provide better funding for their segregated institutions of higher education.[11]

As the institution grew in enrollment and expanded its academic mission, it went from a normal school—that is, a school focused on training Black teachers to work in Texas' segregated public school system—to a full-fledged institution of higher learning offering a wide range of baccalaureate and graduate degrees. With that came several name changes until finally it was renamed Prairie View A&M University in 1973, which was right around the time PVAMU students began fighting for voting rights in Waller County. In 1984, the Texas Constitution was amended to name PVAMU as one of only three "institutions of the first class," alongside Texas A&M University and the University of Texas.

Located about an hour northwest of Houston, PVAMU sits on the land of the former Alta Vista Plantation, owned by Confederate colonel Jared E. Kirby, on which more than 150 enslaved African Americans labored during the plantation's peak, and from whence the College took its original name. Little could these enslaved people have imagined that their descendants could attend a college built for them on the very same land on which they toiled for hours under the blazing sun. Where once they were forcibly held on this land in the slave-owner's firm grip, where they labored, enslaved and disenfranchised, with their destinies determined by others, now, on this same land, there was built an institution of higher learning where their descendants were free to forge their own futures.

Despite being deprived perennially of adequate funding by the state of Texas, PVAMU now boasts an enrollment of nearly 10,000 students with more than 70 degree-granting programs, including 30 Master's and six Doctoral programs. In 2021, PVAMU joined only ten other HBCUs nationwide to have earned the prestigious Research 2 Carnegie Classification. It is known for its highly selective architectural, engineering, and nursing programs. According to *Diverse: Issues in Higher Education*, PVAMU is ranked number one nationwide in producing Blacks with Bachelor's and Master's degrees in Architecture, number three in producing Blacks with Bachelor's degrees in Agriculture, and number four in producing Blacks with degrees in Engineering.[12] During segregation, it was more likely

---

11 Samantha Ketterer, "Enslaved People Toiled at a Plantation where Prairie View A&M Now Stands. Researchers Want to Know their Stories," *Houston Chronicle*, February 29, 2022, https://www.houstonchronicle.com/news/houston-texas/education/article/Enslaved-people-toiled-at-a-plantation-where-16833077.php.

12 "Top 100 Degree Producers—HBCUs 2021–22," *Diverse: Issues in Higher Education*, https://top100.diverseeducation.com/HBCUs-2021-2022/.

than not that a Black nurse in Texas had graduated from PVAMU. But PVAMU also produces productive professionals in many other fields such as juvenile justice, education, psychology, and social work. Since the 1960s, PVAMU has had a highly respected tradition of producing Army and Navy officers who have served their country in multiple wars, contributing no less than six flag officers, including Lt. Gen. Calvin Waller who served as Deputy Commander of U.S. Forces in Operation Desert Storm (the 1990–1991 Persian Gulf War).[13]

PVAMU has a long tradition of enculturating its students with a reverence for the campus' sacred grounds. Unlike many other college campuses around the country, a visitor will never see Prairie View students (or faculty and staff for that matter) walking on the grass. There are no Frisbee games, no impromptu hacky sack competitions, no sunbathers, and certainly no dogs roaming the grounds. Since it is not fully known where all the former slaves were buried or interred on the plantation's grounds, students are taught to respect the memory of the enslaved while revering the land by walking only on sidewalks and in designated areas for fear of walking over an enslaved person's burial site.

It is on this hallowed ground that PVAMU's mostly Black students have struggled for decades to obtain full voting rights in Waller County, Texas, the politics of which were historically dominated by whites. Indeed, PVAMU has a rich history of social and political activism as it relates to voting rights (and other social justice issues).

2 The Right to Vote in Prairie View: Challenges and Responses

PVAMU students historically faced considerable obstacles to cast their ballots in Waller County, despite (or perhaps because of) the passage of the 26th Amendment as well as key legislation such as the Civil Rights Acts, the Voting Rights Act, and the Fair Housing Act. In the early 1970s, tax assessor-collector LeRoy Symm, the elected official who was responsible for administering elections in Waller County, hatched a plan to ostensibly combat voter fraud and ensure that only legal residents of Waller County voted. Part of his plan required only students at PVAMU and no one else in Waller County to fill out a questionnaire regarding their residency status. Symm was first elected in 1956, only two years

---

13 Associated Press, "General Calvin Waller Dies," *The Washington Post*, May 10, 1996, https://www.washingtonpost.com/archive/local/1996/05/11/gen-calvin-waller-dies/3e4c1eb4-5089-43c5-a18d-d23362478dc6/.

after the Supreme Court overturned the legality of segregated public schools in *Brown v. Board of Education*, and at the same time as Martin Luther King's historic rise as leader of the Montgomery Bus Boycott, which marked the beginning of the civil rights movement.

Since only students at PVAMU were required to fill out the questionnaire, the tactic was clearly aimed at Black students who had reached voting age in the wake of the 26th Amendment's passage. Symm used student responses on the questionnaire to unilaterally decide which students could register to vote in Waller County. He did this in open defiance of court rulings that favored the students' interests and continued to defend the practice even after the United States attorney General got involved and sued him. Indeed, many civil legal actions pertain to the PVAMU students' struggle for voting rights. The most important and relevant cases are covered here.

Wilson v. Symm, March 29, 1972

In this case, which first involved PVAMU students litigating for their voting rights, Arthur Ray Wilson, a 22-year-old native of Beaumont, TX who had attended then-named Prairie View Agricultural and Mechanical College for four years, filed suit against LeRoy Symm and Bob Bullock, the Texas secretary of state. Wilson was joined by four other student plaintiffs: Randolph Grayson, 29, of Gulfport, MS, Donnie Gene Young, 22, of Houston, TX, Leodies U.A. Simmons, 19, of Weirgate, TX, and Billy Ray Toliver, 27, of Houston, TX.

As the key election official in Waller County, Symm required students to complete a questionnaire, which he used to determine their residency status and hence whether they could register to vote in Waller County. Symm's questionnaire was not formally approved by any Texas State official, nor was it used in any other Texas voting district. This questionnaire asked, in part:

- Do you intend to reside in Waller indefinitely?
- What do you plan to do when you finish your college education?
- Do you have a job or position in Waller County?
- [Do you] Own any home or other property in Waller County?
- [Do you] Belong to a church, club, or some Waller County organization, *other than college related* (emphasis added).[14]

---

14 *Wilson v. Symm*, 341 F. Supp. 8 (S.D. Tex. 1972). See also *Whatley v. Clark*, 482 F.2d 1230 (1973).

Symm also wanted to know if PVAMU students were married to someone who resided in Waller County.

When Symm denied Wilson and the other four-named plaintiffs' registration applications, they filed suit, claiming such denial was a form of discrimination in violation of the 14th and 26th Amendments. The original student complaint also alleged racial discrimination, but David Richards, a labor and civil rights lawyer who represented the students, dropped this allegation once he encountered Judge James Noel, the presiding judge in U.S. District Court for the Southern District of Texas:

> Given that Prairie View was an all-Black college at the time, there loomed a racial compo-
> nent to this battle, for, not surprisingly, all the elected officials were white ...but after a
> brief exposure to Judge Noel, I withdrew the claim. It was abundantly clear from the court's
> behavior that he would rule against that claim and exonerate Symm and the county from
> any racial bias. ... Judge Noel had been so hostile in our early hearings that I knew I was
> destined to lose in front of him.[15]

Richards notes that Judge Noel's decisions were "venomous in nature," as he criticized the plaintiffs (one of whom he accused of violating state laws), one of the
lawyers for the plaintiffs (whom he derided as "young and inexperienced"), and
Texas State officials like Texas Secretary of State Bob Bullock, whom he said
was "utterly lacking in candor and credibility." Later on, he even took a swipe
at the federal trial court in Texas' Eastern District, implying its ruling in the *Whatley* case (see below) was incorrect in part because the court was "busy."[16]

Richards lamented that he failed to "account for Judge Noel's hostility to the
idea of Prairie View students voting."[17]

Symm argued that his questionnaire was used merely to determine the students' residency. At that time, Texas had a state law that *presumed* students
were not legal residents of the campus wherein they studied and lived, and
hence could not register there. Students therefore bore the burden of proving
otherwise and Symm claimed that he used the questionnaire as a tool by which
students could make their case.

In ruling in Symm's favor, Judge Noel found that Symm acted in "good faith,"[18]
using the questionnaire to fulfill his statutory duty in ascertaining the students'

---

15 David Richards, *Once Upon a Time in Texas: A Liberal in the Lonestar State* (University of Texas Press, 2002), 155.

16 Richards, *Once Upon a Time in Texas*, 158–159.

17 Richards, *Once Upon a Time in Texas*, 157.

18 *Wilson v. Symm*, 341 F. Supp. 8 (S.D. Tex. 1972).

legal residency status for the purpose of voter registration. In its findings, the court held that:

- The plaintiffs indicated to college officials upon their enrollment that their home was elsewhere than Waller County.
- Symm registered other students, some 40 out of 75 who applied, thus demonstrating a pattern showing more than half of the student registration applications being approved.
- "In no case was the determination attributable to the students' age or their status as students" and that "the record contains not the slightest suggestion of discrimination on the basis of race."[19]

The students argued that the Texas statute requiring them to prove their residency status at their college address, "even when correctly applied,"[20] violated their constitutional rights because it singled them out for special treatment, specifically for exclusion from registering, unless they could prove otherwise. However, Judge Noel relied, in part, on *Carrington v. Rash* in ruling against the students. In *Carrington*, the United States Supreme Court in 1965 determined that Texas violated the equal protection clause of the 14th Amendment when it prohibited all military personnel from registering to vote on the grounds that they were transient residents at their base of deployment. The court held that, while states have the right to establish residency requirements, the State of Texas could not ban *all* military personnel from voting without giving them the chance to show they were permanent residents at their duty assignment. So, Judge Noel reasoned that if the *Carrington* ruling said a special class of people (soldiers, students, etc.) could be excluded from registering to vote on the grounds of the transient nature of their residency so long as they were given a chance to prove otherwise, then what Symm was doing in Waller County with the Prairie View students was "constitutionally unobjectionable"[21] and did not violate the equal protection clause of the 14th Amendment. So long as students—or other classes of people—are given the chance to show election officials they are indeed bona fide residents, the court ruled they can be presumed to be non-residents.

The District Court also ruled against the students regarding their 26th Amendment argument. The 26th Amendment, ratified on July 1, 1971, reduced the voting age to 18 years for people voting in national and state elections, and outlawed age discrimination in ballot access. But the court found that the students filing suit—

---

19 *Wilson v. Symm*, 341 F. Supp. 8 (S.D. Tex. 1972).
20 *Wilson v. Symm*, 341 F. Supp. 8 (S.D. Tex. 1972).
21 *Wilson v. Symm*, 341 F. Supp. 8 (S.D. Tex. 1972).

aged 19, 20, 22, 27, and 29—were denied the chance to register in Waller County because of their determined non-residency status and not because of their age. The court concluded that "the presumption of student non-residency is neither irrational nor imprecise,"[22] especially since Texas does allow student applicants a chance to prove their residency in Waller County, by virtue of Symm's questionnaire.

Finally, the court considered the students' claim that Symm's actions were contradictory to the one-man-one-vote principle insofar as it requires Prairie View students be allowed to vote in Waller County because that is where the U.S. Census counts them for purposes of representation. However, Judge Noel was unpersuaded by this line of reasoning and said he was "not inclined to embark upon this pioneering endeavor" because he did not want to lead the federal courts into the "nettlesome wonderland of arithmetical abstractions and judicially unmanageable standards."[23] The court offered that the plaintiffs produced no evidence on this point. This, despite the fact that college students are impacted by local laws, sales taxes, and property taxes.[24]

Whatley v. Clark, August 3, 1973

According to lawyer Richards, he engaged a colleague to file a suit similar to *Wilson*, what became *Whatley v. Clark*, in the adjacent U.S. District Court for the Eastern District of Texas.[25] The suit named T.J. Clark, the Denton County tax assessor, and Bob Bullock, the Texas Secretary of State and chief elections officer, as the main defendants. *Whatley* was like *Wilson* but this time involved students from a predominantly white institution, then named North Texas State University (now called the University of North Texas) in Denton, Texas. The court considered the Texas statute that presumed college students were non-residents of their college-based domicile and ruled that portion of the law unconstitutional. Even though the *Whatley* decision did not involve or consider a formal questionnaire

---

22 *Wilson v. Symm*, 341 F. Supp. 8 (S.D. Tex. 1972).

23 *Wilson v. Symm*, 341 F. Supp. 8 (S.D. Tex. 1972).

24 Gale M. Fjetland, "A Statutory Presumption That a Student Is Not a Resident of the Community Where He Is Attending School Violates the Equal Protection Clause of the Fourteenth Amendment," *Texas Tech Law Review* 5, (1974): 854–855, https://ttu-ir.tdl.org/items/c4cfeb39-0d92-4496-a4dd-c92452eaab74.

25 Richards, *Once Upon a Time in Texas*, 156.

like the one Symm used in Waller,[26] that portion of the Texas State statute on which Symm's questionnaire was at least partially based was ruled unconstitutional.

Having lost the initial decision in *Whatley*, state officials appealed to the U.S. Court of Appeals for the Fifth Circuit—and lost again. Considering the appeal, the Fifth Circuit Court held that "Texas has unquestioned power to restrict the franchise to bona fide residents."[27] But the issue was not whether Texas could verify a voter registrant's residence but rather the *procedures* employed to determine residency. So, the Fifth Circuit Court was asked to consider the constitutionality of the section of Texas law that presumed college students were not residents for the purposes of voter registration unless they could prove otherwise to the satisfaction of state officials. The appellants, Texas State officials, argued that the residence requirement imposed on students in the law was no different from residence requirements imposed on the general populace.

The Fifth Circuit Court disagreed, and for several reasons. First, the federal appeals court questioned why, if students were treated the same, there had to be a separate section in the law carved out just for students. Second, singling out this special class of people—college students—for presumption of non-residence unless they proved otherwise violated their equal protection rights, especially since this additional requirement was not added to the Texas statute until 1967,[28] which happened during the Texas legislative session that came right after passage of the Voting Rights Act in 1965,[29] yet well before the 26th Amendment was ratified in 1971. Third, the Circuit Court rejected the state's argument that *Carrington*, which, as discussed above, dealt with military personnel, applied since the part of the Texas law the students were challenging in *Whatley* was not part of the statute until two years *after* the *Whatley* ruling, so it could not be used precedentially. *Carrington* did not apply because it did not involve a "presumption of nonresidency,"[30] and thus the lower court erred in seeing in *Carrington* a tacit approval of presumption of non-residency for an entire group of people.

---

26 When students attempted to register, the Denton County Registrar asked them if they intended to make Denton their home indefinitely and if they said no, they were not allowed to register. See Fjetland, "A Statutory Presumption," 844.

27 *Whatley v. Clark*, 482 F.2d 1230 (5th Cir. 1973).

28 *Whatley v. Clark*, 482 F.2d 1230 (5th Cir. 1973).

29 The Voting Rights Act was signed by President Lyndon Johnson on August 6, 1965. The Texas State Legislature is a part-time legislature that typically meets every odd year for only 150 days from January-May.

30 *Whatley v. Clark*, 482 F.2d 1230 (5th Cir. 1973).

Moreover, and in stark contrast to Judge Noel's ruling, the Fifth Circuit Court found compelling Texas Secretary of State Bullock's testimony in which he conceded that the intention of the Texas statute was only to discourage students from voting.[31] When he was asked if there were any reason for the law's special classification of students, Bullock testified, "I have yet to find a compelling state reason."[32] Indeed, lawyer Richards asserts, "Whatever the reason, [Bullock's] testimony destroyed the state's case."[33]

The Fifth Circuit Court found it hard to believe that "a presumption that students are not residents of their college communities is *necessary*"[34] to limiting the franchise to bona fide residents, especially since elections in a student's college residence "may have considerably more impact on his life"[35] than elections where he previously resided. In other words, the Texas statute that presumed students were not residents in their college town failed the compelling public interest test since there were other, less restrictive methods that could be used to promote so-called "purity of the ballot box."[36]

Ballas v. Symm, May 24, 1974

Less than a year after Judge Noel issued his ruling in the *Wilson* case, he reiterated his basic findings in *Ballas v. Symm*. Charles Ballas, a white male student at PVAMU, filed a complaint against LeRoy Symm asking for reconsideration of the court's decision in the *Wilson* case. On its face, Judge Noel in the *Ballas* case cited the judicial principle of *res judicata* ('a matter judged') by virtue of his ruling in the *Wilson* case earlier that year. Stating that "the purely legal question of the [Symm] questionnaire's constitutionality was posed and answered in *Wilson*,"[37] the judge was not amenable to reversing his own opinion. Even so, the judge considered Ballas' arguments at length since Ballas challenged the constitutionality of Symm's use of the questionnaire not only on grounds similar to *Wilson*, but with two additional points.

First, Ballas asked Judge Noel to reconsider his *Wilson* ruling based on *Whatley*, which came after Judge Noel's *Wilson* decision. But Judge Noel did not accept

---

31 *Whatley v. Clark*, 482 F.2d 1230 (5th Cir. 1973).
32 Richards, *Once Upon a Time in Texas*, 156.
33 Richards, *Once Upon a Time in Texas*, 157.
34 *Whatley v. Clark*, 482 F.2d 1230 (5th Cir. 1973).
35 *Whatley v. Clark*, 482 F.2d 1230 (5th Cir. 1973).
36 Fjetland, "A Statutory Presumption," 855.
37 *Ballas v. Symm*, 351 F. Supp. 876 (S.D. Tex. 1972).

this and rejected the legal rationales of the *Whatley* ruling altogether. In *Whatley*, the District Court held that the State of Texas placed an unconstitutional burden on students seeking to register using the residence where they attended college. Noel disagreed, first because he asserted that *Whatley* erroneously conflated the meaning of the word "indefinite" in the Texas statute with "permanent" as to a student's future residential status (thus placing an undue burden of proof on the student applicants). Second, Judge Noel found that the *Whatley* decision incorrectly held that the State of Texas had not sufficiently demonstrated a compelling state interest that required the use of the questionnaire. He reasoned that use of the questionnaire to fulfill the statutory requirement of determining residency status did in fact serve a compelling state interest and did not violate "in any sense whatsoever any right of any plaintiff identified in *Whatley, Wilson,* or *Ballas*, guaranteed him under the Equal Protection Clause or under any other provision of the federal constitution."[38]

Second, Ballas requested reconsideration of the *Wilson* ruling based on a bulletin issued by Bullock the day after the *Whatley* ruling, which stated, "No county registrar may require any affidavits or questionnaires in addition to the information required on the application for a voter registration certificate."[39] Symm informed Bullock that he would not comply with the order in the bulletin and would instead continue to apply the *Wilson* ruling. In his telling, lawyer Richards said that Judge Noel was "obviously furious," as Noel summarily dismissed Bullock's bulletin as "clearly erroneous."[40] Moreover, since both the plaintiffs and defendants in *Ballas* agreed that the secretary of state's bulletin was not binding, he held that the "bulletin is not competent evidence" supporting Ballas' contention that the questionnaire violated the 14th Amendment's equal protection clause.[41]

Ironically, Judge Noel did in fact order Symm to register Ballas to vote in the upcoming election, but not for the constitutional reasons Ballas cited in his legal briefs, pleadings, and testimony. Although the court held that the plaintiff was not "entitled to relief under the facts of law,"[42] Judge Noel granted Ballas relief under the Due Process Clause. Specifically, Symm's letter rejecting Ballas' registration application stated that Ballas was entitled to appeal Symm's denial, but "there is no evidence that [Symm] offered or gave [Ballas] the hearing required" under Texas law: "the obvious defect in the defendant's procedure was defendant's failure to

38 *Ballas v. Symm,* 351 F. Supp. 876 (S.D. Tex. 1972).
39 *Ballas v. Symm,* 351 F. Supp. 876 (S.D. Tex. 1972).
40 *Ballas v. Symm,* 351 F. Supp. 876 (S.D. Tex. 1972) and Richards, *Once Upon a Time in Texas,* 159.
41 *Ballas v. Symm,* 351 F. Supp. 876 (S.D. Tex. 1972).
42 *Ballas v. Symm,* 351 F. Supp. 876 (S.D. Tex. 1972).

afford plaintiff a hearing before rejecting the application,"[43] which constitutes a denial of Ballas' due process rights under the 14th Amendment. So, the court granted Ballas—and no one else because the plaintiff's request for class action was denied—relief by ordering Symm to provide him with a registration certificate that was valid only for that upcoming election.

Even so, Ballas appealed the ruling and on May 24, 1974, the U.S. Court of Appeals of the Fifth Circuit upheld Judge Noel's decision.[44] While acknowledging that the Fifth Circuit *Whatley* ruling rendered the Texas statute presuming college students were non-residents unconstitutional, the federal appeals court also held that "use of the questionnaire to determine the residency is not a violation of the Equal Protection Clause or the Voting Rights Act," since the questionnaire "does not appear from the record to be an additional test or requirement for voter qualification."[45] Rather, the questionnaire was seen only as a means to ascertain residency status: "there is no proof that the questionnaire was used as a device to prevent legal residents from voting."[46] Like others in Waller County, students must be residents and the questionnaire was a reasonable way to ascertain their status. As evidenced by the *Symm* litigation described below, that ruling would not be the rule of the land for much longer.

Symm v. United States, January 15, 1979

In 1976, PVAMU student Sydney Hicks took part in a voter registration drive during which nearly 1,000 PVAMU students filled out registration forms, but Symm approved less than 40 of them. Hicks himself ran for Prairie View's City Council—and won, even though he was denied the chance to vote in his own election. In his 2013 interview with Rachel Maddow, Hicks said, "All we wanted was a part of the American dream, that all citizens have the right to vote."[47]

That same year, the U.S. attorney general filed suit against the State of Texas, LeRoy Symm, and Waller County, claiming Symm's use of the questionnaire violated the 14th Amendment's equal protection clause as well as the voting rights guaranteed in the 15th and 26th Amendments. A three-judge panel of the U.S. District Court for the Southern District of Texas considered the challenge, and ruled

---

43 *Ballas v. Symm*, 351 F. Supp. 876 (S.D. Tex. 1972).
44 *Ballas v. Symm*, 494 F.2d 1167 (5th Cir. 1974).
45 *Ballas v. Symm*, 494 F.2d 1167 (5th Cir. 1974).
46 *Ballas v. Symm*, 494 F.2d 1167 (5th Cir. 1974).
47 Rachel Maddow, "Assault on Student Voting Rights."

that Symm's practices, including how he used the questionnaire, violated PVAMU students' 26th Amendment rights.

Before the U.S. Supreme Court finally decided this case, Symm had not only continued his open defiance of the *Whatley* ruling (see above), but also the directives of the Texas secretary of state, who by 1975 had been given clear statutory authority to prohibit the use of the questionnaire. In its filing, the United States did not object to Symm's use of the questionnaire *per se*, but claimed the form's use was part of a pattern intended to deprive students living at PVAMU of their voting rights. Indeed, John Hill, then-Texas secretary of state, asked the court to enjoin Symm from continuing his use of the questionnaire in open defiance of Hill's instructions, and in defiance of an Emergency Rule issued by then-Texas state attorney General Mark White.[48]

The District Court found Symm's position utterly unconvincing, and for several reasons. The United States, represented by the U.S. Attorney General, showed that, of the 70 voting registrars in Texas counties that had institutions of higher learning, only Symm continued to presume that college students were non-residents, despite such presumption having been ruled unconstitutional. Moreover, no other Texas registrar subjected students in their jurisdictions "to any more rigorous scrutiny" than others applying to register to vote.[49] For instance, students from the University of Texas were not subjected to additional scrutiny like that imposed on PVAMU students by Symm. Based on evidence presented by the United States and on testimony given by Symm and his deputies, the court found that "it appears that only Prairie View students or persons with addresses on the campus have been issued the Symm questionnaire and that others not known to Symm are not required to complete the questionnaire."[50]

While the court explained that "the case that controls this controversy is *Whatley v. Clark*,"[51] it went on to cite multiple cases, at the federal level but also at the state level, including Texas, which were consistent with *Whatley* in reaching "virtually identical conclusions" and applying the same legal reasoning.[52] For instance, federal cases in Kentucky and Vermont struck down state officials' practice of requiring students to fill out questionnaires or provide additional proof of their domicile. Supreme Courts in California and New Jersey reached sim-

---

48 *United States v. State of Texas*, 445 F. Supp. 1245 (S.D. Tex. 1978). In early 1976, Mr. White and some of his assistants traveled to PVAMU to assist students in registering to vote: at least one student testified that White's staff was helpful.

49 *United States v. State of Texas*, 445 F. Supp. 1245 (S.D. Tex. 1978).

50 *United States v. State of Texas*, 445 F. Supp. 1245 (S.D. Tex. 1978).

51 *United States v. State of Texas*, 445 F. Supp. 1245 (S.D. Tex. 1978).

52 *United States v. State of Texas*, 445 F. Supp. 1245 (S.D. Tex. 1978).

ilar conclusions, as did courts in Pennsylvania, Mississippi, and Michigan. Ruling in favor of the United States, the court held that "Symm's position is inconsistent both with the Twenty-Sixth Amendment cases discussed above, and also with the relevant Texas cases."[53] In one 1939 Texas case, a state appeals court ruled that a student attending college away from the county where they resided before college *may* retain residency in that county. The "obvious inference," the court in *Symm v. United States* stated, is that students may also lose that residency and instead become residents of the place where they are attending college.[54] Two other Texas cases the court cited are worth noting: one involved a student who left his parents' home to attend college and another considered a woman who left her parents' home for a part-time job. In both cases, even though the new domiciles were obviously not permanent or even 'indefinite,' the two individuals *lost* their residency status in the county of their parents' domicile, thus raising the question as to where the individuals could register to vote. In ruling against Symm, the court said that Mr. Symm's conduct was "inconsistent with the philosophy and trend" of many of the previous cases, while also "directly in contravention to the holdings and language" of others.[55]

Symm appealed, but in *Symm v. United States* (1979) the Supreme Court affirmed the lower court's ruling that using the questionnaire violated students' voting rights under the 26th Amendment. This was a landmark ruling because it was the first time the Supreme Court decided a case involving the 26th Amendment. But the Supreme Court merely stated, "The judgment is affirmed."[56] No majority opinion was issued along with the judgment upholding the District Court's original ruling. Nevertheless, such a summary affirmance has precedential value and is binding precedent.[57] It was a historic victory for the long-suffering student population at PVAMU and while college students across the country unknowingly enjoyed the fruits of the PVAMU students' victory, one might conclude that the fight was over and PVAMU students could rest on their laurels. Alas, Waller County officials continued to present obstacles to PVAMU students attempting to vote locally. The new obstacles ranged from redistricting shenanigans, arrests, intimidation, and even the threat of violence.

---

53 *United States v. State of Texas*, 445 F. Supp. 1245 (S.D. Tex. 1978).

54 *United States v. State of Texas*, 445 F. Supp. 1245 (S.D. Tex. 1978).

55 *United States v. State of Texas*, 445 F. Supp. 1245 (S.D. Tex. 1978).

56 *Symm v. U.S.*, 439 U.S. 1105 (1979).

57 See Yael Bromberg, "Youth Voting Rights and the Unfulfilled Promise of the Twenty-Sixth Amendment," *University of Pennsylvania Journal of Constitutional Law* 21 (2019): 1105, 1134.

3 Post-*Symm* Disenfranchisement: Intimidation, Threats, and the PV-19

In 1980, PVAMU's campus was divided into three separate precincts through gerrymandering to dilute the students' voting strength. The gerrymander was so severe that if students moved across the street from one campus dormitory to another, they were placed into a different voting district:[58] few, if any, students would realize the minor address change put them in a different district, which necessitated them having to re-register to vote. In an interview with the *Texas Observer*, Frank Jackson, a PVAMU graduate who would later go on to elected positions in Waller County and the City of Prairie View, and who became PVAMU's assistant vice chancellor for state relations, said, "They had us carved up like a Christmas turkey."[59] After assistance from the Department of Justice, the entire university was included in one voting precinct in 1990.[60]

As recently as the 1990s, Black candidates for public office in Waller County were rare. However, in 1992 Frank Jackson ran for Waller County Commissioner against a white 16-year incumbent, while another Black candidate, Ellery Stevenson, ran for Waller County Constable.[61] The Waller County Commissioners Court is the managerial or executive governing body of the county and acts as the administrative arm of the Texas State government. It consists of five elected officials, four commissioners, and the county judge, who presides over the Commissioners Court as the spokesperson and ceremonial head. Waller County commissioners

---

58 Kerry Breen, "Midterm Elections 2018: Once Again, Voting Controversies Surface at Prairie View A&M," *Pavement Pieces*, November 2, 2018, https://pavementpieces.com/once-again-voting-controversies-surface-at-prairie-view-am/; and Alexa Ura, "Texas' Oldest Black University was Built on a Former Plantation. Its Students Still Fight a Legacy of Voter Suppression," *Texas Tribune*, February 25, 2021, https://www.texastribune.org/2021/02/25/waller-county-texas-voter-suppression/.

59 Patrick Michels, "The Interview: Frank Jackson," *Texas Observer*, June 20, 2016, https://www.texasobserver.org/prairie-view-mayor-frank-jackson-interview/.

60 Peniel Joseph, Expert Report, *Allen v. Waller* (S.D. Tex.) (dated July 30, 2019, Pls. Trial Exhibit 155), available at https://www.courthousenews.com/wp-content/uploads/2020/10/prairie-view-expert.pdf (describing history of efforts to secure voting rights in Waller County, including those by students, and the history of racial discrimination in voting in Waller County and its specific impact on Black Prairie View students and Prairie View voters). Also see, Rodney Ellis, "Jim Crow Goes to College," *New York Times*, April 27, 1992, https://www.nytimes.com/1992/04/27/opinion/jim-crow-goes-to-college.html.

61 Ellis, "Jim Crow Goes to College" and Peniel Joseph, Expert Report, *Allen v. Waller* (S.D. Tex.) (dated July 30, 2019, Pls. Trial Exhibit 155).

hold significant policy-making authority in areas such as the county's budget, roads, and taxes.[62]

It is important to note that at this point the 5,000 PVAMU students could wield substantial power in shaping local politics in a county that had very few, if any, Black public officials.[63] While both Jackson and Stevenson would go on to win their races, it was not before significant legal and political battles involving PVAMU students, who could effectively tip the balance in these elections, were settled.

Two weeks before the run-off elections in the spring of 1992, 19 Prairie View students were indicted on charges of illegal voting during the March primaries. Five of the 19 students were also additionally indicted on felony charges of aggravated perjury, which, if they were convicted, could have resulted in prison time. Waller County District Attorney A.M. "Buddy" McCaig accused these five students of voting once in their home county of record and once in Waller County.[64]

To many, including Jackson, the indictments resulted from miscommunication between the county elections administrator, the students, and the university.[65] Students frequently move dormitories during their time at the university. If the county mails a voter registration card to the dormitory where the student previously lived, and if the student does not know to pick up the card from that previous dormitory, then the voter registration card gets returned, and the student is removed from the Waller County voter rolls. Because they did not receive their registration cards by mail, many students signed an affidavit at the polls asserting they had registered to vote. However, when the county checked their records, and the students were not on the voter rolls, they were criminally charged.[66]

Additionally, it appears with more than three decades of hindsight that some of these indictments could have been avoided with further due diligence from county officials. Carl Moore Jr. was one of the five students indicted on charges of illegal voting and aggravated perjury because he allegedly voted in two separate

---

62 Waller County, "About Commissioners Court," https://www.co.waller.tx.us/page/CommCourt. About.

63 Mark Langford, "Black Student Voters Allege Harassment in Texas," *UPI*, April 19, 1991, https://www.upi.com/Archives/1992/04/19/Black-student-voters-allege-harassment-in-Texas/7349703656000/.

64 Chandra Baty, "Prairie View 19 Face Arraignment: Students to Plead Not Guilty of Election Fraud," *The Panther*, May 1, 1992, https://digitalcommons.pvamu.edu/cgi/viewcontent.cgi?article=1402&context=pv-panther-newspapers.

65 Baty, "Prairie View 19 Face Arraignment."

66 Baty, "Prairie View 19 Face Arraignment" and Ellis, "Jim Crow Goes to College."

elections in two separate counties. Waller County officials failed to realize that Moore's father, also named Carl Moore, was the person who voted in the other county.[67]

Jackson recalled Moore's parents came from Beaumont, Texas, about two hours east of Prairie View, to see then university president Julius Becton, and prove that Carl Moore Jr. did not vote once in his hometown and then again in Prairie View. According to Jackson, Moore's father, Carl Moore Sr., produced evidence that he was the Carl Moore who voted in Beaumont, not his son, Carl Moore Jr.[68] "But nobody did the correlation," Jackson said, "they just charged the kid with voting twice. He was facing about ten years in prison. But that was to put the spirit of fear into the students."[69]

The wider student community rallied for the 'Prairie View 19,' including by demonstrating at the courthouse the morning of the grand jury session, and by leading a march of hundreds of students who walked and drove caravan-style to Hempstead, shutting down Highway 290, a major thoroughfare which stretches from Houston to Austin. A PVAMU communications student participating in the march reported, "It felt good to be part of a unified effort to improve the rights of students at Prairie View."[70]

During the uproar, McCaig defended his actions by stating that the "permanent residents" of Waller County did not want their legally cast votes to be "diluted by someone who is not a legal voter." McCaig continued, asserting the citizens felt it was: "bad enough being forced to accept the fact that transient students living in a dormitory for a couple of semesters, paying no property taxes, have a right to vote in Waller County (when they should be voting at home) without having county citizens put up with illegal voting on top of that."[71] As it concerned Frank Jackson, McCaig questioned whether Jackson was using his position as a university employee to campaign on officially state-sanctioned business. As a veteran, elected official, university employee, and volunteer fire chief, Mr. Jackson has had an esteemed career as a public servant who has long championed students' voting rights. After graduating from PVAMU in 1973, he was commissioned

67 Langford, "Black Student Voters Allege Harassment in Texas."
68 Langford, "Black Student Voters Allege Harassment in Texas."
69 Frank Jackson, interview by Seamus Heady, July 21, 2023; see also Seamus Heady and Mariia Pankova, "Panthers Vote: The Civic Legacy of Prairie View A&M University," Open Society University Network, January 2025, 19:49, https://vimeo.com/1059082662.
70 Michell Johnson, "Students March in Protest," *The Panther*, April 6, 1992, 1, https://digitalcommons.pvamu.edu/cgi/viewcontent.cgi?article=1391&context=pv-panther-newspapers.
71 Albert M. McCaig, "McCaig on the Prairie View 19," *The Panther*, May 6, 1992, 7, https://digitalcommons.pvamu.edu/cgi/viewcontent.cgi?article=1402&context=pv-panther-newspapers.

as an Ensign in the U.S. Navy, from which he retired as a captain. He returned to work at PVAMU where, over a decades-long career, he held many positions, including government relations officer and vice chancellor for state relations. From the 1990s to the 2010s, he was repeatedly elected to City Council and then as mayor while also serving the City of Prairie View as fire chief. McCaig argued Jackson was deliberately spreading misinformation and "spurring unrest" among the students without a "factual basis." Despite this accusation and veiled threat, Mr. Jackson retained his position at PVAMU.[72]

Indeed, this type of accusation, and the underlying threat that goes with it, helps explain why PVAMU officials have historically been reluctant to wade too heavily into student grievances regarding their voting rights in Waller County. Aside from a posting found in one of the university's webpages announcing the occurrence of a student-led demonstration, there is little record of university officials making strong public stances on behalf of the students. Years later, Jackson reported that the 'Prairie View 19' received public support from political scientists Mack Jones, who himself was expelled for participating in sit-ins at Southern University as an undergraduate, and Dr. Imari Obadele, who was one of the founders of the Republic of New Afrika.[73]

The university's passive approach did not change as the years went on. Priscilla Barbour, the former President of the Student Government Association and one of the primary participants in voting rights activism on campus in the early 2010s, said, "All student-led efforts were truly student-led and students had to see them through from start to finish."[74] As a public institution that's been intentionally starved of state funding, surely university officials must have care as they navigate the prickly thicket involving state and local politicians, on whose largesse the university greatly depends.

But McCaig was not the only person whose ire Jackson drew. The editor of the *Texas Advocate*, Mary Levy, wrote that Jackson needed "a horse-whipping for misconstruing the facts,"[75] a threat whose violent imagery no doubt was intended to strike fear in the hearts of Mr. Jackson and PVAMU's Black students as they were reminded of the horrors their enslaved ancestors were forced to endure.

---

72 McCaig, "McCaig on the Prairie View 19," 7.

73 Mack H. Jones, interview by Jewel Prestage and Twiley Barker, Louie B. Nunn Center for Oral History, University of Kentucky Libraries, July 15, 1994.

74 Jonathan Becker and Erin Cannan, "Institution as Citizen: Colleges and Universities as Actors in Defense of Student Voting Rights," *The Rutgers University Law Review* 74, no. 4 (Summer 2022): 1905.

75 Baty, "Prairie View 19 Face Arraignment."

Jackson responded to these assertions of wrongdoing, arguing that for Levy and McCaig to refer to the students as "transient" and not actual residents of Waller County "is absurd and reflects the mind of a bigot [and it is] unethical and grossly unfair for Mary Levy and Albert (Buddy) McCaig, Jr. to paint a negative picture of these citizens and then turn around and become the first in line to meet dignitaries on campus or to eat bread from the students' table."[76] The charges were dropped after intervention by the United States Department of Justice, citing lack of evidence. However, the indictments drew a long shadow: according to local activist Dwayne Charleston, many of the students chose not to exercise their right to vote in subsequent elections out of fear of being arrested and facing criminal charges.

Those fears were further affirmed in the county a decade later. In the fall of 2003, Waller County District Attorney Oliver Kitzman wrote to the county elections administrator, Lela Loewe, saying:

> Serious inquiries have come to my office this year concerning the actual application of the terms domicile and residency in elections in Waller County. ... Incorrect information about what constitutes residency (and feigned residency) has deprived Waller Countians of fair elections on many occasions in the recent past. Numerous constituents urge me to do something about this. It's my duty to do so, and I will.[77]

Days later, D.A. Kitzman wrote an op-ed in the *Waller Times* threatening to bring criminal charges against any student who did not meet his definition of legal residency.[78] In effect, D.A. Kitzman sought to negate or nullify all the previously discussed court rulings and continued to insist that Prairie View students were not citizens of Waller County and, therefore, were ineligible to vote in local elections. The timing of these threats was peculiar, as a Prairie View student was running for a seat on the Waller County Commissioner's Court in the upcoming spring elections.[79]

---

76 Frank D. Jackson, "Jackson Affirms Commitment to Prairie View Community," *The Panther*, May 6, 1992, https://digitalcommons.pvamu.edu/cgi/viewcontent.cgi?article=1402&context=pv-panther-newspapers.

77 Billy Dragoo, "DA, State at Odds on Student Voting," *Chron*, January 7, 2004, https://www.chron.com/neighborhood/article/DA-state-at-odds-on-student-voting-9787811.php.

78 Barbara Ramirez, "Panthers Defy Intimidation, Weather to Assert Voting Rights," *The Panther*, January 21, 2004, https://digitalcommons.pvamu.edu/cgi/viewcontent.cgi?article=1689&context=pv-panther-newspapers.

79 Breen, "Midterm Elections 2018" and Emmanuel Felton, "Black Students in Texas Filed A Voting Rights Suit but Didn't Get an Answer in Time," *BuzzFeed*, October 30, 2020, https://www.buzzfeednews.com/article/emmanuelfelton/trump-judges-voting-rights-texas-black-students.

Despite affirmations from state leadership, including then-secretary of state Gregg Abbott, that the students had the right to vote in the county,[80] D.A. Kitzman refused to back down. Subsequently the Prairie View NAACP, along with Prairie View undergraduate students Brian Rowland, Neothies Lindley, and Vivian Spikes, filed a lawsuit, alleging Kitzman's statements were akin to voter intimidation. They took to the streets, marching seven miles from PVAMU's main campus to the Waller County courthouse to protest D.A. Kitzman's actions, and initiated an economic boycott of local businesses in the county.[81] The Department of Justice opened an investigation, and the county prosecutor ultimately relented and issued a formal apology to the students:

> I have come to realize that, although it was never my intention, my actions and statements beginning with the letter I sent to Waller County Election Administrator Lela Loewe in November and continuing with my response to the Attorney General opinion earlier this month, taken in the historical context in which they occurred, have been understandably perceived by some PVAMU students as threatening. I want the PVAMU community to know that I apologize, and I welcome them as participants in the democratic institutions in Waller County.[82]

4 From Eligibility to Access

Despite Kitzman's 2004 apology over the eligibility issue, the county then moved to limit Prairie View students' *access* to the polls during the 2004 primary elections by restricting early voting hours on campus to six hours on a single day during spring break, when the vast majority of students would be out of town. Another emergency lawsuit was filed and the county reverted to its original plan for early voting hours. Kitzman's change in early voting hours was not cleared with the Department of Justice, as required by the pre-clearance provision of the Voting Rights Act of 1965.[83] Texas, along with other states and some counties

---

80 Greg Abbott, "Opinion No. GA-0141," Texas Attorney General, February 4, 2004.12, https://www.texasattorneygeneral.gov/sites/default/files/opinion-files/opinion/2004/ga0141.pdf.
81 Ramirez, "Panthers Defy Intimidation" and Nikki Easter, "Students, Community Supporters Boycott Local Businesses," *The Panther*, January 21, 2004.
82 Terry Kliewer, "Waller County DA Apologizes in Vote Flap," *Houston Chronicle*, February 25, 2004, https://www.chron.com/news/houston-texas/article/waller-county-da-apologizes-in-vote-flap-1957246.php.
83 Peniel Joseph, Expert Report, Allen v. Waller (S.D. Tex.) (dated July 30, 2019, Pls. Trial Exhibit 155), and Breen, "Midterm Elections 2018." In its 2018 *Shelby v. Holder* ruling, this provision of the Voting Rights Act was struck down as unconstitutional by the Supreme Court.

and municipalities,[84] was subject to this pre-clearance requirement due to a history of systematic and intentional voter suppression of African American voters in specific jurisdictions. Any change Texas wanted to make to its voting practices, such as early voting hours, the number of polling places, or voter registration requirements, had to be approved by the federal government. This sudden removal of voting access was a direct violation of the pre-clearance provision. More litigation ensued and the county officials honored the previously approved early voting arrangement.

Towards the late 2000s, issues arose again during the period leading up to and after the 2008 presidential election, which saw Barack Obama win a historical election making him the first Black man to win the White House. This understandably created a groundswell of voter registration interest among PVAMU's mostly Black student population.

Many students were registered to vote in the county using Voluntary Deputy Registrars (VDRs). In Texas, VDRs are responsible for registering voters, are appointed by county voter registrars, and according to the Office of the Texas Secretary of State, are "charged with increasing voter registration in the state."[85] But Waller County election officials rejected 'incomplete' voter registrations, many resulting from students forgetting to write down their zip code correctly and/or using outdated registration paperwork. For the students whose registrations the county rejected, the county required VDRs to locate and personally notify the applicants of the rejection. Waller County officials also capped the number of new registrations any VDR could submit for approval, hampering the success of get-out-the-vote initiatives that sought to register Black collegians on PVAMU's campus.[86]

Additionally, prior to the 2008 presidential primaries Waller County planned to reduce its early polling locations from six to one, citing budgetary constraints. This change in polling locations left the county with a lone early voting location, seven miles from PVAMU's campus, creating a prohibitive access issue. Many stu-

---

84 This provision covered some states in their entirety, most of which are in the Deep South, including Alabama, Georgia, Louisiana, Mississippi, and South Carolina. However, counties and municipalities from across the country were also covered, such as Kings County, NY, Monroe County, FL, Clyde Township, MI, and 40 of North Carolina's 100 counties. See U.S. Department of Justice, "Jurisdictions Previously Covered by Section 5," updated May 17, 2023, https://www.justice.gov/crt/jurisdictions-previously-covered-section-5.

85 Texas Secretary of State, "Volunteer Deputy Registrars," https://www.sos.state.tx.us/elections/laws/volunteer-deputy-registrars.shtml.

86 Consent Decree, *United States v. Waller County, TX*, Case 4:08-CV-03022 (S.D. Tex. 2008), https://www.justice.gov/crt/case-document/file/1096926/dl?inline.

dents do not have reliable transportation, and the city and county do not possess public transit, thus creating an impediment to participation. More importantly, the Department of Justice did not approve any of the aforementioned changes as required by section 5 of the Voting Rights Act of 1965, which was still in force at the time. Students marched 7.2 miles from campus to the lone early voting polling in Waller County. Once again, the Department of Justice got involved and entered a consent decree with Waller County, mandating that any change the county sought to make to its registration practices, polling locations, early voting hours, or other changes must be cleared by the Department of Justice. Additionally, in agreeing to the terms of federal oversight, Waller County formally acknowledged that the denial of hundreds of applications from primarily PVAMU students for not using the most updated paperwork or because of other minute errors had not been pre-approved by the Department of Justice. Election officials had to justify denying any voter registration per the 2008 consent decree terms until 2012.[87]

Waller County's decisions to limit early voting on PVAMU's campus continued. In the spring of 2012 and 2013, the closest polling place for PVAMU students was at the City of Prairie View Community Center. This location is just less than a mile from student dorms, and many students do not have automotive transportation. Additionally, this location created an additional barrier of access for students with physical disabilities who did not have cars.[88] Much like in 1992, 2004, and 2008, the students used the one consistent weapon in their arsenal: public protest. Ultimately in the summer of 2013, then-SGA president Priscilla Barbour wrote a letter to Texas Secretary of State John Steen for assistance in securing a polling place on PVAMU's campus. Barbour later remarked, "We've seen the [Waller County] community use the campus for a variety of things. Why not use this as an opportunity to bridge the community and the University to come together and vote?"[89] After assistance from Steen and True The Vote, a conservative organization with focus on stopping voter fraud with origins in the Tea Party movement, the students were finally able to vote on campus in the Memorial Student Center in 2013.[90]

87 Consent Decree, *United States v. Waller County, TX*, Case 4:08-CV-03022 (S.D. Tex. 2008).

88 Reeve Hamilton, "Student Leader Demands On-Campus Polling Place," *The Texas Tribune*, July 31, 2013, https://www.texastribune.org/2013/07/31/prairie-view-m-students-demand-campus-voting/.

89 Priscilla Barbour Randle, interviewed by Seamus Heady, April 5, 2024; and Heady and Pankova, "Panthers Vote."

90 Reeve Hamilton, "Unlikely Coalition Brings On-Campus Voting Location to Prairie View," *The Texas Tribune*, September 30, 2013, https://www.texastribune.org/2013/09/30/prairie-view-campus-gets-long-awaited-voting-locat/.

5 The Struggle Continues: More Recent Developments

In the fall of 2018, the students found themselves back in the headlines and back in the courtroom with yet another lawsuit. Following in the footsteps of previous students, Jayla Allen, along with half a dozen other students, filed a federal civil rights lawsuit against Waller County and its leadership, alleging their 14th, 15th, and 26th Amendment constitutional rights had been violated.[91]

The students sought more access to early voting on campus, which the county refused to provide, citing budgeting concerns. Data from the 2018 primaries in March illustrated that 64% of Prairie View students who voted in the election overwhelmingly utilized early voting, compared with 43% of Waller County voters who utilized early voting in the March primaries.[92] Yet, during the first week of early voting before the November 2018 elections, there were no early voting sites or opportunities in Prairie View. During the second week of early voting, the City of Prairie View had only two early voting locations, the Memorial Student Center (colloquially known as the 'MSC'") on campus, and the Waller County Community Center. The Waller County Community Center is located less than a mile from campus but is rarely used because, according to the plaintiffs, "most students receive their mail on campus." The MSC had early voting for three days from 8 a.m.–5 p.m. from October 29–31, 2018. There were no weekend hours for early voting anywhere in Prairie View. There were no evening hours (i.e., after 5:00 p.m.) for early voting at the MSC during the limited hours that early voting was available on campus.[93]

By contrast, the majority-white City of Waller, whose population was less than half that of the City of Prairie View and had half of the eligible voting-age population of the City of Prairie View, had early voting sites for all 11 days of early voting, which included opportunities to vote during the evenings and on weekends. The City of Brookshire, which had a lower share of voters eligible to vote than the City of Prairie View, had 12 days of early voting, including evenings and weekend hours. The City of Hempstead, whose numerical population is lower than the City of Prairie View's, had 12 days of early voting, including opportunities to vote during weekends and one day of evening accessibility at the Waller County court-

91 *Allen v. Waller County*, 472 F. Supp. 3d 351 (S.D. Tex. 2020), https://casetext.com/case/allen-v-waller-cnty.
92 *Allen v. Waller County*, 472 F. Supp. 3d 351 (S.D. Tex. 2020).
93 *Allen v. Waller County*, 472 F. Supp. 3d 351 (S.D. Tex. 2020).

Figure 1: Student leaders Jayla Allen and Jessica Purnell at a protest in Prairie View, Texas, October, 2018. Photo courtesy of Prairie View A&M University.

house.[94] A few days before the start of early voting, PVAMU students packed a Waller County Commissioners Court meeting, where County Judge Trey Duhon, who is white and head of the Waller County Commissioners Court, acknowledged, "I do think there is an inequity," referring to the disparity in early voting locations and the limited access students have compared with other areas of the county.[95] Despite this concession, Waller County leadership did not approve additional early voting hours on campus for Prairie View students.[96]

This prompted Allen and fellow students Joshua Muhammad, Treasure Smith, Damon Johnson, and Raul Sanchez to sue Waller County Elections Administrator Christy Eason and the Waller County Commissioners Court, including the head of the Commissioners Court, Judge Duhon.[97] The students reached out to the NAACP's Legal Defense Fund (LDF), which responded positively to their request for assistance. Given its previous work in Texas, particularly in the 2012–2013 period

94 *Allen v. Waller County*, 472 F. Supp. 3d 351 (S.D. Tex. 2020).
95 Ura, "Texas' Oldest Black University."
96 Ura, "Texas' Oldest Black University."
97 *Allen v. Waller County*, 472 F. Supp. 3d 351 (S.D. Tex. 2020).

when the NAACP challenged Texas' restrictive photo ID law, which was implemented immediately after the *Shelby* ruling overturned the Civil Rights Act's pre-clearance requirement, the NAACP was receptive to the students' request. "When people from PV call, I answer," said Leah Aden, who is currently the LDF's Director of Litigation and who served as its deputy director during the *Allen* case. "I am not aware of any other group of students at a university that has been serially mistreated using various stratagems by a state or local government over decades," she said.[98] Aden asked, "Why would you do that in a place where you have some of the most active voters in all the county? These are citizens of the country. These are registered voters of the county. Why wouldn't you be putting resources into voting access where past practice shows those opportunities were actually being used?"[99]

Only after this lawsuit had been filed did the county expand the hours of the three on-campus voting days from 7 a.m. to 7 p.m., after previously scheduling early voting at the MSC from 8–5 p.m., and open a Sunday polling place at Prairie View City Hall.[100] The county argued publicly and in court filings that the early voting plan had been approved by both the Republican and Democratic Party Chairs of Waller County, and previously the Chair of the Waller County Democratic Party had asked that early voting on campus be pushed to the second week of early voting, so that it would not coincide with PVAMU's homecoming festivities.[101] Conceding that Waller County had a well-documented issue with student voting rights and voter suppression, Duhon said,

> I understand how this looks. I can understand and appreciate the perception for someone who knows the history of Waller County. I just wish people would take the time to learn the facts and the truth today. This isn't your grandfather's or great-grandfather's county, not even close. It kills me to be painted with a brush that I had nothing to do with.[102]

98 Leah Aden, interview with the authors, January 31, 2025, and email exchanges, February 13, 2025.

99 Leah Aden, interview with the authors, January 31, 2025, and email exchanges, February 13, 2025.

100 Matt Zdun, "Waller County Expands Early Voting for Prairie View A&M Students," *The Texas Tribune*, October 25, 2018, https://www.texastribune.org/2018/10/25/waller-county-expands-early-voting-prairie-view-m-students/. See also Amy Gardner, "In Rural Texas, Black Students' Fight for Voting Access Conjures a Painful Past," *The Washington Post*, September 24, 2019, https://www.washingtonpost.com/politics/in-rural-texas-black-students-fight-for-voting-access-conjures-a-painful-past/2019/09/24/fa18e880-ca69-11e9-a1fe-ca46e8d573c0_story.html.

101 Ura, "Texas' Oldest Black University."

102 Gardner, "In Rural Texas."

Duhon insisted the issue with access to the polls was not the result of racism but merely a county not flush with financial resources trying to do the best it could to provide polling places to its citizens. While defending himself from charges of racism, Duhon again admitted, "I think there's always been this fear that if all the students voted, and they voted in a certain way, they could take over the county."[103]

In 2022, four years after initially filing her lawsuit and long after she graduated, Jayla Allen lost her lawsuit: despite the federal judge being impressed with testimony by Ms. Allen and the other students, the court ruled in favor of Waller County, saying the students had not proved that their constitutional rights were violated. Judge Charles Eskridge, a Trump appointee, wrote in his ruling that, "At best, Plaintiffs establish a mere inconvenience imposed on PVAMU students with respect to the early voting schedule for the 2018 general election. ... In reality, it's rather doubtful that the early voting locations and hours provided by Waller County to PVAMU students can be understood as creating any incremental inconvenience at all."[104]

6 Conclusion

Ever since the arrival of enslaved Africans on the North American continent more than 400 years ago, racial progress in the United States has not been linear; a riptide of white supremacist racial revanchism follows every wave of racial progress. Perhaps no place exemplifies this phenomenon more than Waller County, Texas. Despite orders from Texas State officials, Supreme Court rulings, federal investigations, indictments, and endless marches, it feels as if Waller County, Texas, is stuck in an endless loop of students having their rights affirmed by America's legal institutions and the county quickly adopting new nefarious mechanisms to deny students their constitutional rights. In the late 1960s/early 1970s, it was the residency questionnaire used by LeRoy Symm, then severe gerrymandering, which evolved into indicting students for 'illegally voting' in the spring of 1992, which ultimately evolved to the present day with students engaged in a contentious battle to secure access to polling options on campus that are as equitable

---

103 Gardner, "In Rural Texas."

104 For a more in-depth examination of the most recent installment of PVAMU students fighting for their voting rights, please see Alexander Goodwin, Ronald Goodwin, and Michael J. Nojeim, "The 'Political Science Posse': Voting Rights and Student Activism at Prairie View A&M University," in *The Quest for Justice at Prairie View A&M University*, ed. Will Guzman and William Hoston (Texas Tech University Press, forthcoming).

as those found elsewhere in the county. Racism, covert or overt, has been the animating factor in most of these cases.

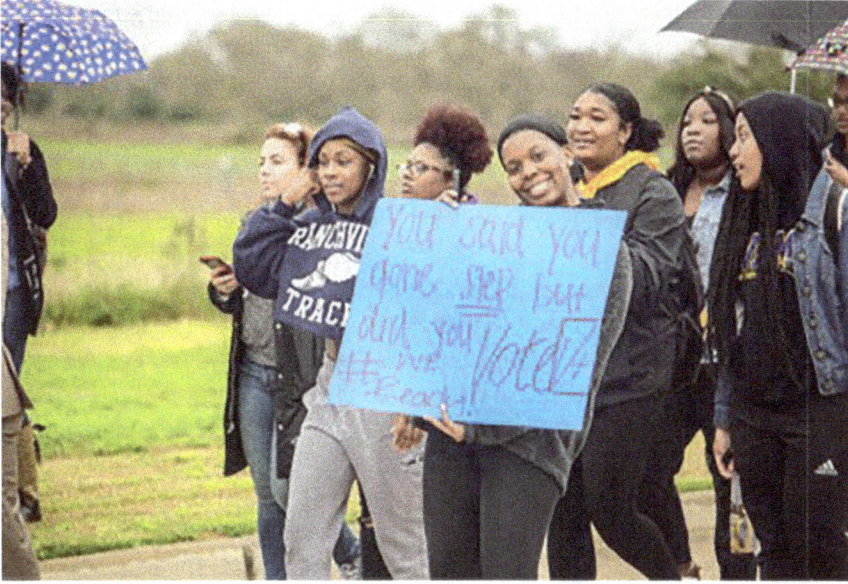

Figure 2: PVAMU Students march in a protest, 2020. Photo courtesy of Prairie View A&M University.

The result has been the same: Prairie View students in Waller County face significant obstacles to casting their votes. As the United States currently navigates one of the most trying periods of its history, this trend of progress and subsequent racial retrenchment seems destined to continue: the only question is not if but when another chapter in the ongoing saga between Waller County versus PVAMU students will be written.

Despite their struggles in accessing voting rights, or perhaps because of them, students at Prairie View A&M University have, for more than a half century, demonstrated a pattern of extraordinary resilience and courage. They have repeatedly stood up and fought against the obstacles that have been placed in front of them, and done so despite being targeted by local officials in a region well known for its ugly, violent, racist past. According to Dr. Melanye Price, who graduated from PVAMU in 1995 and who now serves as the university's Endowed Professor of Political Science and Director of the Ruth J. Simmons Race and Justice Center, it is as if PVAMU students have, for decades proclaimed, "we're never going to stop trying, we're never going to stop suing you, we're never going to stop protesting, we're never going stop registering."[105] Their brave efforts serve as a remarkable example, not only for students elsewhere, but for all who want to engage in social justice.

Indeed, consider some of the PVAMU students who engaged in the most recent struggle. Jayla Allen finished a master's degree in African American Diaspora Studies at Columbia University, currently works as a restorative justice practitioner in New York City, and plans to enter law school in the fall of 2025. Other students from Jayla's time, known as the Political Science Posse (because most of them were Political Science majors), supported the cause by engaging in organizing protests and marches. They remark that their experiences have left them committed to a life in pursuit of social justice.[106] For example, Maydrian-Strozier Lowe was one of the protest leaders in the 2018 period and he is now a civil rights attorney working with the NAACP. Kendric Jones was elected—and still serves as–a member of the Waller County Commissioners Court. Nathan Alexander was elected to Prairie View's City Council and is one of the youngest ever to be elected to a city council in Texas. He left that position and is now finishing law school at the University of Texas. Another Posse member, Kirsten Budwine, works as an attorney for the Texas Civil Rights Project after graduating from the University of Texas Law School, and Maia Young recently completed her law degree at the University of Vermont along with a master's in restorative justice. These students carry on a hopeful legacy of striving for what is right and serve as an inspirational example for others. Perhaps LDF attorney Aden said it best:

> I think [students at PVAMU] have so much to teach this country about how it treats its citizens. I think it's such an example of what Black people do in the face of racial discrimination. ... And the ways the students have responded in terms of running for office, resisting efforts to criminalize their ability to participate politically, registering students, advocating for accessible cites to vote, constantly talking about the value of political participation and much more ... that is so impressive [because Prairie View students] can teach other students how to engage in the face of obstacles, but also engage in a way that affirmatively moves Black people forward.[107]

---

105 Melanye Price, interviewed by Seamus Heady, July 21, 2023; and Heady and Pankova, "Panthers Vote."
106 See Goodwin, Goodwin, and Nojeim, "The 'Political Science Posse.'"
107 Leah Aden, interview with the authors, January 31, 2025, and email exchanges, February 13, 2025.

Bibliography

Abramsky, Sasha. "Just Try Voting Here: 11 of America's Worst Places to Cast a Ballot (or Try)." *Mother Jones*, September/October 2006. https://www.motherjones.com/politics/2006/09/just-try-voting-here-11-americas-worst-places-cast-ballot-or-try/.

Associated Press. "General Calvin Waller Dies." *The Washington Post*, May 10, 1996. https://www.washingtonpost.com/archive/local/1996/05/11/gen-calvin-waller-dies/3e4c1eb4-5089-43c5-a18d-d23362478dc6/.

Baty, Chandra. "Prairie View 19 Face Arraignment: Students to Plead Not Guilty of Election Fraud." *The Panther*, May 1, 1992. https://digitalcommons.pvamu.edu/cgi/viewcontent.cgi?article=1402&context=pv-panther-newspapers.

Becker, Jonathan, and Cannan, Erin. "Institution as Citizen: Colleges and Universities as Actors in Defense of Student Voting Rights." *The Rutgers University Law Review* 74, no. 4 (Summer 2022): 1869–1909. https://rutgerslawreview.com/wp-content/uploads/2023/02/07_Becker_Cannan.pdf.

Breen, Kerry. "Midterm Elections 2018: Once Again, Voting Controversies Surface at Prairie View A&M." *Pavement Pieces*, November 2, 2018. https://pavementpieces.com/once-again-voting-controversies-surface-at-prairie-view-am/.

Bromberg, Yael. "Youth Voting Rights and the Unfulfilled Promise of the Twenty-Sixth Amendment." *University of Pennsylvania Journal of Constitutional Law* 21 (2019): 1105–1166. https://scholarship.law.upenn.edu/jcl/vol21/iss5/1/.

Dart, Tom, and Swaine, John. "Sandra Bland: Suspicion and Mistrust Flourish Amid Official Inconsistencies." *The Guardian*, July 25, 2015. https://www.theguardian.com/us-news/2015/jul/25/sandra-bland-suspicion-mistrust-official-inconsistencies.

Dragoo, Billy. "DA, State at Odds on Student Voting." *Chron*, January 7, 2004. https://www.chron.com/neighborhood/article/DA-state-at-odds-on-student-voting-9787811.php.

Easter, Nikki. "Students, Community Supporters Boycott Local Businesses." *The Panther*, January 21, 2004.

Ellis, Rodney. "Jim Crow Goes to College." *New York Times*, April 27, 1992. https://www.nytimes.com/1992/04/27/opinion/jim-crow-goes-to-college.html.

Equal Justice Initiative. "Lynching in America: Confronting the Legacy of Racial Terror." 3rd Edition. 2017. https://lynchinginamerica.eji.org/report/.

Felton, Emmanuel. "Black Students in Texas Filed a Voting Rights Suit but Didn't Get an Answer in Time." *BuzzFeed*, October 30, 2020. https://www.buzzfeednews.com/article/emmanuelfelton/trump-judges-voting-rights-texas-black-students.

Fjetland, Gale M. "A Statutory Presumption That a Student Is Not a Resident of the Community Where He Is Attending School Violates the Equal Protection Clause of the Fourteenth Amendment." *Texas Tech Law Review* 5 (1974): 851–856. https://ttu-ir.tdl.org/items/c4cfeb39-0d92-4496-a4dd-c92452eaab74.

Gardner, Amy. "In Rural Texas, Black Students' Fight for Voting Access Conjures a Painful Past." *The Washington Post*, September 24, 2019. https://www.washingtonpost.com/politics/in-rural-texas-black-students-fight-for-voting-access-conjures-a-painful-past/2019/09/24/fa18e880-ca69-11e9-a1fe-ca46e8d573c0_story.html.

Good Marable, Karen. "Remembering Sandra Bland's Death in the Place I Call Home." *The New Yorker*, July 13, 2016. https://www.newyorker.com/news/news-desk/remembering-sandra-blands-death-in-the-place-i-call-home.

Goodwin, Alexander, Goodwin, Ronald, and Nojeim, Michael J. "The 'Political Science Posse': Voting Rights and Student Activism at Prairie View A&M University." In *The Quest for Justice at Prairie View A&M University*, edited by Will Guzman and William Hoston. Texas Tech University Press, forthcoming.

Hamilton, Reeve. "Student Leader Demands On-Campus Polling Place." *The Texas Tribune*, July 31, 2013. https://www.texastribune.org/2013/07/31/prairie-view-m-students-demand-campus-voting/.

Hamilton, Reeve. "Unlikely Coalition Brings On-Campus Voting Location to Prairie View." *The Texas Tribune*, September 30, 2013. https://www.texastribune.org/2013/09/30/prairie-view-campus-gets-long-awaited-voting-locat/.

Heady, Seamus, and Pankova, Mariia. "Panthers Vote: The Civic Legacy of Prairie View A&M University." Open Society University Network, January 2025. Video, 19:49, https://vimeo.com/1059082662.

Jackson, Frank D. "Jackson Affirms Commitment to Prairie View Community." *The Panther*, May 6, 1992. https://digitalcommons.pvamu.edu/cgi/viewcontent.cgi?article=1402&context=pv-panther-newspapers.

Johnson, Michelle. "Students March in Protest." *The Panther*, April 6, 1992, 1. https://digitalcommons.pvamu.edu/cgi/viewcontent.cgi?article=1391&context=pv-panther-newspapers.

Ketterer, Samantha. "Enslaved People Toiled at a Plantation where Prairie View A&M Now Stands. Researchers Want to Know their Stories." *Houston Chronicle*, February 29, 2022. https://www.houstonchronicle.com/news/houston-texas/education/article/Enslaved-people-toiled-at-a-plantation-where-16833077.php.

King, Martin Luther Jr. *A Testament of Hope: The Essential Writings and Speeches of Martin Luther King, Jr.* Edited by James M. Washington. HarperCollins, 1985.

Kliewer, Terry. "Waller County DA Apologizes in Vote Flap." *Houston Chronicle*, February 25, 2004. https://www.chron.com/news/houston-texas/article/waller-county-da-apologizes-in-vote-flap-1957246.php.

Langford, Mark. "Black Student Voters Allege Harassment in Texas." *UPI*, April 19, 1991. https://www.upi.com/Archives/1992/04/19/Black-student-voters-allege-harassment-in-Texas/7349703656000/.

Maddow, Rachel. "Assault on Student Voting Rights." *MSNBC*, May 6, 2013. www.youtube.com/watch?v=d4itV4B3E48.

McCaig, Albert M. "McCaig on the Prairie View 19." *The Panther*, May 6, 1992. https://digitalcommons.pvamu.edu/cgi/viewcontent.cgi?article=1402&context=pv-panther-newspapers.

Michels, Patrick. "The Interview: Frank Jackson." *Texas Observer*, June 20, 2016. https://www.texasobserver.org/prairie-view-mayor-frank-jackson-interview/.

Nojeim, Michael J., and Jackson, Frank D. *Down that Road: A Pictorial History of Prairie View A&M University*. Donning Company Publishers, 2011.

Ramirez, Barbara. "Panthers Defy Intimidation, Weather to Assert Voting Rights." *The Panther*, January 21, 2004. https://digitalcommons.pvamu.edu/cgi/viewcontent.cgi?article=1689&context=pv-panther-newspapers.

Rawley, Tom. "Sandra Bland's Death Divides Texas County with Ugly History of Racism." *The Washington Post*, July 27, 2015. https://www.washingtonpost.com/national/ugly-history-of-racism-dogs-texas-county-where-sandra-bland-died/2015/07/27/e69ac168-3317-11e5-8353-1215475949f4_story.html.

Richards, David. *Once Upon a Time in Texas: A Liberal in the Lonestar State.* University of Texas Press, 2002.

Texas Secretary of State. "Volunteer Deputy Registrars." https://www.sos.state.tx.us/elections/laws/volunteer-deputy-registrars.shtml.

"Top 100 Degree Producers—HBCUs 2021–22." *Diverse: Issues in Higher Education.* https://top100.diverseeducation.com/HBCUs-2021-2022/.

Ura, Alexa. "Texas' Oldest Black University was Built on a Former Plantation. Its Students Still Fight a Legacy of Voter Suppression." *Texas Tribune*, February 25, 2021. https://www.texastribune.org/2021/02/25/waller-county-texas-voter-suppression/.

U.S. Department of Justice. "Jurisdictions Previously Covered by Section 5." Updated May 17, 2023. https://www.justice.gov/crt/jurisdictions-previously-covered-section-5.

Waller County. "About Commissioners Court." https://www.co.waller.tx.us/page/CommCourt.About.

Zdun, Matt. "Waller County Expands Early Voting for Prairie View A&M Students." *The Texas Tribune*, October 25, 2018. https://www.texastribune.org/2018/10/25/waller-county-expands-early-voting-prairie-view-m-students/.

Jelani Favors

5 The Road to Democracy: How the Gerrymandering of North Carolina A&T State University Transformed Politics and Protest at the Nation's Largest HBCU

During the summer of 1934, students attending North Carolina Agricultural & Technical College (later renamed North Carolina Agricultural & Technical State University; NC A&T) gathered for their weekly chapel exercises that frequently provided them an opportunity to hear from nationally renowned scholars and politicians. During the month of July, Dr. Harold L. Trigg, the State Inspector of Negro High Schools, greeted over 400 students and faculty and addressed them on the subject "Changing Concepts in Government." As Trigg spoke, the nation was in the clutches of the Great Depression that not only swept in widespread economic despair, but also ushered in an era of political liberalism and radicalism that fundamentally reshaped government and provided a catalyst for the early civil rights movement. "Times bring about new changes and it is the duty of each Negro teacher and principal to be alert to them," declared Trigg. "The future of the nation lies in the hands of the boys and girls that are under your guidance. Therefore, instill in them, and even allow them to participate in those organizations that are making for political goals, for we learn by doing."[1] It is certain that Trigg understood that the participatory democracy that he urged his listeners to become involved in was not accessible to most Black Americans in the South. However, Greensboro, North Carolina offered Black folks a unique sliver of mobility and progressivism that allowed for political participation from which most Black southerners were systematically and violently barred. Trigg also understood that there were few places in America where his advice to Black youth carried more weight and potential than the sacred grounds of Historically Black Colleges and Universities (HBCUs) such as NC A&T.

Black colleges have served as one of the most important laboratories for dissent in higher education. Since the first HBCU was founded in 1837, these institutions have birthed ideals, activists, and powerful social movements that have fought to expand American democracy for all. HBCUs were one of the few Black enclaves where Black youth en masse were exposed to a steady stream of

---

1 "Three Important Addresses Heard," *The Register,* July 6, 1934, https://digital.library.ncat.edu/atregister/24/.

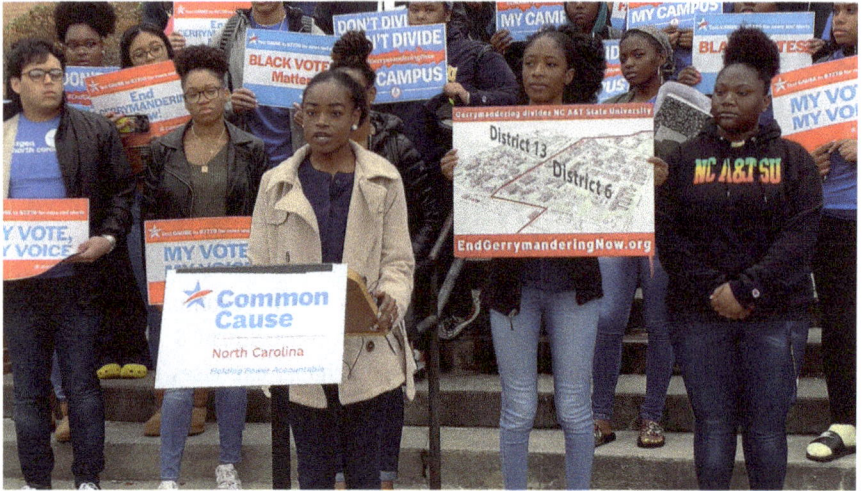

Figure 1: North Carolina A&T student Love Caesar speaking at Common Cause Press Conference, March 26, 2019. Photo Courtesy of Common Cause North Carolina.

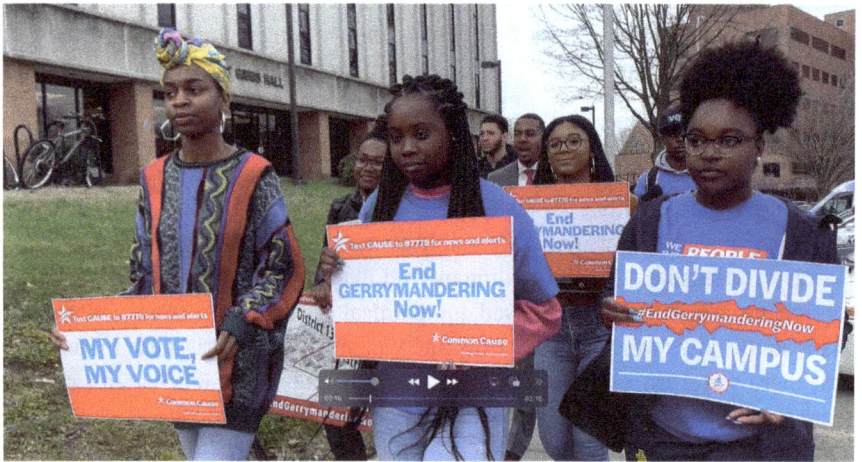

Figure 2: North Carolina A&T student protesters, March 26, 2019. Photo courtesy of Common Cause North Carolina.

race men and women such as Trigg that shaped their political consciousness by arming them with the intellectual tools to wage war against white supremacy. In order to deconstruct the pernicious ideals targeting Black youth, HBCUs were deliberately exposed to a second curriculum. This pedagogy, that was delivered by successive generations of Black college faculty and administrators, countered

Figure 3: North Carolina A&T student protesters, 2019. Photo Courtesy of Common Cause North Carolina.

the corrosive effects of Jim Crow through the promotion of race pride that encouraged Black youth to build and invest in institutions that would serve their community.[2] But perhaps the most important result of this second curriculum was the creation of generations of students who championed the ideals of democracy and citizenship and believed in these sacrosanct values despite being denied them on a daily basis. With Greensboro providing the moderately progressive backdrop, the scene was set for the city's two HBCUs, Bennett College and NC A&T, to serve as a bastion of Black political radicalism throughout the 20th century.

In his classic study entitled *Civilities and Civil Rights: Greensboro, North Carolina and the Black Struggle for Freedom*, historian William Chafe identified the centrality of Black education to the political mobilization taking place in the

---

2 For more on the 'second curriculum,' see Jelani M. Favors, *Shelter in a Time of Storm: How Black Colleges Fostered Generations of Leadership and Activism* (University of North Carolina Press, 2020).

city during the depression. In fact, beginning in 1933, a year before Trigg spoke on NC A&T's campus, Chafe notes that "Blacks ran for city-wide office on a regular basis."[3] This was precipitated by the strong presence of Greensboro's Black educational institutions that turned out a steady stream of conscientious alumni trained to view civic engagement as a necessary tool for agency and activism. While it would still be several years before any African Americans would make a successful run for political office in the city, Chafe documents that "news reports noted the increasing registration of Blacks after 1935, and a new responsiveness by the city council to Black needs as evidenced by construction of a recreation park and a swimming pool in the Black community."[4] African American citizens in Greensboro once again leaned on the burgeoning activist energies stemming from the city's two HBCUs and other traditional Black institutions, such as the city's only Black high school at the time and a myriad of local Black churches. The result was a more concentrated drive for Black voter registration in the city, with students from Bennett College leading the way. In large part, their "Operation Doorknock" campaign in 1951 proved critical in the election of Dr. William Hampton as Greensboro's first Black city councilman. Hampton went on to serve two consecutive terms and his candidacy and subsequent election established a permanent inroad into the political process for the city's Black citizens.[5] As Hampton represented the best interests of his constituents, the 1950s ushered in a new era of Black militancy. Nothing represented that more than the radical mentorship taking place at HBCUs during America's Cold War years.

In December of 1950, students at NC A&T heard from renowned civil rights lawyer and president of Alpha Phi Alpha Fraternity, Belford Lawson, Jr. The university held a "Human Rights Day" that month and the celebrated litigator stood before a packed auditorium to address the students on the subject "Human Rights, the Task at Hand." "We are no longer a meek and lowly people standing in the shadow of a great disappointment," Lawson asserted. "We refuse to believe any longer in some of the hypocrisies of Democracy." Lawson's exhortation was one of the many examples of the radical mentorship and instruction that NC A&T students were receiving that primed the militant atmosphere throughout the decade. By the end of the decade, students at NC A&T were being encouraged to think about "the total emancipation of the people of Africa from foreign domination in every sense—political, economical, social, and cultural." That appeal came from Daniel Chapman, ambassador of Ghana to the United States, who addressed

---

3 William Chafe, *Civilities and Civil Rights: Greensboro, North Carolina and the Black Struggle for Freedom* (Oxford University Press, 1980), 24.
4 Chafe, *Civilities and Civil Rights*, 25.
5 Chafe, *Civilities and Civil Rights*, 23.

a crowd of 3,000 people gathered for NC A&T's 60th commencement. Later the next year, NC A&T students held a mass meeting in the gymnasium to protest budget cuts that the state was making to the already underfunded institution. But nothing better represented the brewing student militancy during the 1950s than the stunning episode that took place on campus in the middle of the decade during the university's Founder's Day observation in November of 1955.[6]

Governor Luther Hodges came to address the student body to honor the 64th anniversary of the campus. As he spoke, Hodges consistently pronounced the word "negro" as the racial slur "niggra" and criticized the work of the NAACP. As Hodges moved deeper into his prepared remarks, the student body grew restless and booed the governor so badly that the Jim Crow politician abruptly stopped mid-speech and left the stage. The campus newspaper reported that students were already on edge due to the lynching of Emmet Till. Hodges merely "threw gasoline on smoldering embers."[7] By February 1, 1960, the campus was more than ready to unleash a social revolution that would rock America to its core and radically reshape youth culture forever.

Time Magazine once referred to American Cold War youth as "the silent generation."[8] As it pertained to Black students being trained at HBCUs, that designation was largely inappropriate and never truly an apt description. Students at NC A&T and other Black colleges had been more than vocal in their distress and anger with Jim Crow policies. Youth chapters of the NAACP grew in number during the 1940s and 50s at HBCUs and campus newspapers were brimming with both incendiary student editorials that called into question white supremacy while also documenting the constant parade of speakers and activists who circulated through Black colleges.[9] The postwar militancy that gave rise to the modern

---

6 "Fraternities are Urged to Fight Tyranny, Injustice," *The Register,* December 1950, https://digital. library.ncat.edu/atregister/111/; "Ghana Ambassador Speaks at A&T 60th Commencement," *The Register,* July 16, 1958, https://digital.library.ncat.edu/atregister/150/; Spurgeon Cameron, "Students Hold Mass Meet in Gymnasium to Rally Against Cuts," *The Register,* April 1, 1959, https://digital.li brary.ncat.edu/atregister/152/.

7 William D. Mason, Jr., "A&T and Gov. Hodges," *The Register,* November 15, 1955, https://digital.li brary.ncat.edu/atregister/141.

8 "People: The Younger Generation," *Time Magazine,* November 5, 1951, https://time.com/archive/ 6794406/people-the-younger-generation/.

9 For more on post-World War II militancy and radicalization of Black youth see Favors, *Shelter in a Time of Storm,* 70–200; Robert Cohen, *When the Old Left Was Young: Student Radicals and America's First Mass Student Movement, 1929–1941* (Oxford University Press, 1993); Johnetta Richards, *The Southern Negro Youth Congress: A History* (University of Cincinnati Press, 1987); Lindsay Swindall, *The Path to the Greater, Freer, Truer World: Southern Civil Rights and Anti-colonialism, 1937–1955* (University Press of Florida, 2019).

civil rights movement only helped to accelerate and intensify elements of dissent that had been increasingly cultivated on Black college campuses since the end of World War II. With the arrival of the sit-ins in 1960, NC A&T students provided an opening salvo in the direct-action phase of the struggle for civil rights. Sit-ins morphed into Freedom Rides, and jail-ins packed local prisons in Greensboro and throughout the South as conscientious objectors to Jim Crow policies placed their bodies and their lives on the line for liberation.

Indeed, Greensboro was a hub of activism throughout the explosive decade of the 1960s. As calls for Black political and economic empowerment grew towards the latter half of the decade, NC A&T students helped to ensure that Black colleges would remain central touchpoints in the freedom struggle. Activists gravitated to the city, launching independent and alternative schools, and creating new student-based organizations like the Student Organization for Black Unity (SOBU) that was founded on NC A&T's campus in 1969. SOBU carried forth the legacy of the Student Nonviolent Coordinating Committee (SNCC), which largely comprised students from HBCUs. SNCC's legacy loomed large over the movement, and as the organization became frayed, SOBU was created in part to safeguard the advancements that SNCC activists had fought so hard for.[10] Among those concerns and interests were the expansions of Black political power. NC A&T's very own alumnus, Henry Frye won a seat to the North Carolina Assembly in 1968, providing some hope that the era would usher in a new wave of Black politicians who would penetrate the citadel of conservatism and bigotry that existed at the state and local levels. According to historian William Chafe, the swell of activist energies that assembled in Greensboro transformed the city into "the center of Black Power in the South," yet the persistence and intractable nature of white supremacy represented significant challenges that threatened to delay, if not derail, the local movement for justice. Much like the rest of the country, "the white response in Greensboro," wrote Chafe, "was resistance, repression, and, subsequently, an effort to separate Black reformers from radicals." As significant as internal squabbles over class and idealism were, it was the external threat of the white power structure that made liberation so elusive for the Black community in Greensboro.[11]

---

10 David Lee Brown, "University to Be Site of First Conference for Black Students," *The A&T Register,* May 2, 1969, https://digital.library.ncat.edu/atregister/364; "Over 600 Attend SOBU Conference," *The A&T Register,* November 7, 1969, https://digital.library.ncat.edu/atregister/373.

11 Brown, "University to Be Site"; Chafe, *Civilities and Civil Rights,* 220, 247. For more on the legacy of independent Black schools during the Black Power movement and the relocation of Malcolm X Liberation University from Durham to Greensboro, see Russel Rickford, *We Are an African People: Independent Education, Black Power, and the Radical Imagination* (Oxford University Press, 2019).

The liberation movement ebbed and flowed in the decades that followed Greensboro's outburst of Black Power radicalism. Expansions in the Black middle class and the removal of de jure segregation laws provided a mirage of hope that was further buoyed by the rise of Black elected officials. However, it was also abundantly clear that systemic racism would not dissipate in Greensboro or throughout the country as Black neighborhoods remained marginalized and neglected, Black institutions such as HBCUs continued to endure historic underfunding that blocked their access to vital resources, and aggressive policing continued to plague Black neighborhoods and target African American leaders.[12] The latter unleashed one of the most violent episodes in the city as Klansmen attacked a peaceful march in 1979, resulting in the death of five activists. Two separate trials acquitted the shooters of any wrongdoing and failed to hold the Greensboro Police Department responsible for their failure to properly protect the marchers.[13] Despite these atrocities and setbacks, many Black citizens of Greensboro continued to place their faith in political progressivism and the expansion of American democracy. The movements towards social justice that arose from the city had largely emanated from Greensboro's two Black colleges that had drilled their students in idealism that bolstered Black youth's faith in the tenets of democracy and citizenship and their belief that these ideals were capable of reclamation and rehabilitation. While conviction in these principles provided the fuel for a moral movement that reshaped the political contours of America, it also increasingly identified the campus of NC A&T as a threat to the political status quo. Moving forward, those seeking to repress and dilute Black political power in the city increasingly saw NC A&T as an essential target.

---

12 Historian Martha Biondi documents the fact that Black colleges were more likely to sustain violence from local and state police and national guardsmen than students at predominately white institutions. This reality resulted in violent outbreaks and often murder at South Carolina State University, North Carolina A&T, Howard University, Voorhees College, Jackson State, Texas Southern, and Southern University. See Martha Biondi, *The Black Revolution on Campus* (University of California Press, 2012), 157. In August of 1972, GAPP organized a 'people's court' that heard a case against the Greensboro Police Department that was charged with several instances of police brutality against the Black community. The case recognized episodes of violence that were inflicted against A&T students and other Black citizens. See "Police Brutality Trial of the Greensboro Black Community," Greensboro Association of Poor People Papers, personal archive of Mr. Lewis Brandon.

13 For more on the impact and legacy of the Greensboro Massacre, see Aran Shetterly, *Morningside: The 1979 Greensboro Massacre and the Struggle for an American City's Soul* (Amistad, 2024) and Sally Avery Bermanzohn, *Through Survivors' Eyes: From the Sixties Through the Greensboro Massacre* (Vanderbilt University Press, 2003).

1 The Path Towards Partition: Gerrymandering the Nation's Largest Black College and the (In) Action that Ensued

The latter half of the 20th century saw most HBCUs in a state of flux. Black colleges entered into a new golden age of growth aided by Hollywood depictions of their unique campus culture. Spike Lee's film *School Daze* was the first on-screen film depiction of HBCUs and the Cosby Show spinoff *A Different World* helped to boost enrollment at HBCUs during the late 1980s and 90s.[14] As Black students registered in greater numbers at schools like NC A&T, the Reagan and Bush eras exacerbated political divisions in the country, a factor that was not lost on Black college students, many of whose families were victims of Reaganomics that slashed funding for vital programs that targeted under-resourced and impoverished communities.[15] NC A&T alumni Jesse Jackson, who was a significant player in the student protests of the 1960s, rose to political prominence and mounted two serious bids to secure the Democratic nomination for president in 1984 and 1988. NC A&T students not only rushed to support his campaign, but the fervor that Jackson's candidacy created also carried over into enthusiastic support for the candidacy of Harvey Gantt. Gantt, a Black politician from Charlotte, unsuccessfully challenged Jesse Helms for his Senate seat in 1990 and 1996 but his campaign injected life and heightened political awareness among Black youth in the state.[16]

---

14 Juan Cherry, "School Daze Stirs Emotions: If Black is Beautiful, What's the Issue?," *The A&T Register*, April 29, 1988, https://digital.library.ncat.edu/atregister/1096/.
15 Audrey L. Williams, "Beware of Reaganomics," *The A&T Register*, January 22, 1982, https://digital.library.ncat.edu/atregister/925/.
16 "Students Start Campaign Fund," *The A&T Register*, January 24, 1984, https://digital.library.ncat.edu/atregister/996/; Jamie C. Ruff, "More Power to Jesse Jackson," *The A&T Register*, March 23, 1984, https://digital.library.ncat.edu/atregister/1004/; James Etheridge, "Jackson Swings Through Triad; Advises Students to Vote," *The A&T Register*, April 27, 1984, https://digital.library.ncat.edu/atregister/1009/; Albert Spruill, "Jackson's Candidacy Offers Sense of Hope," *The A&T Register*, August 28, 1984, https://digital.library.ncat.edu/atregister/1010/; "Students, Faculty Debate Candidacy," *The A&T Register*, November 13, 1987, https://digital.library.ncat.edu/atregister/1084/; "Jackson to Address Commencement," *The A&T Register*, April 8, 1988, https://digital.library.ncat.edu/atregister/1094/; Rhonda Debnam, "Gantt Visits Greensboro," *The A&T Register*, September 21, 1990, https://digital.library.ncat.edu/atregister/1138/; Josephine Kerr, "Gantt Falls Short at Polls Regardless of Increased Aggie Voting Turnout," *The A&T Register*, November 15, 1996, https://digital.library.ncat.edu/atregister/1204/.

Although neither Jackson nor Gantt won their races, it was abundantly clear that NC A&T's campus, when united around a cause and a candidate, could play a significant role in driving and uplifting political agendas. In 2008, this trait dovetailed perfectly into the historic candidacy of Illinois senator Barack Obama, who convincingly won Guilford County by close to 60 % during his presidential run in 2008 and again for his re-election campaign in 2012. Once again, NC A&T students served as a major factor in tipping the scales towards a liberal and progressive agenda. By the end of Obama's second term in 2016, there were two things apparent to NC lawmakers. Conservative legislators throughout the state were well aware of NC A&T's legacy as a seedbed for activism, and any effort to subdue the political agency emanating from the Greensboro campus, that by 2014 had become the largest HBCU in the country, would call for decisive and aggressive action that targeted the institution—right down the middle.

Greensboro had been no stranger to the age-old political tactic of gerrymandering. Through this scheme, both conservative and liberal politicians have historically sought to gain leverage in specific communities by marginalizing their political foes, often with a scalpel-like precision. Perhaps the most absurd example of this in North Carolina was the infamous 12th congressional district that was reestablished and redrawn in 1992 in a serpentine fashion that created the only Black majority district in the state. The district, which included Greensboro, merged and simultaneously reduced the political power of the state's minorities.[17] Following a long run of progressive politics coming out of the city, state legislators took aim at Greensboro once again in 2010. During that year, Republicans took hold of both houses of the state legislature for the first time since 1898, which ironically was the year that white conservative forces violently seized control of the state in order to repress Black political mobility.[18] Republicans also took control of redistricting, thanks in part to a state law that denies the governor the ability to veto any changes made to election maps. Democratic Governor Bev

---

[17] For more on the history and legacy of the North Carolina 12th Congressional District see Gerald L. Ingalls and Toby Moore, "The Present and Future of Racial Gerrymandering: Evidence from North Carolina's 12th Congressional District," *Southeastern Geographer* 35, no. 1 (1995): 58–74, https://dx.doi.org/10.1353/sgo.1995.0009.

[18] The Wilmington Massacre was a seminal moment in the rise of white terrorism during the Nadir. Wilmington, North Carolina is located 200 miles from Greensboro and centered on the southern coast of the state. By the late 19th century, racial violence had become epidemic throughout the South and whatever form of Black political power that existed throughout the region was violently eliminated through the actions of vigilante groups and through the acts of conservative legislators who worked in tandem to reassert white supremacy as the law of the land. For more on the Wilmington Massacre see David Zucchino, *Wilmington's Lie: The Murderous Coup of 1898 and the Rise of White Supremacy* (Grove Press, 2021).

Purdue was rendered powerless as members of the GOP set their sights on Guilford County and conspired a plan to weaken Black political power in the city that had been a consistent source for militancy and mobilization.

Laurel Street is a major artery that runs through the heart of NC A&T's campus. The university experienced a meteoric rise in student population in the first decade of the 21st century which brought the construction of new dorms and facilities on both sides of the campus thoroughfare. In 1969, the university had come under fire from local police and national guardsmen who shot up the campus and drove tanks down Laurel Street following student protests against authoritarian control at a local high school. Conservative white legislators sought to suppress social upheaval coming out of NC A&T's campus in the 1960s by invading the university.[19] By 2010, their focus had shifted to finding new ways to bottle up the threat of political mobilization that the university and its students posed. Gerrymandering became a perfect scheme to subtly enforce their conservative agenda. Aggressively reshaping the political district to produce an outcome in the electorate that favored and empowered the GOP was far less heavy handed than older intimidation tactics of deploying white mobs to uphold Jim Crow policies or sending tanks and soldiers down Laurel Street to terrorize a campus that had long been a force for social and political change in the city and throughout the state. In 2016, in the quiet backrooms of Raleigh and with the silent stroke of a pen, conservative lawmakers attacked the Greensboro campus with the same animus and derision as their predecessors who saw the campus as a threat to the status quo. Their actions would not go unnoticed or unaddressed.

In 2013, the United States Supreme Court rendered a decision in the case of *Shelby v. Holder.* Its ruling added weight to the nefarious actions of North Carolina's state legislators by removing pre-clearance as a provision of the 1965 Voting Rights Act. Under this ruling, states no longer had to receive consent from the federal government in order to make sure changes they made to their voting rights laws did not violate the civil rights of their citizens. With these protections removed, governing bodies such as the North Carolina legislature had an open lane to engage in voter suppression and redraw districts along racial and partisan lines. The Obama administration pushed back against these rulings as much as it could. "This law, we think, will have a disproportionate negative impact on minor-

---

19 For more on the National Guard and local police invasion of A&T's campus in 1969, see North Carolina Advisory Committee to the U.S. Commission on Civil Rights, *"Trouble in Greensboro: A Report of an Open Meeting concerning Disturbances at Dudley High School and North Carolina A&T State University,"* March 1970, 14, https://www2.law.umaryland.edu/marshall/usccr/documents/cr12t75.pdf; "650 Troops Sweep A&T," *Greensboro Daily News*, May 23, 1969; Chafe, *Civilities and Civil Rights*, 185–186.

ity voters," declared acting United States attorney general Eric Holder. "We've looked at these laws across the country. They have a disproportionate negative impact on people who are young, people of color, people who are poor and I think at a minimum have a partisan basis to them." For the next decade, the state would engage in a back-and-forth chess match, with conservatives and progressives countering each other's moves in court. While this was taking place, their efforts had slowly awakened a sleeping giant embodied within the NC A&T student body.[20]

In the same year that the Supreme Court gutted the Voting Rights Act via *Shelby v. Holder*, a young student by the name of Vashti Hinton-Smith arrived as a freshman on the campus of NC A&T. Admittedly, she was not intimately familiar with the long legacy for civil rights that defined the campus that she now called home. She arrived as a marketing major in the College of Business but that, too, was about to change. "And so my freshman year, I took a class with a man named Derick Smith," she recalled. "And this was right after North Carolina had passed the voter ID law. And he's like on the table going off about this voter ID law that's going to restrict early voting, get rid of same day registration, also making it impossible for college students to vote, they're going to need a voter ID. And so he's literally standing on top of the desk, like going off. And I'm like what is happening right now? I felt like something out of *A Different World* or something. And so it was really, I don't say it was cool, but it woke me up."[21]

While Hinton-Smith's recall to the prime-time television show showed its influence and reach for a new generation, it also highlighted the fact that the vibrancy and militancy of the HBCU space that the show attempted to capture, interpret, and broadcast to the world was still very much alive and well at NC A&T. "And so immediately, my interest was piqued," remembered Hinton-Smith. "I can say weeks later, I went and changed my major to political science. And I took every single one of his classes that I could, and I absorbed it all."[22] Professor Derick Smith, who was himself a graduate of Fayetteville State, an HBCU located in the eastern portion of North Carolina, had effectively engaged in the second curriculum that set HBCUs apart as critical sources for the politicization and mobilization of Black youth against the forces of bigotry and intolerance. Hinton-Smith not only changed her major, but she became active in a new student movement against the gerrymandering of the campus and the attempts to suppress the Black vote in Greensboro and beyond. She joined the North Carolina state chapter of Common Cause, a watchdog and advocacy group with chapters across the country whose

20 "NC Republicans Vow to Fight US DOJ Over Voter Laws," *The A&T Register*, October 2, 2013.
21 Vashti Hinton-Smith (former A&T student), interviewed by Seamus Heady, July 19, 2023.
22 Vashti Hinton-Smith, interviewed by Seamus Heady, July 19, 2023.

own tagline states they are dedicated to "holding power accountable" and "upholding the core values of American democracy."[23] Students at NC A&T and all HBCUs had been engaged in that mission since their founding. While Hinton-Smith knew hardly anything about NC A&T prior to her enrollment in 2013, she quickly received a crash course as to why Black colleges were essential to advancing the freedom dreams of Black people in America.

Professor Smith's influence did not stop with Hinton-Smith's recruitment to the cause. Also arriving on NC A&T's campus in 2015 was a student by the name of Nikolaus Knight who had originally come to the university to study theater but had quickly gravitated towards the powerful and timely instruction being provided by the Political Science Department. Knight, a resident of Greensboro, came from a long line of local activists, and his migration over to political science seemed like a natural transition. Derick Smith's lectures on contemporary issues struck a nerve and emboldened students like Knight not to simply digest lessons on how government is structured, but to see themselves as the levers upon which government can and should be changed to justly serve the people. "He mentioned just teaching us about what gerrymandering is, how it was used as a political strategy," recalled Knight. "We were listening to him talk about it. And we had heard that a year prior to us hearing it from him, that they had done this on our campus."[24] As Smith poured race consciousness, cultural nationalism, and idealism into his students, he was utilizing the same second curriculum that had powered previous social movements originating out of Black colleges. Smith's instruction was both revelatory and a catalyst for civic engagement for Knight and his peers. "We began to learn about the gerrymandering," Knight recalled. "And once we learned about it, and students began to talk with each other about it, some of us began working with some training organizations."[25]

Former NC A&T student Tylik McMillan had a similar experience. However, unlike Hinton-Smith and Knight, McMillan was acutely aware of and specifically drawn to the historic campus because of its legacy and reputation as an incubator for activism. He eagerly enrolled as a freshman in 2015, coming to Greensboro with the spirit of activism already in his blood. McMillan had previously worked with the National Action Network and received direct tutelage from nationally

---

23 Common Cause, "Common Cause: Holding Power Accountable," https://actionnetwork.org/groups/common-cause-holding-power-accountable. Notably, Hinton-Smith and her peers are featured on the cover of this book, at an on-campus press conference on March 26, 2019, the day the United States Supreme Court heard oral arguments in Common Cause-North Carolina's partisan gerrymandering challenge in Rucho v. Common Cause.
24 Nikolaus Knight (former A&T student), interviewed by Jonathan Becker, October 21, 2024.
25 Nikolaus Knight, interviewed by Jonathan Becker, October 21, 2024.

known civil rights activist Rev. Al Sharpton. "I always knew I wanted to come to A&T," he recalled. "Not only because of Reverend Jesse Jackson and the history of NC A&T that sparked the sit-in movement in 1960 ... but it was just a rich history that this campus had with civil rights. With Reverend Sharpton being a mentor of mine, and Reverend Jesse Jackson being a mentor of his, it was like it perfectly aligned."[26] As much as it seemed as though McMillan was born for the moment, students don't head off to college with designs of majoring in dissent. Nevertheless, Black students like McMillan enrolled at HBCUs have often carried the inescapable burden of using their intellectual talents and skills that they have honed while attending schools like NC A&T to join in the long struggle for Black liberation. For McMillan and his peers, that massive challenge was finding a way to thwart Republican efforts to divide and dilute the political power of the largest HBCU in the country.

By 2016, (Figure 4) the fight to reverse the redistricting and partition of NC A&T's campus had reached a fever pitch. Also angering students were changes to voter ID laws and efforts to shut down provisions for same-day registration, all of which directly impacted students. While all these efforts were pernicious attempts to suppress young Black voters, it was the redistricting issue that appeared to strike the biggest nerve. As a young student just settling in, McMillan recalled the consternation and confusion that the gerrymandering efforts unleashed. "I think we have this understanding that politicians should not choose their voters, but voters should choose their politicians," declared McMillan. "We were talking about the campus being split down the middle. We were targeted."[27] That same year, the U.S. District Court for the Middle District of North Carolina agreed, ruling that the partitions of the 1st and 12th congressional districts along clear racial lines were unconstitutional. The United States Supreme Court upheld that ruling and informed state legislators that they were required to redraw the electoral map of the district. What happened next fooled no one. Whatever joy NC A&T students felt from this ruling was quickly dashed as they received a hard lesson in the creative and malleable nature of white supremacy and the long tradition of voter suppression.[28]

Republican legislators in North Carolina moved quickly to absorb and deflect the ruling of the high court, unashamedly declaring that their goal was to abandon

---

26 Tylik McMillan (former A&T student), interviewed by Seamus Heady, July 18, 2023.

27 Tylik McMillan, interviewed by Seamus Heady, July 18, 2023.

28 For more on the history of *Cooper v. Harris* that ruled that racial gerrymandering was unconstitutional in the state of North Carolina, see Democracy Docket, "The Decade-Long Fight Against Racial Gerrymandering," May 6, 2021, https://www.democracydocket.com/analysis/the-decade-long-fight-against-racial-gerrymandering/.

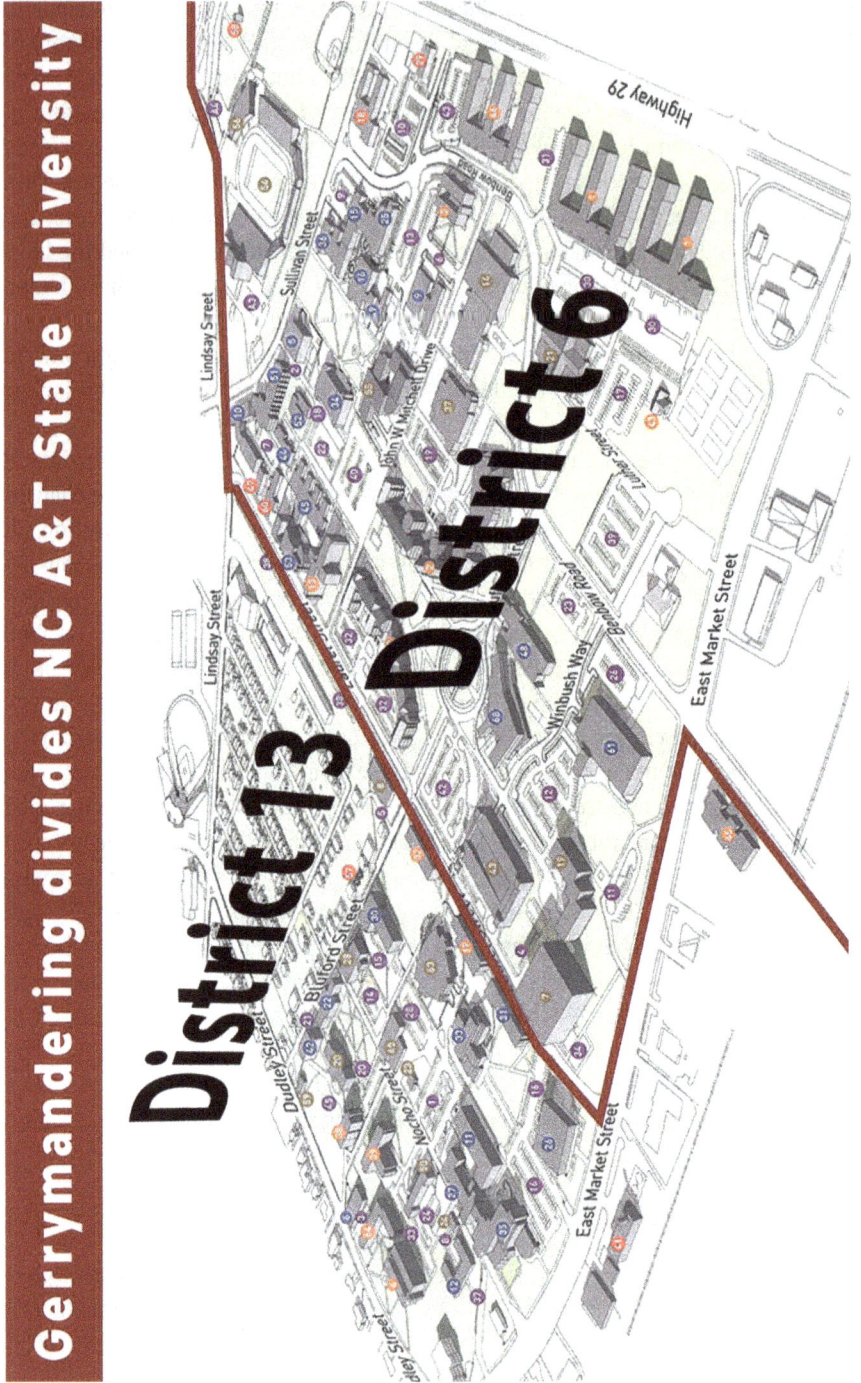

Figure 4: Image of a Common Cause poster sign depicting the North Carolina A&T gerrymander down the middle of campus along Laurel Street. Photo courtesy of Common Cause North Carolina.

racial gerrymandering in favor of partisan gerrymandering. North Carolina State Representative David Lewis became a ringleader in the political circus that was unfolding. "I acknowledge freely that this is a political gerrymander," declared Lewis. Representing Harnett County and the interests of his party, Lewis continued with an explicit description of the power grab to come. "I propose that we draw the map to give a partisan advantage to 10 Republicans and 3 Democrats, because I do not believe it's possible to draw a map with 11 Republicans and 2 Democrats."[29] Lewis' articulation of the GOP effort sent a clear message, and the brash move made two things abundantly clear. The first was that Republicans in the General Assembly were fully committed to use gerrymandering as a tool to leverage and exploit their political power for their own gain. Second was the fact that they still viewed the largest HBCU in the country as a focal point in their efforts to fracture and weaken the Black vote in Guilford County, a move that would reverberate across the Tar Heel state and have a serious impact on local, state, and national elections. NC A&T students concretely understood the racist ramifications of the GOP's actions, despite its disingenuous efforts to describe them as a partisan move rather than a racial one. During a press conference that highlighted the growing resistance on campus to the GOP's moves, NC A&T student Aleecia Sutton astutely observed, "With this university being split into two congressional districts, it undermines and diminishes its political influence and its lobbying power."[30]

The NC A&T student body raised various options to protest the gerrymandering of campus. Long a stalwart of campus activism and mobilization, the Divine 9 organizations, composed of nine historically Black national fraternities and sororities, marshalled their resources to raise political consciousness concerning voter suppression. The 'stroll to the polls' initiative invoked the long tradition and ritual of 'party strolling' for which so many Divine 9 organizations are known. In doing so, they encouraged their members to get out the vote in order to counter voter suppression tactics. Other historic Black institutions responded to the call as well. Black churches across the country have always been pillars of resistance against white supremacy and attempts to politically marginalize the Black community. In Greensboro, several Black churches joined the fight, promoting their own get-out-the-vote campaign that was coined 'souls to the polls.' Black churches were

---

29 "NC Republicans Admit to Partisan Gerrymandering (Part 1)," February 16, 2016, posted October 16, 2017, by Common Cause NC, YouTube, 0:15, https://www.youtube.com/watch?v=scpfpZ-pL8Q.
30 "NC A&T Students Speak Out on Campus Gerrymandering," posted March 22, 2016, by Common Cause NC, YouTube Video, 2:37, https://www.youtube.com/watch?v=01zyvZxY3u8.

no stranger to joining forces with NC A&T students in the long struggle for Black liberation, particularly in the Black communities that surrounded campus that served as the church homes for both students and alumni that lived in the city. "In the past, churches have stopped services to take their entire congregation to voting locations," wrote Allison Gilmore, editor of the NC A&T student newspaper. "Pastors figured if they could get people to come to worship God, they could get them to the polls, too."[31]

As the push to counter voter suppression trudged onward, the Black community in Greensboro increasingly leaned upon each other to chip away at this new surge of aggression coming from political conservatives. NC A&T students couched their position in terms that were familiar with the marginalized communities that they knew so well—the new tactics emerging from the GOP were indeed old strategies, familiar rhetoric, and similar outcomes. Confronting and defeating these measures would take a consolidated and determined community that included traditional sources such as the Black church. But calls for consolidation were careful to make sure that nontraditional sources of protests were not alienated. "Souls to the Polls is not an initiative to only get Christians to vote but rather for all people who believe in the justice system," wrote Gilmore. "Sponsors of the event include churches in the east Greensboro area and the NAACP."[32] As NC A&T students consulted with their traditional allies, they ultimately found new and perhaps unexpected ones in the court system.

Historically, African Americans have always been leery of court rulings dealing with race and the removal of social and political barriers. Indeed, emerging out of slavery, Black folks placed great trust in the judicial system and our nation's system of checks and balances with the hope that these institutions would expand and uphold democracy and justice for all. The result was a pendulum that moved very quickly in establishing swelling optimism in our nation's Reconstruction Amendments that abolished slavery, brought millions of formerly enslaved under the banner of citizenship, and enshrined voting rights for Black men. This trust was utterly dashed with the deliberate undermining of the Reconstruction era that saw America retreat from all of these promises as Jim Crow was codified and crystallized as a fixture of American life and white terrorism went virtually unchecked, wreaking havoc in the lives of Black people. Repeatedly the high courts in America either completely ignored these developments or were complicit in advancing systems of inequality. Although by the mid-20th century, the civil

---

31 Allison Gilmore, "Voter Suppression Hinders Progression of Black Community," *The A&T Register,* October 16, 2018, https://ncatregister.com/14329/the-word/voter-suppression-hinders-progression-of-black-community/.
32 Gilmore, "Voter Suppression."

rights movement had created the necessary pressure to create a thin veneer of justice, many African Americans concretely understood that the system could at any
moment provide either loopholes or full-blown pathways towards their disfranchisement and oppression. Nothing about the court cases surrounding voter suppression in the early 21st century signaled anything different for Black people. The
legal cases that emerged yet again resembled a pendulum that vacillated between
rulings on gerrymandering and redistricting, with cases often being swung back
and forth depending on the political makeup of the court and the justices that
held the fate of the Black community and NC A&T's campus in their hands.

With the position of the courts uncertain and the wheels of justice grinding
ever so slowly, NC A&T students took up lobbying and consolidating their efforts
with external allies. Common Cause became a major source of support as the campus came under attack. Much like Hinton-Smith, who gravitated towards the non-
partisan organization in 2013, Braxton Brewington arrived on campus as a freshman (one year later) and soon infused the intellectual talents he was honing at
NC A&T into the organization that was playing a vital role in the fight against gerrymandering. Brewington lamented the scenario of painstakingly waiting for the
litigation to proceed and found inspiration and an outlet for his talents in the lobbying efforts being employed by Common Cause. Launching a public campaign on
campus to raise awareness of what was taking place became Brewington's mission. "We needed to draw attention to this," he recalled. "Like, can we somehow
politicize this as much as possible? So, part of it was just, like, letting everyone
know. So, we had a lot of events. You know, we did the chalk on the ground,
and we did press. And then, also, a lot of it was just, like, let's just increase
voter turnout."[33] Brewington also became a standout spokesperson on behalf of
Common Cause and his fellow Aggies who were being targeted and victimized
by Republican state lawmakers. On October 17, 2017, Common Cause held a
press conference in Raleigh where Brewington took to the podium to publicly
speak truth to power and to call for transparency and action. "Out of all the places
in Greensboro to separate the districts, lawmakers chose the middle of NC A&T,
the largest public HBCU in the nation," he announced:

> This is not only an unconstitutional gerrymandering, but it's an attack on our campus. Voting
> is the most basic way to make your voice heard, to stand up for what you believe in, and let
> politicians know what issues you care about. And when that power, when that right, when
> that fundamental integrity is stripped, especially from students of color achieving higher ed-
> ucation, that is suppression.[34]

---

33 Braxton Brewington (former A&T student), interviewed by Jonathan Becker, October 31, 2024.
34 Braxton Brewington, "NC A&T Students Speak Out Against Gerrymandering,"

Brewington and his peers were engaged in a public battle against GOP lawmakers in defense of NC A&T. While they were bolstered by the support of community institutions and organizations which were equally appalled by the move to divide the campus, students were often left discouraged by the absence of the ally they had hoped to count on the most during their confrontation with the state —NC A&T's administrative leadership.

In his brilliant study entitled *The Campus Color Line: College Presidents and the Struggle for Black Freedom*, historian Eddie Cole astutely notes that "desegregation, equal educational and employment opportunity, fair housing, free speech, economic disparities—were intertwined with higher education. Therefore, the college presidency is a prism through which to disclose how colleges and universities have challenged or preserved the many enduring forms of anti-Black racism in the United States."[35] Cole's assessment is spot on and few institutions in America have directly impacted policy and popular culture as much as our nation's colleges. Missing from Cole's list was the significant role that higher education has played in shaping and reshaping our fundamental understanding and deployment of democratic principles. For Black colleges, the ability to serve as a spear tip in the fight to preserve and expand American democracy has largely hinged upon the skilled and deft way in which university leaders have approached the complexities that surround their jobs. Throughout the 19th and 20th centuries, Black college presidents, dependent upon private and public funding, walked a tightrope regarding the social and political environment they cultivated for their students. The men and women who led HBCUs were expected to remain largely apolitical and dispassionate, particularly as it related to racial politics.

Yet behind closed doors, Black college presidents played an instrumental role in administering a second curriculum that directly oversaw an active lecture circuit that placed outspoken leaders and activists before their student body, as well as hiring faculty who were militant in their political beliefs and created space for radical mentorship for students who found their voices in the broader fight for liberation. This was the cat-and-mouse game played by HBCU administrators at the height of the civil rights movement that made the freedom struggle's emergence from institutions such as NC A&T possible. But that was during the Jim Crow era. Few Black college students enrolling at NC A&T in the 21st century could have ever imagined that administrators overseeing a school that proudly touted its legacy as birthplace of the sit-in movement would fall under the

press conference, October 17, 2017. Posted October 17, 2017 by Common Cause NC, Facebook, 2:19, https://www.facebook.com/CommonCauseNorthCarolina/videos/10155548174531223/.
35 Eddie Cole, *The Campus Color Line: College Presidents and the Struggle for Black Freedom* (Princeton University Press, 2020), 4.

same constraints and hesitancies as its predecessors. As students sought direction and support in their fight against voter suppression, there was concern that NC A&T's administration did not provide the full-throated endorsement and support for their actions in the way they had originally hoped.

Dr. Harold Martin was appointed Chancellor of NC A&T in 2009, four years prior to the GOP's all-out assault on voting rights in the state that ultimately targeted the Greensboro campus. As an alumnus of NC A&T, Martin was intimately familiar with NC A&T's legacy for activism, having arrived on campus as a student a few months after the campus was invaded by national guardsmen in May of 1969. Nevertheless, the responsibilities and weight of being Chancellor for the largest HBCU in the nation that was beholden to the state of North Carolina for its funding seemed to catch up with Martin, who tried his best to navigate the tense situation that was brewing. Regardless of his intentions for handling the dilemma, student activists felt as though he and other administrators weren't doing enough—a common view of previous HBCU student activists who often saw administrators as a roadblock to their agenda. Commenting on this generational and seemingly ideological divide, Brewington recalled,

> I think once we got an analysis that made sense, we were like, well, wait a minute, the university is not doing its part, because why is the university allowing it to be split? And they haven't said anything. So, we were, like, pressuring them to make a public statement, which we're like, the law is on your side here. Like, you know, you should be saying this is diluting the voting power of your students. This is anti-democratic.[36]

From the perspective of Brewington and his peers, students seemed to have a plethora of ideas that they believed could effectively counter Republican lawmakers' efforts to undermine the political power of the campus, while campus administrators had none. According to Brewington, not only did administrators fail to come to the table with opinions on how to resist, but they also proceeded to deter and delay students' opposition plans. One such plan called for coordinated busing routes to take students to the polls to vote. "And we had a bus system that took you all around campus," recalled Brewington. "And we were like, why don't we have a bus that takes you to a polling place? Like, the university doesn't need to tell people who to vote for, just, like, take them to the polls." However, getting students back and forth to the polls was something that at least initially the university moved very slowly on, much to the disdain of Brewington and his comrades. Student activists became caught up in the campus bureaucracy and what seemed like an endless cycle of deferral. The students were sent to one office

---

36 Braxton Brewington, interviewed by Jonathan Becker, October 31, 2024.

after the other, and never given a straight answer on how to address the problem or even a notion that the administration seemed to care about the partition of the campus in the same way that many of the students did. In one particular meeting, Brewington recalled, "we were in the chancellor's office, and they kept telling us that they couldn't afford it, or it was excuse after excuse after excuse."[37]

The division of the campus and the suppression of young Aggies was clearly a serious situation that Brewington cared deeply about. When the university suggested that the main deterrence was cost, Brewington informed campus administrators that he would pay for it out of his own pocket which, as a struggling college student, wasn't very deep at all. But by this time, Brewington's passion and commitment to the cause were at a point of no return and his primary hope was that the university would get behind the students with equal fervor, or at the very least channel the spirit of activism and righteous idealism that made the institution a critical and celebrated launching point for the modern civil rights movement. "When I offered to pay for it, I think they realized how serious I was, and probably, looking back, that would've been, like, a really bad look," recalled Brewington. "Then they were like, hey, we found some money. And so then they paid for buses. Then they made it a thing, and it was like, get on the A&T bus." Campus administrators' delayed response to creating a busing campaign was disappointing to the students, who were deeply engaged in the fight. Moreover, for students who were well aware of NC A&T's legacy as an incubator for activism, there was a growing sense of betrayal. "I mean, when you tour the campus, they show you bullet holes at the Scott Hall memorial," noted Brewington.

> They show you bullet holes, and you meet the sole living survivor of the NC A&T Four at the breakfast every year. And so, it felt disingenuous for the university to hide behind this history. So I don't know. I think the legacy of A&T both implored us to demand better of the university, but also gave them a shield to hide behind.[38]

Nikolaus Knight was similarly disenchanted by the failure of NC A&T's administration to resist the division of its campus. According to Knight, students not only saw the gerrymandering of the campus as a political stunt, but they also saw it as "evil." Feeling morally violated, students hoped that the administration who had accepted the charge to lead the university and to care for its undergraduates would either put up a direct fight with the political forces assaulting the university, or at least find clandestine ways to support students. Previous NC A&T administrations had employed a variety of schemes and tactics to facilitate the Sit-In

37 Braxton Brewington, interviewed by Jonathan Becker, October 31, 2024.
38 Braxton Brewington, interviewed by Jonathan Becker, October 31, 2024.

movement and Black Power movement during the struggle for liberation in the 1960s and 70s. As Knight saw it, it wasn't as though NC A&T students did not understand the systemic nature of the voter suppression. For Knight and his peers, it was more an issue of expecting the administration to offer some kernel of support or even clandestine advice on how to resist the malicious attempts to disenfranchise students attending the largest HBCU in the nation. "We began to look at these things, like tier by tier," recalled Knight. "And then we also began to point fingers at the UNC Board of Governors at the time, and we pushed back against the university. We wrote an entire statement demanding that the university host or hold a press conference, a press conference stating what's happening, and then also stating that what's happening is racist."[39]

Knight's recollection of the meetings that took place with the chancellor's cabinet was similar to Brewington's. As Knight observed, NC A&T administrators were motivated by self-preservation. Protection of one's job and livelihood were natural impulses that defined the Black experience in America that had also sidelined previous generations of Black folks from becoming more directly involved in a variety of movements for social justice. And much like the historic tensions that often brewed between the young and the old, whatever tacit support was being offered by Chancellor Martin's administration felt insufficient given the pressing nature of the "evil" to which students were being subjected. "I remember specifically when we had a meeting with the chancellor in his cabinet," recalled Knight.

> And they sat down with us and said, look, you know if we say that what's happening here is racist, if we use that terminology and we use that language, someone from the UNC Board of Governors, who might be playing golf with this man [Martin], or playing golf with the folks that drew those lines could potentially gut us, gut our funding, you know.

Much as with Brewington, the chancellor's cabinet attempt to placate the racist forces dividing the campus in order to preserve funding relationships not only failed to register as a sufficient response, but it also felt like a betrayal of the activist branding that the university proudly marketed and displayed. "We heard all of that, and we were like this is A&T, you know," recalled Knight. "Just remember that this is still the school that has a statue of the A&T Four prominently displayed on its campus."[40] For Knight, Brewington, and their peers, whatever quiet, backroom professions of solidarity the Martin administration was making to show support, paled in comparison with the public endorsement that they had hoped for but were being regrettably denied.

---

39 Nikolaus Knight, interviewed by Jonathan Becker, October 21, 2024.
40 Nikolaus Knight, interviewed by Jonathan Becker, October 21, 2024.

Nevertheless, throughout the ordeal that students experienced from voter suppression, the second curriculum thrived at NC A&T and faculty members were able to carve out precious space to foster dialogue and resistance. At the height of the movement against gerrymandering, students had given faculty member Derick Smith the nickname 'The People's Professor,' a designation that fully illustrated their love for and admiration of an instructor who stood atop tabletops to boldly declare the evils of the campus being targeted for voter suppression. Also standing in solidarity with the students was Professor James Steele, a faculty member in the Political Science Department who had been at the university for more than 20 years. Both professors not only encouraged students to use their voices in that crucial moment, but also gave the time-honored and student-cherished provision of extra credit for students using the unfortunate occasion as a laboratory for dissent. "We would hold meetings in the classrooms after classes were over," remembered Knight. "So going to their office, bringing them papers, and they helped us to dissect what the language was saying, what the numbers were saying, what the data was saying. They helped us out with a lot of that, the research side of it, and then helping us put language to it, to tell the story."[41] The traditions of radical mentorship in the midst of oppression had always been the strongest legacy of Black colleges. As the 21st century unfolded and white supremacist actions had yet again targeted the Black community and Black institutions, it was the coordinated and collective response emerging from HBCUs that proved the vitality of the second curriculum as a primary force of resistance.

2 Road to Redemption: How Tragedy, Triumph, and Transition Have Reshaped the Campus of North Carolina NC A&T

As was the case in previous moments of racism targeting the campus of NC A&T, the mobilization and deployment of student activism proved effective in the fight against voter suppression. It was abundantly clear that the Greensboro campus had been targeted and deliberately partitioned along partisan as well as racial lines. The early 2000s rendered several tangible victories that may have caused Republican legislators to set their sights on the campus. In 2008, Senator Barack Obama secured a victory on the national stage, becoming the first Black president in the history of the United States. Students at NC A&T and at HBCUs across the

---

41 Nikolaus Knight, interviewed by Jonathan Becker, October 21, 2024.

nation enthusiastically rushed to volunteer for his campaign and to cast their votes in his favor. NC A&T's meteoric rise in student population began around the same time, and the university's brand had been publicly lifted on a national stage through successive appearances and victories in a nationally televised bowl game that, beginning in 2015, pitted the nation's two top HBCU football programs against each other in a contest that took place in Atlanta. As NC A&T increasingly found its way into the national limelight and friendly debates amongst Black people concerning which was the top HBCU in the nation, so too did GOP lawmakers in North Carolina, who controlled the campus' purse strings, find reasons to highlight and target the historic campus for repression.[42]

The voter suppression and division of NC A&T's campus came to an end in 2019. In that year, a three-judge Superior Court panel heard the case *Harper v. Hall* and ruled that the will of the people was undermined by the establishment of partisan-based gerrymandering that skewed political districts in favor of conservatives. "For nearly a decade, Republicans have forced the people of North Carolina to vote in districts that were manipulated for their own partisan advantage," declared former United States Attorney General Eric Holder. "Now—finally—the era of Republican gerrymandering in the state is coming to an end."[43] Yet in that same year, another three-judge Superior Court panel ultimately ruled that it was far too close to the 2020 elections to order that the congressional maps be immediately redrawn in a way that was just and unbiased. The fight over redrawing districts in North Carolina ultimately reached the United States Supreme Court in *Rucho v. Common Cause* where the justices concluded that the fight was far too partisan for them to get involved, and thus threw the decision back down to the state courts to establish an appropriate approach for redistricting claims. The ultimate victory of reuniting the campus was bittersweet. Students at NC A&T still confronted challenges concerning voter ID, attempts to remove NC A&T's on-campus polling site, and the harsh reality that the Republican-controlled state legislator continued to weaponize gerrymandering by redrawing district lines to favor themselves across the entire state. Nevertheless, as the campus

42 Isaiah George, "An HBCU Bowl Game Wins Out Over NCAA Playoffs," *Andscape*, December 12, 2018, https://andscape.com/features/an-hbcu-bowl-game-wins-out-over-ncaa-playoffs/; Nick Anderson, "Some Large HBCUs are Getting Larger. The Biggest is North Carolina A&T," *The Washington Post*, February 11, 2022, https://www.washingtonpost.com/education/2022/02/11/ncat-enrollment-hbcus/.

43 Gary D. Robertson, "North Carolina Judges Block Current Congressional Map," *Associated Press*, October 28, 2019, https://apnews.com/article/ebe3e179326d41daa5f8da577300299d.

moved into a new decade, there were significant triumphs to celebrate—that even included the embattled Martin administration.[44]

Over the course of the prolonged battles over voter suppression, student activists held the Martin administration at arm's length. While some conceded that the administration was in a difficult position and unable to provide the type of public support that students were looking for, others remained steadfast in their belief that the university could have and should have done more to denounce the targeting of the campus by hostile political forces. The collective history of HBCUs has consistently illustrated the resolve certain college administrators found to subtly advance the freedom dreams of Black youth. This often took place while being confronted with immense political pressure to succumb to the demands of hostile governing bodies that sought to undermine the mission of the institution. For Black colleges in America, that mission has included providing space for youth to be equipped with the intellectual tools to deconstruct bigotry, hatred, and intolerance that marginalized the lives of African Americans. When the sit-ins emerged at A&T in 1960, university president Warmoth T. Gibbs faced intense demands to shut down the protests and bring his students to heel. He famously retorted that "we teach our students how to think, not what to think."[45] He was subsequently fired from his position but left the institution with his head held high, knowing that his actions aided his students in launching a movement that would radically reshape American democracy and civil rights for millions of people who had been denied these rights and freedoms for far too long. The questions confronting the administration of Chancellor Harold Martin were how his administration would answer this new challenge and whether his actions would in any way mirror the courageous steps taken by his predecessor, President Gibbs.

The answers provided a modicum of redemption for the Martin administration. After years of being silently ridiculed by student activists who believed he was not living up to the Aggie legacy as a forbearer for justice, Martin salvaged his reputation by taking key steps that insured that NC A&T would continue to be a space that cultivated and embraced the next generation of activists who could hone their skills and talents for the purpose of forging a more just society. Like other Black college students, young Aggies had always been able to lean upon interstitial spaces such as classrooms and office hours of faculty who endeared themselves to their causes. Beginning in 2020, the Martin administration ensured

44 Michael Wines, "State Court Bars Using North Carolina House Map in 2020 Elections," *New York Times*, October 28, 2019, https://www.nytimes.com/2019/10/28/us/north-carolina-gerrymander-maps.html.

45 Bruce Lambert, "Warmoth T. Gibbs, 101, Educator Who Backed Civil Rights Protests," *New York Times*, April 22, 1993.

that these spaces would become more formal for the growing student population that called NC A&T home. In that year, the campus established the Office of Leadership and Civic Engagement, whose purpose was to expressly link NC A&T students with organizations engaged in the work of preserving and expanding democracy and to apprise students of their voting rights. The office continues to promote the motto and mission of "developing your capacity to change the world." In 2021, the Martin administration moved forward with the establishment of a Center of Excellence for Social Justice (CESJ). The CESJ was funded in part by a generous donation from philanthropist McKenzie Scott, and quickly secured major funding from other private donors and foundations. These private gifts ensured that the center would move forward in its goals to advance NC A&T's enduring commitment to uplifting civil and human rights through the creation of various campus and community-based programs.[46]

Chancellor Harold Martin retired from the university in the spring of 2024; however, these administrative moves largely created through his vision and desire to study and improve the human condition demonstrated that he was cut from the same cloth as those students who led the charge to defend the campus against those who sought to divide it for their political gain. His path to achieve these ends was circuitous, as is often the case for those who must navigate and balance the burdens and expectations of leadership. Nevertheless, Martin's redemption created valuable space that continues to pour elements of leadership, race consciousness, and idealism into the next generation of Aggie activists. In recent years, both the Office of Leadership and Civic Engagement and the CESJ have worked to establish programming that bolsters the identity of their students as civic actors and change agents while also deepening the university's ties with civic organizations in the community that are dedicated to democracy and social justice for all.

The fallout from the political battles over gerrymandering has unquestionably reshaped the makeup of the institution, and political threats to challenge the legitimacy and longevity of NC A&T and the Black community that surround it remain ever present. The history of the United States bears out the painful truth that the road to democracy for African Americans has been neither linear nor easy. Nor has that journey ever been fully achieved. With the gutting of the 1965 Voting Rights Act, the threat of gerrymandering, and a host of other political maneuvers meant to suppress the Black vote, the road remains cluttered with a variety of ob-

---

46 Jamille Whitlow, "N.C. A&T OSD Motivates Students to Vote," *The A&T Register,* October 6, 2020, https://ncatregister.com/17615/the-yard/n-c-at-osd-motivates-students-to-vote/; Markita C. Rowe, "N.C. A&T Establishes Center of Excellence for Social Justice," *Aggie Newsroom,* September 21, 2023, https://www.ncat.edu/news/2023/09/social-justice-center-established.php.

stacles intended to prolong and negate the full political empowerment of historically marginalized communities. Since 1837, Black colleges have served as shelters in a time of storm. Not only have they provided an enclave where Black youth were protected from absorbing messages from the dominant society that were intended to reinforce second-class citizenship and inferiority, but they also provided the most fertile ground for resistance, advocacy, and mobilization. When Dr. Harold Trigg spoke at NC A&T in 1934, he had no way of looking down the corridors of time to see that African Americans would still be encountering the same hostilities that defined the Black experience during the early 20th century. But his counsel for Black educators to remain vigilant in their work in order to advance the freedom dreams of those youth under their charge continues to be prescient and relevant. If this grand American experiment and the democratic ideals that it has professed but rarely practiced are to survive for future generations, then not only must it be open to healing and rehabilitation, but educators within our most valued and treasured institutions must also embrace Trigg's timeless message that "the future of the nation lies in the hands of the boys and girls that are under your guidance."

Bibliography

"650 Troops Sweep A&T." *Greensboro Daily News*, May 23, 1969.

Anderson, Nick. "Some Large HBCUs are Getting Larger. The Biggest is North Carolina A&T." *The Washington Post*, February 11, 2022. https://www.washingtonpost.com/education/2022/02/11/ncat-enrollment-hbcus/.

Bermanzohn, Sally Avery. *Through Survivors' Eyes: From the Sixties Through the Greensboro Massacre.* Vanderbilt University Press, 2003.

Biondi, Martha. *The Black Revolution on Campus.* University of California Press, 2012.

Brewington, Braxton. "NC A&T Students Speak Out Against Gerrymandering." Press conference, October 17, 2017.. Posted October 17, 2017, by Common Cause NC. Facebook, 2:19. https://www.facebook.com/CommonCauseNorthCarolina/videos/10155548174531223/.

Brown, David Lee. "University to Be Site of First Conference for Black Students." *The A&T Register,* May 2, 1969. https://digital.library.ncat.edu/atregister/364.

Cameron, Spurgeon. "Students Hold Mass Meet in Gymnasium to Rally Against Cuts." *The Register,* April 1, 1959. https://digital.library.ncat.edu/atregister/152/.

Chafe, William. *Civilities and Civil Rights: Greensboro, North Carolina and the Black Struggle for Freedom.* Oxford University Press, 1980.

Cherry, Juan. "School Daze Stirs Emotions: If Black is Beautiful, What's the Issue?" *The A&T Register,* April 29, 1988. https://digital.library.ncat.edu/atregister/1096/.

Cohen, Robert. *When the Old Left Was Young: Student Radicals and America's First Mass Student Movement, 1929 – 1941.* Oxford University Press, 1993.

Cole, Eddie. *The Campus Color Line: College Presidents and the Struggle for Black Freedom.* Princeton University Press, 2020.

Common Cause. "Common Cause: Holding Power Accountable." https://actionnetwork.org/groups/common-cause-holding-power-accountable.

Debnam, Rhonda. "Gantt Visits Greensboro." *The A&T Register*, September 21, 1990. https://digital.library.ncat.edu/atregister/1138/.

Democracy Docket. "The Decade-Long Fight Against Racial Gerrymandering." May 6, 2021. https://www.democracydocket.com/analysis/the-decade-long-fight-against-racial-gerrymandering/.

Etheridge, James. "Jackson Swings Through Triad; Advises Students to Vote." *The A&T Register*, April 27, 1984. https://digital.library.ncat.edu/atregister/1009/.

Favors, Jelani M. *Shelter in a Time of Storm: How Black Colleges Fostered Generations of Leadership and Activism*. University of North Carolina Press, 2020.

"Fraternities are Urged to Fight Tyranny, Injustice." *The Register*, December 1950. https://digital.library.ncat.edu/atregister/111/.

George, Isaiah. "An HBCU Bowl Game Wins Out Over NCAA Playoffs." *Andscape*, December 12, 2018. https://andscape.com/features/an-hbcu-bowl-game-wins-out-over-ncaa-playoffs/.

"Ghana Ambassador Speaks at A&T 60th Commencement." *The Register*, July 16, 1958. https://digital.library.ncat.edu/atregister/150/.

Gilmore, Allison. "Voter Suppression Hinders Progression of Black Community." *The A&T Register*, October 16, 2018. https://ncatregister.com/14329/the-word/voter-suppression-hinders-progression-of-black-community.

Ingalls, Gerald L. and Moore, Toby. "The Present and Future of Racial Gerrymandering: Evidence from North Carolina's 12th Congressional District." *Southeastern Geographer* 35, no. 1 (1995): 58–74. https://dx.doi.org/10.1353/sgo.1995.0009.

"Jackson to Address Commencement." *The A&T Register*, April 8, 1988. https://digital.library.ncat.edu/atregister/1094/.

Kerr, Josephine. "Gantt Falls Short at Polls Regardless of Increased Aggie Voting Turnout." *The A&T Register*, November 15, 1996. https://digital.library.ncat.edu/atregister/1204/.

Lambert, Bruce. "Warmoth T. Gibbs, 101, Educator Who Backed Civil Rights Protests." *New York Times*, April 22, 1993.

Mason, William D. Jr. "A&T and Gov. Hodges." *The Register*, November 15, 1955. https://digital.library.ncat.edu/atregister/141.

"NC A&T Students Speak Out on Campus Gerrymandering." Posted March 22, 2016, by Common Cause NC. YouTube, 2:37. https://www.youtube.com/watch?v=01zyvZxY3u8.

"NC Republicans Admit to Partisan Gerrymandering (Part 1)." February 16, 2016. Posted October 16, 2017, by Common Cause NC. YouTube, 0:15. https://www.youtube.com/watch?v=scpfpZ-pL8Q.

"NC Republicans Vow to Fight US DOJ Over Voter Laws," *The A&T Register*, October 2, 2013.

North Carolina Advisory Committee to the U.S. Commission on Civil Rights. "Trouble in Greensboro: A Report of an Open Meeting concerning Disturbances at Dudley High School and North Carolina A&T State University." March 1970. https://www2.law.umaryland.edu/marshall/usccr/documents/cr12t75.pdf.

"Over 600 Attend SOBU Conference." *The A&T Register*, November 7, 1969. https://digital.library.ncat.edu/atregister/373.

"People: The Younger Generation." *Time Magazine*, November 5, 1951. https://time.com/archive/6794406/people-the-younger-generation/.

Richards, Johnetta. *The Southern Negro Youth Congress: A History*. University of Cincinnati Press, 1987.

Rickford, Russel. *We Are an African People: Independent Education, Black Power, and the Radical Imagination.* Oxford University Press, 2019.

Robertson, Gary D. "North Carolina Judges Block Current Congressional Map." *Associated Press*, October 28, 2019. https://apnews.com/article/ebe3e179326d41daa5f8da577300299d.

Rowe, Markita C. "N.C. A&T Establishes Center of Excellence for Social Justice." *Aggie Newsroom*, September 21, 2023. https://www.ncat.edu/news/2023/09/social-justice-center-established.php.

Ruff, Jamie C. "More Power to Jesse Jackson." *The A&T Register*, March 23, 1984. https://digital.library.ncat.edu/atregister/1004/.

Shetterly, Aran. *Morningside: The 1979 Greensboro Massacre and the Struggle for an American City's Soul.* Amistad, 2024.

Spruill, Albert. "Jackson's Candidacy Offers Sense of Hope." *The A&T Register*, August 28, 1984. https://digital.library.ncat.edu/atregister/1010/.

"Students, Faculty Debate Candidacy." *The A&T Register*, November 13, 1987. https://digital.library.ncat.edu/atregister/1084/.

"Students Start Campaign Fund." *The A&T Register*, January 24, 1984. https://digital.library.ncat.edu/atregister/996/.

Swindall, Lindsay. *The Path to the Greater, Freer, Truer World: Southern Civil Rights and Anticolonialism, 1937–1955.* University Press of Florida, 2019.

"Three Important Addresses Heard." *The Register*, July 6, 1934. https://digital.library.ncat.edu/atregister/24/.

Whitlow, Jamille. "N.C. A&T OSD Motivates Students to Vote." *The A&T Register*, October 6, 2020. https://ncatregister.com/17615/the-yard/n-c-at-osd-motivates-students-to-vote/.

Williams, Audrey L. "Beware of Reaganomics." *The A&T Register*, January 22, 1982. https://digital.library.ncat.edu/atregister/925/.

Wines, Michael. "State Court Bars Using North Carolina House Map in 2020 Elections." *New York Times*, October 28, 2019. https://www.nytimes.com/2019/10/28/us/north-carolina-gerrymander-maps.html.

Zucchino, David. *Wilmington's Lie: The Murderous Coup of 1898 and the Rise of White Supremacy.* Grove Press, 2021.

Jonathan Becker

6 Bard College: Jim Crow in Dutchess County

The challenges to student voting rights that have occurred at Bard College, located in a blue state often associated with progressive politics, demonstrate that threats to those rights can occur anywhere. Bard's history involves students, faculty, and the institution acting as engaged citizens, and reveals that a sustained effort is needed to defend those rights when determined actors seek to deny or suppress the student vote.

This chapter explores the history of student voting rights in the period following the passage of the 26th Amendment, which guaranteed the right to vote at age 18 and was ratified July 1, 1971. After an introduction to the college, the first part will focus on the period from mid-1970s until 2013, when students sought the right to vote freely in Dutchess County. The second part will concentrate on the fight for a polling place on the Bard campus, which began in 2005 but took place primarily from 2014 to 2022. The chapter will delve into details of the process to illustrate the role of the key constituencies, faculty, students, and the college, and the methods of collective action used to promote and defend voting rights. As an introduction, it will contextualize Bard as a higher education institution.

1 Background: Bard College

Bard College was founded in 1860 as St. Stephens College, an Episcopalian institution preparing students for a future in the ministry. It became an undergraduate school of Columbia University in 1928, then was renamed Bard College in 1934, and subsequently separated from Columbia when it began admitting women in 1944.

Bard is an unusual institution. On the one hand, it is a traditional 2,000-student residential liberal arts college, situated in the hamlet of Annandale-on-Hudson within the Town of Red Hook, two hours north of New York City along the Hudson River in a rural, predominantly white area. On the other hand, in fulfilling its mission as a "private institution in the public interest," it "acts at the intersection of education and civil society, extending liberal arts and sciences education to communities in which it has been underdeveloped, inaccessible, or absent."[1] It has established a footprint of more than 10,000 students enrolled in programs spread across the United States and the globe. Though its main campus in Annandale-on-Hudson is predominantly white, Bard educates a diverse student body. This is achieved through: the Bard Early Colleges—public institutions which are situated in ten locations across six cities in the US, and which allow students to complete their high school education and earn up to two years of college credit; the Bard Prison Initiative (BPI), a rigorous, liberal arts-in-prison program located in seven prisons in New York State; the Bard Microcolleges, which offer tuition-free community-based education in partnership with local institutions, like the Brooklyn Public Library; and partnerships with higher education institutions in places like Germany, Kyrgyzstan, Myanmar, and Palestine.

These programs have had significant public policy impacts. BPI, for example, played a central role in the reintroduction of government-subsidized Pell grants for incarcerated students in the US and in extending the Tuition Assistance Program and Merit Time sentence reduction for incarcerated students in New York State. Bard Early College in Manhattan was the nation's first public, degree-granting early college high school. In 2001, Bard was directly involved in creating a federal definition of early college programs and Bard's model has since been replicated over 400 times across the US.

Bard's institutional engagement with student voting is consistent with its civic and public interest missions and purposefully is rooted in links between higher education, citizenship, and democracy.[2] Bard's work in the voting sphere has provided a best-practice model of student voter engagement, legal defense and advocacy, and has been shared in meetings, workshops, and communities of practice with organizations such as ALL IN Campus Democracy Challenge, Campus Compact, and Partners for Campus—Community Engagement.

---

1 "Mission Statement," Bard College Mission Statement, Bard College, https://www.bard.edu/about/mission/.
2 Jonathan Becker, "Colleges Should Promote and Defend Student Voting," *Huffington Post*, August 12, 2016, https://www.huffpost.com/entry/american-colleges-should-promote-and-defend-student_b_57ae185fe4b0ae60ff026711.

2 Bard College: The Fight for the Right to Vote Locally

2.1 Student Organizing, Questionnaires, and the Battle over Residency (1976–2000)

In the fall of 1976, Bard students Noel Sturgeon and Sara Caffrey, energized by a tutorial on student voting rights facilitated by political studies professor Robert Koblitz, mobilized other students to register to vote.[3] Their efforts to register were stymied. Republican election commissioner Laura Hodos told them, "students will not be registered," regardless of their specific circumstances, and declared, "We can't have Bard students running the Town of Red Hook."[4] The students sought to fight the decision and through Koblitz were able to obtain representation through the Mid-Hudson Chapter of the New York Civil Liberties Union (NYCLU).

In a lawsuit filed on behalf of the students, which was heard on the eve of the 1976 federal election, State Supreme Court Justice Joseph P. Galliardi sided with Bard student-plaintiffs Robin Caroll, Jan Howell, and Judy R. Robinson, declaring that "they have borne their burden" in establishing residency in the county and were thus "entitled to register."[5]

Unfortunately, the decision did not change the essential dynamic of student voters at Bard or in Dutchess County at large. The decision applied only to the three student litigants and did not address student voters as a class.[6] Although

---

3 In a letter to the editor of the *Poughkeepsie Journal*, Sturgeon and Caffrey explained, "These students fulfill the time requirement for residency and they consider Bard their home. Some students are financially independent from their parents, and do not live with their parents. Therefore, their parents' home is not their legal residence. Some students have not registered in their home towns and cannot register by mail. Some students simply do not have a legal residence. All these students are being denied their right to vote"; Noel Sturgeon and Sara Caffrey, "To the Editor," *Poughkeepsie Journal*, October 8, 1976.
4 *Robin Carroll, Jan Howell, and Judy R. Robinson v. Dutchess County Board of Elections*, 3920 (Dutchess County 1976).
5 *Robin Carroll, Jan Howell, and Judy R. Robinson v. Dutchess County Board of Elections*, 3920 (Dutchess County 1976). Galliardi invoked the 1965 *Carrington v. Rash* Supreme Court decision that "'Fencing out' from the franchise a sector of the population because of the way they may vote is constitutionally impermissible"; *Carrington v. Rash*, 380 U.S. 89 (1965).
6 Marylin Stone, "3 Bard Students Register as a Result of Court Ruling," *Poughkeepsie Journal*, October 28, 1976, 23. Justice Galliardi dismissed the portion of the petition seeking declaratory relief but did so without prejudice, meaning that it could be addressed in another court action.

Bard was a small institution, with fewer than 1,000 students at the time, the lack of continuity among student groups and the absence of engagement by the administration meant that other students could not capitalize on the 1976 success. A year later, Bard students were explicitly excluded from participating in a Red Hook town referendum on nuclear power. Then in 1978, in the run-up to the next federal elections, registrations by a group of more than 100 Bard students were rejected.[7]

There were episodic efforts to allow students to register to vote, but things did not change until the new millennium.[8] Student Activists for Voting Equality (SAVE) was founded by Bard students Marina Smerling and Michael Chameides after hundreds of Bard students had their voter registrations rejected before the 1998 election, when Bard professor Joel Kovel ran as a Green party candidate for the US Senate.[9] That same year, Vassar students had attempted a lawsuit in New York State Supreme Court to gain the right to vote, but their efforts failed because they did not have proper documentation of student registration efforts.[10] Together with a SAVE chapter at Vassar, the Bard students proceeded to press the county on the issue of voting rights.

At the time, Bard students were systematically denied the right to register and vote locally. Dutchess County officials sent Bard and other students in Dutchess County a highly suggestive questionnaire, posing questions such as: "Is your present residence claimed as a student?"; "What year are you in college?"; 'How long do you expect to live at present residence?"; "What is your parents' home address?"; and "To what extent do your parents contribute to your support?"[11] The questionnaire was then used as a basis to deny registration due to residency.

The distribution of the questionnaires, which was overseen by Republican election commissioner William Paroli Sr., who also served as the chairman of the Dutchess County Republican Party, ignored the landmark 1979 Supreme

---

According to the *Poughkeepsie Journal* account, the attorney for the plaintiffs, Stephen M. Lipton, indicated that "further action in this respect will depend on future action of the Board of Elections and the interest of the students."

7 Steven Colatrella 1982 interview by Jonathan Becker, November 1, 2024.

8 The attitude of the Board of Elections varied and was unpredictable. In 1996, some student registrations succeeded, and more after the intervention of students and Bard Director of Student Activities Allen Josey. In 1998 nearly all Vassar and Bard applications were rejected. In 2000, of the 228 students who tried to register, all were sent a questionnaire and nearly all were rejected. See Rafi Rom, "Voting Campaign Heats Up," *Bard Observer*, February 28, 2000, 3.

9 Susannah E. David, "Analyzing Kovel's Defeat in Senate Elections 1998," *Bard Observer*, November 18, 1998, 13–14.

10 Ben Silverbush, "Students Preparing Class Action Lawsuit," *The Miscellany News*, February 18, 2000, 1.

11 Muni Citrin, "Questionnaire Incites Controversy," *Bard Observer*, September 20, 1996.

Court decision in *Symm v. United States* which upheld a ruling finding that the selective and targeted registration practices imposed on students at Prairie View A&M University violated the 26th Amendment. As described in further detail in Chapters one and four, the Symm decision barred the distribution of a questionnaire that asked remarkably similar questions to those posed in Dutchess County, and were used in the same way as a pretext to deny students the right to vote locally.[12]

Paroli's approach also flagrantly ignored a 1984 federal judge's decision in a New York State case, *Auerbach v. Kinley*, a class action suit brought by students from SUNY New Paltz and SUNY Albany with the support of the New York Public Interest Research Group (NYPIRG) and the NYCLU. In this case, Judge Neal P. McCurn ruled that parts of the state constitution which placed added burdens of residency on students (and others, such as seminarians and prisoners) violated the equal protection clause of the 14th Amendment.[13] His decision called on Boards of Election to avoid "requiring any additional documentation from any student beyond that required of all other applicants" and "from adopting or pursuing any registration policy or practice that directly or indirectly discriminates against students or that requires students to do anything more than is required of other applicants."[14] Fifteen years later, Paroli flouted Judge McCurn's admonition that "A student's right to vote should not be contingent upon the whims of the local election officials,"[15] and Dutchess was evidently the only county in New York to distribute a questionnaire targeting students.[16]

SAVE's work picked up steam in the 1999–2000 academic year as the 2000 presidential election was approaching, with Chameides working alongside first-year student Monica Elkinton. SAVE built a coalition consisting of students from Bard and Vassar, several local politicians, and legal defense and advocacy groups including the NYCLU, NYPIRG, and the League of Women Voters. Together, they formed what Chameides called a "grassroots campaign" that "mobilized local ac-

---

12 The Waller County questionnaire asked, for example, "Are you a college student?" "How long have you been a student at such school?" "Where do you live while in college?" "Do you intend to reside in Waller County indefinitely?" "How long have you considered yourself to be a bona fide resident of Waller County?" "What do you plan to do when you finish your college education?" See *Symm v. U.S.*, 439 US 1105 (1979).

13 "After Judge Rules for Students Election Board Changes Tune," *The Journal*, Ogdensburg, New York, October 10, 1984, 2; *Auerbach v. Kinley*, 594 F. Supp. 1503 (N.D.N.Y. 1984).

14 *Auerbach v. Kinley*, 594 F. Supp. 1503 (N.D.N.Y. 1984).

15 "State Limit on Voting By Students Overturned," *New York Times*, October 11, 1984, B2.

16 "Good Progress on Student Vote," *Poughkeepsie Journal*, June 30, 2000, 10 A.

tivists and pressured local officials to follow state and national laws." Students "held protests, press conferences, phone bombs, threatened a lawsuit, and generally pressured Dutchess County officials to stop their discrimination against students."[17] Their efforts were endorsed by both the College Democrats of America and the College Republicans of America.[18]

The Bard students were supported locally by political studies professor Joseph Luders, who gave them advice and focused on the issue in his American government class, and Alan Sussman, a visiting professor with deep links to the NYCLU who taught constitutional law and whose work focused on civil rights issues. Additionally, I published editorials and commentaries in local newspapers, spoke on regional public radio, wrote to local legislators, and lobbied the Bard Board of Trustees in my faculty role as a political studies professor and my institutional role as dean of studies.[19]

The students were also supported by the most senior institutional leadership. Bard President Leon Botstein, together with his Vassar counterpart Frances Ferguson, publicly endorsed the students' efforts.[20] In January, 2000, the Bard College Board of Trustees weighed in, passing this resolution:

> The Board of Trustees of Bard College supports the rights of students at Bard and other colleges in the county to register to vote in Dutchess County where they live, work, and study. The Board of Trustees calls upon the County Board of Elections (BOE) to change any of its practices that impinge upon the rights of students to vote in Dutchess County.[21]

The county legislature,[22] particularly legislators in districts that included Bard and Vassar students, felt pressure and feared litigation. The Dutchess County legislative chair formed a committee to explore the issue. The committee was headed

---

17 "SAVE," *Bard Free Press*, October 4, 2000, 3, https://digitalcommons.bard.edu/cgi/viewcontent.cgi?article=1006&context=bardfreepress.
18 Silverbush, "Students Preparing Class Action Lawsuit," 2.
19 See, for example, Jonathan Becker, "College Students Deserve to Vote Where They Live," *Poughkeepsie Journal*, December 24, 1999. The opinion piece stated: "To welcome them into core community institutions but at the same time to exclude them from exercising their rights as citizens of the same community reeks of hypocrisy. It educates them to be apathetic toward, and cynical about, the political process. This is clearly the wrong message for this community to send to young adults."
20 Silverbush, "Students Preparing Class Action Lawsuit," 2.
21 Bard College Board of Trustees meeting minutes, January 19, 2000.
22 In the New York State system, counties are vested with tremendous power and serve as the interface for many public activities; New York State Department of State Division of Local Government Services, *Local Government Handbook* (Albany, 2018), https://dos.ny.gov/system/files/documents/2023/06/localgovernmenthandbook_2023.pdf.

by Woody Klose, a Republican who represented Bard's Red Hook district; Democrat Kristen Jemiolo, whose Poughkeepsie district included Vassar; and Republican Marcus Molinaro, who was simultaneously a legislator and the mayor of Bard's 'college town' in the village of Tivoli, a position he had held since he was elected at the age of 18.

The committee held public meetings at Bard and Vassar in early 2000. At the Bard meeting, they were faced by well-prepared students and faculty, as well as Arthur Eisenberg from the NYCLU, who had helped litigate the seminal 1984 *Auerbach* case that established residency eligibility for New York State college students. The message to the committee was clear: either support the students or face a lawsuit that they were likely to lose while earning the enmity of a group of previously disenfranchised and soon-to-be-empowered student voters.[23]

The committee's final report was sympathetic to the students' arguments. It recognized that voting is "one of the unique distinguishing marks of an American citizen. ... [It is] the Constitutionally guaranteed right to vote ... [and] ... the single most important cornerstone of our democracy." The committee rejected the need for a questionnaire, and concluded that the county should not create barriers to student voters but should instead "encourage the use of the voting franchise by students."[24]

The opinion of the committee, however, did not settle the issue because the county legislature was not the decision-making body. The ultimate decision on voter registrations fell to the election commissioners, one Democrat and one Republican, appointed by county party committees, conforming to the precedent that both commissioners needed to agree in order to change policy. While Democratic Commissioner William Egan had made his support for student voting clear for some time, there was little indication that Paroli would relent, short of successful litigation. Fortuitously for the students, on the eve of the release of the committee's conclusions, Paroli was convicted in federal court of conspiracy to commit extortion, and was forced to step down.[25] Nevertheless, even then, the issue

---

23 Klose said, "I never felt threatened but I do know that we will lose if they sue"; Anthony Farmer, "Task Force, Let Collegians Vote," *Poughkeepsie Journal*, March 19, 2000, 1 A.

24 Dutchess County Legislator Committee, *Report on Student Voting Questions*, March 13, 2000, https://cce.bard.edu/get-involved/election/files/report-on-student-voting.pdf.

25 Paroli pleaded guilty to one count for activities related to shakedowns of contractors on town projects; John Davis and Emily Stewart, "Disgraced Republican Giant William Paroli Sr. Dies at 86," *Poughkeepsie Journal*, March 22, 2014, downloaded December 17, 2024, https://www.pough keepsiejournal.com/story/news/2014/03/22/william-paroli-sr-controversial-former-gop-leader-has-died/6730283/.

was not settled. Paroli's immediate successor, Dave Gamache, hinted that he would support student registrations. However, he proceeded cautiously and the BOE continued to segregate student registrations and slow-rolled many that were submitted in the spring of 2000. It was only in June of 2000, with the threat of litigation lingering, that Gamache and the BOE committed to registering students without discriminatory barriers, ending a critical chapter in Bard's fight for student voting.[26]

2.2 Implementation Is Everything: Residency and Judicial Threats to Student Voters

The 2000 victory of students was not the end of the story. When the Bard and Vassar students were victorious, Elkinton said, "I am thankful a lawsuit was not necessary," but added presciently, "Students need to keep constant watch over the Board of Elections to protect our right to vote."[27] While the right to vote locally had been achieved, there would be several challenges to it in the coming years.

Fresh off the 2000 victory, Bard began aggressively registering students to vote. Institutionally, Bard went beyond the minimum expected in the Higher Education Reauthorization Act of 1998, which mandated that colleges make "good faith" efforts to register students to vote, whether on campus or at their parents' residences. Voter registration became a mandatory stop on the first day of new student orientation. Bard arranged shuttles to a poll site where registered voters residing on campus cast their ballots, which was situated a mile and a half away from campus at St. John the Evangelist Church in the hamlet of Barrytown (although this led to complaints about 'bussing' students to the polls).

While Bard students generally registered and voted without rancor, there were typical episodic difficulties of America's registration and voting process. These ranged from mistakes with registrations, to spelling mistakes in data input, to voters who had studied away being listed as inactive. Occasionally there were questions over what appropriate forms of identification were acceptable for those who did not provide a social security number while registering. To assist students facing such challenges, Bard began sending its own poll watchers to the poll site,

---

26 Of 150 registrations submitted by students in April and May, only 21 had been approved as of June 1; Jane Berber Smith and Linda Greenblatt, "Progress in Student Voting Questionable," *Poughkeepsie Journal*, July 6, 2000, 6 A.

27 Michael Chameides, "Verdict is In: Dutchess County Students Win Right to Vote," *Bard Free Press* 2, no. 1 (September 2000): 1 – 2, https://digitalcommons.bard.edu/cgi/viewcontent.cgi?article= 1005&context=bardfreepress.

armed with copies of New York State election law, to observe and try to resolve whatever issues emerged, and to explain to students their rights should they be challenged or told that they were in the wrong location.[28]

Tensions grew significantly in 2007. In May of that year, the Town of Red Hook approved a Community Preservation Fund (CPF), which taxed sales of higher-valued homes to preserve open space and farmland, in a special election by 31 votes. The participation of Bard students in the election caused great consternation among some opponents of the CPF and might well have influenced the outcome. It was viewed as an indicator of deeper changes taking place in the town and county, which had been traditional Republican strongholds.[29]

In November of 2007, the once impregnable Republican control of the county legislature was pierced and Democrats won a slim majority for the first time in 30 years. That same election, Micki Strawinski, an employee in Bard's health and counseling center, won a seat on the Red Hook Town Board. In October 2008, for the first time in history, the number of registered Democrats in the county surpassed registered Republicans.[30] In November 2008, after a special election due to the retirement of a town board member, the Town of Red Hook gained a Democratic majority on the town board for the first time in living memory.

The electoral campaign in 2009 was particularly heated. It was the first regular election since the US chose its first Black president, Barack Obama. A March 2009 special election to replace Bard's congresswoman Kirsten Gillibrand, who was appointed to the US Senate after Hillary Clinton became secretary of state, was seen as a referendum on Obama. In that race, Democrat Scott Murphy won a narrow, 401-vote victory that was secured after a month of hard-fought battles over the counting of paper ballots—affidavit and absentee. Such was the level of contention that even Gillibrand's absentee ballot was challenged.[31] These develop-

---

28 On at least one occasion the police were called to the poll site over a vigorous discussion concerning addresses, though it remained unclear who phoned the Dutchess County Sheriff's Office and the sheriff who came seemed perplexed as to why he was there; Jonathan Becker, letter to Dutchess County Sheriff's Department, November 11, 2005. Another time, a local official threatened to call the police because Bard had purchased "I voted" stickers, after student complaints that there were none, and was making them available to voters, whether or not they were college students, at the local poll site.

29 Rasheed Oluwa, "Preservation Tax Squeaks By," *Poughkeepsie Journal*, May 2, 2007.

30 Patricia Doxsey, "Dem Enrollment Tops Republican in Dutchess," *Daily Freeman*, October 10, 2008, downloaded December 12, 2024, https://www.dailyfreeman.com/2008/10/10/dem-enrollment-tops-republican-in-dutchess/.

31 Andrew Bernstein, "Tedisco Team Challenges Gillibrand Ballot," *Troy Record*, April 25, 2009, downloaded December 9, 2024, https://www.troyrecord.com/2009/04/15/tedisco-team-challenges-gillibrands-ballot/.

ments set the stage for more systematic efforts by officials to deprive Bard students of their right to vote, demonstrating both the vulnerability of student voters and the importance of institutional engagement.

On election day in November, 2009, a dubious legal decision created chaos at Bard students' then-off-campus polling place at St. John the Evangelist Church in the neighboring hamlet of Barrytown. Partisan poll watchers descended upon the church to aggressively challenge students on the basis of residency. Again and again, every five or so voters, the Republican poll watchers raised objections. When John Pelosi, a lawyer and Democratic poll watcher who for several years was present at the church to protect student voting rights, pressed for the basis of the challenge, he was told, "I'm challenging for residency, that's all I'm going to tell you."[32]

While under normal circumstances the poll workers overseeing an election would, barring the clear determination of a disqualifying issue, allow a 'challenged voter' to proceed after taking an oath,[33] an extremely problematic judicial decision made earlier that day meant that any Bard student who was challenged on the basis of residency was forced to vote via a paper or 'affidavit' (sometimes called 'provisional') ballot instead of on a machine. This created difficulties, both because Bard students, often voting for the first time, felt intimidated, and because studies have shown that provisional ballots are rejected at a relatively high rate for a variety of technical reasons.[34]

The case emerged out of a complaint centering on Vassar College, located 30 minutes south of Bard in the Town of Poughkeepsie. Vassar drew scrutiny because its campus had been gerrymandered into multiple voting districts (then two, and later three), a tactic which was itself used to suppress student voting, the consequence of which was that some of the students who had changed dormitories

---

32 Patricia Doxsey, "Bard Students Unhappy with Voting Hassle," *Daily Freeman*, November 20, 2009, downloaded December 12, 2024, https://www.dailyfreeman.com/2009/11/20/bard-students-unhappy-with-voting-hassle-with-video/; "Barrytown (District 5) on Election Night," video recording, November 3, 2009, posted November 16, 2009 by BGIAProgram, YouTube, 1:48, https://www.youtube.com/watch?v=ng4QF9lnPds.

33 According to the established procedures, when there was a challenge, the four poll workers would interview the prospective voter and if two of the four thought the voter was eligible, the voter would recite a short oath and proceed to vote on a machine.

34 Yael Bromberg, "Youth Voting Rights and the Unfulfilled Promise of the Twenty-Sixth Amendment," *University of Pennsylvania Journal of Constitutional Law* 21, no. 5 (2019): 1146, https://scholarship.law.upenn.edu/jcl/vol21/iss5/1/. A Florida federal court noted that "In Florida, voters 18–21 had provisional ballots rejected at a rate *four times* higher than the rejection rate of provisional ballots cast by voters ... between the ages of 45 and 64"; *League of Women Voters of Florida, Inc. v. Detzner*, 314, F Supp. 3d 1205, 1219 (N.D. Fla 2018).

would also have been obliged to re-register to vote from their new address and vote at a different polling place because in changing dormitories they had also changed districts.[35] The suit claimed that students were voting in the wrong districts and accused Vassar of encouraging this.[36]

The judge in the case, Poughkeepsie-based Supreme Court Justice James Brands, issued an expansive order that required *any* voters in Dutchess County "who are challenged on the basis of residency" to "cast their ballots as affidavit ballots" or appear before a judge in Poughkeepsie.[37] As a result, a matter that was only relevant to Vassar cascaded to Bard, with Bard students being targeted and deprived of the right to vote on a regular voting machine.

Brands' ruling was procedurally and substantively vexing. Procedurally, the decision was an 'ex parte order,' meaning that not all parties that were impacted were given the opportunity to be represented to argue the case prior to the decision. Indeed, the only people known to be present for the hearing were Justice Brands and attorney John Ciampoli, representing the chair of the Town of Poughkeepsie Republican Committee, Thomas Martinelli. Neither voters nor Democratic election commissioner Fran Knapp were present.[38] Substantively, it ignored the established procedure for addressing challenged voters. It subjected young voters in particular—poll watchers weaponized the decision only at Bard and Vassar—to aggressive tactics by partisan poll watchers. It also took a complaint specific to one location (Vassar was the only college in Dutchess County with more than one voting district) that was filed by a group that had standing in one specific locale (the Town of Poughkeepsie), and applied it to the entire county.

---

35 Kristen Jemiolo, who was part of the county committee that endorsed student voting in 2000, viewed the division of Vassar into multiple legislative districts as clear "party politics;" Patricia Doxsey, "Dutchess Legislature will Shrink in 2004," *Daily Freeman*, November 13, 2002, downloaded December 17, 2024, https://www.dailyfreeman.com/2002/11/13/dutchess-legislature-will-shrink-in-2004/.

36 In his claim, Ciampoli cited communications from the Vassar administration that stated, "Where you vote depends upon the residence you lived in when you registered to vote, not necessarily where you live now"; *Martinelli v. Dutchess County Board of Elections* (N.Y. Sup. Ct. 2009). No Index Number was provided or ever supplied, which was a point of contention as the case was adjudicated and sanctions were later sought against attorney John Ciampoli for "frivolous conduct."

37 Justice James Brands' order, *Martinelli v. Dutchess County Board of Elections* (N.Y. Sup. Ct. 2009).

38 Given the relationships involved, it is certainly possible that Republican commissioner David Gamache was aware of the impending filing. Later that afternoon, attorney Kathleen O'Keefe found Ciampoli in Gamache's office when she went to appeal Judge Dillon's decision. Kathleen O'Keefe, email message to Jonathan Becker, December 2, 2024.

The decision reeked of politics. Democratic election commissioner Knapp described it as an "orchestrated attempt by the Republican Party ... to intimidate college students and suppress voter turnout."[39] There is good reason to think this is correct. Kathleen O'Keefe, attorney for the New York Democratic Assembly Campaign Committee and select Democratic candidates, who would later defend the students, indicated that Judge Brands was known among Republican officials as the judge of choice. It is, moreover, clear that Judge Brands was well aware that there were problems with forcing citizens to vote via an affidavit ballot, having overseen a number of cases where the counting of paper ballots, absentee and affidavit, was vigorously contested, including an extremely close special congressional election earlier in 2009.[40] A few years earlier he had gained a reputation for throwing out paper ballots in tight elections, earning the sobriquet 'pizza stain judge' for disqualifying an absentee ballot due to the presence of an identifying fingerprint that was seemingly from tomato sauce in a Town of Poughkeepsie race that ultimately favored a Republican candidate by two votes.[41]

O'Keefe had been informed of the situation by Knapp and immediately filed an appeal against Brands' decision. The appeal was heard during a conference call with Appellate Division Justice Marc Dillon late in the afternoon on election day. At 7:30 p.m. Judge Dillon issued a handwritten order altering key parts of Brands' decision by restricting the order to the Town of Poughkeepsie, thus removing Bard from its scope, and reinstating the normal course for challenges to voters, which usually allowed them to vote on machines.[42] Unfortunately, by the time the order came down and was distributed, most students had already attempted to vote. In all, 60 Vassar students and a dozen Bard students were forced to vote via affidavit ballot. Presumably others, having heard or witnessed the intimidation that took place at the polls, chose not to vote.

There remained the question of what to do with the affidavit ballots. As stated above, affidavit ballots could be challenged for minor irregularities, especially when elections were highly competitive, as was the case in 2009 with the Town of Red Hook and county legislative majorities at stake. To ensure student votes were counted, Bard, on behalf of the affected students, formally retained and paid O'Keefe, who had previously been working at the behest of Knapp. Institu-

---

39 Doxsey, "Bard Students Unhappy."

40 Bernstein, "Tedisco Team Challenges Gillibrand Ballot."

41 Hudson, "NY-20: Beware of the Pizza Stain Judge," *Daily Kos*, April 15, 2009, downloaded December 9, 2024, https://www.dailykos.com/storyonly/2009/4/14/720054/-NY-20:-Beware-the-Pizza-Stain-Judge.

42 Appellate Division Justice Mark Dillon, Order, *Martinelli v. Dutchess County Board of Elections* (N.Y. Sup. Ct. 2009).

tionally, the College viewed it as a critical moment due to the obvious abuse of the justice system and the egregious intimidation tactics deployed by poll watchers. As I wrote in a letter to the *Poughkeepsie Journal*, "Denying legally qualified citizens the most sacred of rights is reprehensible. The public leaders who have chosen to take this path have failed their communities and the most basic test of leadership."[43]

O'Keefe took testimony from students and filed a motion in State Supreme Court demanding that all Bard students forced to vote via affidavit ballot have their votes counted 'unchallenged,' meaning that they were exempt from the court battles that had taken place in the county over the previous several years during the counting process.[44] In a judgment that further underlined the absurdity of Brands' original ruling, Supreme Court Justice James D. Pagones ordered that all ballots cast by Bard students residing in the district in which they voted be counted by the Dutchess County BOE "without being subject to an objection." Pagones went further, seeking to avoid a repeat event, by permanently enjoining "the Dutchess County BOE from subjecting Bard students who are registered to vote from procedures more rigorous than an average voter when they attempt to vote in a machine."[45]

Coupled with the 1984 *Auerbach* federal court decision, this was the second time a court, this time a state court, had to repeat the basic premise reached by the US Supreme Court in *Symm* in 1979—that students cannot be targeted or subjected to electoral procedures different from the rest of the voter public.

2.3 New Forms of Voter Suppression: Challenging Registration Addresses (2012–2013)

Like the situation at Prairie View A&M University, Dutchess County officials would return to the issue of student voting time and time again. Three years later it was a

---

43 Jonathan Becker, "To the Editor," *Poughkeepsie Journal*, November 20, 2009, 12.
44 *Conti v. Dutchess County Board of Elections*, 9054 (N.Y. Sup. Ct. 2009). Student litigants included Olivia Conti, Sara Kangas, Tanya Sorenson, Casey Asprooth-Jackson, Sarah Bessel, and Iris S.B. Larsen.
45 Hon. James D. Pagones, Order, *Conti v. Dutchess County Board of Elections*, 9054 (N.Y. Sup. Ct. 2009).

new Republican election commissioner, Erik Haight, who targeted student voters.[46]

In 2012, there were federal elections and, as in 2009, races remained close. Two congressional districts situated in the county were tightly fought, as was a critical state Senate seat. In the run-up to the election, Haight, who replaced Gamache in 2011, rejected more than 100 registrations from students from Bard, Marist College, and the Culinary Institute of America due to the failure of the student registrants to provide dorm names and room numbers on their registration forms.[47] The decision appeared to discriminate against college students: such demands were not made of residents of other group quarters, such as at elder-care facilities.[48]

Attention to the issue was brought by Marist College student Daniel Torres. Torres, a communications major who had been registering students in Poughkeepsie, brought registrations to the BOE on the final day of the registration period, only to be told that they did not comply with requirements due to the absence of dorm names and room numbers. He held a press conference to draw attention to the issue, framing it as "a Jim Crow moment in Dutchess County."[49]

Like his predecessor William Paroli, Haight proved obdurate. He was unmoved by a letter jointly authored by the NYCLU and the Brennan Center for Justice, which pointed out that his actions were incompatible with New York State election law, because the registrations in question contained "substantially all of the required information" necessary to determine if someone was an eligible voter.[50] More importantly, he ignored a rare unanimous advisory opinion of the

---

46 Haight himself had been the beneficiary of decisions by Judge Brands in 2005 to disqualify absentee ballots from the Poughkeepsie-based River Valley Care Nursing Home, contributing to Haight's five-vote victory in a seat for the town's city council; Hudson, "NY-20: Beware."

47 Because Vassar was gerrymandered into three districts, its students needed a further identification.

48 Patricia Doxsey, "In Dutchess County, Battle Brews Over Dorm Dwellers' Voting Rights," *Daily Freeman*, October 19, 2012, downloaded December 12, 2024, https://www.dailyfreeman.com/2012/10/19/in-dutchess-county-battle-brews-over-dorm-dwellers-voting-rights.

49 Doxsey, "Dorm Dwellers' Voting Rights." Torres was instructed by representatives at the BOE not to submit the forms, but chose to anyhow, which was critical because the rejection of the forms gave the students standing to pursue a case; Daniel Torres, interviewed by Jonathan Becker, December 10, 2024.

50 The letter from the NYCLU and Brenner Center also raised procedural questions, suggesting that voters should only be denied registration when such a determination is made "by a majority vote of the commissioners"; Arthur Eisenberg and Lee Rowland, New York Civil Liberties Union, letter to Commissioner Erik J. Haight, October 11, 2012, https://www.nyclu.org/uploads/2012/11/Commissioner_Haight_letter_10.11.12.pdf. Haight claimed that the decision was consistent with a 2003 manual of the Board of Elections while Knapp asserted that it was a 'draft' policy and only

New York State BOE that echoed the NYCLU and Brennan Center letter, stressing that "if the registration is from a student where the address is all within a single election district [as was the case for Bard, Marist, and the Culinary Institute] and the address is sufficient for communicating with the voter, that should be deemed substantially complete and the registration should be processed."[51]

Bard became involved as an institution after Democratic Commissioner Knapp reached out to Erin Cannan (author of chapter 8), Bard's vice president for student affairs and deputy director of Bard's Center for Civic Engagement (CCE), which had been founded in 2011 and which coordinated Bard's election efforts. Cannan, who had helped organize student voter registration with a student group, Election@Bard, formed in the late 2000s, identified students whose registrations had been rejected, including some who were willing to serve as litigants. She then arranged for the students to meet with the NYCLU, which was represented by Arthur Eisenberg, a participant in Bard's fight for a poll site in 2000 as well as the *Aurbach* case. The NYCLU staff interviewed the students, and in the end two of the four named litigants selected were from Bard: seniors Alexis Roe and Daniel Roscoe Kern, who joined with the other litigants from Marist and the Culinary Institute.[52]

On October 31, 2012, days before the election, the NYCLU, together with lawyers from Lowenstein Sandler, filed a class action lawsuit with the US District Court for the Southern District seeking injunctive relief because "Commissioner Haight's decision to reject their applications deprives Plaintiffs of their fundamental right to vote."[53] They asked for a declaration that the practice of the Dutchess County BOE was unconstitutional and for preliminary relief to allow students to vote in the upcoming election. On November 5, the day before the election, US District Court Judge Kenneth Karas issued a preliminary injunction, allowing the students to vote and demanding that supplemental poll lists containing the names of student voters be distributed to the appropriate poll sites.

---

relevant for Vassar students because of the division of the campus into different voting districts; Doxsey, "Dorm Dwellers Voting Rights."

51 "06/12/2012 Meeting Transcript," New York State Board of Elections, https://elections.ny.gov/sys tem/files/documents/2023/10/cctranscriptions06122012.pdf.

52 Roe had twice tried to register and both times was sent rejection letters citing "omitted" or "not readable" birth information, only to later be told by phone, after the deadline, that it was due to a missing dorm address. Kern was never informed his registration had been rejected until after the deadline. Naomi Lachance, "Student Votes Challenged," *Bard Free Press* 14, no. 5 (November 2012): 6–7, https://digitalcommons.bard.edu/cgi/viewcontent.cgi?article=1101&context= bardfreepress.

53 Stipulation of Settlement and Consent Decree, *Pitcher v. Dutchess County Board of Elections*, Civil Action No. 12 CV 8017 (S.D.N.Y. 2013).

The following May, a consent decree was signed under the oversight of Judge Karas which "permanently enjoined and prohibited" the Dutchess County BOE from "rejecting an application for registration from a student of Bard College, Marist College or the Culinary Institute of America," if the student met other registration requirements and provided a campus address but did not list a dorm room. The order also required the BOE to pay attorney fees, which amounted to nearly $60,000. It was subsequently decided that all on-campus registrants would use Bard's main address, 30 Campus Road, to register. But in spite of the fact that Haight lost, his opposition to student voting would continue.

3 The Battle for On-Campus Poll Sites (2005 – 2022)

With the question of student voting rights and residency largely settled, the next phase of Bard's fight for student voting rights centered on a different election administration mechanism: an accessible on-campus polling site. Ever since Bard students had earned the right to vote in 2000 they had voted at St. John the Evangelist Church in the hamlet of Barrytown, situated a little less than a mile and a half from main campus. St. John's was known for its hospitality, and for many years on election day the church had held a fundraiser that featured the sale of clam chowder and apple turnovers where locals and the political class of the Town of Red Hook came for lunch.

However, it was not an ideal place for voters, especially Bard students. The voting area was cramped, and those waiting in line at peak times had to wait outside in the dark and sometimes in inclement weather. It was not handicap-accessible or compliant with the Americans with Disabilities Act (ADA). Voters had to climb a stair at the main entry to the polling place and the accessibility ramp for the physically impaired on the other side of the church was replete with problems. There was neither an accessible bathroom nor designated accessible parking. The church's location had other issues that made it dangerous for those without cars: it was on a country road which had no lighting, no sidewalk, and did not even have a verge, making it inaccessible by foot. There was no public transportation that could drop off a voter within half a mile of the site, an expectation articulated in New York State election law.

Bard, on the other hand, offered a myriad of benefits. First, a significant majority of voters in the electoral district lived on the Bard campus, including students, faculty, and staff, and an on-campus poll site would be within walking distance for all of them, including many who did not have their own transportation.

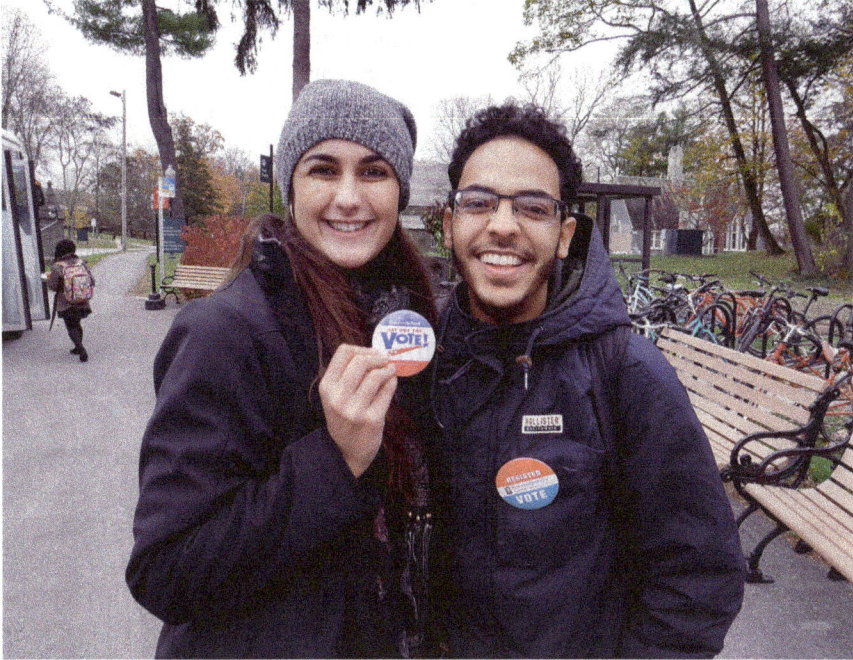

Figure 1: Bard student voters near bus stop, Election Day, November, 2017. Photo by Sarah Wallock '19, courtesy of Bard College.

Second, Bard offered excellent facilities—certainly superior to those at St. John's—including large spaces with ample parking and shelter for those waiting to vote, and all of which were handicap-accessible and compliant with the ADA. Third, an on-campus site would encourage students and young people in general to vote: voting rates for youth are generally low and people who vote when they are young tend to vote throughout their lives. Studies show that the lack of access to poll sites is one of the major barriers to political participation.[54] Finally, Bard was a welcoming place to host non-students. Bard had an open campus and was known as a cultural hub, hosting more than 50,000 visitors per year for numerous public events, including talks, concerts and plays, matches between local high school sport teams, and even the after-prom party for Red Hook High

---

54 "Why Youth Don't Vote: Differences by Race and Education," Center for Information & Research on Civic Learning and Engagement (CIRCLE), August 21, 2018, https://circle.tufts.edu/latest-research/why-youth-dont-vote-differences-race-and-education.

School. It also hosted a Lifetime Learning Institute for several hundred non-traditional and often elderly students in the community.

Efforts to move a poll site to Bard began as early as 2005, when, before local elections, my office (I was then the dean of studies) sent a letter to town officials and candidates seeking a polling place on the Bard campus.[55] This was followed by a 2007 petition prepared by my office that was from students, faculty, and staff.[56] Both documents were sensitive to the tradition associated with St. John's and thus only sought an on-campus poll site: St. John's could be kept if a new site was added or if other sites in town were realigned. The Republican majority on the Town Board demurred, but in 2009, when Democrats won a majority, the Town Board passed a resolution for the first time supporting a poll site on campus in a partisan 3–2 vote.[57] This was repeated in 2016, with four in favor and one not present.

Though the 2009 and 2016 Town Board resolutions underlined local support for a polling place on campus, there was a problem for Bard advocates: a change in poll sites demanded agreement by both commissioners at the bi-partisan BOE, and Erik Haight, who was the Republican election commissioner throughout most of this period, was implacably hostile to a poll site on the Bard campus. Over the years, he invoked numerous arguments about why there should not be a poll site at Bard. He suggested that off-campus voters assigned to a poll site on campus might be hesitant to come to campus (though it should be noted that there were enough registered voters to host a single site at Bard). He suggested that students were unruly, stating: "[c]ollege students are often vocal about political issues," as if this were problematic.[58] His main argument, however, depicted stu-

---

55 Letter from Jonathan Becker to candidates Erin Cannan, Harry Colgen, Sue Crane, Richard Griffiths, Linda Keeling, Sue McCann, Marc Molinaro, Laurie Nash, Vicky Perry, James Ross, and Jonah Triebwasser, November 1, 2005.

56 As a 2007 petition said, "Bard is an open and welcoming community which hosts numerous events that attract people from across Red Hook, be it summer camps, concerts, or high school soccer matches. Bard has handicap accessible facilities suitable for voting"; Bard College Dean of Studies Office, "Petition to Open a Polling Station at Bard College," October 9, 2007.

57 The 2009 resolution echoed the points in the petition, noting, among other things, that "the polling station at St. John's Church in Barrytown is not adequate for the voting needs ... due to the size and location of the site," that "the majority of the voters (in the district) reside in or near Annandale," and there was an absence of "space to shelter resident electors during inclement weather;" Town of Red Hook, *Revision of Polling Stations for the General Elections*, Resolution No. 15, March 10, 2009.

58 Jonathan Becker, "NY State Can Help Overcome Voter Suppression of College Students," *WAMC Northeast Public Radio*, January 27, 2022, 5:30, https://www.wamc.org/commentary-opinion/2022-01-27/ny-state-can-help-overcome-voter-suppression-of-college-students.

dents as second-class citizens. He regularly juxtaposed the terms 'student voters' and 'taxpaying, permanent residents,' implying that the latter were more deserving.[59] He even went so far as to suggest that making it easier for student voters would privilege them in unfair and undemocratic ways: "We don't want a situation where we have a group of voters that are super-enfranchised and a different group of voters in the same election district who are disenfranchised."[60]

Haight's intransigence meant that advocates of a polling place on campus had little hope. The NYCLU, which had been essential to students' victories in 2000 and 2012–2013, was sympathetic to the complaint, and even issued a letter to the BOE in 2016. But given judicial deference to election administrators, it thought the odds of a successful lawsuit unlikely, so its engagement ended there.[61] However, the emergence of Bard's partnership with The Andrew Goodman Foundation (AGF) brought renewed focus. From 2014, the student group Election@Bard became populated by AGF 'Vote Anywhere' ambassadors. It was the Vote Anywhere ambassadors Eva-Marie Quinones and Jonian Rafti who led the appeal to the Town Board in 2016 for a poll site on the Bard campus, making presentations together with Bard administrators from the CCE. Quinones summed up students' assessment of the situation and their commitment to making change thus: "Democracy is based on the concept of one vote, one voice. Right now in the Hudson Valley, one party wants to increase its electoral competitiveness in one of the last swing districts in the nation by disenfranchising an entire demographic. They're fighting dirty. We have one thing to say in response to this: *We'll fight back.*"[62]

A more concerted effort to focus on the poll site issue emerged as the 2020 election approached. From March 2019, AGF Chief Legal Counsel Yael Bromberg,

---

59 Erik Haight, "Commissioner Haight: Set Record Straight with Facts" *Poughkeepsie Journal*, May 28, 2016, downloaded December 10, 2024, https://www.poughkeepsiejournal.com/story/opinion/val ley-views/2016/05/28/commissioner-haight-set-record-straight-facts/84920538/.

60 "Dutchess County Board of Elections, Public Meeting of Dutchess County Board of Elections," virtual meeting, February 25, 2021, posted August 9, 2021, by Bard Center for Civic Engagement, YouTube, 30:32, https://www.youtube.com/watch?v=v8lZDH1Yg1k&t=2s. Dutchess County GOP Committee Chairman Michael McCormack was even more blunt in his assessment: "Bard College is the number one liberal college in all of America—number one, not two, 10, or 15, but number one. Having a polling place on a private institution's campus is stupid"; quoted in Hank Gross, "Agreement Reached on Bard Voting Location," *Mid Hudson News*, October 29, 2020, https://mid hudsonnews.com/2020/10/29/agreement-reached-on-bard-voting-location/.

61 Shannon Wong, NYCLU letter to Election Commissioner Erik Haight, April 11, 2016; *Andrew Goodman Foundation v. Dutchess County Board of Elections*, 52737/20 (N.Y. Sup. Ct. 2020).

62 Eva-Marie Quinones, "The Battle for the Ballot: Inside the Voting Rights Struggle in New York," *Buzzfeed*, May 13, 2016, https://www.buzzfeed.com/evamariequinones/the-battle-for-the-ballot-in side-the-voting-right-2crpl.

a leading 26th Amendment scholar and litigator, met approximately every two weeks with the Election@Bard team, which included Goodman Vote Anywhere ambassadors and staff 'co-champion' Sarah deVeer, the outreach coordinator of CCE. This added systematic engagement, and critical legal focus created a new environment in which they could collectively be more responsive to what proved to be a fast-changing situation. With an eye towards potential litigation, Bromberg recruited Doug Mishkin, who had a long association with the Goodman family and was a senior litigator with decades of experience. He in turn brought in a pro-bono team from his former firm, Venable LLC, headed by Michael Volpe, who also had experience serving in New York local government. They sent a letter to the Dutchess County BOE in early March, prior to the formal assignation of poll sites, outlining the flaws of the St. John's poll site and the benefits of a Bard location, offering to maintain both sites or switching exclusively to one at Bard. Democratic election commissioner Beth Soto responded, saying she supported the move, but pointing out that her counterpart Haight opposed it, meaning that the status quo would remain.[63]

The COVID pandemic which was sweeping the globe brought new impetus to efforts and new opportunities to address the longstanding poll site challenge. While the church poll site posed safety concerns at the best of times, during the pandemic voting in such a small venue was actually dangerous. This spurred a different approach. During the summer of 2020 two changes took place in the way that Bard and AGF/Venable approached the issue of a poll site on campus: first, the focus moved from persuasion to litigation, and, second, the Bard side in meetings with AGF/Venable was expanded beyond the involvement of students and junior administrators to regularly include representatives of the senior administration, including Vice President Cannan, whose work on voting continued; and me, in my capacity as director of CCE and Bard executive vice president/vice president for academic affairs.

The litigation that materialized in August and September 2020, which ultimately became *The Andrew Goodman Foundation v. Dutchess County Board of Elections*, was distinguished by its plaintiffs, who represented cooperation and coordination among students, the institutional leadership, and external advocacy groups: the AGF; the student-led group Election@Bard; its leader and Goodman Vote Everywhere ambassador Sadia Saba; Vice President Cannan, who regularly served as a poll worker at the church; and Bard's long-serving President Leon Botstein, who resided on campus and thus was a district voter. The content covered all

---

63 Elizabeth Soto, Brief, *Andrew Goodman Foundation v. Dutchess County Board of Elections*, 52737/20 (N.Y. Sup. Ct. 2020), https://tools.bard.edu/wwwmedia/files/8850342/71/SotoBrief.pdf.

the complaints over the years about the problems with the church and underlined the advantages of the proposed Bard site—the Multipurpose Room (MPR) of the Bertelsmann Campus Center, and particularly its close proximity to the majority of district voters. However, it zeroed in on two issues that could provide greater legal traction, given the general judicial deference to the decisions of election administrators: disability access and the dangers posed by the pandemic.

While there had long been accusations that the poll site was neither handicap-accessible nor ADA-compliant, the BOE regularly denied this and claimed that its detailed surveys demonstrated that the site was compliant. However, with preparations for a lawsuit taking shape, the Bard team was able to do more research into the issue. CCE requested a copy of the latest accessibility survey, as well as past surveys, through a state public records law ('FOIL') request. The results were astonishing: 17 of 37 questions on the survey were left blank, with "N/A" notations. Among other things, the surveyors failed to answer the entire ramp compliance section, in spite of the fact that the ramp was the only means of entering the building for those with mobility issues. Other questions were answered incorrectly. CCE representatives then visited the site with the head of Bard's Buildings and Grounds, who was responsible for implementing ADA mandates on the Bard campus, and I prepared a report that also incorporated issues raised in the US Department of Justice Civil Rights Division's *ADA Checklist for Polling Places*.[64] The report was then reviewed by Bard's director of accessibility and disability. It was used not only for the purpose of legal filings but was shared publicly, with additional photographic and video documentation of the site's shortcomings.[65] A local disabilities rights organization, Caring Majority Rising, then mobilized, communicating with local politicians and holding a press conference to highlight the challenges the site presented to disabled voters and to underline the BOE's failures.[66]

---

[64] US Department of Justice, Civil Rights Division, *ADA Checklist for Polling Places* (June 2016), https://www.ada.gov/votingchecklist.pdf.

[65] Jonathan Becker, "Report on Visit to Barrytown Polling Site: Red Hook D5," *Andrew Goodman Foundation v. Dutchess County Board of Elections*, 52737/20 (N.Y. Sup. Ct. 2020), https://tools.bard.edu/wwwmedia/files/8850342/78/ADAReport.pdf. For CCE's video on compliance at the poll site, see "ADA Compliance in D5 Red Hook," August 25, 2020, posted April 28, 2021, by Bard Center for Civic Engagement, YouTube, 1:53, https://www.youtube.com/watch?v=jbp69lLmCG8.

[66] The press conference, which was well attended and moving, featured presenters who spoke passionately, highlighting the poll site issue from a disability perspective. See "The Fight for a Polling Place at Bard College," virtual press conference, October 22, 2020, posted October 22, 2020, by Bard Center for Civic Engagement, YouTube, 47:00, https://www.youtube.com/watch?v=ZFp2C8bU7S0.

COVID was an even more salient issue. All of the problems with the church as a polling site were magnified by the pandemic. The idea of cramming six (usually elderly) poll workers into a cramped space was suboptimal at the best of times but frightening during COVID. This was stressed in another presentation before the Red Hook Town Board in August, in which student leaders, backed up by members of CCE, pressed the Board to weigh in. The Town again passed a resolution supporting moving the poll site, underlining both handicap accessibility issues and "an additional and urgent need to provide a polling location with adequate social distancing measures and enhanced safety precautions."[67]

The CCE team also turned to the Bard faculty, asking Professor Felicia Keesing, a world-renowned researcher in infectious diseases, to review the relative safety of the church vs. the proposed space at the campus center. She prepared a report that argued that "the risk of a community member contracting the virus while voting at Bard is at least as low as it is anywhere else in Dutchess County that uses a room of comparable size" and that the risk of COVID transmission at the church was "at least four times higher than at the Bard MPR."[68] CCE representatives who served on Bard's COVID Response Team also worked to incorporate a potential poll site into Bard's robust COVID action plan.

CCE leaders separately approached the church leadership, including a retired professor of biology, to seek their intervention. While they initially demurred, citing the tradition of the church hosting voting and the need to be neutral, Keesing's study helped convince them to take a stand. On September 15, they wrote to the county BOE begging off hosting the poll site and stating, "Our concerns revolve around the current pandemic of COVID-19, and our inability to provide an adequately safe environment for the poll workers as well as the voters. Simply put, our space is too small to support much-needed COVID social distancing, and other sites within District 5 are much larger."[69]

None of this moved Haight. He was not obliged to listen to the college, disability advocates, or scientists. He could even ignore church officials because the

---

67 The presentation featured Student Council president Adrian Costa, Goodman ambassador Sadia Sabia, deVeer, and me; Town of Red Hook, *Resolution Regarding Election District No. 5*, Resolution No. 40, August 26, 2020. For the complete hearing, see "Red Hook Town Council Meeting 08/26/2020 7:30 PM," August 26, 2020, posted August 26, 2020, by Public Access Northern Dutchess (PANDANOW), YouTube, 1:30:05, https://www.youtube.com/watch?v=_BBi9aNJPds#action=share.

68 She stressed Bard's strong safety record and stringent testing regime; *Andrew Goodman Foundation v. Dutchess County Board of Elections*, 52737/20 (N.Y. Sup. Ct. 2020).

69 Mary Grace Williams, Vicar, and John Ferguson, Treasurer, The Church of St. John the Evangelist, letter to Dutchess County Board of Elections, September 15, 2020.

BOE was empowered to require non-profits to host election sites. The commitment to political advantage and hostility to student voters outweighed all arguments about disability compliance and the safety of voters and poll workers. He attempted to refute some specific issues but primarily argued on the basis of procedure and process. He asserted that the objection to disability access should have been filed prior to March, when poll sites are selected. His central argument, however, was that moving the poll site at the late date risked disenfranchising voters who would go to the wrong location.

In the end, Supreme Court Justice Maria Rosa sided with Haight. While she was sympathetic to the substance of the arguments made by AGF and Bard, she indicated that the formal ADA complaints procedurally appeared too late and that, while the use of St. John's as a polling place was "not ideal ... it is not the function of this court to substitute its judgment for that of an administrative agency" barring "arbitrary and capricious actions." She concluded by citing Haight's claim that it would be "too close in time (to the election) to change the polling site" and that doing so would not "be fair" to voters of the district.[70]

The case seemed to be over, however, within two days of the decision, two of the seven other election districts in Red Hook were moved from the Town Hall to a local school in response to COVID concerns. Frustrated by the hypocrisy but sensing an opportunity, the legal team and the plaintiffs regrouped and decided to appeal immediately. Rosa, clearly stung by what she viewed as Haight's deception, reversed herself and ruled in favor of moving the poll site to Bard, stating: "The basis for this court's decision and order has now been eliminated since the primary factor identified by Commissioner Haight and relied upon by this court was simply untrue. Apparently there was, and is, time to move the polling place for District 5 in Red Hook."[71]

Haight in turn appealed to the State Appellate Court, which, after its October 28 hearing, prevailed upon the parties to reach an agreement by which two poll sites would be opened in Red Hook District 5, one in Barrytown and one at Bard. Nearly two decades after the fight for a poll place on the Bard campus had begun, there would be one in time for the 2020 election.

As one might expect, this did not settle the issue. In 2021, there again was litigation over the poll site. Haight asserted that the 2020 agreement for two poll sites in the district did not constitute a precedent and that it was instituted

---

70 Justice Maria G. Rosa, Decision and Order, *Andrew Goodman Foundation v. Dutchess County Board of Elections*, 52737/20 (N.Y. Sup. Ct. 2020), https://tools.bard.edu/wwwmedia/files/8850342/65/Judges%20Decisioon%20September%202020.pdf.
71 Justice Maria G. Rosa, Decision, Order on Motion for Leave to Reargue and Renew, *Andrew Goodman Foundation v. Dutchess County Board of Elections*, 52737/20 (N.Y. Sup. Ct. 2020).

Figure 2: Voters line up early at Bertelsmann Campus Center at Bard College, Election Day, November 2020. Photo courtesy of Jonathan Becker with thanks to Barry Cawston.

only as a one-off measure in response to COVID. Thus, if the two commissioners could not agree on a new poll site, voting would revert to pre-2020 conditions and take place again only at the church. He offered an alternate site on campus, a former restaurant that serves as the alumni center. However, Bard representatives vigorously objected, noting that the location was genuinely dangerous to access since it was situated at a distant point from the main campus across a high-speed rural road with no pedestrian crossings and no access via public transportation.[72] Haight also raised the possibility of using Bard's Fisher Center for Performing Arts, but again Bard representatives objected due to issues of accessibility (the arts center was located at one extreme of the 1,000 acre campus) and the fact that the lobby where Haight proposed to situate the poll site was used for social but never administrative purposes. With a stalemate at the BOE, Bard sued again,

---

72 "Second Public Hearing on District 5 Polling Place," virtual hearing, September 3, 2021, posted September 6, 2021, by Bard College, YouTube, 42:33, https://www.youtube.com/watch?v=HdNY Erw1Xu0.

receiving pro-bono support from Bromberg and Mishkin, as well as attorney Mike Donofrio, who had previously worked with Bromberg on voting issues and policy analysis related to the 26th Amendment.[73] Once again, Election@Bard, Botstein, and Cannan served as litigants, this time joined by four students and a staff member.[74] In this round, Judge Rosa sided with Bard from the start, as did the New York Appellate Division. Henceforth, a polling site would remain at the Bard Bertelsmann Campus Center unless both commissioners agreed to move it.[75]

3.1 Legislative Solutions

While a polling place at Bard seemed set for the foreseeable future, the work was not done. In keeping with its motto of "a private institution in the public interest," Bard pursued the strategy of arriving at a long-term legislative solution to prevent abuses by county Boards of Election, as had occurred in Dutchess County. Bard joined a coalition of voting-rights groups—including Let New York Vote, GenVote, the NYPIRG, the Citizens Union, Common Cause, and the AGF—to advocate for polling places on college campuses across the state. In op-eds and public communications, they used Haight's egregious conduct as a vivid example of the need for a legislative solution.[76] The coalition supported a new law, folded into the state's April 2022 budget, that mandated that county election boards situate polling places on college campuses that had at least 300 registered voters, or at a location mutually agreeable to the board and the college adjacent to the campus. Importantly, the law also said the polling district must be contiguous with the property

---

73 Bromberg worked via her law firm Bromberg Law LLC while Donofrio worked for Stris & Maher LLP. David Vance, "SCOTUS Challenge to Texas COVID-19 Vote by Mail Age Discrimination Draws Amicus from The Andrew Goodman Foundation, Equal Citizens, and Common Cause," *Common Cause*, October 22, 2020, https://www.commoncause.org/press/scotus-challenge-to-texas-covid-19-vote-by-mail-age-discrimination-draws-amicus-from-the-andrew-goodman-foundation-equal-citizens-and-common-cause/.
74 The full case was *Bard College, Election@Bard, Leon Botstein, Erin Cannan, Cynthia Deann Austin Cunningham, Maria Alejandra Rodriguez Ortiz, Sarina Jaqueline Culaj, and Tomas S. Forman v. Dutchess County Board of Elections, Erik J. Haight, and Hannah Black*, 198 A.D.3d 1014 (N.Y. App. Div. 2021) (No. 52777/21).
75 Even after Bard won the second lawsuit over poll sites, it still faced resistance from the County Board of Elections in terms of being supplied fewer poll workers than any other poll site in the county and given one instead of two voting machines. This was explained in the following letter: Jonathan Becker, letter to New York State Board of Elections Enforcement Counsel, August 15, 2022, https://tools.bard.edu/wwwmedia/files/8850342/99/Complaint%20to%20State%20BOE%20August%2015,%202022.pdf.
76 Jonathan Becker, "NY State Can Help."

Figure 3: Bard College President Leon Botstein at Bertelsmann Campus Center poll site, November, 2024. Photo by Robin Kaiküll '26, courtesy of Bard College.

of the campus, thus avoiding situations of gerrymandered campuses like Vassar. Indeed, with the support of Bard and Bromberg, Vassar became the first institution to gain a poll site under the new law, after a faculty member, a student, and the League of Women Voters, represented by Elias Law Group LLP, successfully sued to force a recalcitrant Haight to honor the new law.[77]

These various efforts also informed in part development of the Youth Voting Rights Act, a first-of-its-kind federal proposal designed by Bromberg with the support of American Civil Liberties Union National to cure a variety of impediments to students' voting rights and expand their related access. The measure was introduced to Congress by Senator Elizabeth Warren and US Representative Nikema

---

77 Clara Alger, "Fighting for the Youth Vote in the Hudson Valley," *The River*, November 2, 2023, https://www.chronogram.com/river-newsroom/fighting-for-the-youth-vote-in-the-hudson-valley-19347760.

Williams and, while it has not been passed, it serves as an inspiration for student organizers and is helping to model legislation in different states.

4 Reflections

The Bard case illustrates that the suppression of student votes can happen anywhere and that young people can be targets of voter suppression even in a predominantly white area in a blue state. Despite the 26th Amendment, despite the 1979 Supreme Court ruling in *Symm*, despite the 1984 *Aurbach* decision in New York State, and despite New York State election law, students of Bard and other colleges in Dutchess County were targeted by successive public officials who acted with impunity. They ignored legal precedent and advisory opinions of the State BOE, created discriminatory rules targeted at college students, wielded obviously flawed accessibility surveys to obtain desired conclusions, ignored science, and made false representations at public hearings and even before judges. They were willing to literally risk the health and well-being of elderly poll workers and (primarily student) voters to gain political advantage.

Figure 4: Election@Bard Get Out the Vote Effort, November, 2023. Photo by Jonathan Asiedu '24, courtesy of Bard College.

The Bard case demonstrates that, in order to combat such an approach, there are tremendous benefits to getting student, faculty, and institutional stakeholders to work collaboratively towards a collective goal and to seek, where needed, support from external actors. Bard has created an 'ecosystem of engagement,' which it hopes will serve as an educational model, in which different actors can interact and cooperate, and both respond to fast-changing circumstances and maintain continuity of engagement over long periods of time.[78]

A key distinguishing feature of Bard is that the institution views much of the work related to student voting as a part of its broad educational mission, underlining the link between education, engaged citizenship, and democracy. As Erin Cannan and I argue in our *Rutgers University Law Review* article "Institution as Citizen: Colleges and Universities as Actors in Defense of Student Voting Rights," the institution, from its Board of Trustees on down, has supported students, faculty, and administrators, and used its resources– human, organizational, financial, reputational, and intellectual—to defend students' constitutional rights.[79]

Bard has viewed engagement with voting as part of the educational process. The tools used to promote and defend these rights—letter-writing, petitions, protests, press conferences, state open public records requests, appearances before government bodies, op-eds, research, and litigation—all became lessons for students in engaged citizenship, reaffirming the words of former Congressman and federal Judge Abner Mikva that "democracy is a verb."[80] It has also done so to avoid the pervasive situation in higher education where deeds so often fall short of words. Soaring rhetoric by university leaders and graduation speakers about the virtues of 'making a difference' seem hollow when the institution itself ignores injustice that compromises its broad educational mission.

The role of the institution should not obscure the critical contributions of dedicated students and faculty. Bard students have consistently acted like participatory and justice-oriented citizens as outlined in chapter two, participating in the civic life of the community and calling out and addressing injustice. At the turn of the millennium, justice-oriented students with SAVE mobilized, found allies in the faculty, administration, and local advocacy and legal defense organizations, and were able to win the right of Bard students to vote. Future generations of students under the banner of Election@Bard, many of whom served as Andrew Goodman ambassadors, actively promoted registration, kept the issue of a polling place on campus on the agenda, and served as litigants when their rights were violated. One of the litigants in the 2012–2013 federal case related to residential addresses, Daniel Roscoe Kern, summed up the stakes, stating, "I will either become

78 Jonathan Becker, "Bard College: An Ecosystem of Engagement," *Journal of Community Engagement in Higher Education* 11, no. 1 (2019): 38–52.
79 Jonathan Becker and Erin Cannan, "Institution as Citizen: Colleges and Universities as Actors in Defense of Student Voting Rights," *Rutgers University Law Review* 74, no. 5 (2022): 865–909.
80 Abner Mikva, "About Us," The Mikvan Challenge, https://mikvachallenge.org/about-us/.

completely disheartened and disillusioned with the system or I will say you can actually ... make a bit of a difference."[81]

Bard students who invested in these efforts during their college education went on to achieve great success as active and engaged justice-oriented citizens. For example, Michael Chameides, who founded and led SAVE, serves on the Columbia County Board of Supervisors, due north of Dutchess County, and has served as a community and labor organizer since graduation. Monica Elkinton, who co-led SAVE in 1999, went on to become a state court judge in Alaska. Jonian Rafti, who with Eva-Marie Quinones re-launched efforts to ensure an on-campus polling location, went on to become a national board member of The Andrew Goodman Foundation and a litigator, and Quinones went on to obtain a law degree, works as a litigator, and is also a PhD candidate in political science, where her primary research focuses on voting behavior and disenfranchisement. In other words, their education at Bard College, and their applied focuses in civics and voter engagement, readied them and set them on a professional path for active citizenry.

Faculty also acted as participatory and justice-oriented citizens. Robert Koblitz devoted a tutorial to student voting rights in 1976 in an effort to help students register voters, and his advice and introduction of student organizers to NYCLU representatives helped three students win a lawsuit and vote in Dutchess County. Joseph Luders brought SAVE's work into the classroom. Biologist Felicia Keesing used her scientific expertise to make a case for a polling place at Bard. Bard political studies professor Simon Gilhooley regularly serves as a poll worker at the on-campus poll site. Art professors assign projects with get-out-the-vote themes that adorn campus. Later, the voting rights class taught by me and Gilhooley from which this book emerged created assignments that ultimately formed the basis of a CCE report on the implementation of the new state law mandating polling places on college campuses with 300 or more registered voters. This initiative, at the time of writing, is helping to shape further legislation.[82]

The Bard case also underlines the importance of partnerships. Partnerships with the AGF and ALL IN help register students to vote. Partnerships with the NYCLU and the AGF were critical to obtaining the pro-bono legal representation necessary to establish and defend the right to vote and to gain a polling site on campus. Partnerships with non-profit organizations and networks like GenVote

81 Lachance, "Student Votes Challenged," 6.
82 "Bard Center for Civic Engagement Prepares Report on Poll Sites on College Campuses," Bard Center for Civic Engagement, posted February 16, 2024, https://cce.bard.edu/news/bard-center-for-civic-engagement-prepares-report-on-poll-sites-on-college-campuses-2024-01-06.

and NYPIRG proved essential to passing legislation in New York that will promote polling sites on all New York campuses into the future.

Ultimately, Bard's success was a product of its educational philosophy summed up by President Botstein in his affidavit for the 2020 poll site lawsuit: "Bard College's academic mission is to function in the public interest, and ensure that young voters are civically engaged in the practice of democracy." By not simply rhetorically supporting the link between education and democracy, but serving as a civic actor in its own right, the institution both created an ecosystem in which engagement with voting rights issues was welcome and taught its students important lessons about engaged citizenship in a democracy.

Bibliography

"ADA Compliance in D5 Red Hook." August 25, 2020. Posted April 28, 2021, by Bard Center for Civic Engagement. YouTube, 1:53. https://www.youtube.com/watch?v=jbp69lLmCG8.

"After Judge Rules for Students Election Board Changes Tune." *The Journal*, Ogdensburg, New York, October 10, 1984.

Alger, Clara. "Fighting for the Youth Vote in the Hudson Valley." *The River*, November 2, 2023. https://www.chronogram.com/river-newsroom/fighting-for-the-youth-vote-in-the-hudson-valley-19347760.

Bard Center for Civic Engagement. "Bard Center for Civic Engagement Prepares Report on Poll Sites on College Campuses." Posted February 16, 2024. https://cce.bard.edu/news/bard-center-for-civic-engagement-prepares-report-on-poll-sites-on-college-campuses-2024-01-06.

Bard College. "Mission Statement." https://www.bard.edu/about/mission/.

"Barrytown (District 5) on Election Night." Live footage, November 3, 2009. Posted November 16, 2009 by BGIAProgram. YouTube, 1:48. https://www.youtube.com/watch?v=ng4QF9lnPds.

Becker, Jonathan. "College Students Deserve to Vote Where They Live." *Poughkeepsie Journal*, December 24, 1999.

Becker, Jonathan. "To the Editor." *Poughkeepsie Journal*, November 20, 2009.

Becker, Jonathan. "Colleges Should Promote and Defend Student Voting." *Huffington Post*, August 12, 2016. https://www.huffpost.com/entry/american-colleges-should-promote-and-defend-student_b_57ae185fe4b0ae60ff026711.

Becker, Jonathan. "Bard College: An Ecosystem of Engagement." *Journal of Community Engagement in Higher Education* 11, no. 1 (2019): 38–52.

Becker, Jonathan. "NY State Can Help Overcome Voter Suppression of College Students." *WAMC Northeast Public Radio*, January 27, 2022. 5:30. https://www.wamc.org/commentary-opinion/2022-01-27/ny-state-can-help-overcome-voter-suppression-of-college-students.

Becker, Jonathan, and Erin Cannan, "Institution as Citizen: Colleges and Universities as Actors in Defense of Student Voting Rights," *Rutgers University Law Review* 74, no. 5 (2022): 865–909. https://rutgerslawreview.com/wp-content/uploads/2023/02/07_Becker_Cannan.pdf

Berber Smith, Jane, and Greenblatt, Linda. "Progress in Student Voting Questionable." *Poughkeepsie Journal*, July 6, 2000.

Bernstein, Andrew. "Tedisco Team Challenges Gillibrand Ballot." *Troy Record*, April 25, 2009, downloaded December 9, 2024. https://www.troyrecord.com/2009/04/15/tedisco-team-challenges-gillibrands-ballot/.

Bromberg, Yael. "Youth Voting Rights and the Unfulfilled Promise of the Twenty-Sixth Amendment." *University of Pennsylvania Journal of Constitutional Law* 21, no. 5 (2019): 1105–1166. https://scholarship.law.upenn.edu/jcl/vol21/iss5/1/.

Center for Information & Research on Civic Learning and Engagement. "Why Youth Don't Vote: Differences by Race and Education." August 21, 2018. https://circle.tufts.edu/latest-research/why-youth-dont-vote-differences-race-and-education.

Chameides, Michael. "Verdict is In: Dutchess County Students Win Right to Vote." *Bard Free Press* 2, no. 1 (September 2000): 1–2. https://digitalcommons.bard.edu/cgi/viewcontent.cgi?article=1005&context=bardfreepres.

Citrin, Muni. "Questionnaire Incites Controversy." *Bard Observer*, September 20, 1996.

David, Susannah E. "Analyzing Kovel's Defeat in Senate Elections 1998." *Bard Observer*, November 18, 1998.

Davis John, and Stewart, Emily. "Disgraced Republican Giant William Paroli Sr. Dies at 86." *Poughkeepsie Journal*, March 22, 2014, downloaded December 17, 2024. https://www.poughkeepsiejournal.com/story/news/2014/03/22/william-paroli-sr-controversial-former-gop-leader-has-died/6730283/.

Doxsey, Patricia. "Dutchess Legislature will Shrink in 2004." *Daily Freeman*, November 13, 2002, downloaded December 17, 2024. https://www.dailyfreeman.com/2002/11/13/dutchess-legislature-will-shrink-in-2004/.

Doxsey, Patricia. "Dem Enrollment Tops Republican in Dutchess." *Daily Freeman*, October 10, 2008, downloaded December 12, 2024. https://www.dailyfreeman.com/2008/10/10/dem-enrollment-tops-republican-in-dutchess/.

Doxsey, Patricia. "Bard Students Unhappy with Voting Hassle." *Daily Freeman*, November 20, 2009, downloaded December 12, 2024. https://www.dailyfreeman.com/2009/11/20/bard-students-unhappy-with-voting-hassle-with-video/.

Doxey, Patricia. "In Dutchess County, Battle Brews Over Dorm Dwellers' Voting Rights." *Daily Freeman*, October 19, 2012, downloaded December 12, 2024. https://www.dailyfreeman.com/2012/10/19/in-dutchess-county-battle-brews-over-dorm-dwellers-voting-rights/.

"Dutchess County Board of Elections, Public Meeting of Dutchess County Board of Elections." Virtual meeting, February 25, 2021. Posted August 9, 2021, by Bard Center for Civic Engagement. YouTube, 30:32. https://www.youtube.com/watch?v=v8lZDH1Yg1k&t=2s.

Dutchess County Legislator Committee. *Report on Student Voting Questions.* March 13, 2000. https://cce.bard.edu/get-involved/election/files/report-on-student-voting.pdf.

Election@Bard. *Bard College's ALL-IN Campus Democracy Challenge Action Plan.* Created December 15, 2021, revised December 10, 2023. https://allinchallenge.org/wp-content/uploads/Bard-College-2024-Action-Plan.pdf.

Farmer, Anthony. "Task Force, Let Collegians Vote." *Poughkeepsie Journal*, March 19, 2000.

"Good Progress on Student Vote." *Poughkeepsie Journal*, June 20, 2000.

Gross, Hank. "Agreement Reached on Bard Voting Location." *Mid Hudson News*, October 29, 2020. https://midhudsonnews.com/2020/10/29/agreement-reached-on-bard-voting-location/.

Haight, Erik. "Commissioner Haight: Set Record Straight with Facts." *Poughkeepsie Journal*, May 28, 2016, downloaded December 10, 2024. https://www.poughkeepsiejournal.com/story/opinion/valley-views/2016/05/28/commissioner-haight-set-record-straight-facts/84920538/.

Hudson. "NY-20: Beware of the Pizza Stain Judge." *Daily Kos*, April 15, 2009, downloaded December 9, 2024. https://www.dailykos.com/storyonly/2009/4/14/720054/-NY-20:-Beware-the-Pizza-Stain-Judge.

Lachance, Naomi. "Student Votes Challenged." *Bard Free Press* 14, no. 5 (November 2012): 6 – 7. https://digitalcommons.bard.edu/cgi/viewcontent.cgi?article=1101&context=bardfreepress.

Mikva, Abner. "About Us." The Mikvan Challenge. https://mikvachallenge.org/about-us/.

New York State Board of Elections. "06/12/2012 Meeting Transcript." https://elections.ny.gov/system/files/documents/2023/10/cctranscriptions06122012.pdf.

New York State Department of State Division of Local Government Services. *Local Government Handbook*. Albany, 2018. https://dos.ny.gov/system/files/documents/2023/06/localgovernmenthandbook 2023.pdf.5186103850

Oluwa, Rasheed. "Preservation Tax Squeaks By." *Poughkeepsie Journal*, May 2, 2007.

Quinones, Eva-Marie. "The Battle for the Ballot: Inside the Voting Rights Struggle in New York." *Buzzfeed*, May 13, 2016. https://www.buzzfeed.com/evamariequinones/the-battle-for-the-ballot-inside-the-voting-right-2crpl.

"Red Hook Town Council Meeting 08/26/2020 7:30 PM." August 26, 2020. Posted August 26, 2020, by Public Access Northern Dutchess (PANDANOW). YouTube, 1:30:05. https://www.youtube.com/watch?v=_BBi9aNJPds#action=share.

Rom, Rafi. "Voting Campaign Heats Up." *Bard Observer*, February 28, 2000.

"SAVE." *Bard Free Press*, October 4, 2000. https://digitalcommons.bard.edu/cgi/viewcontent.cgi?article=1006&context=bardfreepress.

"Second Public Hearing on District 5 Polling Place." Virtual hearing, September 3, 2021. Posted September 6, 2021, by Bard College. YouTube, 42:33. https://www.youtube.com/watch?v=HdNYErw1Xu0.

Silverbush, Ben. "Students Preparing Class Action Lawsuit." *The Miscellany News*, February 18, 2000.

"State Limit on Voting By Students Overturned." *New York Times*, October 11, 1984.

Stone, Marylin. "3 Bard Student Register as a Result of Court Ruling." *Poughkeepsie Journal*, October 28, 1976.

Sturgeon, Noel, and Caffrey, Sara. "To the Editor." *Poughkeepsie Journal*, October 8, 1976.

"The Fight for a Polling Place at Bard College." Virtual press conference, October 22, 2020. Posted October 22, 2020, by Bard Center for Civic Engagement. YouTube, 47:00. https://www.youtube.com/watch?v=ZFp2C8bU7S0.

U.S. Department of Justice, Civil Rights Division. *ADA Checklist for Polling Places*, June 2016. https://www.ada.gov/votingchecklist.pdf.

Vance, David. "SCOTUS Challenge to Texas COVID-19 Vote By Mail Age Discrimination Draws Amicus from The Andrew Goodman Foundation, Equal Citizens, and Common Cause." *Common Cause*, October 22, 2020. https://www.commoncause.org/press/scotus-challenge-to-texas-covid-19-vote-by-mail-age-discrimination-draws-amicus-from-the-andrew-goodman-foundation-equal-citizens-and-common-cause/.

Jonathan Becker

7 Lessons Learned: Summary of the Cases

The ratification of the 26th Amendment did not end the fight over youth voting rights in the country. While there was clear agreement that citizens aged 18 to 21 could vote free of age discrimination, there was no consensus on where they could vote, nor clarity on how rules governing the processes of registration and voting would translate for populations such as students, who by nature are more itinerant.[1] As foreshadowed in the congressional debate over the passage of the Amendment, this fight was particularly virulent on college campuses.

Nowhere was this more so than at Historically Black Colleges and Universities (HBCUs), which were attractive targets for voter suppression and disenfranchisement because they represent the intersection of potential Black and youth power and illuminate broader questions of what it means to live in a representational democracy, and what it means to teach and engage youth citizenry. In the framework offered by civil rights theorist Lani Guinier, racialized communities can serve as a "miner's canary," offering a "diagnostic, signaling need for more systemic critique" based on "early warning signs of poison in the social atmosphere."[2] Like a miner's canary, the poisonous impact of voter suppression at HBCUs offers a diagnosis to aid democratic renewal for the general population at large, and especially the class of youth voters. Since the passage of the 26th Amendment, youth voter suppression has not only impacted HBCUs, but also other higher educational institutions, public and private, including primarily white institutions. The case studies examined in this book illustrate that remarkably similar tactics were used to suppress the student vote across institutions, time, and geographies. It is also worth noting that youth voter suppression also exists in non-college settings, including at the high school level. All of this works against the spirit of the Amendment, which aspired to "encourage greater political participation on the part of the young," not simply to remove barriers to access.[3]

This chapter will review the case studies featured in this book and attempt to identify some common themes that emerged. It will begin by exploring the mech-

---

1 For details of the legislative history of the Amendment and manifestations of its as-yet unfulfilled promise, see Yael Bromberg, "Youth Voting Rights and the Unfulfilled Promise of the Twenty-Sixth Amendment," *University of Pennsylvania Journal of Constitutional Law* 21, no. 5 (2019): 1105–1166, https://papers.ssrn.com/sol3/papers.cfm?abstract_id=3442198.
2 Lani Guinier, *The Miner's Canary* (Harvard University Press, 2003), 11–12.
3 Bromberg, "Youth Voting Rights," 1133.

anisms of voter suppression, and particularly how local election officials used their positions of power to implement discriminatory practices that targeted students. It will then examine the motivations for such actions, including the intersection between youth, race, and political power. Finally, it will analyze how students, faculty, and administrators fought back to promote voting and defend student voting rights, incorporating the adaptation of Westheimer and Kahne's typology of citizenship discussed in chapter two.

1 Voter Disenfranchisement and the Student Vote

The four case studies demonstrate that there have been—and continue to be—many similarities in terms of methods deployed to restrict voting. While the Voting Rights Acts and a flurry of legal decisions have meant that some of the most notorious and egregious methods of voter suppression used in the Jim Crow era are no longer viable, one lesson of the case studies is that local and state officials in America's decentralized election system have tremendous latitude to shape the voting process.

The cases were selected so as to demonstrate the evolution of the right to vote, and how it has been restricted over time on college campuses as sites of voter suppression; accordingly, they tell the story of good, bad, and sometimes ambivalent government officials. On the front line are local election administrators, whether they are referred to as registrars, election commissioners, or, as in the case of Texas in the 1970s, tax accessor-collectors who served as ex-officio voter registrars. It also includes publicly elected local and state officials—mayors, town and county supervisors, and state and county legislators—responsible for oversight of local election administrators and making laws that govern voting and shape districts and municipalities; as well as governors who appoint key officials, approve laws, and often control purse strings of public institutions. Finally, it includes district attorneys responsible for enforcing voting rules and the judiciary, which is meant to impartially adjudicate rules and regulations and honor precedent in a non-partisan manner.

In the worst instances, key public officials in positions of power invented rules, implemented practices, and created voting districts all designed to disenfranchise voters and dilute student voting power. At times, these officials acted with impunity while relying on government coffers to defend their actions when they were sued for violating the rights of vulnerable and often impecunious populations.[4] They were on a few occasions aided by judges who ignored precedent and/or made decisions that triggered the targeting of student voters. Often they were supported, silently or otherwise, by others in positions of power, as well as by populations for whom the ends too readily justified the means. In the best instances, as discussed in the next section, civic actors, often coming from college communities, were able to fight restrictions and demonstrate the best of active American citizenry.

Fueled by community suspicion of student voters, residency-based challenges were a common starting point of efforts to disenfranchise student voters. Students are vulnerable because of the potentially limited duration of stay in their college communities. At Prairie View A&M University (PVAMU) in Waller County, Texas, and at Bard College in Dutchess County, New York, students, unlike other populations, were singled out with questionnaires which were regularly used as a pretext to disqualify them. The approach was reminiscent of the method used to winnow the participation of Black voters in Tuskegee and the rest of Alabama when the legislature imposed a questionnaire through The Voter Qualification Amendment in 1951.[5] Twenty years later, in Waller County, tax-assessor LeRoy Symm's use of questionnaires led to the landmark *Symm v. U.S.* case in 1979, the only substantive Supreme Court ruling on the 26th Amendment, which resolved the question of law after years in which U.S. District Court Judge James Noel of the Southern District of Texas obdurately refused to recognize other court decisions and the views of the Texas Secretary of State, Texas Attorney General, and U.S. Attorney General.[6] Two decades later, Dutchess County Election Commissioner William Paroli, Sr. displayed the impunity felt by local officials by targeting students in the county with questionnaires very similar to those used by *Symm*, ignoring rulings by

---

4 For example, Dutchess County commissioner Erik Haight cost the county nearly $130,000 in legal fees between 2012 and 2021 in three losing court cases; Jonathan Becker, "DC Legislature Public Comments on Nov. 4, 2021," recorded Dutchess County Legislature committee meeting, November 4, 2021, posted November 5, 2021 by Bard Center for Civic Engagement, YouTube, 7:57, https://youtu.be/kjZ-vgiQ248.

5 Robert J. Norrell, *Reaping the Whirlwind: The Civil Rights Movement and Tuskegee* (Alfred Knopf, 1985), 83. Norrell wrote that the questionnaire was "an ambiguous, legalistic form sprinkled with words and phrases like 'bona fide,' 'priority,' 'secular,' and 'moral turpitude,'" that would "prove to be difficult for many applicants, both black and white, though most registrars tended to help whites fill it out." For the full questionnaire, see also United States Commission on Civil Rights, *Hearings Before the US Commission on Voting Rights*, 85th Cong., 1958–1959, https://www.usccr.gov/files/historical/1958/58-001.pdf.

6 David Richards, *Once Upon a Time in Texas: A Liberal in the Lonestar State* (University of Texas Press, 2002), 155.

both the U.S. Supreme Court and New York federal and state courts in the process.[7] The policy changed only after Paroli was convicted federally for conspiracy to commit extortion and another commissioner was appointed; even then it took some months of intensive public lobbying by Bard and Vassar students, backed up by the threat of litigation to ensure that the law was followed.[8] As noted above, while the laws of the land have changed dramatically since the middle of last century, the methods used by local officials to disenfranchise student voters have, in the worst of cases, been consistent.

Gerrymanders were another favorite tool for diluting voting power. In Alabama, State Senator Samuel Engelhardt ushered through the unanimous passage of Act 140, which gerrymandered the municipal boundaries of Tuskegee from a square into a 28-sided, sea dragon-shaped figure that removed nearly all Black voters and Tuskegee Institute itself from the city boundaries.[9] In other cases, local leaders divided college campuses into multiple election districts, creating confusion about the correct polling locations and causing havoc with voter registration efforts by forcing students to re-register when they moved dormitories. After *Symm*, in the 1980s, the PVAMU campus was divided into multiple districts until the Justice Department intervened at the end of the decade.[10] The North Carolina A&T State University (NC A&T) campus was divided in two after the implementation of newly drawn congressional maps created in 2016.[11] Although a gerrymander was informally proposed but never implemented at Bard, it was deployed in the southern part of Dutchess County at Vassar College, which was divided into three electoral districts.[12] This rebounded on Bard after Dutchess County Supreme

---

7 Rafi Rom, "Voting Campaign Heats Up," *Bard Observer*, February 28, 2000, 3; Michael Chameides, "Verdict is In: Dutchess County Students Win Right to Vote," *Bard Free Press* 2, no. 1 (September 2000): 1–2, https://digitalcommons.bard.edu/cgi/viewcontent.cgi?article=1005&context=bardfreepress.

8 Chameides, "Verdict is In."

9 Lewis Jones and Stanley Smith, *Tuskegee, Alabama: Voting Rights and Economic Pressure*, Field Reports on Desegregation in the South (Anti-Defamation League of B'nai B'rith, 1958).

10 In 1990, thanks to enforcement by the Department of Justice, students were regrouped into one district. See Rodney Ellis, "Jim Crow Goes to College," *New York Times*, April 27, 1992, https://www.nytimes.com/1992/04/27/opinion/jim-crow-goes-to-college.html. See also Alexa Ura, "Texas' Oldest Black University Was Built on a Former Plantation. Its Students Still Fight a Legacy of Voter Suppression.," *The Texas Tribune*, February 25, 2021, https://www.texastribune.org/2021/02/25/waller-county-texas-voter-suppression/.

11 Elizabeth Thompson, "The Legal Fight Over NC Gerrymandering Isn't Over. How We Got Here, and What's Next," *The News & Observer*, June 27, 2019, https://www.newsobserver.com/news/politics-government/article231422113.html.

12 Jyotsna Naidu, "Local Independent Redistricting Could Challenge Gerrymandered Campus," *The Miscellany News*, February 9, 2022, https://miscellanynews.org/2022/02/09/news/local-indepen-

Court Justice James Brands' 2009 ex-parte order, issued on election day solely based on a complaint filed by a notorious attorney, empowered partisan poll watchers to challenge student voters from Bard and Vassar outside of established practices. As a result, bewildered students were challenged at the polls and, with no evidence of wrongdoing, forced to vote via affidavit ballots, significantly increasing the risk that their votes would not be counted.[13]

Another mechanism for suppressing student votes common to our cases is the restriction of poll sites on college campuses. On-campus poll sites are important because they are familiar and comfortable places for students, regularly within easy walking or biking distance for large populations of student voters, accessible through public transportation, and situated in handicap-accessible buildings. A 2016 survey of 'undermobilized'—registered but not voting—youth indicated that two of the most important reasons for their failure to vote were that they were "too busy" (47%) or lacked transportation (19%) to poll sites.[14] PVAMU, NC A&T, and Bard all experienced difficulty with the establishment of poll sites, be they for early or election-day voting. Indeed, Dutchess County Election Commissioner Erik Haight was so committed to preventing a polling place on the Bard College campus that during COVID he insisted voting take place in a small church a mile and a half from campus. In so doing, he dismissed concerns of the church elders and a world-class infectious disease expert who all agreed that the church was unsafe for voters and poll workers, lying to a New York State Supreme Court judge about the challenges of moving the poll site in the process.[15] Even when on-campus poll sites are established there can be challenges. At PVAMU, the hours of operation for early voting were significantly restricted, leading to recent litigation.

---

dent-redistricting-could-challenge-gerrymandered-campus/. Note, an April 2022 change in New York State law outlaws campus gerrymandering. See Press Release, "New Legislation Will Bring Polling Places to New York College Campuses," Bard College, April 9, 2022, https://www.bard.edu/news/new-legislation-will-bring-polling-places-to-new-york-college-campuses-2022-04-09.

13 Patricia Doxsey, "Bard Students Unhappy with Voting Hassle," *Daily Freeman*, November 20, 2009, downloaded December 12, 2024, https://www.dailyfreeman.com/2009/11/20/bard-students-unhappy-with-voting-hassle-with-video/.

14 The survey polled 18–29- year-old undermobilized voters. The figures cited refer to those with college experience. For those without college experience, a slightly lower percentage (44%) indicated that free time was a problem but a higher number (35%) indicated that transportation was an impediment: Center for Information & Research on Civic Learning and Engagement, "Why Youth Don't Vote: Differences by Race and Education," August 21, 2018, https://circle.tufts.edu/latest-research/why-youth-dont-vote-differences-race-and-education.

15 Jonathan Becker, "NY State Can Help Overcome Voter Suppression of College Students," *WAMC Northeast Public Radio*, January 27, 2022, 5:30, https://www.wamc.org/commentary-opinion/2022-01-27/ny-state-can-help-overcome-voter-suppression-of-college-students.

The NC A&T poll site, which was first established in 2019 after tremendous student efforts, has been threatened twice with removal by the local Board of Elections.[16]

Intimidation is another common tactic used to suppress the student vote. It is particularly impactful given the vulnerability of the student voting population, which consists of many first-time voters unfamiliar with voting processes.[17] This was most extreme in Prairie View. In 1992, well after the *Symm* decision, Waller County District Attorney Buddy McCaig erroneously charged members of the 'Prairie View 19' with voting fraud and in some cases aggravated perjury.[18] In 2004, local Assistant District Attorney, Oliver Kitzman, accused students of "feigned residency" and published threats to arrest and fine them if they voted locally, even ignoring pushback from Texas attorney general (and future governor) Greg Abbott.[19] Although not as extreme, at Bard, after Judge Brands' 2009 decision based on a complaint originating at Vassar College, poll watchers descended upon the poll site where Bard students voted and aggressively challenged bewildered students, bashing the camera of a local lawyer recording their actions in order to defend the students in the process.[20] Police were also sent to the

---

16 Sterling Bland, "On-Campus Polling Place at North Carolina A&T State University," The Andrew Goodman Foundation (2022), /https://andrewgoodman.org/wp-content/uploads/2023/05/North-Carolina-AT-State-University-Case-Study.pdf. The case study was developed in an academic collaboration led by Cornell Brooks and Yael Bromberg with the Harvard Kennedy School's William Trotter Collaborative for Social Justice. For more resources, see "Toolkit: Securing On-Campus Polling Places," The Andrew Goodman Foundation (2022), https://andrewgoodman.org/wp-content/uploads/2022/10/A-Toolkit-For-Securing-On-Campus-Polling-Places.pdf.
17 Yael Bromberg, "The Future Is Unwritten: Reclaiming the Twenty-Sixth Amendment," *Rutgers University Law Review* 74, no. 5 (Summer 2022): 1671–1696, https://papers.ssrn.com/sol3/papers.cfm?abstract_id=4378484.
18 Caleb Brookins, "Historical Consciousness and the PV 19," *The Digital PV Panther Project*, October 11, 2022, https://pvpantherproject.com/2022/10/the-pv19-voter-suppression-and-historical-consciousness-in-2022/.
19 Eric Hoover, "Students at Prairie View A&M U. File Federal Lawsuit to Protect Their Voting Rights," *The Chronicle of Higher Education*, February 9, 2004, https://www.chronicle.com/article/students-at-prairie-view-a-m-u-file-federal-lawsuit-to-protect-their-voting-rights/. Abbott declared at a news conference, "College students cannot be targeted for discriminatory residency requirements and nothing prevents them from voting where they attend school." Kitzman only backed down after being sued by a group of students backed by the NAACP and the Lawyers' Committee for Human Rights, leading him to sign a consent decree. See Lianne Hart, "D.A. Challenge of Student Voters Is a Civil Rights Lesson," *Los Angeles Times*, February 15, 2004, https://www.latimes.com/archives/la-xpm-2004-feb-15-na-prairie15-story.html. For Abbott's opinion, see: Greg Abbott to Rodney Ellis, opinion letter, "Residency Requirements for Voting in an Election in Texas (RQ-0157-GA)," February 4, 2004, Texas Attorney General Opinion Files, https://www.texasattorneygeneral.gov/sites/default/files/opinion-files/opinion/2004/ga0141.pdf.
20 Doxsey, "Bard Students Unhappy."

newly established poll site at Bard in 2020 by Election Commissioner Haight over the implementation of state-imposed COVID guidelines, although the assigned officer acknowledged the rules were being followed and was apologetic about his presence.[21] The point of such actions was not simply to intimidate those who may be directly implicated, but to send a message to all students about the potential dangers of voting locally. What is noteworthy in these instances is that the source of the intimidation was a figure of legal and/or regulatory authority; whether in law enforcement or in elections oversight roles, figures to whom students may have looked for guidance in seeking to vote.

Threats were also extended to institutions. Engelhardt threatened Tuskegee with budget cuts in response to Charles Gomillion's voting rights advocacy through the Tuskegee Civic Association (TCA). Dutchess County authorities implicitly threatened to withdraw from negotiations with Bard over control of traffic on a county road that bisects campus due to the College's push for an on-campus poll site.[22] The Presidents of PVAMU and NC A&T did not have to be threatened: they understood that they were always in danger of losing funds if they upset state officials, so they were naturally disincentivized from rocking the boat.

2 Why Restrictions?

Although the 26th Amendment was ratified with overwhelming cross-partisan support, the congressional debates surrounding the youth vote illustrated that there were already fears concerning the disruptive impact that large groups of youth voters in college towns could have on local governance. Town–gown tensions go back centuries and, as Tuskegee illustrates, are far more acute at HBCUs given their makeup and history as venues of autonomy and resistance to white supremacy.[23] While motives cannot be discreetly distilled easily, the case studies suggest restrictions on student voters emerged for three primary and overlapping reasons: desire for political advantage, fear of student voting power, and racism.

It is no coincidence that the most egregious attempts to limit student voting emerged at times of intense political competition that threatened established po-

---

21 Linda Greenblatt, Democratic Inspector Co-ordinator, Town of Red Hook, unpublished report submitted to Board of Elections and shared with author, November, 2020.
22 Erin Cannan, Bard College vice president for civic engagement, interviewed by Jonathan Becker, February 19, 2025.
23 United States Commission on Civil Rights, *Report of the United States Commission on Civil Rights*, 86th Cong., 1st sess., September 9, 1959, 76.

litical and racial hierarchies. The Tuskegee gerrymander did not happen in a vacuum. Nationally, it came three years after *Brown v. Board of Education* challenged the central tenets of Jim Crow and less than a month after Dr. Martin Luther King's "Give Us the Ballot" speech.[24] Locally, it emerged after a 1954 school board race in which a Black candidate and Tuskegee Institute employee Jessie P. Guzman won enough votes, in part due to increased Black voter registration, to instill fear in many white residents over the future voting power balance.[25] Indeed, Engelhardt, the chief architect of the gerrymander—who was also the executive secretary of the state's White Citizens Council—made it very clear that one of the main reasons he entered politics was to prevent Black people from gaining political power.[26]

Similar dynamics of political competition can be observed in our other case studies. In Waller County, the indictment of students who were part of the 'Prairie View 19' occurred two weeks prior to a 1992 run-off election in which two Black candidates, one a PVAMU alum, were vying for political office that had long been controlled by the white establishment, including the positions of county commissioner and county constable.[27] In North Carolina, the gerrymander occurred not long after the *Shelby* decision, as a newly empowered Republican majority was seeking, once again, to further their grip on the state legislature after prior redistricting maps were overturned for racial discrimination. As the chief architect of changes in district mapping, North Carolina State Assemblyman David Lewis, put it, "I propose that we draw the maps to give a partisan advantage to

---

24 King himself visited the Tuskegee Civic Association on July 2, 1957, meaning that in a six-week period he issued the "Give Us the Ballot Speech," the gerrymander was launched, and King visited Tuskegee.

25 C.G. Gomillion, "The Tuskegee Voting Story," *Clinical Sociology Review* 6, no. 1 (1988): 25, https:// digitalcommons.wayne.edu/cgi/viewcontent.cgi?article=1117&context=csr. As Gabriel Smith wrote, "Guzman's run for an otherwise harmless seat on the School Board represented the first real indication to Tuskegee's whites that their Black neighbors were seriously interested in ascending to political power in the town and county. Not only did Guzman's blackness pose a serious threat to the segregationist political landscape of Tuskegee of that time, but it also inspired more Black people to register to vote. With more Black citizens attempting to enter the political process in Tuskegee, the need for Engelhardt's gerrymander became much more apparent to those at the top of Tuskegee's white power structure"; Gabriel Antwan Smith, "A Hollow Inheritance: The Legacies of the Tuskegee Civic Association and the Crusade for Civic Democracy in Alabama" (MA Thesis, Auburn University, 2016), 88–89.

26 Bernard Taper, *Gomillion Versus Lightfoot: The Right to Vote in Apartheid Alabama* (University of Alabama Press, 2003), 49; Smith, "A Hollow Inheritance," 53; Norrell, *Reaping the Whirlwind*, 86.

27 Mark Langford, "Black Student Voters Allege Harassment in Texas," *United Press International*, April 19, 1992, https://www.upi.com/Archives/1992/04/19/Black-student-voters-allege-harass ment-in-Texas/7349703656000/.

ten Republicans and three Democrats because I do not believe it's possible to draw a map with eleven Republicans and two Democrats."[28] Finally, in Dutchess County, Judge Brands' 2009 *ex parte* order allowing aggressive challenges to student voters occurred just as Dutchess County became majority Democrat for the first time in 30 years, and just as the majority on the Red Hook Town Board, where Bard is situated, swung Democrat for the first time in living memory.[29] The shifting political grounds no doubt also helped explain Haight's 2012 decision to reject registrations of students from Bard, Marist College, and the Culinary Institute of America who failed to include dorm addresses on their forms, which was set aside on the eve of the midterm election by a federal court.[30] The fear of student voting power echoes across the language used by elections officials whose actions have discouraged student voting: Dutchess County Election Commissioner Haight was unusually candid in expressing his views of student voters, invoking similar language to that of District Attorney McCaig when he prosecuted the 'Prairie View 19,' comparing Bard students with "taxpaying, permanent residents."[31] He openly committed to ensuring the students would not have access to a polling place on campus, even if they constituted the vast majority (nearly 70%) of voters in the district, because he did not want them to be "super-enfranchised," even if this endangered voters and poll workers and saddled the taxpayers of Dutchess County with tens of thousands of dollars in legal fees from losing court battles.[32]

It is important to underline that our studies demonstrate that it was not simply political competition and fear of student voting power that drove attempts to disenfranchise: for the HBCU cases, race also played an intersecting and often central role.

---

28 Thompson, "The Legal Fight Over NC Gerrymandering Isn't Over."

29 Patricia Doxsey, "Dem Enrollment Tops Republican in Dutchess," *Daily Freeman*, October 10, 2008, downloaded December 12, 2024, https://www.dailyfreeman.com/2008/10/10/dem-enrollment-tops-republican-in-dutchess/.

30 Patricia Doxsey, "In Dutchess County, Battle Brews Over Dorm Dwellers' Voting Rights," *Daily Freeman*, October 19, 2012, downloaded December 12, 2024, https://www.dailyfreeman.com/2012/10/19/in-dutchess-county-battle-brews-over-dorm-dwellers-voting-rights.

31 Erik Haight, "Commissioner Haight: Set Record Straight with Facts," *Poughkeepsie Journal*, May 28, 2016, downloaded December 10, 2024, https://www.poughkeepsiejournal.com/story/opinion/valley-views/2016/05/28/commissioner-haight-set-record-straight-facts/84920538/. McCaig stated that the "permanent residents" of Waller County did not want their legally cast votes to be "diluted by someone who is not a legal voter."

32 "Dutchess County Board of Elections, Public Meeting of Dutchess County Board of Elections," virtual meeting, February 25, 2021, posted August 9, 2021, by Bard Center for Civic Engagement, YouTube, 30:32, https://www.youtube.com/watch?v=v8lZDH1Yg1k&t=2s.

The Tuskegee gerrymander was fundamentally about race, which is why it resulted in 98% of registered Black voters, and the entire Tuskegee Institute, being removed from the redrawn city lines. As Engelhardt, who used the slogan "I stand for White Supremacy and Segregation," told a journalist, "That was my angle—to protect ourselves. Not only me, but my family. My aunts, uncles, and cousin owned land. If you have a [pejorative racist expletive] tax assessor, what would he do to you?"[33] Similar racist views permeated the state government. When Tuskegee's county Board of Registrars resisted being hauled before the newly formed U.S. Commission on Civil Rights to testify as to the appalling Black voter registration rates in the county, it was Alabama State Attorney General John M. Patterson who advised them to resist participating in the hearing all together. Patterson campaigned on white fear and white supremacy and was elected governor, only to continue his mantra against federal intervention. In 1960, he advocated before the U.S. Senate against a federal proposal (which had been inspired by events in Tuskegee) to assign federal registrars to southern jurisdictions resistant to local Black registration.[34]

At the time of the arrest of the 'Prairie View 19,' District Attorney Peter Speers insisted that racism has "nothing to do" with the arrest of the students,[35] but few from the Prairie View community bought that. As one student commentator pointed out: "No one has ever questioned the rights of students at the University of Houston or Texas A&M to vote, but the issue is continually raised about the students who attend PVAMU."[36] The suggestion by *The Texas Advocate*'s editor Mary Levy that Frank Jackson, who at the time was running for the seat of county commissioner, be "horsewhipped" over his support for the arrested students underlined the racist dynamic at play.[37] State Senator Rodney Ellis from Houston, who filed a complaint with the Justice Department about the treatment of students, put it succinctly: "It looks like there's a number of ghosts of Jim Crow walking around Waller County. ... At some point, you have to draw the line."[38]

The case study of NC A&T showed similar contours. Assemblyman Lewis was conspicuous in his attempts to make the 2016 gerrymander appear partisan and

---

33 Norrell, *Reaping the Whirlwind*, 86; Smith, "A Hollow Inheritance," 53; Taper, *Gomillion Versus Lightfoot*, 49.

34 During the boycott, Patterson denounced the "so called leaders" whom he accused of taking contributions "to buy expensive cars, silk suits and pay for expensive trips." Norrell, *Reaping the Whirlwind*, 98, 114; Taper, *Gomillion Versus Lightfoot*, 20.

35 Langford, "Black Student Voters."

36 Brookins, "Historical Consciousness and the PV 19."

37 Brookins, "Historical Consciousness and the PV 19."

38 Langford, "Black Student Voters." See also Ellis, "Jim Crow Goes to College."

not racial in order to avoid judicial blowback, stating, "I acknowledge freely that this would be a political gerrymander, which is not against the law."[39] And yet the history of North Carolina suggests that when an HBCU is targeted, the role of race cannot be dismissed. Braxton Brewington, an NC A&T student leader and Common Cause fellow, articulated the view of student activists when he said, "How could you separate partisan gerrymandering from racial gerrymandering given the makeup of Democrats and Black people ... specific to the state of North Carolina?"[40] Moreover, it is telling that in addition to NC A&T, another HBCU, Fayetteville State University, was a target of gerrymandering in 2016, with students divided between the 8th and 9th congressional districts.[41]

In this manner, youth voter suppression can often stand alone, or be intertwined with racial and/or partisan voter suppression. And, as seen in the Bard College on-campus polling site case, where the disability rights community championed for the on-campus polling site—because it was far more accessible than the small church where Bard students had previously voted and, unlike the church, comported with Americans with Disabilities Act guidelines—disability discrimination may be intertwined as well. And yet, there is something unique about youth voter suppression in terms of its universalism. As Yael Bromberg wrote, "Simply put, all voters *age*—independent of partisanship, race, gender, or class. Age is both fixed as a state of being for a class, or perhaps a generation, and yet, ever-changing on an individual basis."[42] In other words, a conceptualization of age-based discrimination may offer a starting point to build bridges where others see polarization.

---

39 Brennan Center for Justice, "Current Partisan Gerrymandering Cases," Court Case Tracker, published April 26, 2017, https://www.brennancenter.org/our-work/court-cases/current-partisan-gerrymandering-cases.

40 Braxton Brewington, interviewed by Jonathan Becker, October 31, 2024.

41 Prabhat Gautam, Nancy Thomas, and Rebecca Stein, "Student and Minority Communities of Interest for Shaping Voting Districts," *Institute for Democracy and Higher Education*, October 21, 2021, 4. Unlike NC A&T, the campus was not divided down the middle, but the lines, with Fayetteville State abutting two district lines, left many students, the majority of whom lived off campus, divided between two districts.

42 Bromberg, "Youth Voting Rights," 1112. See also Alexander A. Boni-Saenz, "Age, Time and Discrimination," *Georgia Law Review* no. 53 (2019): 845–904, https://papers.ssrn.com/sol3/papers.cfm?abstract_id=3276514#.

3 The Resistance

The case studies of the four institutions demonstrate that it is possible to resist attempts by public officials to disenfranchise voters. If we turn again to our adaptation of Westheimer and Kahne's typology of 'personally responsible,' 'participatory,' and 'justice-oriented' citizens discussed in chapter two, we see many students, faculty, and institutions playing participatory and justice-oriented roles, engaging robustly with voting issues, and drawing "explicit attention to matters of injustice and to the importance of pursuing social justice."[43]

3.1 Student Citizens

Many students at the four institutions examined acted as participatory citizens, meaning they helped other students register to vote, supported get-out-the-vote efforts, organized and distributed petitions, and participated in boycotts and marches. The participatory citizen approach among these students often entailed more protest-focused mobilizations, which tended to ebb and flow, and although such actions may serve as legitimate forms of awareness-raising activism, they are often disconnected from longer-term strategic campaign planning. While there is no perfect demarcation line, the justice-oriented students were closer to the nexus of organizing, advocacy, and litigation efforts that were necessary to overcome entrenched voter suppression and effect longer-lasting institutional and legal reforms. The justice-oriented students organized campaigns to promote voting rights often in coordination with other organizations and advocates who sought to effect lasting change. They attempted to resolve access challenges with poll sites on campus. They participated in lawsuits against public officials who deprived students of voting rights and advocated for changes to state and federal laws that protect student voters and facilitate student voting.

Tuskegee students played a supportive role in responding to the gerrymander, participating in the boycott and organizing a 400-student protest in 1960.[44] They would come to the fore later in the 1960s, when the campus became a vibrant cen-

---

43 Joel Westheimer and Joseph Kahne, "What Kind of Citizen? The Politics of Educating for Democracy," *American Educational Research Journal* 41, no. 2 (2004): 237–269.
44 Thomas Fortuna, "Black Citizens Boycott White Merchants for U.S. Voting Rights, Tuskegee, Alabama, 1957–1961," Global Nonviolent Action Database, November 9, 2011, https://nvdatabase. swarthmore.edu/content/black-citizens-boycott-white-merchants-us-voting-rights-tuskegee-alaba ma-1957-1961#:~:text=By%20the%20end%20of%201959,"100%20per%20cent%20effective.

ter of student organizing and protest. Tuskegee students played a particularly energetic role in registering rural Black voters and, in so doing, helped to realize the long-held aspirations of Gomillion and the TCA.[45]

At PVAMU, several generations of student leaders have acted as justice-oriented citizens, remaining actively engaged to ensure voting rights. Numerous students participated in litigation. Arthur Ray Wilson and Charles Ballas served as named student litigants when Symm, a local election administrator, would not register them due to residency.[46] After Waller County Assistant District Attorney Kitzman threatened to arrest students for voting locally, PVAMU student Neothies Lindley Jr. and others participated in the 2004 litigation against the county brought by the Prairie View chapter of the NAACP.[47] Student Council President Priscilla Barbour led the fight in 2012 and 2013 for a poll site on campus that helped secure the site at the Memorial Student Center for early voting and election day.[48] PVAMU student Jayla Allen sued in the 2018 fight for equal early voting poll sites[49] and testified before Congress on the history of disenfranchisement at PVAMU.[50] Generations of PVAMU students organized and participated in major marches that took place in 1992, 2004, 2008, 2018, and 2020 to protest arrests, fight threats and intim-

---

45 Norrell, *Reaping the Whirlwind*, 179; Brian Jones, *The Tuskegee Student Uprising: A History* (New York University Press, 2022). Gomillion and others at the TCA were ultimately left behind by many students who felt that their gradualist approach to integration was too slow and insufficiently radical for the times; Smith, "A Hollow Inheritance," 126–132.
46 All litigants included Arthur Ray Wilson, Randolph Grayson, Donnie Gene Young, Leodies U.A. Simmons, and Billy Ray Toliver; *Wilson v. Symm*, 341 F. Supp. 8 (S.D. Tex. 1972), https://law.justia.com/cases/federal/district-courts/FSupp/341/8/1456867/.
47 *Prairie View Chapter of the NAACP, Neothies Lindley, JR., K. Thanes Queenan, Vivian Spikes, and Brian Rowland v. Oliver S. Kitzman, Waller County Criminal District Attorney*, Civil Action No. H 04 0459 (S.D. Tex. 2004), https://lawyerscommittee.org/wp-content/uploads/2015/08/040205-PV-NAACP-v.-Kitzman-complaint.pdf.
48 Reeve Hamilton, "Student Leader Demands On-Campus Polling Place," *The Texas Tribune*, July 31, 2013, https://www.texastribune.org/2013/07/31/prairie-view-m-students-demand-campus-voting/.
49 Besides Allen, litigants were: Damon Johnson, Joshua Muhammad, Raul Sanchez, and Treasure Smith; *Jayla Allen, Damon Johnson, Joshua Muhammad, Raul Sanchez, and Treasure Smith v. Waller County, Texas*, Civil Case No. 4:18 CV 3985 (S.D. Tex. 2018), https://www.naacpldf.org/wp-content/uploads/Complaint-Allen-v.-Waller-County-filed-1.pdf.
50 United States House of Representatives Committee on the Judiciary Subcommittee on the Constitution, Civil Rights, and Civil Liberties, *Hearing on the Enforcement of the Voting Rights Act*, 116 Cong., 2019 (statement of Jayla Allen, Chair, Rock the Vote, Prairie View A&M University), https://docs.house.gov/meetings/JU/JU10/20190503/109387/HHRG-116-JU10-Wstate-AllenJ-20190503.pdf.

idation, and to advocate for poll sites and extended voting on campus.[51] The 2008 march alone involved more than 1,000 students and allies marching seven miles from campus to the early voting site after Waller County officials cut the number of early voting sites in the county from half a dozen to one during the March presidential primaries.[52] The student commitment to promoting voting and protecting voting rights has been such a prominent feature of Prairie View student life that it has been internalized as an essential function of student government.

In North Carolina, a group of committed NC A&T students, including Nick Knight, Braxton Brewington, Love Caesar, and Delaney Vandergrift, worked hand in hand with Common Cause and IGNITE North Carolina to fight the 2016 campus gerrymander. They distributed petitions, held press conferences, and attended Board of Elections meetings to advocate for change.[53] Vandergrift and others led the successful fight for a polling place on campus. Students also established a "Real Aggies Vote" campaign, and partnered with organizations like The Andrew Goodman Foundation and the ALL IN Campus Democracy Challenge, as well as a newly founded Office of Leadership and Civic Engagement, to promote student voting.[54] Students were particularly shaped by the history of activism at NC A&T during the Second Reconstruction, and felt the inspiration and burdens of following the A&T (Greensboro) Four.

At Bard, Student Activists for Voting Equality (SAVE), led by Michael Chameides and Monica Elkinton, fought for the right of students to register and vote locally after student registrations had been systematically denied. Partnering with students from Vassar College, they pressured local representatives in county government, organized protests at the Board of Elections, held press conferences, and presented their case at public hearings.[55] They collaborated with Bard faculty and administrators to strategize and ensure public institutional support. Their threat of litigation in 2000 played an important role in pushing the county and

51 Lucio Vasquez, "Prairie View A&M Students Combat Voter Suppression by Marching to Early Voting Site," *Texas Public Radio*, October 15, 2020, https://www.tpr.org/news/2020-10-15/prairie-view-a-m-students-combat-voter-suppression-by-marching-to-early-voting-site.

52 Helen Eriksen, "Thousands March in Prairie View for Voting Rights," The Ruckus Society, February 25, 2008, https://ruckus.org/thousands-march-in-prairie-view-for-voting-rights-2/; Hamilton, "Student Leader Demands."

53 Braxton Brewington, interviewed by Jonathan Becker, October 31, 2024; Niklaus Knight, interviewed by Jonathan Becker, October 23, 2024.

54 Bland, "On-Campus Polling Place."

55 "SAVE," *Bard Free Press*, October 4, 2000, 3, https://digitalcommons.bard.edu/cgi/viewcontent.cgi?article=1006&context=bardfreepress.

Board of Elections to finally register student voters. [56] After this victory, students at Bard formed an organization called Election@Bard, which not only organized student voter registration and get-out-the-vote efforts, but also began public lobbying for a polling place on campus. Students like Jonian Rafti and Eva-Marie Quinones, partnering with The Andrew Goodman Foundation and the Bard Center for Civic Engagement, used many of the same tactics as SAVE to promote the on-campus poll site. [57] Several generations of students have served as litigants in court cases since the turn of the millennium, including the 2009 state case to count votes when students were erroneously forced to vote via affidavit ballots, the 2012 federal case over the rejection of registrations that did not include dorm addresses, and the two rounds of litigation in 2020 and 2021 that focused on a polling site on campus. [58]

3.2 Faculty Citizens

Faculty at the four institutions studied served as participatory citizens, advising students on strategies, offering community-based learning courses and tutorials, and publicizing voting rights issues. They have also acted as justice-oriented citizens, serving as litigants, conducting research that exposes inequities in voting rights, and disseminating that research publicly.

Charles Gomillion of the Tuskegee Institute is the model justice-oriented faculty member, not only teaching but also working for decades as the President of the TCA. In pursuing this work, he helped organize efforts for Black citizens of Macon County to register to vote despite a myriad of impediments and ubiquitous threats, wrote public letters to fellow citizens, and confronted local officials, publicly challenging Governor Jim Folsom to "relieve us of the embarrassment we are

---

56 "SAVE," 3; Anthony Farmer, "Task Force, Let Collegians Vote," *Poughkeepsie Journal*, March 19, 2000, 1 A.

57 Eva-Marie Quinones, "The Battle for the Ballot: Inside the Voting Rights Struggle in New York," *Buzzfeed*, May 13, 2016, https://www.buzzfeed.com/evamariequinones/the-battle-for-the-ballot-inside-the-voting-right-2crpl.

58 Bard students constituted all of the litigants: Olivia Conti, Sara Kangas, Tanya Sorenson, Casey Asprooth-Jackson, Sarah Bessel, and Iris S.B. Larson in *Conti v. Dutchess County Board of Elections*, 9054 (N.Y. Sup. Ct. 2009); Alexis Roe and Hans Kern in *Pitcher v. Dutchess County Board of Elections*, Civil Action No. 12 CV 8017 (S.D.N.Y. 2012); Sadia Saba in *Andrew Goodman Foundation v. Dutchess County Board of Elections* 52737/20 (N.Y. Sup. Ct. 2020); and Maria Alejandra Rodriguez Ortiz, Sarina Jaqueline Culaj, and Tomas S. Forman in *Bard College v. Dutchess County Board of Elections*, 198 A.D.3d 1014 (N.Y. App. Div. 2021) (No. 52777/21).

now experiencing and the political disfranchisement we are now suffering."[59] He even testified before the Senate Judiciary Committee as it was considering the impact of segregation in the run-up to the Civil Rights Act of 1957. In response to the gerrymander, he helped organize the Tuskegee local economic boycott, which helped model future economic mobilization in defense of civil rights. He helped document the systematic disenfranchisement of Black voters in Macon County and Alabama more broadly and captured numerous indictors or impediments to social development and political participation in his 1958 dissertation, "Civic Democracy in the South."[60] Finally, he served as the lead litigant in what became *Gomillion v. Lightfoot*, the first important Supreme Court case over racial gerrymandering, and a break-through case which set a stepping stone for gerrymander claims even outside of the racial context.

Though Gomillion sets the bar for faculty involvement, there were several other faculty members from Tuskegee who worked as a part of the TCA to secure the franchise, including historian Frank Toland, sociologist Stanley Smith, and pioneering researcher in the study of Black people in the rural south Lewis Wade Jones, who, together with Smith, prepared an important research report in 1958, sponsored by the the Anti-Defamation League of B'nai Brith, on voting, the gerrymander, and the boycott, particularly the attitudes of white citizens.[61] William Andrew Hunter, Dean of the Institute's School of Education, spoke on the first day of public hearings before the United States Commission on Civil Rights in 1958, following Gomillion's former student and TCA executive director William Mitchell.[62] Political scientist Charles V. Hamilton drafted a bill providing for federal voting registrars when local boards are inactive, planting ideas, like Gomillion and Mitchell, that helped shape the Civil Rights Act of 1960 and the Voting Rights Act of 1965.[63]

Faculty at the other institutions examined also stepped forward as participatory and justice-oriented citizens, although it should be acknowledged that their work was often in the background, doing what good faculty members do: engaging with students within and outside of the classroom and trying, where appropriate, to make lessons inside the classroom relevant to student experiences. This role was especially important at HBCUs, where the 'second curriculum,' which emphasized idealism, cultural nationalism, and race consciousness, was so critical to stu-

59 Smith, "A Hollow Inheritance," 35.
60 Charles Gomillion, "Civic Democracy in the South" (PhD diss., Ohio State University, 1959).
61 Jones and Smith, *Tuskegee, Alabama.*
62 United States Commission on Civil Rights, *Hearings Before the US Commission on Voting Rights,* 11–36.
63 Norrell, *Reaping the Whirlwind,* 119.

dents' identity as civic actors.[64] Political scientists Mack Jones and Imari Obadele at PVAMU, Derick Smith and James Steele at NC A&T, and Joseph Luders at Bard played more direct advisory roles, guiding students about voting rights issues and at times intervening in conversations with administrators. Smith, known as the 'People's Professor,' inspired students and helped them understand their legacy, channeled the second curriculum, and taught them about gerrymandering. Luders made public statements and incorporated issues of student voting into his American politics class during the initial fight for student voting at Bard. Robert Koblitz and Alan Sussman at Bard also served as bridges to legal defense groups, linking students with the New York Civil Liberties Union. The Tuskegee faculty demonstrated the importance of engaged research on voting through their extensive documentation of numbers and attitudes. The research of Bard biology professor Felicia Keesing on the relative safety of an on-campus poll site during COVID demonstrates that faculty from a variety of disciplines can deploy their research skills in efforts to defend and preserve democracy.

3.3 Institution as Citizen

Universities as institutions face dilemmas when they address issues of voting. On the one hand, they invoke the link between democracy and education, and frequently encourage students to contribute to society and become agents of change. On the other hand, they are situated in communities which might not want students to vote locally. Leaders have a responsibility not simply to do what is right, but to preserve and protect the institution (and are often fearful for their own positions). They sometimes find themselves navigating between students and faculty who are agitating to promote justice, and concerns about the impact that their actions may have on governmental decisions about everything from planning and zoning to state budgets.

The four institutions studied reflect different circumstances and different approaches. As public institutions that are often the target of government officials, and dependent on state budgetary allocations, PVAMU and NC A&T are more vulnerable, and the leadership of both have taken much more tepid approaches to advocating for student voting rights. In the voting sphere, they have acted more like personally responsible institutions than participatory or justice-oriented insti-

---

64 Jelani M. Favors, *Shelter in a Time of Storm: How Black Colleges Fostered Generations of Leadership and Activism* (University of North Carolina Press, 2020), 4.

tutions, remaining largely neutral as students and outside groups have pressed them to take action against attempts to suppress the student vote.

Priscilla Barbour, who led the 2012 efforts to secure a poll site on PVAMU's campus, bemoaned a lack of involvement of university administration.[65] However, it could be argued that while the administration did not always directly embrace students' work, it was supportive in the sense that it retained Frank Jackson, the Prairie View alum who became city mayor while simultaneously serving as assistant vice chancellor for state relations. Jackson is a revered figure who served as a regular sounding board and advisor to students, but was distant enough from the university leadership and sufficiently discreet in his interactions to give the university plausible deniability.[66] And in 2020, PVAMU's President Ruth Simmons participated in the march organized by student government to an early polling site a mile from campus, which protested the absence of an on-campus site.[67]

Students involved in the fight against the 2016 gerrymander at NC A&T met with the university leadership and felt that they were hostile to their efforts, particularly when the president insisted that he would not openly describe the gerrymander as racist.[68] In their mind, the conservative approach betrayed the legacy of activism that the institution so often trumpeted. Ironically, they also noted the institution's subsequent embrace of the registration and voting process, and were almost wistful about the creation of an Office of Leadership and Civic Engagement, which helped take the lead on such efforts.[69]

Tuskegee and Bard are private institutions, though the former is more dependent on the state for funds. At Tuskegee, the Gomillion period witnessed a form of passive support for the TCA's efforts, with the institution operating publicly as personally responsible citizen, but sometimes privately as a participatory citizen. There was open knowledge that the work of Tuskegee Institute faculty and staff affiliated with the TCA entailed a degree of danger for the institution, but successive presidents Frederick Douglass Patterson (1935–1953) and Luther Hilton Foster (1953–1981) tacitly approved of Gomillion and others' work to fight discrimination.[70] Patterson ignored Engelhardt's threats to cut funds due to Gomillion's ef-

65 Jonathan Becker and Erin Cannan, "Institution as Citizen: Colleges and Universities as Actors in Defense of Student Voting Rights," *Rutgers University Law Review* 74, no. 5 (Summer 2022), 1905.
66 Patrick Michels, "The Interview: Frank Jackson," *Texas Observer*, June 20, 2016, https://www.texasobserver.org/prairie-view-mayor-frank-jackson-interview/.
67 Vasquez, "Prairie View A&M Students Combat Voter Suppression."
68 Niklaus Knight, interviewed by Jonathan Becker, October 23, 2024.
69 Braxton Brewington, interviewed by Jonathan Becker, October 31, 2024.
70 As Jones and Smith put it, "Both presidents' styles of leadership were heavily criticized and blamed because they both allowed Charles Gomillion, Lewis Jones, and other Institute faculty the

forts and when Alabama Governor Gordon Persons confronted him about Gomillion's work, he insisted that Gomillion was "simply exercising his duties as a citizen. He's not acting officially for Tuskegee Institute."[71] Patterson recalled that
the only time he cracked down on Gomillion was when he and others at the
TCA used Tuskegee stationery in their work.[72] As Jones recalled years later, the
leadership of Tuskegee played a sort of shell game with Gomillion, moving him
from position to position, be it head of department or division or dean of students,
to deflect attention from his civic role.[73] Having been gerrymandered out of Tuskegee in Act 140, Foster was more open in his support of the boycott, stating, "Now
that they don't want us in the city of Tuskegee, I have no reason to trade there."[74]

Bard's leadership took an even more aggressive approach in acting as a justice-oriented citizen. The institution regularly devoted resources—organizational,
human, financial, and reputational—to promote and defend students' right to
vote. Bard's President Leon Botstein and the Bard Board of Trustees publicly endorsed students' right to vote locally, and institutional leaders regularly published
op-eds and commentaries on student voting rights, even encouraging other higher
education institutions to join in. The institutional leadership arranged and bank-
rolled a lawsuit in 2009 which forced the county to count the votes of students required to vote via affidavit ballot as 'unchallenged,' and President Botstein and
Vice President for Student Affairs Erin Cannan served as litigants in the battle

---

freedom to pursue civil rights and community activism without fear of termination or chas-
tisement as long as they continued to be productive faculty members and further the University's
mission"; Jones and Smith, *Tuskegee, Alabama*, 76. While the institution's founder, Booker T.
Washington, is often criticized for his paternalistic view of racial accommodation and separa-
tionist preparedness during the early 20th century, less known or acknowledged is his support
behind the scenes. As detailed by Louis R. Harlan, Washington leveraged his Tuskegee network of
philanthropists and "secretly paid for and directed a succession of court suits against discrimination in voting, exclusion of Negroes from jury panels, Jim Crow railroad facilities, and various
kinds of exploitation of the black poor ... he took every precaution to keep information of his
secret actions from leaking out." Indeed, he kept this work separate from the Institute where he
was known for his tight control of faculty and students. Louis R. Harlan, "The Secret Life of
Booker T. Washington," *The Journal of Southern History* 37, no. 3 (August, 1971), 396.
71 Smith, "A Hollow Inheritance," 111, citing Frederick D. Patterson, Martia G. Goodson, and
Harry V. Richardson, *Chronicles of Faith: The Autobiography of Frederick Douglass Patterson*
(University of Alabama Press, 1991), 109–110.
72 When Gomillion used the stationery, Patterson recalled telling him: "Don't do that. I don't
object to what you are doing but don't identify your movement officially with Tuskegee Institute,
because Tuskegee Institute isn't a civil rights movement, it's an educational institution." Smith, "A
Hollow Inheritance," 112.
73 Jones and Smith, *Tuskegee, Alabama*.
74 Fortuna, "Black Citizens Boycott White Merchants."

for a polling place on campus in 2020 and 2021. This institutional engagement has extended to include best practices for student voter registration, with mandatory stops at a voter registration station during student orientation, and elaborate registration and get-out-the-vote efforts. These efforts include stationing of college officials as poll workers and poll watchers at the on-campus poll site in order to protect student voters and be responsive to any challenges that might emerge. Bard's Center for Civic Engagement, led by Bard's executive vice president and vice president for academic affairs, even coordinated with an alliance of voting rights organizations to successfully advocate for changes in New York State law to situate polling sites on college campuses with 300 or more registered voters, and at the time of writing is working to refine the law to ensure that more campuses host poll sites.[75]

3.4 External Organizations

Finally, it should be noted that in each of the cases, key actors received critical assistance and guidance from outside advocacy groups and legal defense organizations. The NAACP shaped PVAMU students' response to Assistant District Attorney Kitzman's threats to arrest student voters and consistently since, including recent litigation for equal early voting opportunities led by Leah Aden, then-deputy director of litigation for the NAACP Legal Defense and Education Fund; good government group Common Cause was critical in mobilizing NC A&T students' reaction to the campus gerrymander, as a part of its larger efforts in North Carolina through the Common Cause-North Carolina HBCU Student Action Alliance; and nonpartisan student organization The Andrew Goodman Foundation helped galvanize the students' and institution's fight for an on-campus poll site at Bard and on other colleges throughout the country with the legal and academic support of Yael Bromberg, the Harvard Kennedy School Trotter Collaborative or Social Justice, and the Rutgers International Human Rights Clinic. Legal support was further offered, and sometimes wholly driven, by the plaintiffs' bar. Lawyers who left their mark included: Fred Gray, who worked on behalf of Gomillion and the TCA in Tuskegee, a mainstay lawyer in the Alabama civil rights movement; Texas labor and civil rights lawyer David Richards, who litigated the case on behalf of PVAMU students in *Symm*; and Bromberg, Doug Mishkin, Michael Volpe,

---

75 Bard Center for Civic Engagement, "Bard Center for Civic Engagement Prepares Report on Poll Sites on College Campuses," February 16, 2024, https://cce.bard.edu/news/bard-center-for-civic-engagement-prepares-report-on-poll-sites-on-college-campuses-2024-01-06.

and Mike Donofrio, who represented Bard College and The Andrew Goodman Foundation to secure an on-campus polling location. While there exist various models of legal defense, these public interest attorneys tend to embrace a litigation approach known as 'People's Lawyering,' which prioritizes client and movement empowerment through the legal process, rather than an arm's-length transactional client relationship. This approach seeks a legal victory in the courts, of course, but also seeks to advance the cause itself. Legendary constitutional rights attorney Arthur Kinoy defined the term, explaining: "[T]he test of success for a people's lawyer is not always the technical winning or losing of the formal proceeding ... the real test was the impact of the legal activities on the morale and understanding of the people involved in the struggle."[76]

This chapter, in many ways, is a product of not only people's lawyering, but also people's teaching. The book project is born as an outgrowth of an academic collaboration to synchronously and collectively teach an undergraduate course bringing together faculty and students from the institutions of higher education across four states which have shaped the nation's voting rights jurisprudence with emphasis on the youth vote. The analysis for this chapter's comparison of the four case studies is a product of multidisciplinary academic course collaboration engaging with historians, political scientists, litigators and legal scholars, guest speakers, including youth leaders, and not least the students who have participated in the classes.

4 Conclusion

The case studies show that colleges and universities can realize the link between higher education and democracy that is often celebrated but which, to borrow from Dr. King, too often shows a "high blood pressure of words and anemia of deeds."[77] Idealistic and determined justice-oriented students, faculty, and administrators have, across multiple institutions in different environments, fought to promote and defend the most essential of democratic rights.

The primary locus of engagement varied. Tuskegee's fight was led by a faculty member, sociologist Charles Gomillion, who led the TCA to protect the institution. PVAMU's efforts were anchored in generations of student leaders, so much so that promoting voting and the protection of voting rights has become an essential com-

---

76 Arthur Kinoy, *Rights on Trial: The Odyssey of a People's Lawyer* (Harvard University Press, 1984), 57.
77 Martin Luther King, Jr., *A Testament of Hope: The Essential Writings and Speeches of Martin Luther King, Jr.*, ed. James M. Washington (HarperCollins, 1985), 198.

ponent of student government and the school's fraternity and social culture. Bard's efforts began with students from the Student Activists for Voting Equality, but the administration, in the form of the Center for Civic Engagement, has guided successive generations of Election@Bard students and placed institutional resources, and partnerships with organizations such as The Andrew Goodman Foundation and the local chapter of the League of Women Voters, squarely behind voting rights efforts. Common Cause-North Carolina mobilized and guided NC A&T students' fight against the gerrymander, but the students were also inspired by the "People's Professor" Derick Smith.

These efforts often took considerable time and tenacity. Gomillion and the TCA's work to gain voting rights for Black citizens in the City of Tuskegee and Macon County took place over a quarter of a century. Bard's fight for student voting rights and a polling place on campus, which included four lawsuits, one federal and three state, took place over a similar time frame. PVAMU's work to defend student voters and gain an accessible and available poll site have been ongoing since the 1970s and promise to continue. In this manner, the process of participatory democracy and democratic engagement is a journey, and not a destination.

It is important to note that the impact of these efforts has rippled out beyond individual campuses. Gomillion and the TCA's thorough documentation of discriminatory practices and the violation of voting rights in Macon County, and the impact of the Tuskegee gerrymander, helped shape the Civil Rights Acts of 1957 and 1960, and the Voting Rights Act of 1965. The suits filed by Prairie View students led to *Symm v. United States* (1979), the only Supreme Court decision concerning the 26th Amendment, which is regularly cited in litigation of student voting cases. Bard's protracted fight for a polling place on campus and its publicizing of the egregious acts of the Dutchess County Board of Elections helped galvanize a coalition of voting rights organizations and members of state government to take such decisions out of the hands of local election boards and mandate polling places on or near college campuses with large groups of registered voters. The cumulative experiences of youth voter infringements across the nation have shaped development of the Youth Voting Rights Act, a comprehensive federal bill to fulfill the promise of the 26th Amendment. But these ripples did not just occur. They emerged from the hard work, dedication, and organization of justice-oriented students, faculty and administrators and their allies, who demonstrated that systemic change is possible.

Bibliography

Abbott, Greg. Greg Abbott to Rodney Ellis, opinion letter. "Residency Requirements for Voting in an Election in Texas (RQ-0157-GA)." February 4, 2004. Texas Attorney General Opinion Files. https://www.texasattorneygeneral.gov/sites/default/files/opinion-files/opinion/2004/ga0141.pdf.

Bard Center for Civic Engagement. "Bard Center for Civic Engagement Prepares Report on Poll Sites on College Campuses." February 16, 2024. https://cce.bard.edu/news/bard-center-for-civic-engagement-prepares-report-on-poll-sites-on-college-campuses-2024-01-06.

Becker, Jonathan. "DC Legislature Public Comments on Nov. 4, 2021." Recorded Dutchess County Legislature committee meeting, November 4, 2021. Posted November 5, 2021, by Bard Center for Civic Engagement. YouTube, 7:57. https://youtu.be/kjZ-vgiQ248.

Becker, Jonathan. "NY State Can Help Overcome Voter Suppression of College Students." *WAMC Northeast Public Radio*, January 27, 2022. 5:30. https://www.wamc.org/commentary-opinion/2022-01-27/ny-state-can-help-overcome-voter-suppression-of-college-students.

Becker, Jonathan, and Cannan, Erin. "Institution as Citizen: Colleges and Universities as Actors in Defense of Student Voting Rights." *Rutgers University Law Review* 74, no. 5 (Summer 2022): 865–909. https://rutgerslawreview.com/wp-content/uploads/2023/02/07_Becker_Cannan.pdf.

Bland, Sterling. "On-Campus Polling Place at North Carolina A&T State University." The Andrew Goodman Foundation, 2022. https://andrewgoodman.org/wp-content/uploads/2023/05/North-Carolina-AT-State-University-Case-Study.pdf

Boni-Saenz, Alexander A. "Age, Time and Discrimination." *Georgia Law Review* no. 53 (2019): 845–904. https://papers.ssrn.com/sol3/papers.cfm?abstract_id=3276514#.

Brennan Center for Justice. "Current Partisan Gerrymandering Cases." Court Case Tracker. Published April 26, 2017. https://www.brennancenter.org/our-work/court-cases/current-partisan-gerrymandering-cases.

Bromberg, Yael. "Youth Voting Rights and the Unfulfilled Promise of the Twenty-Sixth Amendment." *University of Pennsylvania Journal of Constitutional Law* 21, no. 5 (2019): 1105–1166. https://scholarship.law.upenn.edu/jcl/vol21/iss5/1/.

Bromberg, Yael. "The Future Is Unwritten: Reclaiming the Twenty-Sixth Amendment." *Rutgers University Law Review* 74, no. 5 (Summer 2022): 1671–1696. https://papers.ssrn.com/sol3/papers.cfm?abstract_id=4378484.

Brookins, Caleb. "Historical Consciousness and the PV 19." *The Digital PV Panther Project*, October 11, 2022. https://pvpantherproject.com/2022/10/the-pv19-voter-suppression-and-historical-consciousness-in-2022/.

Center for Information & Research on Civic Learning and Engagement. "Why Youth Don't Vote: Differences by Race and Education." August 21, 2018. https://circle.tufts.edu/latest-research/why-youth-dont-vote-differences-race-and-education.

Chameides, Michael. "Verdict is In: Dutchess County Students Win Right to Vote." *Bard Free Press* 2, no. 1 (September 2000): 1–2. https://digitalcommons.bard.edu/cgi/viewcontent.cgi?article=1005&context=bardfreepres.

Doxsey, Patricia. "Dem Enrollment Tops Republican in Dutchess." *Daily Freeman*, October 10, 2008. Downloaded December 12, 2024. https://www.dailyfreeman.com/2008/10/10/dem-enrollment-tops-republican-in-dutchess/.

Doxsey, Patricia. "Bard Students Unhappy with Voting Hassle." *Daily Freeman*, November 20, 2009. Downloaded December 12, 2024. https://www.dailyfreeman.com/2009/11/20/bard-students-unhappy-with-voting-hassle-with-video/.

Doxey, Patricia. "In Dutchess County, Battle Brews Over Dorm Dwellers' Voting Rights." *Daily Freeman*, October 19, 2012. Downloaded December 12, 2024. https://www.dailyfreeman.com/2012/10/19/in-dutchess-county-battle-brews-over-dorm-dwellers-voting-rights.

"Dutchess County Board of Elections, Public Meeting of Dutchess County Board of Elections." Virtual meeting, February 25, 2021. Posted August 9, 2021, by Bard Center for Civic Engagement. YouTube, 30:32. https://www.youtube.com/watch?v=v8lZDH1Yg1k&t=2s.

Ellis, Rodney, "Jim Crow Goes to College." *New York Times*, April 27, 1992). https://www.nytimes.com/1992/04/27/opinion/jim-crow-goes-to-college.html.

Eriksen, Helen. "Thousands March in Prairie View for Voting Rights." The Ruckus Society, February 25, 2008. https://ruckus.org/thousands-march-in-prairie-view-for-voting-rights-2/.

Farmer, Anthony. "Task Force, Let Collegians Vote." *Poughkeepsie Journal*, March 19, 2000.

Favors, Jelani M. *Shelter in a Time of Storm: How Black Colleges Fostered Generations of Leadership and Activism.* University of North Carolina Press, 2020.

Fortuna, Thomas. "Black Citizens Boycott White Merchants for U.S. Voting Rights, Tuskegee, Alabama, 1957–1961." Global Nonviolent Action Database, November 9, 2011. https://nvdatabase.swarthmore.edu/content/black-citizens-boycott-white-merchants-us-voting-rights-tuskegee-alabama-1957-1961#:~:text=By%20the%20end%20of%201959,"100%20per%20cent%20effective.

Gautam, Prabhat, Thomas, Nancy, and Stein, Rebecca. "Student and Minority Communities of Interest for Shaping Voting Districts." *Institute for Democracy and Higher Education*, October 21, 2021, 1–13.

Gomillion, Charles. "Civic Democracy in the South." PhD diss., Ohio State University, 1959. https://etd.ohiolink.edu/acprod/odb_etd/ws/send_file/send?accession=osu1486476430056701&disposition=inline.

Gomillion, C.G. "The Tuskegee Voting Story." *Clinical Sociology Review* 6, no. 1 (1988): 22–26. https://digitalcommons.wayne.edu/cgi/viewcontent.cgi?article=1117&context=csr.

Guinier, Lani. *The Miner's Canary.* Harvard University Press, 2003.

Haight, Erik. "Commissioner Haight: Set Record Straight with Facts." *Poughkeepsie Journal*, May 28, 2016. Downloaded December 10, 2024. https://www.poughkeepsiejournal.com/story/opinion/valley-views/2016/05/28/commissioner-haight-set-record-straight-facts/84920538/.

Hamilton, Reeve. "Student Leader Demands On-Campus Polling Place." *The Texas Tribune*, July 31, 2013. https://www.texastribune.org/2013/07/31/prairie-view-m-students-demand-campus-voting/.

Harlan, Louis R. "The Secret Life of Booker T. Washington," *The Journal of Southern History* 37, no. 3 (August 1971): 393–416.

Hart, Lianne. "D.A. Challenge of Student Voters Is a Civil Rights Lesson." *Los Angeles Times*, February 15, 2004. https://www.latimes.com/archives/la-xpm-2004-feb-15-na-prairie15-story.html.

Hoover, Eric. "Students at Prairie View A&M U. File Federal Lawsuit to Protect Their Voting Rights." *The Chronicle of Higher Education*, February 9, 2004. https://www.chronicle.com/article/students-at-prairie-view-a-m-u-file-federal-lawsuit-to-protect-their-voting-rights/.

Jones, Brian. *The Tuskegee Student Uprising: A History.* New York University Press, 2022.

Jones, Lewis, and Smith, Stanley. *Tuskegee, Alabama: Voting Rights and Economic Pressure.* Field Reports on Desegregation in the South. Anti-Defamation League of B'nai B'rith, 1958.

King, Martin Luther, Jr. *A Testament of Hope: The Essential Writings and Speeches of Martin Luther King, Jr.* Edited by James M. Washington. HarperCollins, 1985.

Kinoy, Arthur. *Rights on Trial: The Odyssey of a People's Lawyer.* Harvard University Press, 1984.

Langford, Mark. "Black Student Voters Allege Harassment in Texas." *United Press International*, April 19, 1992. https://www.upi.com/Archives/1992/04/19/Black-student-voters-allege-harassment-in-Texas/7349703656000/.

Michaels, Patrick. "The Interview: Frank Jackson." *Texas Observer*, June 20, 2016. https://www.texasobserver.org/prairie-view-mayor-frank-jackson-interview/.

Naidu, Jyotsna. "Local Independent Redistricting Could Challenge Gerrymandered Campus," *The Miscellany News*, February 9, 2022. https://miscellanynews.org/2022/02/09/news/local-independent-redistricting-could-challenge-gerrymandered-campus/.

Norrell, Robert J. *Reaping the Whirlwind: The Civil Rights Movement and Tuskegee*. Alfred Knopf, 1985.

Patterson, Frederick D., Goodson, Martia G., and Richardson, Harry V. *Chronicles of Faith: The Autobiography of Frederick Douglass Patterson*. University of Alabama Press, 1991.

Quinones, Eva-Marie. "The Battle for the Ballot: Inside the Voting Rights Struggle in New York." *Buzzfeed*, May 13, 2016. https://www.buzzfeed.com/evamariequinones/the-battle-for-the-ballot-inside-the-voting-right-2crpl.

Richards, David. *Once Upon a Time in Texas: A Liberal in the Lonestar State*. University of Texas Press, 2002.

Rom, Rafi. "Voting Campaign Heats Up." *Bard Observer*, February 28, 2000.

"SAVE." *Bard Free Press*, October 4, 2000. https://digitalcommons.bard.edu/cgi/viewcontent.cgi?article=1006&context=bardfreepress.

Smith, Gabriel Antwan. "A Hollow Inheritance: The Legacies of the Tuskegee Civic Association and the Crusade for Civic Democracy in Alabama." MA Thesis, Auburn University, 2016.

Taper, Bernard. *Gomillion Versus Lightfoot: The Right to Vote in Apartheid Alabama*. University of Alabama Press, 2003.

Thompson, Elizabeth. "The Legal Fight Over NC Gerrymandering Isn't Over. How We Got Here, and What's Next." *The News & Observer*, June 27, 2019. https://www.newsobserver.com/news/politics-government/article231422113.html.

"Trailing N.C. Supreme Court Candidate Asks Court to Get Involved in Race." *Spectrum News*, December 18, 2024. https://spectrumlocalnews.com/nc/charlotte/news/2024/12/19/trailing-n-c--supreme-court-candidate-asks-court-to-get-involved-in-race.

United States Commission on Civil Rights. *Hearings Before the US Commission on Voting Rights*. 85th Cong., December 8, 1958, December 9, 1958, and January 9, 1959. https://www.usccr.gov/files/historical/1958/58-001.pdf.

United States Commission on Civil Rights. *Report of the United States Commission on Civil Rights*. 86th Cong., 1st sess., September 9, 1959. https://www.crmvet.org/docs/ccr_rights_us_6100.pdf.

United States House of Representatives Committee on the Judiciary Subcommittee on the Constitution, Civil Rights, and Civil Liberties. *Hearing on the Enforcement of the Voting Rights Act*. 116 Cong., May 3, 2019. https://docs.house.gov/meetings/JU/JU10/20190503/109387/HHRG-116-JU10-Wstate-AllenJ-20190503.pdf.

Ura, Alexa. "Texas' Oldest Black University Was Built on a Former Plantation. Its Students Still Fight a Legacy of Voter Suppression." *The Texas Tribune*, February 25, 2021. https://www.texastribune.org/2021/02/25/waller-county-texas-voter-suppression/.

Vasquez, Lucio. "Prairie View A&M Students Combat Voter Suppression by Marching to Early Voting Site." *Texas Public Radio*, October 15, 2020. https://www.tpr.org/news/2020-10-15/prairie-view-a-m-students-combat-voter-suppression-by-marching-to-early-voting-site.

Westheimer, Joel, and Khane, Joseph. "What Kind of Citizen? The Politics of Educating for Democracy." *American Educational Research Journal* 41, no. 2 (2004): 237–269.

Erin Cannan

8 A Practical Guide to Encouraging Student Voting

While much of this book focuses on battles over the right of students and others in college communities to vote, that right is not meaningful unless it is realized. This chapter synthesizes the best practices and frameworks for how college communities address student voting. Here you will find practical step-by-step guidance on building a voting action plan that embeds the work of voter registration and voting within a campus culture of democratic engagement and learning. The recommendations are drawn from voter action plans used by colleges and universities and recommendations from national organizations. I also highlight the activities and strategies employed by the campuses featured in this book: Prairie View A&M University (PVAMU), North Carolina Agricultural & Technical State University (NC A&T), Tuskegee University, and Bard College.

   The 1998 reauthorization of the Higher Education Act of 1965 requires institutions to make a "good faith effort to distribute a mail voter registration form ... to each student enrolled in a degree or certificate program and physically in attendance at the institution, and to make such forms widely available to students at the institution."[1] Institutions often interpret the "good faith effort" as minimal engagement with voter registration that might simply include an emailed link to students or the distribution of hard copy registration forms in designated areas on campus. This chapter draws instead from "Institutions as Citizen: Colleges and Universities as Actors in Defense of Student Voting Rights," where Jonathan Becker and I argued that "institutions need to expand (or create) strategic voter action plans for elections" to move institutions from "passive action" typical of a "personally responsible citizen" to "participatory" or "justice-oriented" active engagement with students and the protection of their rights.[2] A well-developed voter action plan grounds voter registration, engagement, and protection in the institution's civic mission, moving an institution from a 'passive citizen' approach (simply making voter registration available) to 'participatory' (linking voter registration to administrative processes, leading get-out-the-vote (GOTV) campaigns, transporting students to polling sites, promoting voter education campaigns), or 'justice-orient-

---

1 Jonathan Becker and Erin Cannan, "Institution as Citizen: Colleges and Universities as Actors in Defense of Student Voting Rights," *The Rutgers University Law Review* 74, no. 5 (2022): 1884; *Higher Education Amendments of 1998*, Public Law 105–244, Sec. 489.
2 Becker and Cannan, "Institution as Citizen," 1891.

ed' (actively protecting student voting rights by monitoring and challenging attempts to disenfranchise student voters, actively promoting on-campus poll sites, and advocating for legislation which promotes student voting).

Without institutional support and planning, the responsibility for promoting voting and protecting student voting rights is informally left to student groups or community organizations. This ignores the explicit links between voting, voting engagement, and the democratic purpose of higher education, as well as the powerful learning associated with early engagement with voting. This chapter is directed at students, faculty, and administrators who are advancing engagement on their own campuses, and seeks to answer three questions. What is a campus voter action plan? What are core elements for successful planning? And, how can institutions actively engage with students to encourage participation and learning? I conclude the chapter by exploring the role of campus coalitions and senior leadership, and highlighting key considerations when advocating for institutional resources.

1 What is a Campus Voter Action Plan?

1.1 Institutions as Citizens: Moving to a Justice-Oriented Model

One of the challenges related to youth voting is that many young people register and/or vote for the first time when they are enrolled in college. As with any new experience, they are more likely to successfully navigate the voter registration process with help. What that help looks like depends on the local ecosystem and requires universities to understand the local structural and informational barriers experienced by students, whether they are voting in person at a campus address, in the local community as a resident, or by absentee ballot. Having a plan that anticipates potential challenges to the voter registration process can combat restrictions to the franchise while addressing logistical and motivational barriers to student participation.

Since the passage of the 26th Amendment, youth voting, defined either as 18- to 24-year-olds or 18- to 29-year-olds, has consistently lagged behind other demographics. Voter registration rates for this group trail older voters, and the yield rates for youth voters have remained low with under 40 % of Gen Z voters (age 18–28) registering compared with almost twice that for Boomers (age 60–89).[3]

---

3 Julian Ramos, "Voter Registration Rates by Generation," Berkeley Initiative for Young Ameri-

However, not every young voter who sits out an election does so on purpose. What impacts the successful engagement of young people? Voting rules themselves are barriers for many youth voters and disproportionately impact youth of color who report the lack of access to transportation, proper ID, and long lines as barriers.[4] First, there are 'experience' and 'information' gaps. Most high school students are eligible to register to vote before they graduate. Although there is little data available, The Civics Center, an organization focused on registering high school students across the country, estimates that very few high school students encounter voter registration before graduating and that proactive policies in schools and states increase registration numbers.[5] This leaves many students entering college with little understanding of the process despite being eligible to register prior to matriculating into college.

The call to action for institutions is to facilitate the process to make it as accessible as possible as soon as possible. According to the Center for Information & Research on Civic Learning and Engagement's (CIRCLE's) Alberto Medina and Katie Kilton, youth voter turnout rates correlate to the accessibility of voter registration in a given state. The easier the voter registration process, the more likely a young person will successfully cast a vote.[6] Once a registration form has been completed and a successful vote has been cast, the more likely a new voter will become a consistent voter because voting behavior is habitual and best established as a young person.[7] As Eric Pulzer says, "A citizen's voting history is a powerful predictor of future behavior."[8] The barriers faced by young people can delay the development of that voting habit and demotivate them from participating in other areas of democracy.

cans Democracy Policy Lab, April 23, 2024, https://youngamericans.berkeley.edu/2024/04/voter-reg istration-rates-by-generation.

4 Center for Information & Research on Civic Learning and Engagement, "Why Youth Don't Vote: Differences by Race and Education," , August 21, 2018, https://circle.tufts.edu/latest-research/why-youth-dont-vote-differences-race-and-education; Movement Advancement Project and The Civics Center, "A Silenced Generation: How the Power of the Youth Vote Collides with Barriers to Voting," January 2024, https://www.mapresearch.org/file/MAP-2024-Youth-Voting-Report.pdf.

5 Movement Advancement Project and The Civics Center, "A Silenced Generation"; The Civics Center, "The Importance of High Schools," https://www.thecivicscenter.org/why-high-school.

6 Alberto Medina and Katie Hilton, "New Data: Nearly Half of Youth Voted in 2024," Center for Information & Research on Civic Learning and Engagement, April 14, 2025, https://circle.tufts.edu/latest-research/new-data-nearly-half-youth-voted-2024.

7 Eric Plutzer, "Becoming a Habitual Voter: Inertia, Resources, and Growth in Young Adulthood," *American Political Science Review* 96, no. 1 (March 2002): 41–56, https://doi.org/10.1017/S0003055402004227.

8 Plutzer, "Becoming a Habitual Voter," 43.

What gets in the way of registering to vote? Many young people who did not register in the 2024 election indicated that they did not know how to register or experienced problems with completing forms, ran out of time, or missed critical deadlines.[9] Students often assume that they can register through apps or online and are not aware of registration deadlines, ID requirements for first-time registrants, restrictions on absentee voting, or minutiae like proper campus addresses or finding the appropriate postage. Many students are living away from home for the first time, and have fewer resources and unpredictable schedules.[10] The 'information or experience gap' makes it easier for young people to make mistakes in the registration process, yet at the same time it is becoming increasingly difficult for third parties to register voters.[11] The likelihood that students have moved from their home communities where social networks are more readily available contributes to this gap.

Voting action plans developed with these barriers in mind can operationalize how institutions choose to place resources both human and financial. Without a plan, even well-intentioned institutions are likely to struggle to sustain student voting over time or understand what barriers are preventing students from successfully casting a ballot.

Campus voting action plans can range in specificity, sophistication, and responsibility. Minimally, a plan should identify the goals (e. g., reach 100 % participation of eligible voters), strategies, and actions for student voter registration, voter education, and a GOTV campaign. Institutions striving for more 'participatory' or 'justice-oriented' goals can use the voter action plan to more explicitly link participation to the role education plays in democracy and the advancement of civic learning while also preparing to protect students' right to vote, if threatened. Planning establishes the infrastructure and identifies responsible campus units and coalitions who lead and monitor registration and voter participation from year to year. Organized coalitions can more easily identify localized challenges, improve voter registration and voter turnout over time, and link the work to educational goals and pedagogical objectives in order to establish campus constituent buy-in to make the work sustainable over time.

---

9 Alberto Medina, Kelly Siegel-Stechler, Sara Suzuki, Ruby Belle Booth, and Katie Hilton, "Young People and the 2024 Election: Struggling, Disconnected, and Dissatisfied," Center for Information & Research on Civic Learning and Engagement, January 15, 2025, https://circle.tufts.edu/latest-research/2024-poll-barriers-issues-economy.
10 Movement Advancement Project and The Civics Center, "A Silenced Generation," 4–6.
11 Brennan Center for Justice, "Voting Laws Roundup: 2024 in Review," January 15, 2025, https://www.brennancenter.org/our-work/research-reports/voting-laws-roundup-2024-review.

Since 2012, national partners like ALL IN Campus Democracy Challenge, Vote Friendly Campus, Campus Vote Project, Fair Election Center, Institute for Democracy and Higher Education (IDHE), and Students Learn Students Vote Coalition (SLSV), among others, have offered institutions guidance on how to build a plan and developed iterative rating systems to provide direct feedback to institutions to improve planning. Each offers resources and tools that can be incorporated into the planning process. In the case of ALL IN, an individualized, iterative process includes ongoing feedback with "structure (program design and accountability), support (consultation, training, resources, and networking), and recognition (awards and accolades)," which help with long-term success.[12]

Post-election resources, like those available through Tufts' National Study of Learning Voting and Engagement (NSVLE), report data that examines over 1,000 U.S. institutions' voter registration and turnout rates to understand and improve student voting turnout.[13] CIRCLE, under which NSVLE is situated, closely follows youth voting trends. The investment in using these resources for planning works. Campuses that were considered highly engaged with ALL IN had 2022 voter turnout rates that were an average of five percentage points higher than other campuses.[14]

Partnerships can support the advocacy work that might be necessary if an institution needs to protect and/or expand student voting rights. In the case of Bard, regional partnerships not only helped with the various challenges to voting rights, but were also integral in helping pass New York State legislation requiring, with the institution's approval, the establishment of polling sites on campuses with more than 300 registered voters living on campus. These regional or statewide coalitions can improve access to the polls and challenge restrictive rules that make it difficult for students to vote.

Without a plan or appropriate partnerships, institutions are left to guess year to year how many and which students are successfully casting a ballot and what barriers might be preventing other students from voting. The how and why of a plan moves institutions towards 'participatory' or 'justice-oriented' action as resources are committed to help track data, facilitate voter registration and voting, and build protections to overcome efforts to suppress student voters. Voter protec-

---

12 ALL IN Campus Democracy Challenge, "The ALL IN Campus Democracy Challenge," April 4, 2025, https://allinchallenge.org/wp-content/uploads/ALL-IN-Theory-of-Change.pdf.

13 Institute for Democracy and Higher Education, "National Study of Learning, Voting and Engagement (NSLVE) Data Portal," https://nslve.tufts.edu/research/national-study-learning-voting-and-engagement-nslve/nslve-data-portal.

14 ALL IN Campus Democracy Challenge, "2024 Annual Report," January 2025, 13, https://allinchallenge.org/impact/.

tion establishes an institution as 'justice-oriented' and communicates to the campus and local/regional community that efforts to interfere with voting rights will be challenged. The more a plan moves beyond logistics and links the work to institutional and educational missions, the more likely the plan can be sustained over time.

2 The Planning Roadmap

As the Aggies say … Vote with Clarity
(NC A&T Voter Action Plan)

Campuses must account for their unique ecosystems when planning, evaluating the opportunities and challenges within the local context. A planning roadmap helps institutions establish where they fall on the engagement spectrum and identify strategic actions that move their campus culture towards more 'justice-oriented' approaches. As demonstrated by the battles over voting rights described in this book, there are always new challenges. Without campus buy-in, resources, and ongoing planning and monitoring, it is impossible to ensure full access, participation, or long-term sustainability.

This Planning Roadmap outlines specific actions for each step of the planning process. The steps can be used in part or as a whole depending on institutional resources and goals. Users of the roadmap can be individual students, faculty, or staff, whether they are working on campuses with little to no existing voter support or as part of a designated campus coalition already working on enhancing or expanding existing voting infrastructures.

Each section of the roadmap includes a corresponding table with sample activities and timelines that can help campus teams develop more comprehensive voter action plans at each stage of the voting process. The activities reflected in these tables are a compilation of the kinds of activities organized on each of the four campuses featured in this volume. The tables are practical guides that can be used to support campuses at any stage of planning.

2.1 Voter Registration

Registering students to vote is at the core of any voter action plan, and planning prepares campuses to meet the logistical and motivational challenges when engaging student voters. According to CIRCLE, more than one-third of youth voters in 2024 indicated that they were uninterested in engaging with the election. Many lacked information and motivation to register, citing dissatisfaction with candidates as the biggest barrier to participation while others did not see voting as important or felt "politically adrift with no party home."[15] Addressing these barriers starts at voter registration.

Critical to this process is coordination by a planning team responsible for voter registration and the monitoring of whether those registrations are successfully processed. Minimally, a campus voting action plan should establish a baseline for the number of students registered and the number of students voting. The team can use this list to target the most at-risk registrations. Young people have lower turnout in states without facilitative voting laws, and report missing deadlines or running out of time when online registration, automatic registration, or same-day registration are not available.[16] Therefore, targeting voter registration at the youngest voters (18- to 19-year-olds), that is, incoming college freshmen and sophomores, whose voter turnout traditionally trails their slightly older (ages 20–29) peers, can begin to address the most acute gaps in experience and information.[17]

The planning for voter registration can be organized by senior leadership, student groups, the faculty, or staff in administrative departments but ideally involves some combination of all four. When and how voter registration occurs depends on the voting options available to students on a given campus: non-residential colleges with mostly local or regional students have different voter registration processes from large state schools with primarily in-state voters. Many campuses manage both local registrations as well as in-state and out-of-state registrations. Organizers should start by assessing the types of voters they will encounter to prepare information and resources and provide training for teams responsible for the voter registration drives. In the case of a commuter campus, for example, this means preparing to register voters in multiple local precincts or counties within a given geographic range. Campuses with a large percentage of out-of-state voters need to prepare for the rules governing local voter registration and statewide and out-of-state voter registrations.

15 Medina, Siegel-Stechler, Suzuki, Booth, and Hilton, "Young People and the 2024 Election."
16 Center for Information & Research on Civic Learning and Engagement, "State-by-State Youth Voter Turnout Data and the Impact of Election Laws in 2022," updated May 2, 2023, https://circle.tufts.edu/latest-research/state-state-youth-voter-turnout-data-and-impact-election-laws-2022.
17 Center for Information & Research on Civic Learning and Engagement, "Youth Turnout Among Teens Shows Need for Growing Voters," September 19, 2019, https://circle.tufts.edu/latest-research/youth-turnout-among-teens-shows-need-growing-voters.

Since a myriad of state rulings and the *Symm*[18] decision, students are eligible to register at either their college address (on or off campus) or at the address of their home of origin. Determining which option best fits the student's needs can be confusing, especially for new voters who are unfamiliar with complicated absentee voter registration systems in their home states or may not know that they are eligible to register at a school address. New voters often have questions about where they should register and how to register. To help each student complete and submit a voter registration form at the address that makes sense for that individual student, teams should begin communicating with students prior to arrival on campus. As restrictions to first-time voter registration and absentee voting mount, institutions should consider advocating for students to register at their campus address in order to provide clearer assistance under changing legislation, or at least make clear that this is an option. Bard has shifted messaging since establishing an on-campus polling site, actively encouraging students to consider in-person voting to make sure they can successfully cast a ballot (while informing them, of course, of their right to vote from their home-of-origin address should they satisfy the residency requirements there). For students opting to vote by absentee ballot, institutions should attempt to ensure that election-related mail is accessible and prioritized in campus mailing systems, and even proactively communicate with students when such mail arrives in order to avoid common issues stemming from strict election-related deadlines.

How voter registration drives are organized and how voter registrations are processed will be determined by local laws. In some states, voter registration drives are limited by restrictive laws and can carry heavy fines or even threats of criminal charges.[19] In Florida, for example, a 2023 law, Bill 7050, requires organizers to register annually with the state and follow numerous rules or face fines of up to $250,000.[20] In Alabama, it is a crime to assist a voter in obtaining or returning a mail application. At the time of writing, both are being challenged in court.[21] To be sure, restrictions such as these are rare. However, knowledge is power. A comprehensive annual review of rules governing voter registration

---

18 *Symm v. United States*, 439 U.S. 1105 (1979), affirming *United States v. Texas*, 445 F. Supp. 1245 (S.D. Tex. 1978).

19 Brennan Center for Justice, "Voting Laws Roundup."

20 Florida State Senate, An Act Relating to Elections, SB 7050, introduced April 11, 2023, https://www.flsenate.gov/Session/Bill/2023/7050.

21 Johanna Alonso, "A Florida Law Has Nearly Killed Campus Voter Registration Drives," *Inside Higher Ed*, July 8, 2024, https://www.insidehighered.com/news/government/politics-elections/2024/07/08/florida-voter-registration-law-has-major-impact#; Florida State Senate, An Act Relating to Elections, SB 7050, introduced April 11, 2023, https://www.flsenate.gov/Session/Bill/2023/7050.

can be incorporated into training for teams to strategize how to manage potential barriers. And, when appropriate, institutions can decide to join a regional or state coalition to challenge state rules or highlight restrictive laws during voter registration drives or educational events.

How to manage voter registration drives within the local ecosystem must be determined by the campus team. In cases like Bard, where voters are from across the country, teams must track voter registration deadlines and regulations across the United States. A well-coordinated, well-trained voter registration team can manage multiple types of voter registrations while also keeping track of who has successfully registered (and where), and troubleshoot options when registration forms are not successfully processed. Schools can maintain an up-to-date list of registered voters (including location of registration) with the cooperation of the local Board of Elections (BOE) to help teams coordinate educational programs, outreach, and GOTV efforts. To manage the challenges of large-scale and/or complicated voter registrations, a campus might elect to invest in digital tools like Motivote that gamify the process to help voters register, find information about elections and candidates, and encourage peer-to-peer networking to increase participation. Rock the Vote, Vote.org, and The Andrew Goodman Foundation's VoteEverywhere offer similar digital tools. Planning teams should consider the most effective tools for their particular campus and advocate for more resources when needed.

Although voter drives can emerge from different parts of campus, the most sustainable and effective organizing is done by cross-campus coalitions (see section 3.1). In order to effectively reach all students, voter registration is linked to important bureaucratic processes in which all students participate. This can include first-year and returning student check-ins, orientation, course registration, room selection, and student billing. Integration into annual student events can reach students who might not engage with traditional registration campaigns. These events can include student club fairs, student government elections, homecoming, athletic or Greek Life events, or other campus traditions that draw large numbers and a diverse range of students. Faculty can disseminate information about opportunities to register or sponsor class visits by voter registration teams in a first-year seminar or other course where new voters are likely to be enrolled. NC A&T's plan, for example, pushes to "get voter registration and education in the classroom (separate from the first-year experience curriculum) and virtual/electronic platforms (links and information on the University website, virtual student union, Aggie Access, in Housing application and Orientation material, etc.)."[22] Ultimately, the goal is to have multiple touchpoints for all eligible voters

---

22 North Carolina Agricultural & Technical State University, "Voter Engagement 2.4: Aggies Vote

every academic year of a student's time at an institution. These touchpoints can act as building blocks to expand students' knowledge not only about elections and maintaining voter status (hopefully with increasing independence), but also to develop their sense of civic agency within the American context.

Bard's updated 2024 plan incorporates more structured touchpoints on an annual basis. Campus teams have a required check-in at all arrival days, voter registration is connected to Housing Selection and other routine processes, and regular registration drives happen through the Fall. Students are asked to complete a form that includes a voter registration status look-up (encouraging independence) and information about primaries and requesting absentee ballots. Students opting out of Housing Selection are prompted to re-register with their new off-campus address. Student orientation includes a Democracy Day, a day-long event centered on readings and panel discussions related to elections, politics, and civics. PVA-MU's voting plan calls for "In-person voter registration drives, in-person voter education events (e.g. film screenings, debates, lecture series, etc.), classroom voter registration presentations (in-person or virtual), [and] virtual voter registration drives (e.g. Couch Party text banking events), virtual voter education events (e.g. film screening, debates, lectures series, etc.)."[23] Each moment is an opportunity for engagement that builds students' confidence.

Tapping into student energy and knowledge makes the planning more responsive and connected to student needs. Relational, peer-to-peer organizing that leverages personal networks is most effective in reaching a diverse range of voters. Relationships between the voting advocate (canvasser, organizer) and the potential voter matter.[24] Beyond social networks, young voters seek inspiration and connection. Tuskegee's Andrew Goodman Foundation Fellows Xadia Cherrie and Paige Henry reflected on how important it was for them to connect with community leaders and organizers who looked like them and with whom students could relate.[25] When asked what universities should consider when building a plan, they recommended that organizers focus on voter education, things like bringing can-

---

with Clarity, Seeing Beyond the Polls," June 2024, 13, https://allinchallenge.org/wp-content/uploads/North-Carolina-AT-State-University-2024-Action-Plan.pdf.

23 Crystal Edwards, "2020 Democratic Engagement Action Plan," Prairie View A&M University, 2020, 3, https://allinchallenge.org/wp-content/uploads/Prairie-View-AM-University-ALL-IN-Challenge-Action-Plan.docx.pdf.

24 Cassandra Handan-Nader, Daniel E. Ho, Alison Morantz, and Tom A. Rutter, "The Effectiveness of a Neighbor-to-Neighbor Get-Out-the-Vote Program: Evidence from the 2017 Virginia State Elections," *Journal of Experimental Political Science* 8, no. 2 (Summer 2021): 145–160, https://doi.org/10.1017/XPS.2020.11.

25 Xadia Cherrie and Paige Henry, interviewed by Erin Cannan, February 26, 2025.

didates to campus, teaching logistics about voting, and advocating for students to vote at school. However, they both described how powerful it was to connect with the community and with the history around them. Xadia reflected on how moved she was to hear the intergenerational stories during a Bloody Sunday commemoration in Selma, saying "I came to understand that success has its ups and downs. Hearing intergenerational stories at the Bloody Sunday events in Selma gave me inspiration because older people are still fighting for young people. They reminded me to not stop fighting even if discouraged."[26]

For further information regarding activities related to this section, see Table 1.

Table 1: Sample timeline for a voter registration drive.

Pre-arrival
– Communicate with new students (post-enrollment) about voter registration options in the local context.
– Send communications to new students from campus leaders about the link between education and democracy, endorsing voting as a critical way to participate in democracy.
– Coordinate with local or national partners to build a voter registration plan for the semester.
– Set planning goals (for instance, register 100 % of eligible voters).
– Request current voter lists from BOE to establish the baseline of participation.
– How many eligible student voters are on campus?
– How many are registered and where are they registered?
– Who is not registered (or registration is unknown)?
– Link registration to enrollment processes (billing, housing forms, move-in information).

Arrival
– Require voter registration check-in for first year and transfer arrival day. Students can determine where and if they want to register to vote.
– Distribute information at orientation sessions or during course registration processes.
– Table at the opening of school check-ins and events to confirm voter registration status for returning students.
– Send campus communications about available voter registration options and upcoming deadlines.
– Send campus text to returning students whose registration status is unknown, with link to the form and supporting resources, requesting updates.

Fall semester
– Utilize federal work-study funding to hire peer leaders to coordinate.
– Support opportunities for students to engage with voter registration, either peer-led or in partnership with organizations in voter fellowships, or support courses/research on elections and voting.

---

26 Xadia Cherrie, interviewed by Erin Cannan, February 26, 2025.

- Celebrate civic holidays such as National Voter Registration Day, with tabling, academic, and co-curricular programming.
- Faculty host student voter registration teams in a class (especially targeting courses with younger students).
- Provide sample language for faculty to use in class announcements and in emails to their students with educational information on voter registration and programming.
- Identify faculty champions to educate other faculty on voter registration information in various settings like faculty committees, departmental meetings, or in faculty meetings.
- Offer students fellowship or other opportunities to support the voter registration process by developing savvy peer-to-peer voter education materials, such as social media memes and videos. Teach students how to check voter registration rolls independently or using digital tools.
- Track and communicate voter registration deadlines, especially for out-of-state voters. Disseminate posters or other visuals that map deadlines.
- Host voter registration drives in partnership with athletics, residence life, graduate schools, off-campus offices.
- Schedule voter registration classroom visits during established civic holidays in September.
- Text, email, and phone communications to eligible voters whose voter registration status is unknown.
- Coordinate regular team check-ins to track registrations.
- Hold open office hours, table at key events, and programming
- Coordinate educational efforts to teach people how to track their own voter registration status online.
- Offer last-chance events to help students register at the final deadline available to them based on residency.

Spring semester

- Require voter registration check-in for mid-year entering students, including transfer arrivals.
- Host voter registration tabling to align with primaries, local, or special elections.
- Coordinate with senior services to provide information for graduating students moving from the area.
- Coordinate with the study abroad office to confirm voter registration and voting services for voting from overseas.
- Provide faculty advisors with information on how to update voter registrations to be used during advising meetings; especially for students moving off campus or graduating.
- Re-register students who are moving out of district or off campus in compliance with local election law.

2.2 Monitoring Voter Registration

Bard's voter registration process focuses on more than just the successful submission of registration forms. Members of the team are assigned to closely track registration forms to ensure that they are correctly and fully processed by the local BOE to troubleshoot errors made by students or detect systemic efforts to reject student forms that should be successfully processed. In the case where students are making errors, campus teams can work with individual students and train teams to watch for specific errors that are causing forms to be rejected. If it is the case that student forms are not being processed as they should by the BOE, the monitoring team can address using a variety of strategies including discussions with BOE officials, advocacy with appropriate state offices, or by taking legal action.

Monitoring begins at voter registration. Election@Bard has organized an institutionally sponsored voter registration team that monitors and tracks student voter registration forms after they have been submitted to the BOE to ensure that they have been successfully processed. The team identifies problems at two critical times: prior to the end of registration and prior to election day. This is supplemented by efforts to strongly encourage student voters to check their voter registration status. This early monitoring can often catch registrations that are rejected due to misspelled names, missing information, or other defects. Around election deadlines and election day itself, monitoring efforts can shift towards helping students avoid missing absentee voter deadlines, participate in early voting, or, in more extreme cases, preparing them to complete affidavit ballots or even to appear before a judge on election day if appropriate.

This form of monitoring is also critical in allowing an institution to be 'justice-oriented.' Tracking the cycle provides mechanisms for early detection of more systemic problems. Teams can monitor rolls for frequency of denied forms (are student voters being targeted and how?) to identify efforts to disenfranchise student voters, whether intentionally or unintentionally. Appropriate officials can then consult with the Board of Elections, or sympathetic lawyers, to identify the appropriate response.

Teams can measure improvements in turnout by tracking the percentage of eligible voters who are registered and the percentage of voters who come out to the polls. This allows for long-term planning and the refinement of voter plans.

For further information regarding activities related to this section, see Tables 2 and 3.

Table 2: A sample timeline for monitoring voter registration.

Pre-arrival

- Meet with BOE to check in and obtain the most up-to-date voter rolls.
    - Identify returning students who may have been made inactive or been dropped from the rolls.
    - Follow up with students about their status.
- Coordinate with college enrollment offices to identify all eligible voters (over 18, U.S. citizenship, residency).
    - Compare eligible voter information from campus officials with BOE voter registration rolls.

Arrival

- Coordinate outreach for eligible voters whose registration status is unknown.
- Develop predetermined time frame to request updated voter rolls (weekly is recommended) to track successful registrations.
    - Note any rejected voter registration forms and reasons for the rejection.
    - Follow up with the voter to address the issue.
- In some states, colleges and universities offer local BOEs a list of on-campus student registrants, to offer an additional proof of residency, where required. Early coordination with the local BOE helps the overall youth electoral process.

Before deadlines for voter registration

- Text, email, and phone eligible voters whose status is unknown.
- Text, email, and phone voter registration status to eligible voters whose address has changed and requires re-registration.
- Coordinate peer-to-peer outreach to voters who have not yet registered.
- Host open office hours, tabling at key events, and programming with voter registration teams to field questions about voter registration status.
- Monitor why and how many voter registration forms are rejected and for what reason.
- Troubleshoot options for voters whose forms were not successfully processed, especially those whose forms were rejected after a registration deadline (i.e., voters living in New York State can register ten days prior to election day, which may provide time to register locally).

Before election day

- Confirm final voter registration rolls for local polls after voter registration deadline.

Table 3: A practical guide to encouraging student voting.

College-sponsored voter registration must be led by non-partisan teams.
- Campus teams should not advocate for candidates, parties, or positions.
- The responsibility of the team is focused on empowering and teaching student voters how to participate in an election to encourage a lifelong practice.

Residency eligibility considerations:

Does the length of time at a student's address meet eligibility requirements for that state?
- Voter registration teams should be aware of requirements and deadlines for absentee voting in all states where students are registering. In cases where polls are on or near to campus, teams might make a determination to recommend that students register locally to avoid confusing absentee ballot processes, especially for campuses with on-site polls. Absentee voting has severe restrictions for new voters in some states. Ultimately, teams should advise students that the determination of where they decide to vote is subjective and that they should take into account a range of considerations including residency and eligibility.
- Campuses which are able should consider advocating for a single voter registration address for on-campus voters to avoid confusion with listing dorm names or numbers on voter registration forms. Where this is not possible, campuses should work with the local BOE to offer proof of on-campus student residencies (such as lists provided by the college to the BOE) to avoid erroneous denials of voter registration forms.
- Students voting at their campus address must mark the address correctly otherwise forms can be rejected based on residency. Bard's lawsuits were in some cases driven by challenges to residency. A single campus mailing address is now used by all on-campus students at Bard.

Forms must be completed by the voter, filled out accurately (correct spelling, birthdates, etc.), and mailed prior to registration deadlines (which vary) to the local Board of Elections.
- Teams can provide sample forms at all voter registration drives to help minimize mistakes and should be trained to review completed forms to address mistakes on site.
- Where possible, teams can process voter registration forms for voters or help voters complete and mail forms directly. Distributing forms or QR codes with links to forms or information is likely going to result in a fewer number of successfully processed forms.

Registration forms should be tracked.
- Where allowed, forms should be copied and then sent via certified mail and/or dropped at the BOE to obtain receipts for hand delivery. In-person drop-offs to the BOE are particularly important when delivering forms close to deadlines, as deadlines for mailed forms vary.

Maintain records of completed forms (make copies where allowed, track numbers) to compare with updated voter rolls and to troubleshoot in cases where forms are rejected.
- For campuses with local voters, teams should regularly request (through Freedom of Information Law requests, if needed) updated voter rolls from the BOE to ensure registrations are processed.
- The BOE can provide information on why forms are rejected. Having copies of submitted forms can help in cases where concerns might arise.

2.3 Getting Out the Vote

Not every successfully processed voter registration form translates into a vote. In the 2024 election, some states experienced an uptick in new voters registered, yet youth participation dropped nationally.[27] Persuading a student to register to vote,

---

27 Medina, Siegel-Stechler, Suzuki, Booth, and Hilton, "Young People and the 2024 Election."

which is a largely easy and quick process (without voter obstruction), may not be enough to convince them to commit time and resources to cast a ballot. GOTV campaigns must be targeted, responsive, compelling, and focused on the needs and interests of the voters. Without a plan, GOTV efforts may not motivate reluctant voters to participate on election day.

GOTV efforts are part logistics and part a call to action. The logistics are focused on tracking if eligible voters are voting. The call to action is a strategy to motivate reluctant voters to go to the polls. At first glance, sitting out an election might be attributed to apathy when in fact logistics, confusion, and complicated attitudes towards voting or candidates might be playing a role.[28] In some cases, students may not trust the system or trust that elections will have outcomes that will impact their lives. According to NSLVE, the overall student voting rate in 2022 was down from the 2018 midterms.[29] As a whole, institutional voting rates went down, with minority-serving and women's colleges experiencing the biggest decreases.[30] GOTV teams should take these trends into account, and the trends on their own campuses, when considering how to frame GOTV efforts.

GOTV involves two types of strategies. The first focuses on the mobilization of voters who are likely to vote and preparing them for what to expect at the polls. This aspect of planning involves education about who and what is on the ballot, including overlooked issues like referendums (often called 'ballot proposals,' 'propositions,' or 'initiatives') and about what the process of voting actually looks like (whether voting in person or by absentee ballot). This educational programming can come in many forms. How to vote is certainly important; what the ballot looks like and what to expect at the polls are critical. However, programming is often more successful when students can learn about the issues connected to a particular election. This can be done in a variety of ways. Meeting candidates is one of the most direct ways to connect with an election. This can be coordinated through a class or sponsored as a campus-wide program. Visits can come in many forms, including candidate and/or representative forums and debates and/or individual 'meet and greets.' This is particularly useful for smaller local, regional, and/or state candidates. Student debates focused on issues represented on the ballot or debate watch parties for bigger elections can be linked to courses and sponsored by student groups. Faculty-led panels, teach-ins, and class visits (even opening certain relevant classes to the entire campus) can help students understand how

---

28 Medina, Siegel-Stechler, Suzuki, Booth, and Hilton, "Young People and the 2024 Election."
29 Adam Gismondi, Matthew Nelsen, Mariani German, Victoria Tse, and Amanda Sahar d'Urso, "Democracy Counts 2022: Student Engagement in a Midterm Year," National Study of Learning, Voting, and Engagement, 2024, 3, https://tufts.app.box.com/v/democracy-counts-2022.
30 Gismondi, Nelsen, German, Tse, and d'Urso, "Democracy Counts 2022," 8.

their future work sector might be impacted by election outcomes. Student newspapers, student government, or election teams can produce voter guides that include candidate responses to questions relevant to youth voters. Websites, social media posts, emails, and fliers with election information including links to candidate websites, volunteer, or internship opportunities with campaigns can encourage broader participation. Coordination with off-campus partners like the League of Women Voters who might sponsor regional events can connect students to local GOTV efforts and can provide additional learning opportunities. Finally, students can sign up to work elections as poll workers or poll watchers.

The second strategy is more complicated. It is focused on persuading reluctant voters that they should vote and involves appealing to emotions and shared values. GOTV campaigns need to stir people's emotions, inspire and encourage a sense of belonging, and connect the power of voting with issues that the individual voters care about. The more targeted, individualized, and personalized a campaign, the more effective the outcomes.[31] This is where peer-to-peer organizing is most critical. Connecting with trusted peers may have the largest impact on a reluctant voter's decision to come out to the polls. Taking the time to listen to why students are reluctant to come out to vote, and finding ways to help address their concerns, requires multiple in-person touchpoints that focus on relational organizing through student networks, student-only programs, and student-to-student messaging. Such is the case with PVAMU's annual March to the Poll, which experienced the largest turnout of students when the planning was shared with the major campus organizations.[32] PVAMU's Kala Washington describes how each student organization plays a critical role within the voter engagement ecosystem: "Student participation is almost entirely dependent on student-driven efforts. Without a strong desire or call to action from students, engagement remains minimal. However, for civic engagement to be truly effective and sustainable, it must be recognized and supported as a core institutional priority. The level of staff and administrative involvement directly correlates with the number of students who participate."[33]

NC A&T takes a different approach through a student-organized volunteer group called Research Revolutionaries, who work to tie what's on the ballot to research.[34] For example, Research Revolutionaries created an Aggie voter guide based on student interest that emphasized how issues might impact fields of in-

---

31 Yale University Institution for Social and Policy Studies, "Lessons from GOTV Experiments," https://isps.yale.edu/research/field-experiments-initiative/lessons-from-gotv-experiments.
32 Kala Washington, email with author, March 16, 2025.
33 Kala Washington, email with author, March 16, 2025.
34 Tiffany Seawright, interviewed by Erin Cannan, February 25, 2025.

terest or their future sectors. Student groups created programs based on the research and the outreach team created infographics and materials for social media while a student street team coordinated live events. These efforts act as invitations to a diverse range of students, encouraging participation and establishing a campus as a place where voting is expected and encouraged.

For further information regarding activities related to this section, see Table 4.

Table 4: A sample plan for a campaign to get out the vote.

Strategizing

- Coordinate campus surveys to understand why students are voting or not voting. What issues do students consider to be important? Is that compelling them to vote?
- Invite candidates, organize debates, sponsor issue-based discussions.
- Create student-developed voter guides (what's on your ballot).
- Troubleshoot how many students who registered chose not to vote. How many eligible voters chose not to register? Why?
- Engage trusted groups like athletic teams, clubs, Student Government Association, fraternities and sororities, student groups, scholarship offices, faculty advisors (why voting matters by major/industry) to organize networks. Likely more in-person, smaller group discussions and engagement. Consider hiring peer ambassadors to coordinate targeted campaigns.
- Centralize resources on websites with relevant messaging for all voters on campus.
- Coordinate educational programs with faculty, student groups/organizations, campus departments, or off-campus partners that help students translate what is on the ballot to issues that they care about.
- Link educational programming to relevant courses in collaboration with academic departments.

Messaging

- Coordinate messaging from senior leadership: public statements from the president/senior leadership affirming students' right to vote; reinforce link between education and democracy.
- Coordinate messaging to families to support new voters.
- Coordinate social media campaigns and messaging and begin prior to first-year arrival. Include evidence-based strategies like personalized, student-to-student communications on why voting matters. These peer-to-peer communications are key to voter outreach, since students know best how to engage their peers and how to capture their attention.
- Make civics a class, encouraging faculty to link one class with a topically relevant focus to the election (provide resources for speaker, travel, screening, etc.).
- Establish an early voting initiative.
- Offer a campus-wide voting challenge or 'friends don't let friends stay home' campaigns.
- Promote accountability pledges like ALL INs 'Triple your Pledge' campaigns.

Counting down
– Create a comprehensive communication strategy to launch in the summer that includes key dates and deadlines. Campaigns should be targeted based on what phase of the election cycle (voter registration, absentee ballot requests/mail-in deadlines, and early voting/election day). – Link issues to programming for civic holidays such as National Voter Registration Day and Early Voting week, focused on student interest. Consider providing resources for student groups to coordinate group-specific programs (i.e., residence hall programs, athletic teams, student clubs). – Create a 'make your voter plan campaign' (each voter asked to make their plan for election day, can include a 'take a friend' or 'remind a friend' strategy). – Distribute information and announcements for faculty with information on deadlines, early voting, or absentee dates and where to find more information

Preparing for election day
– Focus specifically on messaging to registered voters through peer-led and individualized texting, emailing, calling, and door-knocking. – Support a peer-led campus postering campaign encouraging students to vote and informing them where their polling sites are located. – Prepare messaging and announcements for faculty to distribute and/or discuss in class just before the election. – Host faculty panel on 'disciplines on the ballot,' educating voters on what types of issues are represented on the ballot (this could be campus-wide or departmental). – Coordinate with campus partners on 'make your voting plan' to help students schedule when they will vote and if they will bring a friend. This can be discussed in smaller cohorts, including in classes with faculty, in athletic teams with coaches, and in residence halls with residence life staff. – Coordinate GOTV reminders one week prior to early voting (text, email, calls, dorm storms, tabling). – Work with monitoring teams who track voters to coordinate individualized outreach via coaches, team captains, peer ambassadors, etc. 48/24 hours prior to election day. – Include emails, notes, and calls that promise a follow-up communication that will ask about the voting experience. – Offer programs focused on 'beyond the ballot' initiatives to engage students.

2.4 Voting Plan and Election Day

All election day plans should focus on preparing voters for what to expect, whether they are voting absentee or in person at a polling site, during the early voting period and/or on election day depending on the state. Every voter should have an individualized voting plan which includes contingency plans in case they face challenges. But just as with voter registration, planning for early voting and/or election day looks very different on campuses with different types of voters. Campuses exclusively working with commuting students should focus on identifying applicable polling sites, hours, and sample ballots. These teams may want to emphasize early voting options to account for how work and class schedules on election day might conflict with plans to vote. For residential campuses without a poll site on campus, arrangements should be made to provide regular shuttles to the polls for locally registered voters, including transporting students to early polling sites. If students vote at multiple locations based on residency (campus is split between districts or off-campus students vote in different local polls), then early education will be key, and coordinated plans to transport students to multiple sites might be necessary.

Election day efforts ramp up on the first day students can request an absentee ballot: this is when voting begins. Periods to request absentee ballots vary wildly, ranging from three to twenty-one days in advance of election day.[35] Return deadlines fluctuate as well. Some states allow absentee ballots to be received within designated times following election day while others require ballots to be received by or on election day. Absentee ballots can often require additional steps. For instance, voters might be asked to include a signature from a witness (in some instances required to be a voter from that same state) or notary. Other ballots might require copies of state-issued IDs. Rules governing absentee ballots in the states where students are registered should be confirmed annually on websites that aggregate this information but it should be noted that rules should be double checked by teams in advance of GOTV efforts. The most up-to-date information should appear on individual secretary of state websites.

Once voter registration deadlines have passed, monitoring teams can turn their attention to tracking the voter experience at the polls in order to track how many voters are successfully casting a ballot. This effort can include campus officials, faculty, and students signing up to be poll workers and poll watchers at sites where the majority of students are voting. In Bard's case, faculty, staff, and students all work the polls both on campus and at local off-campus sites where students are most likely to be voting. Given past experiences, Bard has developed relationships with attorneys who have agreed in advance of election day to represent students in the case of difficulties. Bard transportation is prearranged to take students to the county seat where student voters can appear before a judge in the case that they believe they have been inappropriately turned away from the polls.

The size and makeup of the election day team depends on the campus. Larger campuses must train and deploy much larger teams and are likely supporting voters who are casting ballots at multiple local polling sites. However, the organizing principles for the teams are largely the same. For instance, NC A&T's coalition in-

---

35 Vote.org, "Absentee Ballot Deadlines," https://www.vote.org/absentee-ballot-deadlines/.

cludes over 30 campus and local partners with the goal to reach 50 % higher voter participation.[36] In Bard's case, the election day team is divided into multiple subgroups. A centrally located campus team helps educate students heading to the polls by providing sample ballots, answering logistical questions, and troubleshooting issues for voters who might be turned away from the polls inappropriately, like misspellings of names. They track and reach out to eligible voters who have not yet turned out. This team coordinates day-of-GOTV efforts, answers questions, and encourages students to come out. A second team is trained to monitor students who may experience difficulties at the poll or who are turned away. These team members are trained to troubleshoot issues and advise students on their options.

Inevitably, young voters will make mistakes on voter registration forms and not appear in the voter rolls. Voters will have been made 'inactive' because, for example, they have studied abroad and a BOE mailer sent to their mailing address is sent back. Helping students understand what to expect at the polls is important, including teaching them what their rights are in the case that something goes wrong (e. g., options to complete a provisional or affidavit ballot). And, if a voter does not have any remaining options to help them vote, explaining what went wrong and what to do for the next election cycle can help ensure they can cast a ballot next election. However, it is the case that sometimes voters are inappropriately challenged when trying to vote and legal expertise is needed.[37] Monitoring teams can coordinate with lawyers who can advise students on options to respond to the challenge.

2.5 Post-Election Debrief

Following every election, teams should debrief to determine if they met their goals. This is where yield rates for voters can help teams assess their plan. Post-election campus teams can call, email, or text voters with surveys to assess students' experiences at the ballot (or mailbox) and review NSLVE comparative data which comes out after midterm and presidential elections. NSLVE data provides campus-specific, detailed data about who voted based on multiple criteria and includes comparative data. Insights gained by the team can be embedded into future plans, making the whole process evidence-based, more effective, and

---

36 North Carolina Agricultural & Technical State University, "Voter Engagement 2.4," 5, 15.
37 Election@Bard, "Bard College's ALL IN Campus Democracy Challenge Action Plan," revised December 10, 2023, https://allinchallenge.org/wp-content/uploads/Bard-College-2024-Action-Plan. pdf, 13.

sustainable. Post-election educational programs like 'beyond the ballot' or 'now what' sessions can make more explicit the link between elections and ongoing civic engagement opportunities year-round.

For further information regarding activities related to this section, see Table 5 and Appendix A.

Table 5: A sample of activities for monitoring before and after election day.

Before election day and during early voting
– Support establishment of teams setting up in high-traffic areas on and off campus to help students determine rules in their state and troubleshoot, especially in the week leading up to the early voting period.
– Coordinate with campus mailroom to provide postage and answer questions regarding postmarks, and to ensure that election materials are prioritized in campus mailing systems, even during the spring break period in connection with the primary elections.
– Remind voters about ID requirements (if needed, what type of IDs are accepted, and facilitate access to student ID if accepted).

On election day
– Coordinate with GOTV team to monitor which eligible voters have voted and manage election day messaging to voters, including outreach to voters who have not yet voted.
– Establish and coordinate centralized teams set up in designated areas to provide information, track voter experiences, and troubleshoot issues at the poll. Inform voters of their rights, including how to complete provisional ballots in the case that a voter might not appear, has been made inactive, or has been removed from the rolls. Troubleshoot voters who are not appearing on the rolls, who have been made inactive, or who might have a misspelled name.
– Transport voters to appear before a judge in the case that the voter believes the roll is incorrect. In some states, voters have the option to appear in front of a judge when they believe they are being prevented from voting for a reason they consider to be illegitimate (i. e., challenged by an election poll watcher).
– Establish on-site legal support to advise voters who may need representation.

After election day
– Survey voters to solicit feedback on their election day experience.
– Review NSLVE data analysis to identify students who are not participating.
– Inform students who voted provisionally about how to cure provisional ballots.
– Track students' ability to cast a successful vote by mail or in person on election day, and provisional ballot.
– **Support** students and faculty interested in studying voter trends and systems design analysis.

3 Implementing Plans: Building an Ecosystem of Engagement

3.1 Cross-Campus Coalition-Building

In their "Strengthening American Democracy" guide, SLSV recommends the establishment of campus-wide coalitions as the second step in the planning process.[38] These coalitions or campus teams can originate from different departments, programs, or student groups. The most effective plans are directed and led by peers, supported by staff, partnered with community members, and explicitly endorsed by leadership. Each of the four campuses represented in this volume demonstrates different types of planning, yet all coordinate the work using cross-campus coalitions composed of students, staff, faculty, senior leadership, and community partners. It is important to note that for those campuses experiencing active voter disenfranchisement, it is especially important to have campus coalitions that can take on different aspects of the work. In Bard's case, the small Election@Bard team had to be in court multiple times just before election day. Much of the team was preoccupied with the legal challenges, making it hard to implement planning strategies for GOTV and voter education.

PVAMU's and NC A&T's voter action plans are designed by a coalition of faculty, staff and students. NC A&T's Director of Leadership and Engagement and External Affairs/Office of Strategic Partnerships, works closely with a large number of student leaders, the student government and clubs, while much of PVAMU's has been largely student led. Bard's plan is based out of The Center for Civic Engagement under the student-led Election@Bard team, which receives institutional support from the executive vice president and (former) vice president for student affairs. Tuskegee's team is led by powerful student clubs and the Student Government Association in coordination with Student Life and Development.

Teams can originate from different departments, programs, or student groups. Larger cross-campus coalitions can help alleviate the pressure on smaller teams and ensure that students are participating in elections by reaching more students through a diverse network of academic departments, student services offices, and student organizations. Coordination with multiple academic depart-

---

38 Students Learn Students Vote Coalition, "Strengthening American Democracy: A Guide for Developing an Action Plan to Increase Civic Learning, Political Engagement, and Voter Participation Among College Students," 4th ed., August 2023, https://allinchallenge.org/wp-content/uploads/StrengtheningAmericanDemocracyGuideVOL4.pdf.

ments to incorporate the work into the classroom can help realize the mission to link voting and democratic learning. Coalitions can build momentum across campus, build a voting campus culture, and act as a check and balance to a potential shift in institutional or leadership priorities. Without a cross-campus coalition, institutional commitments can waver as changes in leadership occur or external pressures work to erode institutional priorities. This body can build on lessons learned from tracking student voting habits, provide 'on the ground' messaging that reflects student interests, and maintain the archival record of actions. The collaborative nature and multi-stakeholder approach can help realize the institutional commitments made in the planning and meet the evolving needs of student voters over time.

The Civic Engagement Coalition (CEC), the main organizing body for NC A&T's voter engagement, distributes planning across faculty, student groups, administrators, and off-campus partners.[39] NC A&T's director of leadership and engagement, Tiffany Seawright, a key organizer and author of NC A&T's Student Voting Action plan, collaboratively leads the team with the Office of the Chancellor and the Student Government Association. The CEC is charged with the oversight of the planning work, revisiting the student voting plan every year, assessing what worked and what didn't, and establishing short- and long-term goals aiming "to achieve institutionalization and 100% participation supported through concrete and achievable annual goals with a system of monitoring."[40] NC A&T's system of phased planning uses different focus areas for deeper engagement with the issues represented on the ballot.[41] The group monitors trends in new students' civic literacy as they enter the university to be responsive to the needs of the evolving student body.

The responsibilities of a campus coalition can vary widely and depend on how a group is authorized to act. The most effective implementation should include careful consideration of the structure of the group, including its leadership, organizing principles, primary goals, and communications strategies. Members of the coalition can work together to track and monitor voter registration forms and participation, as well as managing reporting, archiving, and evaluation of the annual election cycle to determine what is working and what needs to change. This kind of engagement also allows members of the coalition to determine if challenges to students' access to the polls is occurring.

---

39 North Carolina Agricultural & Technical State University, "Voter Engagement 2.4," 4.
40 North Carolina Agricultural & Technical State University, "Voter Engagement 2.4," 12.
41 North Carolina Agricultural & Technical State University, "Voter Engagement 2.4," 14.

Seawright and the CEC support a variety of student-led organizing efforts, including the Student Social Action Coalition, a body of students composed of representatives from different student groups and committees on campus whose work incorporates civic engagement as a pillar within their mission. The work has raised student political awareness and social action and the continuous dialogue helps when there is a call to action or a threat to student voting rights, as was the case a few years ago.

Tuskegee's dean of students, Tameka Harper cites the collaborative nature of the campus voting efforts for a successful 2024 student voting outcome.[42] She attributes the success to multiple partnerships, from student government and Greek organizations, to staff offices, to the NAACP and local and state-elected officials. The goal of the 2024 plan was to register students to vote and "change the narrative on how HBCU students perceive voting and the political process."[43] This effort resulted in the Tuskegee University Royal Court winning the "Vote Loud HBCU Voter Registration Challenge," receiving the most voter registration submissions among 100+ HBCU campuses.[44] These efforts would not be possible without the coordination of large campus coalitions.

3.2 Campus Polling Sites

Once a campus has successfully managed multiple elections, it might be time to consider campaigning to secure a campus polling site. Accessing polls off campus can be difficult and creates logistical barriers to voting. On-campus polling sites increase student access and eliminate barriers. Institutions should consider local BOE requirements and consult with campus leaders, local partners, and legal teams to determine the path forward. Institutional leaders should identify and make available appropriate locations for voting that are accessible and centrally located. Campaigns should align diverse groups and demonstrate the logistical and civic value of establishing a polling site on campus.[45] Access to polling sites on campus is especially helpful for young, newly registered voters.[46] Success-

---

42 Tameka Harper, email with author, February 19, 2025.

43 Tameka Harper, email with author, February 19, 2025.

44 Tameka Harper, email with author, February 19, 2025.

45 The Andrew Goodman Foundation, "Toolkit: Securing On-Campus Polling Places," 2, https://andrewgoodman.org/wp-content/uploads/2022/10/A-Toolkit-For-Securing-On-Campus-Polling-Places.pdf.

46 See, for example, Daniel A. Smith, "On-Campus Early In-Person Voting in Florida in the 2018 General Election," The Andrew Goodman Foundation, August 9, 2019, 10, https://andrewgoodman.

ful campaigns include an understanding of the support of the local BOE. Strategies will largely depend on the cooperation of the BOE. If BOE officials are receptive, then the focus might be on meeting polling site requirements (like registering the number of required voters, as is the case in New York State). However, if BOE officials are reticent or even hostile to hosting a site on campus, campus coalitions need to build strategies that challenge restrictions that can range from state laws, like the one proposed in Texas in 2023 which attempted to prohibit campuses from hosting early voting or election day sites, or uncooperative officials, as in the Bard polling site case.[47]

3.3 Leadership

Leadership plays a critical role in the activation and long-term sustainability of a voter action plan. ALL IN's 2023 "Nonpartisan Student Voting Group Report" identified some troubling trends to watch for in future elections.[48] This includes lower engagement by stakeholders, including senior campus leaders, with less election messaging and coordination by campus leadership and lower financial support.

We have argued that not only should "leadership ... be willing to promote the view that students not only have the right to vote" but that they should actively encourage students to vote locally where their vote is more likely to be counted.[49] Campuses whose leadership actively engages experience better outcomes, with higher voter turnout on campuses whose president signed ALL IN's Presidents' Commitment to Full Voter Participation.[50]

IDHE's executive director Nancy Thomas recognizes that "institutional leaders may be reluctant to wade into political waters" but advises that "'political' and 'partisan' are not interchangeable terms" and senior leaders should "reimagine election seasons as opportunities to bridge differences; strengthen community and inclusion; improve political discourse; cultivate student activism, leadership

---

org/wp-content/uploads/2019/08/On-Campus-Early-In-Person-Voting-in-Florida-in-the-2018-Gener al-Election-FINAL-8-9.pdf.

47 Becky Fogel, "A Texas Republican Says Banning College Polling Places is About Safety. Students Don't Buy It," *KUT News*, March 1, 2023, https://www.kut.org/education/2023-03-01/a-texas-republi can-says-banning-college-polling-places-is-about-safety-students-dont-buy-it.

48 ALL IN Campus Democracy Challenge, "ALL IN Nonpartisan Student Voting Group Report," 2023, https://allinchallenge.org/wp-content/uploads/ALL-IN-Student-Voting-Group-Report-and-Toolkits.pdf.

49 Becker and Cannan, "Institution as Citizen," 1894.

50 "ALL IN Campus Democracy Challenge, "2024 Annual Report."

and collaboration; make political learning more pervasive; and encourage informed participation in democracy."[51] Senior leadership can harness campus resources, set expectations, message broadly, connect large networks, and explicitly connect the work to institutional missions, strategic plans, educational learning outcomes, and institutional priorities. Although voting registration efforts can emerge from any point on campus, long-term sustainability requires senior-level endorsement. Without it, plans can be sidelined or abandoned.

4 Conclusion

At the foundation of this kind of work is the belief that institutions themselves must act with the values we hope our students embody. Activating students is the challenge. Appealing to students who are feeling like their voices do not count is the most vexing problem to plan around, especially when candidates and issues may not motivate voters to work through the barriers that are placed on young voters. Successful planning must combine education, logistics, strategies, emotional intelligence, and empathy. For the 2024 election, young people reported that issues, especially the economy, were the biggest factors in the election—not candidates or a sense of civic duty.[52]

Planning must respond to the students we have on campus today, and each new year brings new students. A careful planning process allows campus communities to be responsive to the evolving needs of students. Voting is emotional and taps deeply into a civic imagination. However, without planning, the ability to reach and inspire all students to register and to vote is unlikely. As new voters come to college, so will new concerns and challenges. It is the responsibility of institutions of higher education to prepare students in active citizenry, today and tomorrow. Institutional planning for voter registration and engagement, including building processes for communications, monitoring, curing, and cross-coalition support, are key to satisfying the mission of higher education.

---

[51] Nancy Thomas, Margaret Brower, Ishara Casellas Connors, Adam Gismondi, and Kyle Upchurch, "Election Imperatives Version 2.0," Institute for Democracy and Higher Education, August 2020, 4, https://dgmg81phhvh63.cloudfront.net/content/user-photos/Initiatives/IDHE/idhe-election-imperatives-v2.pdf.

[52] Center for Information & Research on Civic Learning and Engagement, "Poll: Economic Struggles, Varied Issue Priorities, and Dislike of Candidates Shaped the Youth Vote in 2024," https://circle.tufts.edu/poll-economic-struggles-varied-issue-priorities-and-dislike-candidates-shaped-youth-vote-2024.

Appendix A. Questions to Consider for Managing and Monitoring Election Day

- How close are local polling sites for students? Is there a polling site on or near campus? If not, how far are the polling locations? Are they accessible via public transportation? Are they actually handicap-accessible?
- What is the experience of students at polling sites during early voting or on election day?
- Do students have to travel far from campus?
- Are polling sites accessible by public transportation and are they handicap-accessible?
- Are students turned away by poll workers or forced to vote via provisional ballot (a vote normally cast on paper and not on a machine and reviewed later for eligibility) due to concerns about ID or for other reasons?
- Do student voters know what their rights are if they are challenged or if they are asked to vote provisionally?
- Are student absentee ballots or mail-in forms counted or challenged?
- What does the data reveal about the students missed during campus outreach?
- Have students been disproportionately purged from the rolls and/or made 'inactive'? If so, for what reason?
- Are local voter registrations being properly processed? Why or why not?
- How many students are casting a ballot and how are they casting those ballots (mail in, absentee, in person, affidavit aka provisional)?
- What challenges are students facing when casting a vote? Are they being turned away at the polls? Did they understand how to mail in an absentee ballot?
- At what rate do students turn out to vote during early voting or on election day? What challenges emerge on election day? Are students' absentee ballots or mail-in forms counted or challenged?

Appendix B. Considerations for Building Campus Coalitions

- Where does the campus planning emerge from?
    - Bottom-up (student-led and driven with little administrative support).
    - Top-down (directives issued by institutional leadership, vice presidents, chancellors or presidents).
    - Middle-out (faculty or administratively driven coalitions with some institutional supports).
- What cross-campus coalitions exist or can be developed, and does their work align with voting goals?
- Who can charge a coalition with the authority and resources to do the work?
- How can cross-constituent groups align the work with existing strategic or learning goals?
- What is the primary focus and mission of the group (i.e., voter registration, voter participation or ongoing civic participation, removing obstacles to youth voting)? How is that mission articulated to the campus community?

Appendix C. Considerations for Engaging and Activating Campus Leaders

Considerations for engaging campus leaders
- Have campus leaders signed national commitments on behalf of student voting rights? Are they engaged in any way in national discussions or academic spaces related to student voting rights?
- What demonstrated commitment is available that is in support of student voting rights or, more importantly, links the work to the institutional mission to educate for democracy? Are those commitments up to date, publicly available, and articulated to the campus community on a regular basis?

Considerations for activating senior leadership
Leadership has a range of options to demonstrate institutional commitment:
- Link student voting and engagement to educational outcomes related to democracy and connect the work to ongoing efforts to teach civic participation, including where appropriate clinical or applied learning work so that students may study and analyze engagement trends of their peers.
- Public articulation in support of students' right to vote in annual communications to all constituencies, including to families.[53]
- Public articulation of the institutional commitment to defend students' right to vote.[54]
- Articulate and define the work related to the institution's third mission.
- Actively work towards creating an enabling environment for student voting:
  - Designate resources to support the work, including campus facilities to host an accessible and centrally located on-campus polling site.
  - Create and publicly support cross-campus, intergenerational teams charged with the development of voter action plans.
- Bind words and deeds through ongoing and repeated articulation that student voting rights are not only supported but are an institutional priority:
  - Write opinion pieces linking voting and higher education's link to democracy.
  - Annually encourage students to vote, and where appropriate to vote with their campus address.
  - Actively defend students' right to vote when threatened.

---

53 Becker and Cannan, "Institution as Citizen," 1894.
54 Becker and Cannan, "Institution as Citizen," 1894.

- Explore local, state, and federal-based solutions such as those offered by the Youth Voting Rights Act and analogous state proposals, and monitor proposed potential restrictions.

Appendix D. Voting Terms Defined

The rules governing voter registration vary widely by state and, in the case of local elections, by counties, towns, and villages. The process of registering to vote, how and where to register, is confusing and often intentionally inconvenient, especially for new voters. What and how to plan for a voter action plan are determined by the types of voting available in the local campus context. The following are definitions of key words that campus teams should be familiar with when planning.

Voter Registration: Eligible voters complete required paperwork which identifies them as living within a certain voting district and confirms their eligibility to vote. That paperwork enrolls them in that district's electoral roll. The paperwork is sent to the local Board of Elections. Requirements for voter eligibility vary widely across the country.

Once a voter is registered at their local district they can vote in person, absentee, or in some states, by mail-in ballot. In-person voting has set dates and a voter is typically required to vote at designated polling sites. Absentee voting requires voters to request a ballot by a certain date. This is often done through the mail. In many cases, online or digital processes are not available.

Boards of Elections (BOEs) are state-run, local, bi-partisan government agencies charged with overseeing election-related activities as dictated by state law. BOEs process voter registrations, manage polling sites, and count voters to determine election results.

Voter Rolls are the voter registration lists of voters in a given district eligible to vote in an upcoming election. Voter rolls are public and voters can use digital tools to find out if they are registered.

Ballots are how voters cast their votes. Ballots are pre-printed by the local BOE and can include candidates running for local, state, or national elections. Often ballots also include voting for or against proposed legislation or other actions (like school board budgets).

Absentee Voting requires voters to request a paper ballot from their BOE. Rules governing absentee voting vary widely state by state and in some cases require a state-approved excuse (i.e., being out of district for the election day). If a request is approved, the voter completes the ballot and mails the ballot back as required.

Mail-in ballots are used by some states for all voters. Ballots are mailed to all voters in the state directly and returned by mail. At the time of publication, eight states allow all elections to be held by mail: California, Colorado, Hawaii, Nevada, Oregon, Utah, Vermont, and Washington State (see https://www.ncsl.org/). Other states allow counties to opt in or use mail-in for only some elections.

Early Voting is available in some states where voters can vote in person on designated days and at certain locations prior to the federal election day.

Election Day occurs annually for federal, state, and local public offices and is set as "the Tuesday next after the first Monday in November." Smaller elections like Boards of Education may occur on different dates, depending on local election law. Many states now hold early voting in some elections. Dates, locations, and timing of polling sites can vary.

Casting a Ballot is the process of voting. Voters must be registered in advance (same-day registration is rare) and typically cast a ballot at a designated site(s) unless a state is a mail-in-only state. Voters complete ballots by hand at designated privacy booths and cast their votes on official election machines which read a voter's ballot.

Provisional Ballots are available in all states except those that offer same-day registration. Required by the National Voter Registration Act 1993, voters who do not appear on the voter registration list at their designated polling place but believe that they are properly registered can vote via a provisional ballot. The ballot is the same pre-printed form received by other voters but is placed in a special sealed envelope instead of cast by machine. Following election day, registration status is confirmed and votes counted for voters whose registrations can be confirmed.

Bibliography

ALL IN Campus Democracy Challenge. "ALL IN Nonpartisan Student Voting Group Report." 2023. https://allinchallenge.org/wp-content/uploads/ALL-IN-Student-Voting-Group-Report-and-Toolkits.pdf.

ALL IN Campus Democracy Challenge. "2024 Annual Report." January 2025. https://allinchallenge.org/impact/.

ALL IN Campus Democracy Challenge. "The ALL IN Campus Democracy Challenge." April 4, 2025. https://allinchallenge.org/wp-content/uploads/ALL-IN-Theory-of-Change.pdf.

Alonso, Johanna. "A Florida Law Has Nearly Killed Campus Voter Registration Drives." *Inside Higher Ed*, July 8, 2024. https://www.insidehighered.com/news/government/politics-elections/2024/07/08/florida-voter-registration-law-has-major-impact#.

Becker, Jonathan, and Cannan, Erin. "Institution as Citizen: Colleges and Universities as Actors in Defense of Student Voting Rights." *The Rutgers University Law Review* 74, no. 5 (2022): 1869–1909.

Brennan Center for Justice. "Voting Laws Roundup: 2024 in Review." January 15, 2025. https://www.brennancenter.org/our-work/research-reports/voting-laws-roundup-2024-review.

Center for Information & Research on Civic Learning and Engagement. "Why Youth Don't Vote: Differences by Race and Education." August 21, 2018. https://circle.tufts.edu/latest-research/why-youth-dont-vote-differences-race-and-education.

Center for Information & Research on Civic Learning and Engagement. "Youth Turnout Among Teens Shows Need for Growing Voters." September 19, 2019. https://circle.tufts.edu/latest-research/youth-turnout-among-teens-shows-need-growing-voters.

Center for Information & Research on Civic Learning and Engagement. "State-by-State Youth Voter Turnout Data and the Impact of Election Laws in 2022." Updated May 2, 2023. https://circle.tufts.edu/latest-research/state-state-youth-voter-turnout-data-and-impact-election-laws-2022.

Center for Information & Research on Civic Learning and Engagement. "Poll: Economic Struggles, Varied Issue Priorities, and Dislike of Candidates Shaped the Youth Vote in 2024." January 15, 2025. https://circle.tufts.edu/poll-economic-struggles-varied-issue-priorities-and-dislike-candidates-shaped-youth-vote-2024.

Edwards, Crystal. "2020 Democratic Engagement Action Plan." Prairie View A&M University. https://allinchallenge.org/wp-content/uploads/Prairie-View-AM-University-ALL-IN-Challenge-Action-Plan.docx.pdf.

Election@Bard. "Bard College's ALL IN Campus Democracy Challenge Action Plan." Revised December 10, 2023. https://allinchallenge.org/wp-content/uploads/Bard-College-2024-Action-Plan.pdf.

Fogel, Becky. "A Texas Republican Says Banning College Polling Places is About Safety. Students Don't Buy It." *KUT News*, March 1, 2023. https://www.kut.org/education/2023-03-01/a-texas-republican-says-banning-college-polling-places-is-about-safety-students-dont-buy-it.

Gismondi, Adam, Nelsen, Matthew, German, Mariani, Tse, Victoria, and d'Urso, Amanda Sahar. "Democracy Counts 2022: Student Engagement in a Midterm Year." National Study of Learning, Voting, and Engagement. 2024. https://tufts.app.box.com/v/democracy-counts-2022.

Handan-Nader, Cassandra, Ho, Daniel E., Morantz, Alison, and Rutter, Tom A. "The Effectiveness of a Neighbor-to-Neighbor Get-Out-the-Vote Program: Evidence from the 2017 Virginia State Elections." *Journal of Experimental Political Science* 8, no. 2 (Summer 2021): 145–160. https://doi.org/10.1017/XPS.2020.11.

Institute for Democracy and Higher Education. "National Study of Learning, Voting and Engagement (NSLVE) Data Portal." https://nslve.tufts.edu/research/national-study-learning-voting-and-engagement-nslve/nslve-data-portal.

Medina, Alberto, Siegel-Stechler, Kelly, Suzuki, Sara, Booth, Ruby Belle, and Hilton, Katie. "Young People and the 2024 Election: Struggling, Disconnected, and Dissatisfied." Center for Information & Research on Civic Learning and Engagement. January 15, 2025. https://circle.tufts.edu/latest-research/2024-poll-barriers-issues-economy.

Medina, Alberto and Hilton, Katie. "New Data: Nearly Half of Youth Voted in 2024." Center for Information & Research on Civic Learning and Engagement. April 14, 2025. https://circle.tufts.edu/latest-research/new-data-nearly-half-youth-voted-2024.

Movement Advancement Project and The Civics Center. "A Silenced Generation: How the Power of the Youth Vote Collides with Barriers to Voting." January 2024. https://www.mapresearch.org/file/MAP-2024-Youth-Voting-Report.pdf.

North Carolina Agricultural & Technical State University. "Voter Engagement 2.4: Aggies Vote with Clarity, Seeing Beyond the Polls." 2024. https://allinchallenge.org/wp-content/uploads/North-Carolina-AT-State-University-2024-Action-Plan.pdf.

Plutzer, Eric. "Becoming a Habitual Voter: Inertia, Resources, and Growth in Young Adulthood." *American Political Science Review* 96, no. 1 (March 2002): 41–56. https://doi.org/10.1017/S0003055402004227.

Ramos, Julian. "Voter Registration Rates by Generation." Berkeley Initiative for Young Americans Democracy Policy Lab. April 23, 2024. https://youngamericans.berkeley.edu/2024/04/voter-registration-rates-by-generation.

Smith, Daniel A. "On-Campus Early In-Person Voting in Florida in the 2018 General Election." The Andrew Goodman Foundation. August 9, 2019. https://andrewgoodman.org/wp-content/up loads/2019/08/On-Campus-Early-In-Person-Voting-in-Florida-in-the-2018-General-Election-FINAL-8-9.pdf.

Students Learn Students Vote Coalition. "Strengthening American Democracy: A Guide for Developing an Action Plan to Increase Civic Learning, Political Engagement, and Voter Participation Among College Students." 4th ed. August 2023. https://allinchallenge.org/wp-content/uploads/StrengtheningAmericanDemocracyGuideVOL4.pdf.

The Andrew Goodman Foundation. "Toolkit: Securing On-Campus Polling Places." https://andrewgoodman.org/wp-content/uploads/2022/10/A-Toolkit-For-Securing-On-Campus-Polling-Places.pdf.

The Civics Center. "The Importance of High Schools." https://www.thecivicscenter.org/why-high-school.

Thomas, Nancy, Brower, Margaret, Casellas Connors, Ishara, Gismondi, Adam, and Upchurch, Kyle. "Election Imperatives Version 2.0." Institute for Democracy and Higher Education (IDHE). August 2020. https://dgmg81phhvh63.cloudfront.net/content/user-photos/Initiatives/IDHE/idhe-election-imperatives-v2.pdf.

Vote.org. "Absentee Ballot Deadlines." https://www.vote.org/absentee-ballot-deadlines/.

Yale University Institution for Social and Policy Studies. "Lessons from GOTV Experiments." https://isps.yale.edu/research/field-experiments-initiative/lessons-from-gotv-experiments.

Yael Bromberg and Jonathan Becker

Conclusion: From the 26th Amendment to the 2024 Election and Beyond

Democracy is at a crossroads, and America once again finds itself in a time of upheaval.

The Supreme Court has long declared that the right to vote is fundamental because it is preservative of all other rights. Yet, for most of this country's history, the voting rights of many Americans have been denied or diluted. For youth voters specifically, it was not until 1971 when the 26th Amendment was ratified that they secured their right to vote. Through this process, they would gain recognition as a protected class of voters with respect to access to the ballot: "The right of citizens of the United States, who are eighteen years of age or older, to vote shall not be denied or abridged by the United States or by any State on account of age." Although introduced over 150 times in Congress in a 30-year period, it was not until a nationwide youth-led coalition was formed—the Youth Franchise Coalition, consisting of prominent civil rights, education, labor, and youth organizations—that their access to suffrage was constitutionalized.

Like many of the steps on the road to American democracy, the ratification of the 26th Amendment did not resolve all issues related to youth voting rights. As foreshadowed in the congressional debate over the Amendment, the battle over the youth vote was particularly virulent on college campuses, and particularly so at Historically Black Colleges and Universities (HBCUs). These were attractive targets for voter suppression efforts because they represent the intersection of the political power of both youth and Black voters. And while it would be an exaggeration to equate the fight for the youth vote with the battle against white supremacy and the struggle for freedom and civil rights experienced by African Americans in the United States, the two share familiar and sometimes intersecting elements, even when race is not centrally involved, both in terms of the attitudes, behaviors, and practices of those seeking to limit the suffrage, and in terms of the tools used to defend democratic freedoms.

A little more than a half century since the ratification of the 26th Amendment, challenges to student voting remain. The bipartisan commitment to expand voting rights, which shaped the Second Reconstruction and was manifested in the overwhelming support in Congress for the Voting Rights Act of 1965 (passing the House 328–74 and the Senate 79–18), and even greater support for the 26th Amendment in 1971 (passing the Senate 94–0 and then the House 401–19), has now evaporated.

The 2013 *Shelby* decision by the United States Supreme Court dismantled key protections of the Voting Rights Act. Attempts to repair and modernize it in the form of the John Lewis Voting Rights Act passed the Democratic Party-led House twice with increasingly slim margins: in 2019 (228–187) and in 2021 (219–212), but the pro-voter measure has yet to achieve full support by both chambers of Congress.

Political polarization has taken over American society, evident in the increased politicization of the fundamental right to vote. Prior successful amendments to the Voting Rights Act once passed with wide support: in 1970 (passing in the Senate 64–12 and in the House 272–132), 1975 (Senate 77–12, House 346–56), 1982 (Senate 85–8, House unanimous), 1992 (House 237–125, Senate 75–20), and 2006 (House 390–33, Senate 98–0). Yet, by 2015, on the second anniversary of *Shelby*, then-House Judiciary Chairman Bob Goodlatte refused to so much as hold a committee hearing on the Voting Rights Act, allowing a previously introduced bill to amend it to languish in committee.

In the midst of the COVID pandemic, as students in 2020 were temporarily displaced from their campus residences during a consequential and unprecedented election season, the Youth Voting Rights Act was born. The proposal was originally conceived by Yael Bromberg, with strong support from D.C.-savvy Sonia Gill, then-senior legislative counsel with American Civil Liberties Union (ACLU) National, and steadfast leadership from the congressional offices of Representative John Lewis and Senator Elizabeth Warren. It was introduced in 2022 and 2023 by Senator Warren and Representative Nikema Williams, gaining 68 co-sponsors in the House.

The Youth Voting Rights Act is the first comprehensive proposal to enforce the 26th Amendment by:
- designating public institutions of higher education as voter registration agencies, therefore imposing greater voter registration obligations on the institutions;
- allowing young people aged 16 and 17 in every state to pre-register to vote before turning 18, setting them up on the pipeline to civic engagement;
- requiring institutions of higher education to host an on-campus polling site, and a system of regulation and support, with an opportunity to waive-out;
- codifying the right to vote from a college domicile;
- guaranteeing that states accept student identification cards to meet voter ID requirements;
- creating a grant program dedicated to youth electoral involvement, including paid fellowships for young persons to work with state and local officials to support youth civic and political engagement among their peers;

-   removing age-based restrictions on access to voting by mail in federal races; and
-   empowering federal officials to gather data to study voter engagement by age and race to inform efforts to improve youth involvement in elections.

Despite the massive cross-partisan history of the 26th Amendment, it is extremely unlikely that the Youth Voting Rights Act will advance in the current political climate. That is not to say that the federal initiative should not be pursued, of course, but that it should set an organizing and policy framework and goalpost. Indeed, grassroots advocates in various states across the nation are beginning to explore state-based versions of the proposal. In this manner, an eventual federal statutory proposal may perhaps follow the historical experience of the Amendment, where a handful of states lowered the voting age prior to ratification (Georgia, Kentucky, Alaska, Hawaii) and informed the congressional debates for ratification.

The present federal view is particularly bleak where the current proposals have shifted from advancement and modernization to outright suppression. The 2025 GOP-led House of Representatives in April passed the Safeguard American Voter Eligibility (SAVE) Act, under the false myth of noncitizen voting. The proposal mandates documentary proof of citizenship for any voter registration applicant, such as a U.S. passport or U.S. birth certificate, placing enormous burdens on married women who have changed their names (and therefore their birth certificates may not match their current legal name) and young people, who are particularly mobile and do not travel to school with their U.S. passport or their U.S. birth certificate; nor are they likely to appear in person with such proof at an election agency prior to voter registration deadlines, as would be required under the Act. This radical measure, which is supported by the President, passed the House with unanimous Republican support, and though it faces an uphill challenge in the Senate because of the filibuster, it is a fire alarm that the right to vote is under attack. Elements of it have already been taken up in state legislatures.

There is something downright nihilistic about these efforts. It is un-American to attack voters' access to the ballot based on a presumption of their partisan affiliations. *Why not play by the rules and appeal to the voters based on your candidacy and platform?* Nonetheless, the most recent attacks on the vote seem to attack voters *regardless* of their partisan affiliation. The University of Maryland's Center for Democracy and Civic Engagement conducted three surveys to analyze the impact of voter registration laws like the SAVE Act proposal requiring documentary proof of citizenship.[1] They found that men—and especially young men

---

1 Sam Novey, Jillian Andres Rothschild, and Michael Hammer, "Which U.S. Citizens Lack Easy

aged 18 – 29—are the least likely to be able to easily access such proofs, and that in certain Republican states such as Texas, access to these proofs was harder for Republicans than for Democrats. Older voters were less likely to own documentary proof of citizenship as well.

The same destructive trend has emerged as to limitations on access to vote-by-mail. Here, the GOP has advanced false narratives claiming that vote-by-mail is insecure and contributes to election fraud. It has pursued multiple legal challenges to restrict the voting mechanism across the nation, although the strong majority of votes cast in 2020 relied on this mechanism (69.4 %), a considerable jump from 2016 (40 %), with increased rates continuing even after the pandemic.[2] According to Pew, in 2024 a quarter (26 %) of Republican voters said they voted by mail or absentee ballot.[3]

More recently, in 2025, an unprecedented effort sought to disenfranchise voters who already lawfully cast their duly counted votes in an election for a seat on the North Carolina Supreme Court. There, Judge Jefferson Griffin, a candidate for the high court bench who sits on the state appeals court, lost his bid for higher office. Rather than concede, Griffin waged a months-long effort to toss 65,000 lawfully cast ballots, including those cast by over 5,000 military personnel, overseas civil servants, and missionaries, which became the center of the legal challenge six months after the election. The challenge was unprecedented on multiple counts: the contest was not limited to votes that had been cast but not yet counted, such as outstanding absentee or provisional ballots, but went after votes that were both lawfully cast and lawfully counted—essentially operating as a post-election months-long audit. It also sought to change the requirements for voter identification after the election, requiring military voters to offer proper identification even though they followed the rules and cast a lawful ballot for election day. The Fourth Circuit Court of Appeals temporarily blocked the beginning of a massive, unprecedented review period, initially approved by the state's high court, until the federal constitutional claims could be further addressed.[4] Finally, in May, nearly seven

Access to Documentary Proof of Citizenship?" University of Maryland Center for Democracy and Civic Engagement, April 10, 2025, https://cdce.substack.com/p/which-us-citizens-lack-easy-access.

2 Ivan Pereira, "Early Voting Options Grow in Popularity, Reconfiguring Campaigns and Voting Preparation," *ABC News,* September 4, 2024, https://abcnews.go.com/Politics/early-voting-options-grow-popularity-reconfiguring-campaigns-voting/story?id=112682514.

3 Pew Research Center, "Voters Broadly Positive About How Elections Were Conducted, in Sharp Contrast to 2020," December 4, 2024, 17, https://www.pewresearch.org/wp-content/uploads/sites/20/2024/12/PP_2024.12.3_election-2024_REPORT.pdf.

4 Kyle Ingram, "Federal Judges Block NC Supreme Court Election 'Cure' Process—For Now," *The Raleigh News & Observer,* April 22, 2025, https://www.newsobserver.com/news/politics-government/article304819896.html.

months after the election, a federal judge, a Trump appointee, ruled that the process would violate the equal protection because it would subject voters to different rules. Two days later, Griffin finally conceded, and Riggs was duly sworn in.

Former GOP governor Pat McCrory, who admitted he voted for Griffin, criticized the approach:

> I wanted the Republican judge to win because his philosophy more aligns with me. But in order to take the seat, you've got to earn the seat and win the seat. And in this case, he was defeated. ... You abide by the rules before the election. It's like changing a penalty call after the Super Bowl is over. You don't do that. And the military personnel, I think are special. And that's why an exception was made for ID, that we trusted the military to do what's right. And they voted based upon the rule set.[5]

In sum, we find ourselves in a new age of body politic, where hyper-political polarization has warped into an anti-democracy bent.

This lawless whirlwind directly impacts youth voters, and is a far cry from the times when Senator Barry Goldwater (R-Arizona), the leader of the modern national conservative movement, stood up against youth discrimination in ballot access, persuading his conservative peers in Congress to join him to support youth enfranchisement, first via the 1970 Amendment of the Voting Rights Act, and then via constitutional ratification. Senator Goldwater implored Congress to embrace the youth vote:

> They are not allowed to vote. ... This attitude is outmoded and archaic. It is literally based on a tradition which dates back to medieval times. Perhaps, in the days around the turn of the century, it once had meaning. In 1900 only 6% of Americans who had reached 18 were high school graduates. In fact, as late as 1940, only half of all 18-year-olds had completed high school.
>
> But this is 1970. This is the age of instant communications, all-news radio stations, T.V. news, and the most avid political concern on the part of young Americans that I have ever witnessed.
>
> Today fully 81% of Americans have graduated from high school before they reach 18. Almost 50% of 18-, 19- and 20-year-olds are enrolled in college. And the education which they are receiving is more advanced and intense than in any time in our history.
>
> In short, youth today is better informed and better equipped than any previous generation. They are without a doubt equally mature, both mentally and physically, as the average citizen who had reached 25 when I was growing up. In fact, they may be better able to com-

---

5 Tom George, "Military and Overseas Voters at Center of Challenges in Riggs–Griffin NC Supreme Court Race," *ABC News*, April 20, 2025, https://abc7ny.com/post/military-overseas-voters-center-challenges-north-carolina-supreme-court-race-between-allison-riggs-jefferson-griffin/16209562/.

prehend the dramatic technological advances and changing perspectives of modern life than many of their parents.

Therefore, I hold that there is no sensible reason for denying the vote to 18-year-olds. What's more, I think we have studied the issue long enough. The voting age should be lowered and lowered at once across the entire nation.[6]

In contrast, at every step of the election administration process today—from voter registration, to vote-by-mail applications, to in-person voting, to ensuring that vote-by-mail or provisional ballots are adequately counted—young people experience unique and disproportionate obstacles.

For example, ahead of the 2024 election, Idaho passed a law removing student identification cards from permissible forms of voter ID. The law came on the heels of Idaho boasting the largest rate of increase (66%) in youth voter registration in the nation between 2018 and 2022.[7] The removal was upheld unanimously by the Idaho Supreme Court, which reasoned that young voters' fundamental rights to vote were not infringed, because students could sign an affidavit in lieu of voter ID.[8] Just two weeks earlier, the Montana Supreme Court had issued a landmark ruling, invalidating four 2021 laws that uniquely impacted youth voters.[9] The Montana legislature had ended same-day registration (which allows voters to register and vote on the same day, a key policy for highly mobile youth voters); stripped student identification from the list of eligible forms of voter ID, although it had allowed student voter IDs for almost two decades; prohibited paid third-party ballot collection (a measure that directly impacted Native American voters living on reservations); and barred county officials from distributing mail-in ballots to minors who would turn 18 and be eligible to vote by Election Day.[10]

In 2024, the Board of Elections serving Purdue University, an Indiana public university home to approximately 40,000 undergraduate students, announced that for the first time in nearly two decades an on-campus polling site would

---

6 Senator Barry Goldwater, Testimony, 116 Cong. Rec. S.3216 (March 9, 1970).

7 Ruby Belle Booth, "Youth Voter Registration Has Surpassed 2018 Levels in Many States, but It's Lagging for the Youngest Voters," Center for Information & Research Civic Learning and Engagement (CIRCLE), September 14, 2022, https://circle.tufts.edu/latest-research/youth-voter-registration-has-surpassed-2018-levels-many-states-its-lagging-youngest.

8 *Babe Vote and League of Women Voters of Idaho v. McGrane*, 546 P.3d 694 (Idaho 2024).

9 *Montana Democratic Party v. Jacobsen*, 545 P.3d 1074 (Montana 2024). In prior phases of the litigation securing a preliminary injunction of these laws, Bromberg served as an expert witness on their youth impact and the state's constitutional convention history vis-à-vis the 26th Amendment.

10 Alicia Bannon, "Montana Strikes Down Voting Restrictions," State Court Report, April 10, 2024, https://statecourtreport.org/our-work/analysis-opinion/montana-strikes-down-voting-restrictions

not be provided.[11] The board claimed that low student voter registration rates informed the decision. However, after backlash, a limited site—only for the early voting period—was situated on campus. The board declined the university administration's efforts to bring the polling site back on campus on Election Day.[12] In April 2025, the state passed a new law prohibiting the use of student identification as voter identification, rolling back 20 years of state policy.[13]

At Franklin and Marshall College in Pennsylvania, student registrations were delayed ahead of the 2024 general elections. Some students were told they should vote where their parents lived and that they could not register in Pennsylvania without providing proof that they had cancelled previous registrations; the use of Franklin and Marshall's main address was also challenged.[14] The Lancaster Board of Elections tried to silence the college through a highly unusual cease-and-desist order, though the Secretary of State's office intervened to ensure that students could register.[15]

In Texas, a bill was proposed in 2023 to outright ban polling locations on college campuses across the state. A similar endeavor had been pursued in Florida by the secretary of state in 2018, but a federal court judge found that it plainly vio-

11 Johanna Alonso, "Removal of On-Campus Voting on Election Day Sparks Uproar at Purdue," *Inside Higher Ed*, October 3, 2024, https://www.insidehighered.com/news/government/politics-elec tions/2024/10/03/purdue-loses-long-standing-campus-polling-place.

12 Purdue University, "Purdue University Statement on Campus Voting Locations," September 17, 2024, https://www.purdue.edu/newsroom/2024/Q3/purdue-university-statement-on-campus-voting-locations-sept-17-2024/.

13 Kayla Dwyer, "Gov. Mike Braun Signs Bill Banning Student IDs at Voting Booth," *Indy Star*, April 16, 2025, https://www.indystar.com/story/news/politics/2025/04/16/gov-mike-braun-senate-bill-10-student-voter-id-laws/83030092007/.

14 Matt Klinedinst, "Lancaster County Election Officials Accused of Misleading Voters about Their Registration Status," *Fox43*, October 22, 2024, https://www.fox43.com/article/news/local/lan caster-county-election-officials-accused-misleading-voters-registration-status-lancaster-county/521-3bc14754-6e79-4150-8fb9-b0416a29f4c8; Russ Walker and Tom Lisi, "F&M Voter Organization Alleges Lancaster County Elections Staff Misled on Registration Rules," *Lancaster Online*, October 19, 2024, https://lancasteronline.com/news/local/f-m-voter-organization-alleges-lancaster-county-elec tions-staff-misled-on-registration-rules/article_8e2a9904-8e66-11ef-bf47-df1e4cfcd3e8.html.

15 Steve Ulrich, "Department of State Intervenes in F&M Votes/Lancaster County Voter Registration Dispute," *PoliticsPA*, October 21, 2024, https://www.politicspa.com/department-of-state-inter venes-in-fm-votes-lancaster-county-voter-registration-dispute/139616; Brett Sholtis, "Lancaster County Commissioners Send 'Cease and Desist' Letter to F&M College over Voter Registration Claims," *Lancaster Online*, October 29, 2024, https://lancasteronline.com/news/politics/lancaster-county-commissioners-send-cease-and-desist-letter-to-f-m-college-over-voter-registration/article_ e51a4dae-9578-11ef-8394-4f60feb393b8.html.

lated the 26th Amendment.[16] The case arose when trained student ambassadors with The Andrew Goodman Foundation began raising awareness of the measure in Florida, leading to the creation of new federal precedent on the 26th Amendment. Judge Walker therein recognized "voting is the beating heart of democracy" and that the state action targeted "a discrete class of individuals—nearly 830,000 individuals who live and work on public colleges and university communities, i. e., overwhelmingly young voters ... the *only* class in Florida facing such a prohibition." He found the state action to be "unexplainable on grounds other than age" and barred the action pursuant to the 26th Amendment.[17]

While there are glimmers of hope, such as the 2024 ruling by the Montana Supreme Court and the 2018 ruling by the Florida federal court, there is reason to think that things will get worse. A large proportion of the American electorate falsely believes the 2020 election was stolen, and with a second Trump administration advocates for 'election integrity' will no doubt seek to impose new limits on voting. The Voting Rights Act continues to be the target of constant attacks to further dilute its efficacy. Potential new Executive Orders are rumored to be en route, to attack basic election adminsitration tools such as the use of vote-by-mail or auditable voting machines. Key figures close to the administration have spoken of targeting election officials who actively promote voter registration or who make it easier for citizens to vote. They even resist legislation protecting election workers, citizens who are the linchpin of the sprawling American electoral system.[18] It does not bode well that many close to the current administration seek to model their behavior on figures like authoritarian Hungarian prime minister Victor Orban, who has not only manipulated electoral rules and stacked the judiciary, but also targeted universities, including closing a thriving and distinguished private American institution.[19] Meanwhile, efforts are underway to endeavor to normalize the idea of a third-term presidency.

---

16 *League of Women Voters of Florida Inc. v. Detzner*, 314 F.Supp.3d 1205 (N.D. Fla. 2018). Bromberg served as co-counsel for plaintiff The Andrew Goodman Foundation in subsequent phases of the litigation.

17 *League of Women Voters of Florida Inc. v. Detzner*, 314 F.Supp.3d 1205 (N.D. Fla. 2018).

18 Miles Parks, "What 'Election Integrity Advocates' Have Planned for 2025," *NPR*, December 20, 2024, https://www.npr.org/2024/12/20/nx-s1-5217816/what-election-integrity-advocates-have-planned-for-2025.

19 Ferenc Laczó, "Westernization by Preemptive Rejection: How Viktor Orbán Sells to U.S. Conservatives their own Obsessions," *The Review of Democracy*, July 12, 2022, https://revdem.ceu.edu/2022/12/07/westernization-by-preemptive-rejection-how-viktor-orban-sells-to-us-conservatives-their-own-obsessions/; Jeremy Shapiro and Zsuzsanna Végh, "The Organisation of America: Hungary's Lessons for Donald Trump," *European Council on Foreign Relations*, October 9, 2024, https://ecfr.eu/publication/the-orbanisation-of-america-hungarys-lessons-for-donald-trump/.

The highly unusual aforementioned post-election challenge in the 2024 State Supreme Court race in North Carolina further demonstrates the continued vulnerability of young voters, particularly college students. A study by the Student Voting Rights Lab at Duke and North Carolina Central Universities found that voters 18–25 years old were disproportionately represented in Griffin's challenge to the election results. Among the 60,000-plus voters with allegedly "incomplete voter registrations," young voters were 3.4 times more likely than those over 65 to have their vote challenged. Additionally, young Black voters were 5.28 times more likely to be challenged than white men over 65. Notably, Griffin's challenges to overseas ballots included just four counties—Durham, Guilford, Forsyth, and Buncombe—each home to large numbers of college students. Large proportions of students from Duke University, North Carolina Central, and NC A&T were targeted, with HBCU-enrolled students disqualified at particularly high rates.[20]

Despite efforts of committed and sometimes heroic students and faculty, the occasional intervention of institutions, and the emergence and growth of important organizations like Students Learn Students Vote, the ALL IN Campus Democracy Challenge, and The Andrew Goodman Foundation, youth and student voting remain precarious, with only 50% of young people age 18–29 voting in the 2020 election, and 47% in 2024. While this is an improvement compared with 2016 (39%), the fact of the matter is that approximately half of young voters nationally are just not participating at the ballot box.[21] (Figure 1). Moreover, gaps persist based on race and gender. For example, Tuft's Center for Information & Research Civic Learning and Engagement (CIRCLE) found that 58% of young white women voted in the 2024 presidential election, compared with 25% of young Black men. CIRCLE found a discrepancy in youth voter participation ranging from 33% (in Oklahoma and Arkansas) to 62% (Minnesota). Importantly, CIRCLE concluded that state-by-state trends in youth turnout vary based on the role of election policies

---

20 Gunther Peck, "Documenting the Damage of Judge Jefferson Griffin's Supreme Court Election Challenge," *NC Newsline*, February 6, 2025, https://ncnewsline.com/2025/02/06/documenting-the-damage-of-judge-jefferson-griffins-supreme-court-election-challenge/; Katherine Gallagher, "How the Grinch Is Stealing Our Voting Rights," *Duke Chronicle*, December 23, 2024, https://www.duke chronicle.com/article/2024/12/grinch-is-stealing-our-voting-rights. The Duke research and more extensive research submitted on behalf of Justice Riggs demonstrated that missing information was overwhelmingly due to recording and other clerical errors or due to coding errors. See Rusty Jacobs, "Board Analysis Shows Griffin's Ballot Challenges are Based on Inaccurate Assumptions," *WUNC North Carolina Public Radio*, February 16, 2025, https://www.wunc.org/politics/2025-02-16/board-analysis-jeffersongriffin-ballot-challenges-inaccurate-assumptions.
21 Alberto Medina and Katie Hilton, "New Data: Nearly Half of Youth Voted in 2024," Center for Information & Research on Civic Learning and Engagement (CIRCLE), April 14, 2025, https://circle.tufts.edu/latest-research/new-data-nearly-half-youth-voted-2024.

in facilitating or hindering youth participation, policies like automatic, online, and same-day registration.[22]

Another CIRCLE survey of 18–34-year-olds indicates that many who did not vote were not registered. Nearly 1 in 8 youth said that they "did not know how to register" or "had trouble" with their voter registration forms. Nearly one-third of those surveyed (32%) said they were "too busy," "ran out of time," or "missed the registration deadline." Just over 10% simply "forgot," while an astounding 36% of unregistered youth said simply that voting is "not important to me."[23]

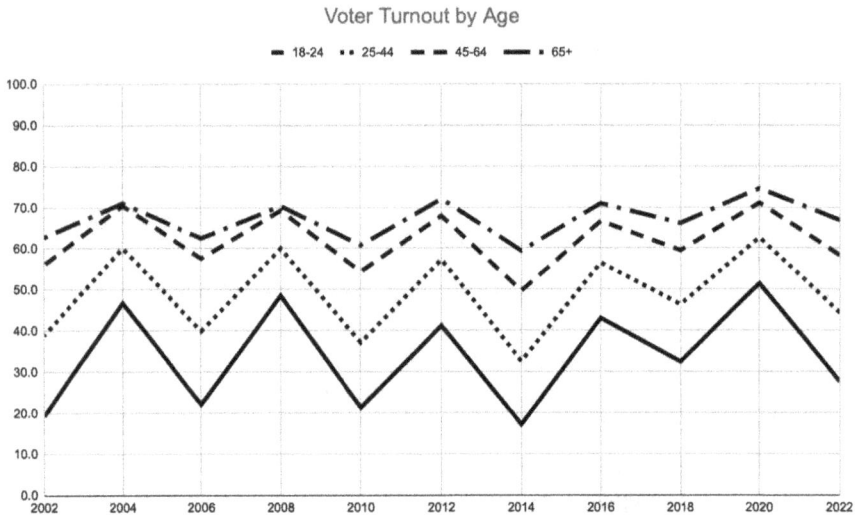

Figure 1: Percentage voted by age.
Source: US Census Bureau: https://www.census.gov/topics/public-sector/voting/data/tables.html.

All told, less than half of young voters in 2024 voted in the general election, compared with a national turnout of all ages of nearly 64%, which itself is lower than the majority of advanced industrial democracies.[24] While voter suppression laws

22 Medina and Hilton, "New Data."

23 Alberto Medina, Kelly Siegel-Stechler, Sara Suzuki, Ruby Belle Booth, and Katie Hilton, "Young People and the 2024 Election: Struggling, Disconnected, and Dissatisfied," Center for Information & Research on Civic Learning and Engagement (CIRCLE), January 15, 2025, https://circle.tufts.edu/latest-research/2024-poll-barriers-issues-economy.

24 Ballotpedia, "Election Results, 2024: Analysis of Voter Turnout in the 2024 General Election," https://ballotpedia.org/Election_results,_2024:_Analysis_of_voter_turnout_in_the_2024_general_election; Drew Desilver, "Turnout in U.S. Has Soared in Recent Elections but by Some Measures Still

and regulations should be resisted at every turn, and we should embrace the full spirit of the 26th Amendment for increased political participation of youth, it is daunting to outrun non-participation altogether.

Challenges associated with voting and voter apathy are indicative of more pressing concerns about American democracy, of which voting and free and fair elections are necessary but insufficient conditions. Survey after survey have shown declining trust in institutions and belief in democracy. In one recent survey of 30 countries that asked whether "it is important to live in a country that is democratically governed," only 80% of Americans responded in the affirmative, leaving it fourth from the bottom, ahead of only Pakistan, Saudi Arabia, and Russia.[25] The growing disenchantment of young Americans, and youth around the globe, with democracy is particularly alarming: several studies demonstrate not only that young Americans are dissatisfied with state democracy, but also that their belief in democracy compared with authoritarian alternatives is declining, both in absolute terms and in relative terms compared with what older generations believed at comparable stages of life.[26]

There is also reason to be concerned about the civic commitment of American institutions of higher education. The most wealthy and powerful institutions in the country, which remain predominantly white, continue to celebrate the fundamental link between education and democracy, but remain hesitant to engage institutionally with the fight for the most fundamental of democratic rights. As the students from Ivy League Votes succinctly put it, "student voting is not where it should be," and institutions share part of the blame.[27] The gap between word and deed only promises to grow as calls for institutional 'neutrality' and growing threats from the federal government translate into timidity and restraint in the face of injustice. While the civic mission of HBCUs remains intact, they are chron-

---

Trails That of Many Other Countries," Pew Research Center, November 1, 2022, https://www.pewresearch.org/short-reads/2022/11/01/turnout-in-u-s-has-soared-in-recent-elections-but-by-some-measures-still-trails-that-of-many-other-countries/.

25 Open Society Foundations, "Open Society Barometer: Can Democracy Deliver?", launched September 2023, https://www.opensocietyfoundations.org/focus/open-society-barometer.

26 R.S. Foa, A. Klassen, D. Wenger, A. Rand, and M. Slade, *Youth and Satisfaction with Democracy: Reversing the Democratic Disconnect?* (Centre for the Future of Democracy, 2020), https://www.cam.ac.uk/system/files/youth_and_satisfaction_with_democracy.pdf; Open Society Foundation, "Open Society Barometer"; Zach Hrynowski and Stephanie Marken, "Gen Z Voices Lackluster Trust in Major U.S. Institutions," *Gallup*, September 14, 2023, https://news.gallup.com/opinion/gallup/510395/gen-voices-lackluster-trust-major-institutions.aspx.

27 Members of Ivy League Votes, "Student Voting is Not Where it Should Be," *Inside Higher Ed*, January 2, 2022, https://www.insidehighered.com/views/2022/01/03/college-students-face-many-unnecessary-obstacles-voting-opinion.

ically underfunded and remain vulnerable both to the malevolent acts of state lawmakers and a growing neoliberal ethos in academe which deemphasizes the social sciences and humanities, and which may ultimately diminish the 'second curriculum' that fostered race consciousness, cultural nationalism, idealism, and resistance to white supremacy.

Looking Forward

Students at the four institutions that are the focus of this book participated jointly in a course entitled "Student Voting: Power, Politics, and Race in the Fight for American Democracy," that was offered simultaneously across the four campuses. The discussions with students at the end of the course in Fall 2023 were largely positive, but stood starkly compared with the mixed reaction for students at the end of the Fall 2024 course. Many of the students were disappointed with the 2024 election. Their disappointment was rooted in many things, including the defeat of their preferred candidates, the decline in youth voting overall, and the fact that there was an increase in college-age voters supporting a candidate who made election denialism a core element of his identity. Some were frustrated that the United States did not elect its first female president. Many of the students, particularly from HBCUs, were stung not just by the defeat of the first major-party presidential candidate who was a graduate of an HBCU, but by the victory of a presidential candidate whose racism, manifested in a history of discriminatory business practices, the promotion of birther conspiracy theories against America's first Black president, and association with white supremacist groups, appeared so obvious to them. They expressed a palpable disappointment in fellow youth, including those with a college education, who voted for Trump in greater numbers than in 2016 or 2020, and with predominantly white higher education institutions which apparently produced many students who were evidently unconcerned with Trump's racism.

But that was not the entire story. Many of the students in the course were inspired and in awe of work done by generations of students who, together with faculty, administrators, and outside groups, had fought and continued to fight for the most essential of democratic rights. Students were moved and motivated when they engaged with past youth leaders like Judy Richardson, who played a central role in the Student Nonviolent Coordination Committee, and David Goodman, whose brother Andy was assassinated by the Klan in Mississippi during Freedom Summer, which guided the creation of The Andrew Goodman Foundation, a national organization dedicated to youth voices and voters.

Students were also inspired by recent graduates who continued the fight after leaving college, like David Hogg of Leaders We Deserve which is working to elect young political leaders, and of March for Our Lives, a youth-led organization focused on gun control, created in the wake of the Parkland, Florida high school massacre. Evan Marlbrough of Atlanta, Georgia offered insights of his college leadership experience in securing the first all-student-operated on-campus polling site with The Andrew Goodman Foundation. Upon graduation and in the midst of the pandemic, Marlbrough then expanded this model and established the Georgia Youth Poll Worker Project to recruit and train 1,000 young poll workers for polling sites across the state, a program later acquired by the ACLU of Georgia. Jahnavi Rao, our youngest guest speaker, shared her work establishing the 501c3 New Voters, which civically engages over 800,000 high school students across the country. Brianna Cea described her efforts co-founding and leading non-profit GenVote, which engages college youth in organizing and advocacy.

Students also benefitted from hearing from their peers who were active with contemporary student voting rights efforts on campus. For example, Bard student Sierra Ford, an Andrew Goodman Foundation Vote Everywhere ambassador, and other Goodman ambassadors and student leaders from the course's participating colleges, offered short presentations at the beginning of the course on how the respective student bodies were engaging students in securing voter access.

The course's students were often moved to find ways to participate in the process of democratic participation itself, sometimes in an individual manner by ensuring that they registered by the deadline and voted; sometimes in a participatory manner outside of the course room by voluntarily canvassing their peers to register to vote; and sometimes moving towards a justice-oriented approach by voluntarily joining civics organizations beyond the classroom.

The pendulum may yet swing again. While much is made of this generation's dissatisfaction with traditional politics, as the voting numbers above illustrate, too little attention is paid to other forms of civic engagement which have been steadily growing among America's youth according to a 2022 survey by the Center for Information & Research Civic Learning and Engagement, and which may ultimately help grow youth voters, such as volunteering for political campaigns, donating money, attending protests, signing petitions, and joining boycotts.[28] Americans

---

28 Ruby Belle Booth, "Youth Are Interested in Political Action, but Lack Support and Opportunities," Center for Information & Research Civic Learning and Engagement (CIRCLE), January 30, 2023, https://circle.tufts.edu/latest-research/youth-are-interested-political-action-lack-support-and-opportunities. See also A. Kiesa, R.B. Booth, N. Hayat, A. Medina, and K. Kawashima-Ginsberg, "Growing Voters: Building Institutions and Community Ecosystems for Equitable Election Paraged 18–24 still overwhelmingly believe in the potential for democracy to create change and three-quarters agree that "voting is an important way to have a say in the future of the country."[29] One cannot but imagine that motivated young people, looking on as America reflects more and more the political stagnation of gerontocracy and kleptocracy, will channel their energies into further political engagement.

The 26th Amendment was adopted not only in reaction to the paradox that young Americans were old enough to die fighting for their country yet too young to determine who should govern. It was also adopted out of a hope that youthful energy and idealism could propel the nation to a better future. It passed not simply because politicians in Washington, D.C. decided that it was time for change, but because of the tremendous organizing and planning of students and advocacy groups who worked tirelessly for its passage, and who engaged in states across the nation, especially in Appalachia and middle America. That tradition, as our case studies show, has been kept alive as students, faculty, administrators, and allies have fought to realize the 26th Amendment's promise on college campuses. As Jayla Allen of Prairie View A&M University put it, "One thing I always said is that we're watching, we're listening, we want to be involved, we know that we are the future, we know that we can have the impact to make the changes that we need … [to make the] world that we want to see."[30] The lesson of our case studies is not that voting and democracy are synonymous, but that citizens, including students, have agency and that they can deploy the tools of democracy to promote equity and advance democratic freedoms in the hope of a better future.

Bibliography

Alonso, Johanna. "Removal of On-Campus Voting on Election Day Sparks Uproar at Purdue." *Inside Higher Ed*, October 3, 2024. https://www.insidehighered.com/news/government/politics-elections/2024/10/03/purdue-loses-long-standing-campus-polling-place.
Ballotpedia. "Election Results, 2024: Analysis of Voter Turnout in the 2024 General Election." https://ballotpedia.org/Election_results,_2024:_Analysis_of_voter_turnout_in_the_2024_general_election.

---

ticipation," Center for Information & Research Civic Learning and Engagement (CIRCLE), 2022, https://circle.tufts.edu/circlegrowingvoters

29 Booth, "Youth Are Interested."

30 Jayla Allen, interviewed by Seamus Heady, May 24, 2024.

Bannon, Alicia. "Montana Strikes Down Voting Restrictions." *State Court Report*, April 10, 2024. https://www.insidehighered.com/news/government/politics-elections/2024/10/03/purdue-loses-long-standing-campus-polling-place.

Booth, Ruby Belle. "Youth Voter Registration Has Surpassed 2018 Levels in Many States, but It's Lagging for the Youngest Voters." Center for Information & Research Civic Learning and Engagement (CIRCLE), September 14, 2022. https://circle.tufts.edu/latest-research/youth-voter-registration-has-surpassed-2018-levels-many-states-its-lagging-youngest.

Booth, Ruby Belle. "Youth Are Interested in Political Action, but Lack Support and Opportunities." Center for Information & Research Civic Learning and Engagement (CIRCLE), January 30, 2023. https://circle.tufts.edu/latest-research/youth-are-interested-political-action-lack-support-and-opportunities.

Desilver, Drew. "Turnout in U.S. Has Soared in Recent Elections but by Some Measures Still Trails That of Many Other Countries." Pew Research Center, November 1, 2022. https://www.pewresearch.org/short-reads/2022/11/01/turnout-in-u-s-has-soared-in-recent-elections-but-by-some-measures-still-trails-that-of-many-other-countries/.

Dwyer, Kayla. "Gov. Mike Braun Signs Bill Banning Student IDs at Voting Booth." *Indy Star*, April 16, 2025. https://www.indystar.com/story/news/politics/2025/04/16/gov-mike-braun-senate-bill-10-student-voter-id-laws/83030092007/.

Foa, R.S., Klassen, A., Wenger, D., Rand, A., and Slade, M. *Youth and Satisfaction with Democracy: Reversing the Democratic Disconnect?* Centre for the Future of Democracy, 2020. https://www.cam.ac.uk/system/files/youth_and_satisfaction_with_democracy.pdf.

Gallagher, Katherine. "How the Grinch Is Stealing Our Voting Rights." *Duke Chronicle*, December 23, 2024. https://www.dukechronicle.com/article/2024/12/grinch-is-stealing-our-voting-rights.

George, Tom. "Military and Overseas Voters at Center of Challenges in Riggs–Griffin NC Supreme Court Race." *ABC News*, April 20, 2025. https://abc7ny.com/post/military-overseas-voters-center-challenges-north-carolina-supreme-court-race-between-allison-riggs-jefferson-griffin/16209562/.

Hrynowski, Zach and Marken, Stephanie. "Gen Z Voices Lackluster Trust in Major U.S. Institutions." *Gallup*, September 14, 2023. https://news.gallup.com/opinion/gallup/510395/gen-voices-lackluster-trust-major-institutions.aspx.

Ingram, Kyle. "Federal Judges Block NC Supreme Court Election 'Cure' Process—For Now." *The Raleigh News & Observer*, April 22, 2025. https://www.newsobserver.com/news/politics-government/article304819896.html.

Jacobs, Rusty. "Board Analysis Shows Griffin's Ballot Challenges are Based on Inaccurate Assumptions." *WUNC Northern Carolina Public Radio*, February 16, 2025. https://www.wunc.org/politics/2025-02-16/board-analysis-jeffersongriffin-ballot-challenges-inaccurate-assumptions.

Kiesa, A., Booth, R.B., Hayat, N., Medina, A. and Kawashima-Ginsberg, K. "Growing Voters: Building Institutions and Community Ecosystems for Equitable Election Participation." Center for Information & Research on Civic Learning and Engagement (CIRCLE), 2022. https://circle.tufts.edu/circlegrowingvoters.

Klinedinst, Matt. "Lancaster County Election Officials Accused of Misleading Voters about Their Registration Status." *Fox43*, October 22, 2024. https://www.fox43.com/article/news/local/lancaster-county-election-officials-accused-misleading-voters-registration-status-lancaster-county/521-3bc14754-6e79-4150-8fb9-b0416a29f4c8.

Laczó, Ferenc. "Westernization by Preemptive Rejection: How Viktor Orbán Sells to U.S. Conservatives their own Obsessions." *The Review of Democracy*, July 12, 2022. https://revdem.

ceu.edu/2022/12/07/westernization-by-preemptive-rejection-how-viktor-orban-sells-to-us-conservatives-their-own-obsessions/.

Medina, Alberto and Hilton, Katie. "New Data: Nearly Half of Youth Voted in 2024." Center for Information & Research on Civic Learning and Engagement (CIRCLE), April 14, 2025. https://circle.tufts.edu/latest-research/new-data-nearly-half-youth-voted-2024.

Medina, Alberto, Siegel-Stechler, Kelly, Suzuki, Sara, Booth, Ruby Belle, and Hilton, Katie. "Young People and the 2024 Election: Struggling, Disconnected, and Dissatisfied." Center for Information & Research on Civic Learning and Engagement (CIRCLE), January 15, 2025. https://circle.tufts.edu/latest-research/2024-poll-barriers-issues-economy.

Members of Ivy League Votes. "Student Voting is Not Where it Should Be." *Inside Higher Ed*, January 2, 2022. https://www.insidehighered.com/views/2022/01/03/college-students-face-many-unnecessary-obstacles-voting-opinion.

Novey, Sam, Andres Rothschild, Jillian, and Hammer, Michael. "Which U.S. Citizens Lack Easy Access to Documentary Proof of Citizenship?" University of Maryland Center for Democracy and Civic Engagement, April 10, 2025. https://cdce.substack.com/p/which-us-citizens-lack-easy-access.

Open Society Foundations. "Open Society Barometer: Can Democracy Deliver?" Launched September 2023. https://www.opensocietyfoundations.org/focus/open-society-barometer.

Parks, Miles. "What 'Election Integrity Advocates' Have Planned for 2025." *NPR*, December 20, 2024. https://www.npr.org/2024/12/20/nx-s1-5217816/what-election-integrity-advocates-have-planned-for-2025.

Peck, Gunther. "Documenting the Damage of Judge Jefferson Griffin's Supreme Court Election Challenge." *NC Newsline*, February 6, 2025. https://ncnewsline.com/2025/02/06/documenting-the-damage-of-judge-jefferson-griffins-supreme-court-election-challenge/.

Pereira, Ivan. "Early Voting Options Grow in Popularity, Reconfiguring Campaigns and Voting Preparation." *ABC News*, September 4, 2024. https://abcnews.go.com/Politics/early-voting-options-grow-popularity-reconfiguring-campaigns-voting/story?id=112682514.

Pew Research Center. "Voters Broadly Positive About How Elections Were Conducted, in Sharp Contrast to 2020." December 2, 2024. https://www.pewresearch.org/wp-content/uploads/sites/20/2024/12/PP_2024.12.3_election-2024_REPORT.pdf.

Purdue University. "Purdue University Statement on Campus Voting Locations." September 17, 2024. https://www.purdue.edu/newsroom/2024/Q3/purdue-university-statement-on-campus-voting-locations-sept-17-2024.

Shapiro, Jeremy and Végh, Zsuzsanna. "The Organisation of America: Hungary's Lessons for Donald Trump." *European Council on Foreign Relations*, October 9, 2024. https://ecfr.eu/publication/the-organisation-of-america-hungarys-lessons-for-donald-trump/.

Sholtis, Brett. "Lancaster County Commissioners Send 'Cease and Desist' Letter to F&M College over Voter Registration Claims." *Lancaster Online*, October 29, 2024. https://lancasteronline.com/news/politics/lancaster-county-commissioners-send-cease-and-desist-letter-to-f-m-college-over-voter-registration/article_e51a4dae-9578-11ef-8394-4f60feb393b8.html.

Ulrich, Steve. "Department of State Intervenes in F&M Votes/Lancaster County Voter Registration Dispute." *PoliticsPA*, October 21, 2024. https://www.politicspa.com/department-of-state-intervenes-in-fm-votes-lancaster-county-voter-registration-dispute/139616.

U.S. Congress. *Congressional Record.* 91st Cong., 2nd sess., 1970. Vol. 116, pt. 5. https://www.congress.gov/bound-congressional-record/1970/03/09/116/senate-section.

Walker, Russ and Lisi, Tom. "F&M Voter Organization Alleges Lancaster County Elections Staff Misled on Registration Rules." *Lancaster Online*, October 19, 2024. https://lancasteronline.com/

news/local/f-m-voter-organization-alleges-lancaster-county-elections-staff-misled-on-registration-rules/article_8e2a9904-8e66-11ef-bf47-df1e4cfcd3e8.html.

Jonathan Becker, Lisa Bratton, Yael Bromberg, Jelani Favors,
Simon Gilhooley, Melanye Price

Afterword: Reflections on the Course "Student Voting: Power, Politics, and Race in the Fight for American Democracy"

1 Jonathan Becker, Bard College

In 1976, as a 12-year old, I volunteered on the congressional campaign of Illinois congressman Abner Mikva, knocking on doors and tracking voters as a part of 'get out the vote' efforts. Mikva won in what was an incredibly tight race: he was declared the winner two weeks after the election by a mere 201 votes. His victory was affirmed a year and a half later when the Illinois Supreme Court rejected a "Petition for Recount" by his opponent, Samuel Young, who had alleged errors, irregularities, and fraud. One of the keys to Mikva's success was the strong support of college students. His election was just five years after the 26th Amendment lowered the voting age to 18. Indeed, Mikva, who was a strong advocate of the 26th Amendment, strategically cultivated the college vote and relied heavily on student voters from Northwestern University and the absentee ballots of college students studying out of district to carry him to victory.

I spent much of the subsequent 20-plus years abroad, studying in Canada and the United Kingdom, doing research in the Soviet Union, and working in Ukraine, the Czech Republic, and Hungary after 'people power' had torn down the Berlin Wall. In Central and Eastern Europe, I was part of a cadre of idealistic young Americans aspiring to forge a world that respected human rights, abided by the rule of law, and recognized the will of the people as expressed in free and fair elections. I witnessed some amazing things in my time abroad, including Russia's first competitive elections in 1989, where turnout was nearly 90%.

I returned to the United States where I began to work at Bard College. With the 1998 mid-term elections approaching, Bard's director of student activities, Allen Josey explained to me that the Dutchess County Board of Elections (BOE) did not allow Bard students to vote locally. This did not immediately resonate with me: I had lived abroad since I was 17 and had only voted absentee. Then I met with student organizers who were determined to fight for their right to vote locally. Many were passionate about their place in the community, volunteering for local organizations and identifying the Hudson Valley as home. Some literally had nowhere else to vote because they were born nearby or because their parents had moved from where they grew up. But none of this mattered to the BOE, which acted with impunity and simply rejected student registrants. Thus began a nearly 25-year journey to fight for democracy at home.

Figure 1: Students and faculty from "Student Voting: Power, Politics and Race in the Fight for American Democracy," in front of statue of A&T (Greensboro) Four, October 16, 2024. Photo courtesy Seamus Heady.

The idea for the course "Student Voting: Power, Politics, and Race in the Fight for American Democracy" emerged from the lessons learned during this quarter century. The structure of the course was modeled on courses Bard had conducted with international partners in which faculty from around the globe co-designed a course and students did common assignments. Although a discrete course is offered at each institution, all of the students and faculty gather together in an online classroom multiple times during the semester so that students can learn with and from each other and benefit from the diverse knowledge of the course faculty. Students enrolled in these courses regularly report that the learning environment allows them to gain unique insights because they are exposed to different perspectives. In the case of student voting, although all of the institutions are situated in the United States, the diversity of students and faculty produced a vibrant learning environment. In informative and stimulating dialogue that linked young people across the country, students presented each other with insights gleaned from interviews with older family members about their voting experiences, described their voting rights role models, and more.

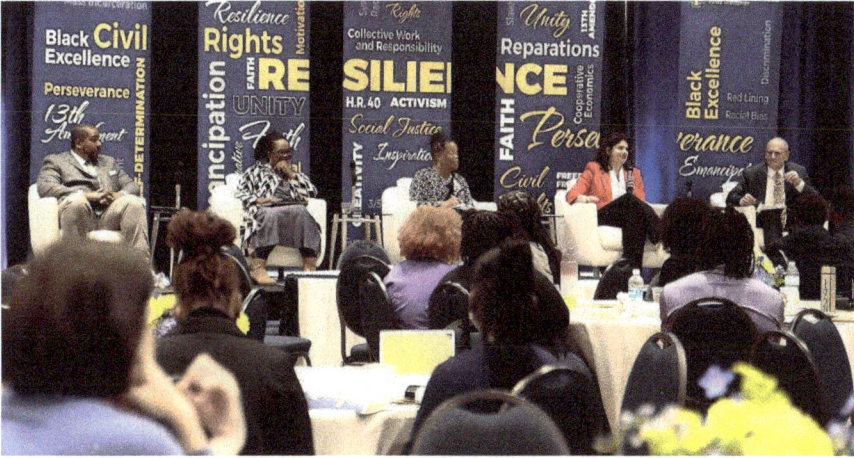

Figure 2: Faculty from "Student Voting: Power, Politics and Race in the Fight for American Democracy," HBCU Democracy Day at North Carolina A&T State University, October 16, 2024 (from left: Jelani Favors, Melanye Price, Lisa Bratton, Yael Bromberg, and Jonathan Becker). Photo courtesy of Seamus Heady.

The most stirring moments were classes in which students were exposed to the amazing work of past generations of student leaders who fought for their right to vote. Students were taught that they can be more than passive observers. This is especially important today, as the United States falls further into the grip of authoritarianism and the right to vote is challenged more than at any point since the Second Reconstruction. The most important things that we can teach our students today is that they have agency and that their capacity to make an impact as citizens is enhanced when they act collectively.

The current moment represents, in many ways, the antithesis of the idealistic spirit which marked the start of my professional career. One can only hope that the lessons from the class and in this book, culled from generations of engaged and determined students, faculty, administrators, and their allies, will help highlight the path to a better and more democratic future.

2 Lisa Bratton, Tuskegee University

This class on voting was more than just a class to me—it was personal.

I have missed two elections in my life: one when I lived in Taiwan and one when I was unexpectedly delayed out of town on family business. Voting was also personal for my parents. I grew up in Vallejo, California and when I was a child, voting took place in private homes. My parents took me to vote with them in the home of our family friends, the Norrises. While I did not understand that they were exercising a newly won constitutional right, I knew it was important from dinnertime conversations.

My great-great-grandfather, Green Bratton, was born enslaved at Historic Brattonsville in York County, South Carolina. While writing a book on resistance at Brattonsville, I found a document indicating that he was a registered voter in 1868. My father, who was born in the same county in 1917, could not vote until 1965.

When Shirley Chisholm made her bid for president in January 1972, I was ten years old. I vividly recall asking my mother if she was going to vote for her. She replied, "America is not ready for a Black president." Fast forward to 2008, and both she and I have lived to see the election of Barack Obama.

This class gave me the opportunity to share my passion for voting which I hope has inspired my students to become lifelong voters. Students learned of Tuskegee's extraordinary role in securing voting rights for all. The class was offered during the Harris/Trump election, one of the most contentious in U.S. history, and we were able to discuss some of the implications of each outcome. Students have shared with me the impact that this class has had on them—including their decisions to become lifelong voters. I am humbled to have been a part of their experience.

3 Yael Bromberg, Esq.

Designing and teaching "Student Voting: Power, Politics, and Race in the Fight for American Democracy" has been a dream. The course brought together professors and students from different departments across four colleges and four states. This resulting book is better for the thought-provoking questions posed by our students over the last two years teaching this course together, and by the ongoing interrogation of the subject matter by my fellow faculty members.

Over 20 years ago, I was an active student and community organizer, spearheading and supporting various voter registration and advocacy campaigns. Those involved in similar efforts, no matter the locale, know the truism all too well: freedom is an endless meeting. The work is hard, and the labor required is far from glamorous and often unseen. But the difficulty and bitterness of loss is staved off by the rewards of the participatory process. The sweetness of wins is long-lasting. It demands celebration, no matter how small or how large. The process itself shapes us. I had no idea how foundational this early exposure to democratic engagement would be for me or my peers, and have since witnessed and supported generations of young people navigating their own democratic practice.

When I was a young constitutional rights attorney, I worked in the D.C. headquarters of Common Cause, and then taught and supervised voting rights litigation at the Georgetown Law Civil Rights Clinic. The absence of the 26th Amendment vexed me. Mention of the issue was bare—if mentioned at all—in election law textbooks and materials. I found myself poring through the archives at the Library of Congress, leading to my legal scholarship on the 26th Amendment, *The Unfulfilled Promise.* Through these efforts, I had the privilege of befriending, and endlessly interviewing, the then-youth organizers (now in their 70s) who led the successful ratification of the Amendment in 1971. Those organizers and congressional staffers went on to do great things, joining the Carter administration, international peace and democracy efforts, and other causes for the public good. While most people may not know their names, they were the young sheroes and heroes who made the seemingly impossible happen.

Through these various works, I also befriended David Goodman, brother of slain Freedom Summer civil rights worker Andy Goodman, who encouraged me to start my own law firm. Seven years later, the firm continues to support practitioners of democracy, securing ballot reform and voter access in multiple precedential litigations in New Jersey, and engaging young voters, faculty, and administrators across the country in search of solutions for electoral access. One of my first clients was The Andrew Goodman Foundation, whose mission is to make young voices and votes a powerful force in democracy, with its vast network of over 60 campuses across the country.

Over 50 years after ratification of the 26th Amendment, obstacles to the youth vote persist, intentionally or otherwise. These are described in further detail in the first legal volume on the Amendment, published by *The Rutgers University Law Review,* for which I worked alongside student-editors as a faculty advisor. The volume features contributions by a range of critical voices in the field. A part of this systemic problem is academia's shortcoming, ripe with opportunity, to ready and support young voters as they inherit the franchise.

To my surprise, the students primarily attracted to this course were not activists and organizers. So why did they sign up for the course? Word clouds generated on the first day of class in Fall 2023 and Fall 2024 revealed similar responses: *democracy, elections, rights, power, ideals, sacrifice, choice, president.* Our classroom discussions unearthed a deep curiosity about the democratic and political process, especially as it relates to their own demographic group on the question of youth political power. Thus, even though they were not all (or perhaps, not yet) democracy practitioners, they sought to study the process and the history, in the context of contemporary struggles. More, as the semester progressed, and as we heard back from students who had completed the course, they found ways to engage, several in leadership capacities.

We endeavored, as much as possible, not to idolize civil rights heroes and litigators whose work we studied in class, but to humanize them and emphasize agency and community. In addition to our course readings, we brought into the classroom the past, and the present, hearing in Fall 2023 from North Carolina Supreme Court Justice Allison Riggs and Georgia youth organizer Evan Marlbrough, and in Fall 2024 from organizer of the Student Nonviolent Coordinating Committee, Judy Richardson, and David Goodman. In Fall 2023, David Hogg joined us, a young man launched into youth organizing by a tragic gun massacre at his high school, who champions young candidates to run for office. These speakers brought our readings to life, and motivated students to carry their learnings outside of the classroom.

This book cracks the shell, revealing the yolk America's college communities have served in furtherance of democracy. It is written primarily for an undergraduate and academic audiences, and provides a legal framework to explore the historic role of college communities, and especially youth, as constitutional architects in shaping the right to vote.

4 Jelani Favors, University of North Carolina A&T

In 1948, Dr. Rodney Higgins, a newly hired political scientist at Southern University, a historically Black college in Baton Rouge, was asked to outline his goals for leading his academic unit on campus. In his letter to the campus president, Higgins declared, "The university must set the standards of individual freedom, national development and world citizenship. Adequate education of its youth is the life blood of democratic society." Higgins' comments amid the background of a socially and politically oppressive Cold War illustrate how potent Black colleges were in the fight to expand and defend democracy while also planting seeds for the modern civil rights movement. Since 1837, Historically Black Colleges and Universities (HBCUs) have 'set the standards' in promoting civic engagement among their students by cultivating a pedagogy rooted in the deliberate interrogation of America's political shortcomings. Through the advancement of a 'Second Curriculum,' that emphasized race consciousness, cultural nationalism, and idealism, HBCUs served as the epicenter of social movements that have radically reshaped the social and political contours of our nation.

I am honored to have served alongside my colleagues at Bard, Tuskegee, and Prairie View A&M as we engaged our students in our collaborative course entitled "Student Voting: Power, Politics, and Race in the Fight for American Democracy."

This class examined the challenges and barriers to galvanize the youth vote and centered its focus on the 26th Amendment to the Constitution that lowered the voting age to 18 in 1971. There have been direct challenges and attempts to undermine the voting rights of our students on these respective campuses, and our ability to find synergy and commonalities in these experiences has presented a unique opportunity to further explore the power and significance of student voice. Through a series of classroom projects, guest speakers, and robust discussion, this class has been one of the most important highlights in my career as a college instructor and has been thoroughly enjoyed by students who enrolled. These comparative case studies provided our students with a new understanding of how critical the fight for American democracy is, and how the university still 'sets the standard' for civic engagement and remains an essential battleground in the preservation and expansion of these ideals.

5 Simon Gilhooley, Bard College

> ... Bard offers unique opportunities for students and faculty to study, experience and realize the principle that higher-education institutions can and should operate in the public interest.
> Bard College Mission Statement

As part of its self-understanding as a private institution operating in the public interest, Bard College has taken a particular interest in student voting rights. Over the last quarter century Bard College has participated in four successful lawsuits, one federal and three state, grounded in the 26th Amendment, that have established student voting eligibility and a polling site on campus, and contributed to the adoption of a New York state law mandating polling sites on college campuses with more than 300 registered voters and outlawing campus gerrymanders. Beginning in Fall 2023, it has directly connected these efforts to curricular offerings through its iteration of the undergraduate course, "Student Voting: Power, Politics, and Race in the Fight for American Democracy," in which I have taught.

We are fortunate at Bard College to have an administration that is highly supportive of efforts to embed civics education across the College, valuing the ideal of the College as a civic actor. Prior experience through a struggle for student voting rights and an institutional center in the form of Bard's Center for Civic Engagement has provided an experiential and institutional foundation for addressing the contemporary challenge of civics education. It is indicative of this tendency that I have co-taught the course at Bard with our executive vice president—and it has been to the class's benefit to have someone who has spearheaded the struggle for voting rights on our campus lead the course. I also think that in our case, having a 'regular' American faculty member co-teach with faculty in a senior administrative role has opened up discussion on these issues in unique ways—at times conversations in the classroom have represented the perspectives of three distinct groups of 'stakeholders'—students, faculty, and administration—allowing for the convergences and tensions between different interests to be identified and explored. For the students, that has exposed the workings of the university as an institution in ways that I don't think students often appreciate. It was interesting for them to see that what they often regard as a singular institution is a complex of distinct interests, and striking to think about how that complexity can play out in the historical moments that we examined in the class.

It has been a highlight of the last two years to be involved in the design and instruction of this course. Its undoubted strength is the opportunity for students to interact with figures who have direct experience and/or expert knowledge of the struggle for voting and civil rights. The joint meetings between the campuses are the jewels of this course, enabling students to hear from those who can share an expertise that is not readily replicable in the act of reading a text. A highlight of the Fall 2024 semester was a session with Judy Richardson, David Goodman, and Johnavi Rao. Students heard from two individuals who were active in the civil rights movement and from a contemporary youth activist, and were able to learn how those individuals came to be involved, what challenges they identified, and what they thought were the areas of challenge today. The session provided a bridge between history and the current moment, enlivening the struggle for students and highlighting the thread that joins the past and today. Students are hungry to understand what successful activism requires and looking for spaces of hope in the current moment, and the ability to hear from those who have faced and overcome challenges to civil and political rights is in that sense priceless.

But if that cross-historical connection is invaluable, so too is the cross-national connection between campuses. The ability of students to see that a struggle for voting rights is not limited to one region or state, and that despite distinct conditions, similarities in the forms of suppression are evident in different spaces, offers them a way of thinking about the struggle that would not be possible if we were to attend to only one case. Here, I cannot overstate the contribution of my colleagues who bring an expertise to each discussion that is irreplaceable. However, it is the students themselves who bring a feel for, and investment in, their own campus' struggles who make vivid that cross-national connection. Having recently graded the final projects for our own class, it is striking the degree to which students have become the owners of a campus struggle that pre-dates their presence —both in terms of their deep consideration of that struggle as a historic artifact and in terms of their willingness to further and secure the gains that such struggles have produced.

That is perhaps, for me, the ultimate success of this course—that students leave the class understanding their own positionality within an ongoing struggle for voting rights; that they see themselves as historical actors who have the opportunity of stepping into a role of fighting for greater voting rights. It is unfortunate that at this moment history calls out for such actors, but a source of real hope to see a crop of students ready to pick up the mantle of those who came before them.

6 Melanye Price, Prairie View A&M University

In 1992, I was a sophomore at Prairie View A&M University (PVAMU) and preparing to vote for the first time and *I was extremely excited.* I had been told my whole life that my ancestors had died for my right to vote and now it was my moment to fulfill that obligation. I possessed both hubris and naiveté about how impactful my vote would be when I first engaged the political process.

Additionally, it was Bill Clinton's first election. Voting for Bill Clinton meant that a Democrat would be President for the first time since I was very young, *and I* could help make that happen. For students at my HBCU and Blacks across the nation, he was viewed as having a particular affinity to African Americans. I registered to vote at Prairie View because there were students canvassing the dorms and tabling around campus. In the most anticlimactic fashion possible, I cast a ballot for Bill Clinton using a pencil and bubble sheet in a forgettable building near campus. Imagine my surprise days later when 19 PVAMU students were indicted for voter fraud. In the weeks that followed I would learn about a history of antagonism between university students and the political leaders of Waller County, where PVAMU is located, that started before I was born. I learned about voter discrimination in real life and in real time. The fights that I thought ended with the civil rights movement were happening right in front of me. I learned that we—PVAMU students—were engaged in a fight about whether the students at my historically Black college were legitimate residents of a county where we lived for nine months of every year for at least four years of our lives.

Nearly 30 years after my voter experience, in 2019, I became a professor at my alma mater and taught a Black politics class where one of the students, Jayla Allen, was the lead plaintiff in a voter discrimination case (*Allen v. Waller*) against Waller County that emerged from the 2018 election cycle. With representation from the NAACP Legal Defense Fund, five students petitioned the government over infringement upon their ability to equally access early voting. In 2020, just before the presidential election, the students were deposed about an election two years earlier.

They explained to lawyers and court officials how their rights had been violated in an election that had already been decided and certified, and for which people had been doing the job for nearly two years.

In the 1979 *Symm* case, PVAMU students opened the door for future PVAMU students and all students across the country to register to vote as legal residents of the jurisdiction where they attend college, including from their dormitories and other on-campus residences. Though few people know much about Prairie View students' voting history, their battle for voting rights is one of the most important examples of student voting activism in this nation's history, and certainly since the passage of the 26th Amendment. This case is essential to establishing youth and students as a protected class in voter discrimination law. Unfortunately, this triumphant end for students nationally masks the continued struggle for voting rights by the students at Prairie View. Every successive generation since the *Symm* case has had to fight a new or recycled form of discrimination and assault on their voting rights. The hard truth is that neither the Voting Rights Act nor the 26th Amendment could shield students at Prairie View from the dogged hostility aimed at them by county officials, but at least someone was watching and periodically intervening.

I have taught Black politics for decades but it is only in the last ten years that I have begun to incorporate this history into my lectures. More people should know our story. More of our own students should learn it before they experience voter discrimination. This is why the course "Student Voting: Power, Politics, and Race in the Fight for American Democracy" has been invaluable. The impact of this course for my students has been immense. Universities often do a great job of expanding students' worldview, but we should also be more adept at helping them understand their potential to be change-makers in their immediate environment. Prairie View students have played an outsized role in expanding ballot access for students; however, there is no systematic way for successive generations of students to learn this history. This course has filled a void in our curriculum. As we work to infuse Prairie View history into more of our curriculum, these students get to learn that history and connect it to other campuses while also meeting new students and faculty. The fact that the course last year overlapped with a presidential election season also gave it more meaning. Students were able to study this history and develop strategies to mobilize and energize other students based on what they had learned in class. At the end of the course, they were excited about how they would apply what they had learned for the rest of their time on campus. They also had ideas about what the PVAMU administration could do to help facilitate student participation. I see all of these outcomes as a win for the students and a sign that the goals of the course were achieved.

Index

www.ingramcontent.com/pod-product-compliance
Lightning Source LLC
Chambersburg PA
CBHW050335270326
41926CB00016B/3467